Music and the Poetics of Production in the Bolivian Andes

Music and the Poetics of Production in the Bolivian Andes

HENRY STOBART

ASHGATE

Published by

Ashgate Publishing Limited
Gower House
Croft Road
Aldershot
Hants GU11 3HR
England

Ashgate Publishing Company
Suite 420
101 Cherry Street
Burlington, VT 05401-4405
USA

Ashgate website: http://www.ashgate.com

British Library Cataloguing in Publication Data
Stobart, Henry, 1958–
    Music and the poetics of production in the Bolivian Andes.
    – (SOAS musicology series)
    1. Music – Social aspects – Bolivia – Kalankira 2. Quechua
    Indians – Bolivia – Kalankira – Music 3. Kalankira (Bolivia)
    – Social life and customs
    I. Title
    781.6'29832308414

Library of Congress Cataloging-in-Publication Data
Stobart, Henry, 1958–
    Music and the poetics of production in the Bolivian Andes / Henry Stobart.
        p. cm. – (SOAS musicology series)
    Includes bibliographical references.
    ISBN 0-7546-0489-6 (alk. paper)
    1. Folk music – Bolivia – Potosí (Dept.) – History and criticism. 2. Potosí
(Bolivia) – Social life and customs. I. Title. II. Series.

    ML3575.B6S76 2006
    781.62'9832308414–dc22

                                                                              2005032594

ISBN-10: 0-7546-0489-6   ISBN-13: 978-0-7546-0489-1

This book is printed on acid-free paper

Typeset in Times by Express Typesetters Ltd, Farnham

Printed and bound in Great Britain by MPG Books Ltd, Bodmin

Contents

List of Figures

List of Musical Examples – Transcriptions

CD track numbers are in **bold**

A Note about the CD Recording

The sequence of tracks on the accompanying CD is organized to follow the unfolding year rather than to reflect the order that these recordings are discussed in the book. Wind and guitar song repertoires, linked to particular times of year, are often alternated in order to provide variety whilst at the same time respecting the seasonal alternation of genres and instruments. The intention is that the CD can be enjoyed alone as well as in conjunction with reading the book. In most cases, recordings of speech or of short analytical excerpts are located towards the end of the disc. This CD is provided free of charge with this book; it may be copied, but must not be sold or used for any commercial purpose without written permission of the author.

CD Recording Details

Track		Minutes
1	Men dancing to the *panti charango* (*cruz* genre) at the *calvario* shortly before removing the cross. *Zapateo* dancing at end of recording. Feast of the Holy Cross 1am, 3.5.91 (Ex. 4.2)	1.31
2	*Suna* played on *julajula* panpipes at *calvario*. High-pitched *wiswi* size played by boy clearly audible. Feast of the Holy Cross 3.5.91 (Ex. 6.5)	1.24
3	*Charango* song with *zapateo* dancing in a bar in Macha, performers from San Lazaro. Feast of the Holy Cross 4.5.91 (Ex. 3.1)	0.54
4	*Kuwla* on *julajula* panpipes. Players kneel and face the sun at dawn following the night of *San Juan* – the winter solstice. Ch'uslonkari community, near Sacaca (Map 3) 25.6.91 (Ex. 6.1)	1.03
5	*Cruz* song performed during 'urbanization' festivities in Tumaykuri. Performers from P'uytukuri, Tumaykuri 8.4.91 (Ex. 4.6)	1.33
6	Sounds of *tinku* fighting and a *suna* played on *julajula* panpipes by men from Milluri community. Chayrapata, Feast of Easter 1.4.91 (Chapter 6)	1.20
7	*Cruz* song verses performed with the *charango* at the *alférezes'* llama corral in Kalankira. Feast of the Holy Cross 5.5.91 (Ex. 5.3)	1.52
8	Church bells and *suna* played on *julajula* panpipes by men from Jamach'iri community entering Chayrapata, Feast of Easter (Ex. 6.7)	1.40
9	Wedding verses sung during the *asintu* ceremony. Santosa Beltrán: voice, Asencio Jara: *charango*. Kalankira. (Ex. 5.5)	2.04
10	*Huayño* played on *siku* panpipes during the feast of Guadalupe. Kalankira 1.9.91 (Ex. 7.1)	1.46
11	*Huayño* played on *siku* panpipes during the feast of Exultación. Wak'an Phukru 16.9.91 (Ex. 7.3)	1.28
12	*San pedro* song verses sung following the *asintu* ceremony. Kalankira 17.8.91 (Ex. 5.1)	2.15
13	*Marcha* played on *siku* panpipes during the feast of Exultación. Wak'an Phukru 16.9.91 (Ex. 7.2)	1.16
14	*Kuwla* played on *siku* panpipes during the feast of Exultación. Wak'an Phukru 16.9.91 (Chapter 7)	1.07

30	Massed llama mating on mountain peak above Kalankira (*Q'ala walaychu*). Approximately 70 animals mating simultaneously. Christmas day 25.12.92 (Chapter 8)	1.14
31	Hungry llama sounds, release of animals from corral beside homestead, and hostess requests recording stop ('*basta compadre*'). 27.3.96 (Chapter 8)	0.31
32	*Wayñu* song with *kitarra* (*Uray mayunta rishani*). Feast of Carnival, Kalankira. 13.2.91 (Ex. 5.2)	1.10
33	*Pinkillu* flute *wayñu* with voices and *pututu* trumpets, during the *alma kacharpaya* ('despatch of soul') ceremony. It accompanies *pukllay* and *qhata* dancing. Feast of Carnival, Kalankira 11.2.91 (Ex. 9.2)	2.06
34	*Wayñu* song with *kitarra* (*Ayranpuni*) performed during the *alma kacharpaya*. Feast of Carnival, Kalankira 11.2.91 (Ex. 9.1)	1.37
35	*Pinkillu* flute *wayñu*, singing and *qhata* dancing, in *pinkillu kacharpaya* ('despatch of the *pinkillus*') ceremony. Carnival, Kalankira 15.2.91 (Ex. 9.3)	1.17
36	*Salaki* song (Asunta Beltrán: voice, Paulino Jara: *charango*). Recorded in family cooking hut 25.5.91 (Ex. 9.4)	2.19
37	*Salaki* singing and dancing with sounds of *sirinu* whistles. *Jatun kacharpaya* ('great despatch') ceremony. Carnival, Kalankira 17.2.91 (Chapter 9)	1.14
38	Bell stones on Kanqali hill – sounded by Asencio Jara and author. 30.8.91 (Chapter 2)	0.46
39	Imitations of bird and animal sounds connected to their names by Paulino Jara (a) *juqu* – 'owl', (b) *wiskacha* – Andean rodent (Chapter 2)	0.19
40	*Charango* strumming in *cruz* genre on large *panti* style instrument by Paulino Jara. 12.4.02 (Ex. 4.4 and 4.5, Fig. 4.7)	1.09
41	*Charango* strumming in *san pedro* genre on large *panti* style instrument by Paulino Jara. 12.4.02 (Ex. 4.4, Fig. 4.7)	0.52
42	*Charango* strumming in *san lazaro* variant of *cruz* genre on a small Betanzos style instrument by Paulino Jara. 12.4.02 (Ex. 4.7)	0.52
43	*Qhaliyu* song performed by Mariano Beltrán (c. 75 years). 4.7.91 (Chapter 3)	0.47
44	*Hiyawa* verses sung by young people from *ayllu* Pukwata in a bar. Easter Saturday, Colquechaka 31.3.91 (Chapter 3)	1.27
45	*Charango* strumming in *san pedro* genre on small *k'ullu* style instrument by Paulino Jara. Asymmetric 3:2:2 ratio. 28.7.91 (Ex. 4.1)	0.41
46	The Battle for Water – a Quechua story told by Adrian Chura. 15.5.91 (Chapter 7, Appendix 1)	2.04

Musical Transcription and Orthography

Musical transcription

The musical transcriptions in this book are intended to support analysis and aid listening to the accompanying CD recording. Most of Kalankira's music is built on fairly short repeated structures, sometimes incorporating internal repeats, which are subject to many forms of variation during performance. My transcriptions usually present a single rendition of the principal repeated form; often shown as a single line, despite octave doublings and varying degrees of heterophony according to genre. As I have tended to eliminate obvious 'mistakes' and to include more typical versions there is a danger of 'synoptic illusion', where other renditions might appear 'as imperfect, impoverished performances' (Bourdieu 1977:98). In other words, these transcriptions should not be imbued with authority or seen as representative; they are simply starting points in the process of listening to and engaging with this music – for use in conjunction with the accompanying CD recording. In the interests of clarity, key signatures with multiple sharps or flats are avoided through transposition (usually up or down one semitone) and no attempt is made to represent the complex asymmetrical rhythmic ratios, subtle pitch fluctuations, or timbral richness so characteristic of Andean musical expressions (see Stobart & Cross 2000).

Orthography

Quechua and Aymara orthography has been a source of fierce debate ever since these languages first began to be written down in the sixteenth century. Although many attempts have been made to reach an orthographic standard much disagreement remains. The version I have learned, which is commonly used for Bolivian Quechua and is partially based on Spanish orthography, uses an allophonic three vowel system A, I, U and the following consonants: Ch, Ch', Chh, J (or H), K, K', Kh, L, Ll, M, N, Ñ, P, P', Ph, Q, Q', Qh, R, S, T, T', Th, U, W, Y, several of which are combined with ejectives or aspirates. As in other parts of the Andes, the Quechua speakers of Kalankira use numerous Spanish loan words, some of which retain Spanish phonology whereas others become highly distorted by Quechua inflexion and incorporate Quechua suffixes. For the most part, in my transcriptions of texts, I follow Quechua orthographic convention for words of both Quechua and Spanish origin. However, I have also adopted a pragmatic approach: in some cases I use Spanish spelling for Spanish words that are especially difficult to render in Quechua. For the main text and in my translations I often adopt more familiar Spanish spellings. For example, *charango* and *cruz*, which appear in my Quechua transcriptions as *charanku* and *kurus*.

In this book I use the following abbreviations: Que. (Quechua), Aym. (Aymara) and Sp. (Spanish).

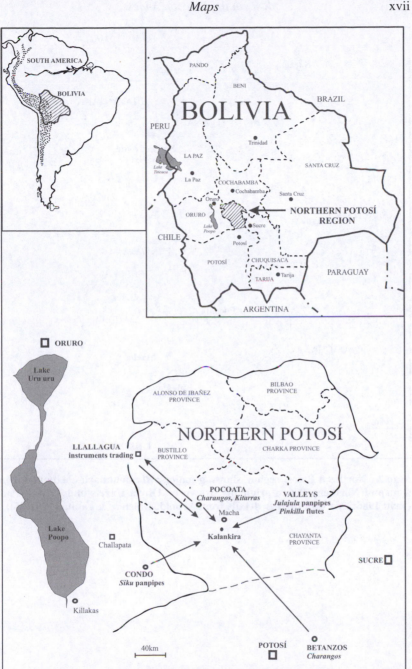

Map 1   Provinces of Northern Potosí and regional towns, in the context of Bolivia and South America. Shows the places where the musical instruments played in Kalankira are made or obtained.

Map 2   Northern Potosí region, showing major *ayllu* boundaries. Adapted from a map of Northern Potosí originally drawn by Olivia Harris and Tristan Platt (Platt 1986:234) with further details from Arnold, Jiménez & Yapita (1992:35).

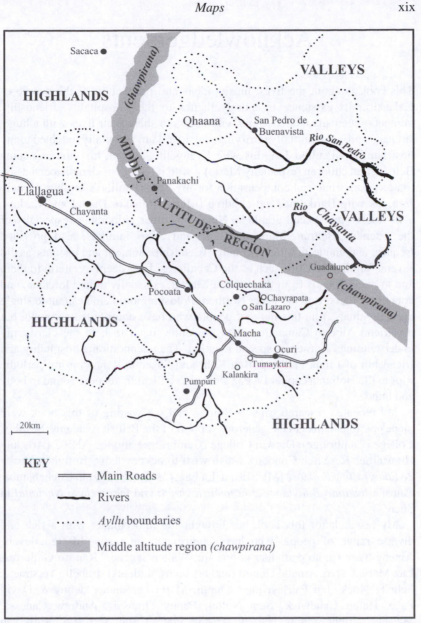

Map 3 Northern Potosí region. Shows primary ecological/altitude division, rivers, main roads and locations mentioned in the text. Adapted from a map of Northern Potosí originally drawn by Olivia Harris and Tristan Platt (Platt 1986:234) with further details from Arnold, Jiménez & Yapita (1992:35).

Acknowledgements

This book is about the lives, music, ideas and production of the people of Kalankira. Its existence is entirely thanks to their hospitality, friendship, humour, generosity, patience and willingness to share their lives with a huge, strange, a probably initially terrifying, outsider. I am especially indebted to my host family – Paulino Jara, his wife Evangelia Anarata, his mother Asunta Beltrán, and children (especially Mario) – who it took considerable persuasion to accept any financial compensation for my keep. Paulino's brother Asencio Jara, his wife Bardolina, and children (Maria, Reneko, Daniel and Carlos), also deserve my special gratitude. Numerous other individuals, especially of the extended Beltrán, Mamani, Chura and Suyo families, also provided frequent and unquestioning hospitality, friendship, humour and insights, as did several families in Titiri, such as the Caballeros. I am deeply grateful to them and to many friends from the town of Macha, especially doña Florencia, and countless others from the wider Northern Potosí region. I am hesitant to single out individuals from this mass of people who have contributed so much, but my friend Alberto Camaqui – who has done much to help me clarify my understandings – deserves special mention. The unconditional hospitality and friendship of Linda Farthing, Ben Kohl and Susanna Rance on my periodic trips to the Bolivian capital La Paz were also critical to keeping sound in body and mind.

My repeated research trips to Bolivia and the writing of this book were made possible thanks to the generous support of the British Academy, St Johns College (Cambridge), Darwin College (Cambridge) and the AHRC (Arts and Humanities Research Council). I also wish to acknowledge Bolivia's *Museo de Etnografía y Folklore* (MUSEF) in La Paz, *Centro Portales* in Cochabamba, Potosí's *Instituto Boliviano de Etnomusicología* and the *Archivo Nacional* in Sucre.

My research for this book has brought me into contact with a rich and diverse range of people who have contributed on many different levels. Among these (in no particular order) are: Wálter Sánchez, Ramiro Gutierrez, Luz-Maria Calvo, Arnaud Gerard (and his many students), Isabelle Verstraete, Felicity Nock, Jan Fairley, Lucy Duran, Maria Fernandez, Jenny & David Page, Helen Chadwick, Sara Nuttal, Penny Dransart, Andrew Canessa, Melanie Wright, Penny Harvey, Tristan Platt, Colin McEwan, Ruth van Velzen, Peter Gose, Cassandra Torrico, Kenneth Mills, Denise Arnold, Juan de Dios Yapita, Maggie Bolton, Michelle Bigenho, Ian Cross, Ruth Davis, Martin Clayton, Tina Ramnarine, Mark Holmes and Mike Skeet. Special gratitude goes to Bill Sillar, Rosaleen Howard and Olivia Harris for their ongoing friendship, support, enthusiasm and critical perspectives. The encouragement, interest and support of colleagues in the Music Department of Royal Holloway, University of London is also much appreciated.

My students – past and present – have been a constant source of inspiration, helping me develop and challenge a range of the ideas presented here; the enthusiasm and dedication of many for playing Andean music has also provided many insights and immense mutual enjoyment. My work as a performer in the Early/World Music ensemble *SIRINU*, alongside such imaginative and impressive musicians as Jon Banks, Sara Stowe and Matthew Spring, has been very important over the gestation of this book, keeping performance alive, vital and critical to my approach. Jon Bank's astute comments on various chapters are warmly appreciated.

This book has benefited enormously from the insightful editing of Linda Farthing, the thought-provoking feedback of Bonno Thoden van Velzen (my father-in-law), and the detailed reading and critical comments of Hettie Malcomson. I am also grateful to Rosaleen Howard, Pedro Plaza and Lindsey Crickmay for their guidance and comments on my Quechua translations.

Finally thanks to my family: my parents-in-law for sharing such enthusiasm for ethnography; my aunt, Mary Oliver, for loaning me the money that enabled me to travel to Bolivia in the first place; my parents and brothers for instilling a love and fascination for agriculture, music and so much else (especially William for transferring my video shots to photos); my children and constant teachers – Bonno and Laurence; and my wonderful wife Diura, for sharing the trials and tribulations of bringing this book to fruition.

Part I
Creating Context

Chapter 1

Introduction

The poetics of production

It comes as no surprise that much ethnography is shaped by the passions and experience of the ethnographer and this book is no exception. Its point of departure is the relationship between music and agricultural production, a perspective that is informed by my own experience of growing up on a farm in Cornwall in South West England combined with a passion for playing music and growing plants. This has undoubtedly led me to notice things and make connections that might not seem so obvious or significant to others. However, this book is neither about 'agriculture' in a narrow material and economic sense nor about 'music' as an autonomous sphere of activity and knowledge. Rather it explores the ideas and processes that underlie and connect these activities, leading us well beyond the immediate products of fields and herds to a much broader and richer conception of production and reproduction.

When I first travelled to South America in 1986 for a year, I was already aware that many Bolivian peasant communities play a diverse range of regionally and calendrically differentiated musical instruments, some explicitly related to agricultural activities.[1] That year I attended over forty feasts in the Bolivian countryside (some lasting over a week) and visited many instrument makers, which afforded me a broad comparative perspective. The experience highlighted just how little I really understood about how music fits into the lives of the peasant farmers and herders who play it. The existing ethnomusicological literature was largely descriptive and usually based on brief encounters with the musicians.[2] It became abundantly clear that to

---

[1] My curiosity was aroused by Max Peter Baumann's superb calendrically organized recordings *Music of the Bolivian Highlands* (1982a) and some of Louis Girault's classic 1955–73 (1987) recordings (analysed in Raul & Marguerite d'Harcourt 1959), as well as Hans Buechler's book *The Masked Media* 1980) and Joseph Bastien's *Mountain of the Condor* (1978). I was also especially inspired by the pioneering work in the Northern Potosí region of Bolivia by the British anthropologists Olivia Harris and Tristan Platt.

[2] Among the few individuals engaged in music-focused fieldwork in a single community over more than a few weeks in the 1980s was André Langevin (1987, 1992). Excellent work on music of the Bolivian highlands from this period, based on shorter encounters, includes that of Wálter Sánchez (1988, 1989a, 1989b, 1996) and Luz Maria Calvo (Calvo & Sánchez 1991) – both based at Centro Portales, Cochabamba – Ramiro Gutiérrez (1991) and a little later Rosalía Martínez (1990, 1994, 1996). Subsequently much superb work has appeared from Arnaud Gerard (1996a, 1996b, 1997), Isabelle Verstraete, Erlinda Zegarra (c. 1997), Omar Laime (2002) and others based in Potosí (Universidad de Tomás Frias). Also of note are the publications of Michelle Bigenho (2002) and Thomas Solomon (1994a, 1994b, 1997, 2000), and the wide-ranging work of the

expand my understanding I had to learn an indigenous language and spend an extended period deeply involved in a community and its music. This led me to Kalankira, a Quechua speaking community of farmers and herders of *ayllu* Macha, Northern Potosí in 1991. My life has been deeply interwoven with them ever since.

Rather than seeking a community in some way remarkable for its music, I sought to explore how a group of people whose lives are dominated by small-scale agricultural production approach music. Kalankira is like countless other communities of the region, where music making is a normal and expected skill, closely linked to calendrical ritual, agriculture and courtship. Yet at the same time this community's particular conjunction of individuals, knowledge, customs and histories is also unique. Almost every man plays (or has played) a minimum of four seasonally differentiated instruments, while women are the principal singers. Men sometimes sing, but women do not play instruments – although no rigid prohibition is maintained against women touching instruments, comparable to those reported in Amazonia.[3] Musical participation peaks with courtship and diminishes following marriage. As in many other parts of the Bolivian Andes, Kalankira's musical instruments, genres and dances alternate seasonally and are explicitly connected with regulating atmospheric conditions and the cycle of agricultural production.

Despite its evident importance to them, initially people in Kalankira were bemused by my aim to find out about their 'music'. Firstly, they are not in the habit of talking about their various instruments and genres as a single category, equivalent to the English word 'music' – a term without a true equivalent in either of the principal indigenous languages of the Andes, Quechua and Aymara.[4] Secondly, musical genres, dances and instruments tend to be closely connected with particular performance contexts. For most people the mention of an instrument or genre locates it within broader cycles of transformation, alternation or (re)production, such as the human life cycle, the agricultural year, Catholic feast calendar or shifting relations with other groups. Finally, the majority of music making takes place during calendrical feasts – sensory explosions that contrast vividly with the austerity of daily life. Although usually integral and albeit privileged at certain moments, music is just one of a variety of ingredients that contribute synaesthetically to the festive event (Stobart 2002a:97–99).

---

anthropologist Denise Arnold (with Juan de Dios Yapita and Domingo Jiménez), based on extensive fieldwork in Qaqachaka.

[3] See Stobart (forthcoming) for discussion of musical instruments and gender.

[4] Both languages include a wealth of terms to describe a multiplicity of instruments, genres, dance forms, contrasted sound qualities and timbres, but no single word conveys equivalent semantic space to either the English 'music' or 'sound'.

Music, poetics and production

Musical knowledge, discourse and practices in Kalankira are not neatly separated from other spheres, but are deeply integrated into more general ideas about 'production'. Yet scholarly approaches to 'production' have tended to be subject to what Herzfeld calls 'economic reductionism', whereby – in 'a Cartesian division of labor' – supposedly non-material aspects of social life, such as narrative, gesture and music, are omitted (1997:23). It is also surprising, given the extent to which growing crops and herding have dominated human history, how few ethnomusicological studies have dedicated more than passing reference to relations between agricultural and musical production.

The 'Poetics of Production' in this book's title aims to stress the mutual interdependence of musical and socio-economic production, and of what might be called the 'mundane, and the 'aesthetic'.[5] However, this expression is perhaps a misnomer; literally I suppose meaning 'the production of production'– (where 'poetic', from the Greek *poieō*, means 'to make, produce or create').[6] Ultimately, my motivation for using the word 'poetics' in this title probably owes more to Andean ritual practices than to scholarship – although both inform my approach. For example, when people drink alcohol or chew

---

[5] Feld puts this rather well: 'The poetic is an emergent figure that reframes an everyday ground, both strengthening that ground and contributing to its solidity and fluidity. Likewise the everyday ground stands ready to be reframed, to take on new heights or depths, to *evoke more than signify*, to move more forcefully into the realm of feeling and sensation' (1996:114).

[6] The term poetics, which 'conjures up an automatic series of misunderstandings' (Herzfeld 1997:142), is most often encountered in the context of poetic language and its analysis (Jacobson 1960), its relationship to music (Hill 1993, Feld 1990 [1982]), or for example architecture (Bachelard 1994 [1958]). The confusion surrounding the term may be traced back to Aristotle's *Poetics* in which he differentiated 'production', as processes in the natural world that were worthy of his new philosophical enquiry, from artistic 'production' with its focus on affect through invoking similarities or resonances as metaphor. This was a polemical move on Aristotle's part to distance himself from his predecessors, especially the poets (Lloyd 1990:23). By the Renaissance, Aristotle's influence had led 'musical poetics' to refer to the 'art of setting down a completed work that had a coherent design and unity' (Palisca 1993:viii) and, over the centuries, poetics came to imply 'the separation of knowledge about art from the conditions which made it possible, from context' (Samson 1999:36). However today, in the social sciences, poetics has come to mean almost precisely the reverse. For example 'cultural poetics' specifically 'rejects the privileging or bracketing of a self-contained realm of art within society' (Dougherty & Kurke 1998:5), while Krims defines his 'musical poetics' as a means to ground musical analysis within social praxis; a process of demystification (2000:202). Herzfeld has stressed the etymology of poetics in the Greek verb for action, arguing that it should not be conflated with 'poetry', as some kind of 'romantic mysticism of seeing poetry in social life' (1997:22, 142). My own interest in poetics lies precisely in exploring the interdependence of the 'mundane' and 'aesthetic', but unlike Herzfeld, I prefer not to entirely lose sight of poetry; evocation is critical to my approach.

coca leaves[7] in Kalankira, each sip or ingested wad of leaves is treated as an offering to the powers, places, crops, domestic animals and other objects that ensure human well being. These spirit beings are invoked using epithets or alternative names of endearment, remembered one after another in memorised sequences or *thakis* ('pathways').[8] In such ritual contexts, people refer to the 'house' (*wasi*) as 'nest' (*thapa*), to the 'field' (*chajra*) as 'virgin' (*wirjin*), and to the 'potato' (*papa*) as *chaskañawi* ('starry/bushy eyes') – a term also used in songs to refer to a lover. This affective language stresses close empathetic – even sentimental – relations, serving as a means to appeal to the generative power or spirit (*animu*) of the object, being or place, and to set it into 'communicative mode'.[9] Playing music and dancing also open these lines of communication and invoke particular modes of relationship – where well being and (re)productive potential are largely understood in terms of the quality of relations with the various personified places, objects or beings.[10] For example, when we played flutes and danced ankle-deep in rain-sodden dung in a sheep corral, I was assured that this would make the animals reproduce well.

This is a good example of what I mean by a poetics of production, where there was nothing in the least 'poetic' – in a romantic literary sense – about this miserably damp and uncomfortable experience. However, I do not limit my notion of the poetic to those times when epithets are used or music is played. Rather the poetics of production also encompass the alternation between different names, the orchestration of shifting forms of musical sounds and silences, and the play of shifting identities, that all contribute to social, economic and cultural production. Evocation is also central to the very idea of a 'poetics of production', where meanings are *evoked by*, not *embodied* in cultural symbols – a point that has also informed my approach to ethnographic writing (Keesing 1989:463, Tyler 1986:123, Clifford 1986:25–6). Similarly, music, dance and musical artefacts might be said to 'afford' rather than simply embody meanings (Clayton 2001:6–9), thereby shifting our attention to the knowledge and experience of those involved in musical production, reception and exchanges.

---

[7] Although the drug cocaine is produced from coca leaves it is important that the reader does not confuse this powerful narcotic, which has no place in Andean rural communities, with coca leaves which are a mild stimulant, immensely sacred and a fundamental aspect of socio-ritual interaction (Allen 1988:220–225).

[8] See for example Arnold, Jiménez & Yapita 1991, Abercrombie 1998:320, 350.

[9] Cf. Feld [1982] 1990:131.

[10] Such practices may also be seen to form part of a kind of 'sentient ecology' (Anderson 2000:116–17), the broader framework for what Ingold calls a *poetics of dwelling* (2000:26). 'In the past', he observes, 'there has been a tendency to write off such poetics as the outpourings of a primitive mentality that has been superseded by the rise of a modern scientific worldview'. On the contrary, he argues, 'scientific activity is always, and necessarily, grounded in a poetics of dwelling' (2000:110).

The word 'production' is probably most widely encountered in connection with economics, such as the manufacture of goods or cultivation of crops through the application of human energy (labour), technique and knowledge (Keesing 1981:178).[11] The word 'production' is also commonly heard in reference to the creation or preparation of something for (public) presentation, such as a piece of music, play, film or radio broadcast. It is notable that this term is often associated with presentational aspects of a work, object or phenomenon and its reception, rather than earlier stages in its creation. Similarly, when we talk about the 'production' of sound by a voice, instrument or piece of audio equipment, this highlights the close connection between the processes by which the sound is created and the experience and evaluation of its reception.

In its most literal sense, *production* refers to 'bringing' something 'forward, forth or out', and offering it for 'inspection or consideration'. In other words production is in essence a communicative process that brings beings or things into relation with one another. The products, such as sounds, harvested food crops, commodities or radio broadcasts, are not simply cast out into a void; rather they embark upon and give rise to social lives (Appadurai 1986). From this perspective the notion of 'production' becomes a useful way of thinking about identity and processes of relatedness (Carsten 2000).

A central argument in this book is that these various forms of 'production' are deeply interwoven and that in Kalankira music is critical to their articulation. This leads us to consider how the production of sound, especially in music, relates to other forms of material production: productions that must necessarily be approached in terms of both (shifting) relationships and (cyclical) processes through time. In terms of the production of relationships, Kalankira's seasonally alternated musical instruments can be understood as iconic of bodies that shape sound as *animu*, the animating energy of all living things (see Chapter 2). The idea of a metaphorical 'body', its cycles of transformation and its relationships with others, not only draws on imagery from the human body, but also from the (life) cycles of the potato, and from the animated earth and cosmos. Kalankira's music can in part be seen as a way

---

[11] For many decades, scholarly work on the theme of production has been dominated by Marxist economic determinism. Marx's interest focused on the way surplus value, beyond the needs of subsistence, is extracted from the labour process, arguing that for the capitalist mode of production, only labour that accumulates capital is deemed 'productive'. Marx's approach, developed as a means of differentiating historical periods through their economic organization, may be seen to have contributed to economic reductionism which characterized much anthropology, especially up until the 1980s. For example, from an anthropological perspective, Keesing characterizes 'production' as 'the process whereby the world is engaged and transformed by human labor' (1981:178). Agency is built into the very structure of the verb 'to pro*duce*' (as the Latin *ducere* to 'lead'), but clearly humans are not always directly involved in everything that we might call 'production' (for example, in the 'production' of flowers or fruit by a wild plant or of sound by a waterfall).

to invoke, transform or communicate between these various bodies and their shifting forms; where the body is animated from within and may serve as 'a model that can stand for any bounded system' (Douglas 1994 [1966]:116). Thus, we shall see that relations between bodies of people, as 'imagined communities' (Anderson 1991 [1983]), are also critical to local expressions of production, where the invocation of social insiders and outsiders alternates with the seasons.

The isolated community?

For outsiders Kalankira is well off the beaten track. Even getting to Macha, the nearest town, from Bolivia's larger urban centres involves a major journey along hazardous and vertigious dirt-track roads. Up until the mid 1990s, when daily buses to Macha began, this typically involved being tightly packed with dozens of locals and an array of animals in the back of an open truck. From the sleepy town of Macha follows an ascent by foot of over 1000m, taking at least four hours (halved if one is lucky enough to catch a truck to the top of the hill above Macha). In the late 1990s, the town of Macha acquired a single public telephone and electricity in many households, followed almost immediately – as if by default – by a television.

Yet, Kalankira and other nearby communities seem very unlikely to acquire such services and communications in the forseeable future. Many families in Kalankira own radio-cassette players but the cost of batteries – not usually a priority – means that these are rarely heard. The Kalankiras converse almost exclusively in the indigenous language Quechua and in the early 1990s only a few men were able to speak more than quite elementary Spanish, the dominant national language, and therefore lacked any voice in the machinery of state.[12] Since the construction of an elementary school below the hamlet of Pata ('Upper') Kalankira in 1994, most children now attend school and general competence in Spanish has probably increased. Before this time, some children attended classes in Palqa uyu, well over an hour's walk for short legs. Many men spend several months each year working in the larger towns of the region, as builders' labourers or in other forms of manual work to acquire cash, but the principal economic activities for most Kalankiras are locally based agriculture and herding. In many respects, Kalankira might be characterized as a paradigmatic 'isolated rural setting'.

Thomas Turino, referring to his own fascinating research on music and urban migration between the rural highlands of Southern Peru and the urban sprawl of Lima, writes that:

---

[12] See Howard-Malverde (1990a) on the use and implication of the Quechua word *upa* ('deaf and dumb'), used in central Peru to refer to individuals who are unable to speak, read or write Spanish.

...in Peru, at least, and I would guess more generally, bounded, synchronic
musical ethnography in an isolated rural setting is no longer a tenable
methodology because of the circular links between these different types of
spaces (1993:13).

Turino is not alone in connecting fieldwork in rural settings with an
uncritical approach to history and broader socio-political dynamics; indeed
there is a sense that fieldwork in such places has become unfashionable. But
rural settings are not in themselves a problem; rather what should be stressed
is the need to be wary of ethnographic invocations of isolation, purity,
authenticity and cultural stasis, and the ways that these can contribute to
stereotypes and prejudice.[13] In reality, very few ethnomusicologists have lived
in Andean peasant communities for extended periods, let alone experienced a
year of music making.[14]

The word 'isolated' is subjective. For its inhabitants, Kalankira is the centre
of the known world, and shapes the primary experience through which other
people, places, things and knowledge are in turn known.[15] Although often
characterized as resistant to the cash economy, recent research demonstrates
that Andean peasants have been deeply involved in urban markets since the
sixteenth century (Larson & Harris 1995).[16] Yet, it is also their very lack of
reliance on markets that tends to differentiate the peasants of communities,
such as Kalankira, from the *mestizos* (*cholos*), of towns like nearby Macha,
who usually derive much of their income from commerce (Harris 1995a:351).
Since the European invasion Andean peasants have been continuously
involved in markets but from a disadvantaged position, with only the most
poorly paid and lowest status jobs made open to them. In turn, this
disadvantage and consequent limited potential to accumulate has come to
define Indian identity and values. The contrast between accumulation and
circulation, a central theme in this book, is critical to understanding local ideas
about sound and the organization of musical performance.

The idea of Kalankira as untouched by history or economically and
culturally isolated seems especially hard to maintain given its proximity to
Potosí; some sixty miles away. During the sixteenth and seventeenth centuries,

---

[13] For example, see Nettl (1985:15) who notes an earlier ethnomusicological tendency to view
'non-Western' musics as static, or the attempts to introduce a historical dimension to the discipline
in the essays in Blum, Bohlmann & Neuman (1993). Philip Bohlman, in particular, has been a key
figure in this historicization process.

[14] However the anthropologists Olivia Harris (1988) and Denise Arnold (1992) with Juan de dios
Yapita (1998a, 1998b) have written on the theme of music and undertaken long-term fieldwork.

[15] Like the notion of *world view*, this enables us to move towards a more ego-centred analysis,
whilst making the point that although many members of a given group may hold shared world
views, these might not be shared by every individual (Hodder 1987:4).

[16] Alongside the requirement to pay monetary tribute to the colonial authorities (Saignes
1995:168), in the late sixteenth century native people supplied the bulk of foodcrops to Potosí
(Larson 1995:16).

Potosí was home to the world's richest silver mines and one of its largest cities (Escobari 1985 and 1996:55).[17] To supply labour for the mines, Viceroy Francisco de Toledo imposed the *mita* in 1575; requiring a seventh of the adult male Indian population to travel to Potosí each year (Bakewell 1984, Cole 1985), a practice finally abolished in the nineteenth century. In an account of a procession during a Potosí fiesta in 1622, Bartolemé Arzáns de Orsua y Vela invokes the mixed emotions – fascination and terror – with which Indian *mitayos* must have approached Potosí (1965, I:349):

> … then entered as many as 200 Indians, as when they come to perform the *mita* in this rich Mountain each year, yet this entrance was of rejoicing and the other of tears. They entered with various trumpet-like instruments, bamboos and calabashes, all silvered and decorated with ribbons, which are the same instruments with which they enter when coming from their provinces, though their sound is not very pleasing, at least it is not unpleasant. They also brought some little tubes of silver placed sequentially in the manner of an organ (which the Indians call *ayarichis*) and which make a smooth harmony.

This description features instruments still played in the countryside around Potosí today, suggesting considerable continuity in musical practices.[18] But *mitayos*, including numerous from *ayllu* Macha, could hardly fail to be touched by what they encountered. The extravagence of Potosí's feasts was legendary, as evoked in Arzáns' account of riotous wedding celebrations in 1643, which included a mock battle (1965, II:93):

> Finally, the clarins, cornetts, animal-horns with bamboos of the type used by the Indians, together with horns, trumpets, drums, shotguns, blunderbuses, and various other types of din, produced a noise so confused and horrible that many of those present were stunned in terror.
> With this confusion past, a new harmony of delightful instruments was to be heard and enjoyed in various parts; now of harps, vihuelas and guitars; now *rabeles*, *gaitas* [pipe and tabors] of Zamora, tamborines, hornpipes, *zampoñas*,[19] *sonajas* [rattles], albokas and other rustic instruments. Then entered, on rich and beautiful floats, first the god of love, blind and naked; then Apollo and his muses, followed by the lively performances of gods from the ancient fables.

---

[17] Hemming observes that by the late 1590s Potosí had fourteen dance halls, thirty-six gambling houses, seven to eight hundred professional gamblers, a theatre, one hundred and twenty prostitutes, and dozens of churches (1983:407).

[18] These are, firstly the *pululu* (*pulu* or *chujlla*), a bamboo and calabash (gourd) trumpet played at sacred sites, such as beside the church door, during major feasts (Stobart 1987, Sanchez 1989b:19–20, Cavour 1994:74–5), and secondly the *ayarichi* panpipes, of which there are many other colonial references. Today *ayarichis* (or *ayarachis*) are widely played during dry season feasts to the south and east of Potosí (Baumann 1985:36, Stobart 1988:15, Flety & Martínez 1992:32, Cavour 1994:50–54) – but these are not constructed from silver.

[19] This probably refers to the Spanish hurdy gurdy or bagpipes (*gaita*). However, the Spanish word *zampoña* is widely used in the Andes today to refer to *siku* panpipes (played in pairs of eight and seven, or seven and six tubes).

The vivid sense of a cultural melting pot is invoked by this juxtaposition of diverse sounds, created by instruments from the full gamut of Spanish society and its provinces, alongside Indian trumpets and imagery from classical literature. The impact of Potosí and the *mita* on the rural communities of the region was profound, both as a cultural and economic powerhouse, and due to the immense numbers who perished working the mines. Agriculture and herding have dominated the economic production of highland communities such as Kalankira over many centuries, but this does not mean that such groups are bounded or isolated. Rather, Kalankira's production of people (identities), crops and music are understood in relation to outsiders. Indeed, music, dance and dress emerge as particularly important media for articulating and shaping emic notions of inside and outside to productive ends.

Ethnographic fictions

The name 'Kalankira' used in this book is a 'true fiction'. Most official documents or maps use the Spanish spelling *Cayanguera* or Quechua/Aymara *Qayankira* (Mendoza & Patzi 1997:101).[20] According to several local people the name is derived from the *kalan kalan* sound produced by the ringing rocks situated on Qanqali hill high above the hamlet of Pata Qayankira (Chapter 2). Thus, in the name 'Kalankira' I bring together local beliefs about sound production and its link with identity – central concerns in this book – with Quechua, rather than Spanish, orthography. My hope is that this fiction opens up emic perspectives, in terms of place, sound, language and identity. It also serves as a constant reminder that this, like all ethnographic accounts, is a construction that cannot avoid some distortion – however reflexive and true to both my hosts and myself I try to be. 'Even the best ethnographic texts – serious, true fictions – are systems, or economies, of truth. Power and history work through them, in ways their authors cannot fully control' (Clifford 1986:7).

To avoid burdening the reader with a multiplicity of place names and shifting affiliations, I often use the name Kalankira loosely, as a kind of ethnographic shorthand, to refer to the group of hamlets and dispersed homesteads where my hosts lived. In certain contexts most of the individuals living in this district, perhaps a total of 250, would probably identify with this group and with the name Kalankira (*Qayankira*).[21] This would be just one of a range of context-sensitive ways of thinking about and expressing ethnic, political and territorial identity; thus Kalankira should not be thought of as some kind of fixed, unitary and homogeneous 'organic whole' (Turino

---

[20] In the 1619 revista of the Macha region it appears as 'Caanquira' (Platt, Boysse-Cassagne and Harris, 2006:538, 574).

[21] It is principally in the feast of the Holy Cross (May 3) that this group is manifested – notably through musical performance (Chapter 6).

1996:469). In the early 1990s three hamlets each of some 40 to 60 souls dominated the district: Pata Kalankira ('Upper *Qayankira*), Ura Kalankira ('Lower *Qayankira*) and Wak'an Phukru.[22] I lived in Pata Kalankira (Figure 1.1), which is situated beside the district's small colonial church and graveyard, and made almost daily visits to Wak'an Phukru, which nestles on a hill some 12 minutes walk above Pata Kalankira. My trips to Ura Kalankira – a good 25 minute walk including a very steep hill – and to the many dispersed homesteads were less frequent.[23] However I did make many visits to the home of don Adrian Chura, the oldest man and foremost storyteller of the district who lived with his nephew Pedro Chura, in Apacheta; nearly an hour's walk away (see Character Glossary). When I use phrases such as 'in Kalankira' or refer to 'the Kalankiras', it is usually my subjective experience of these places and people that I have in mind – once more a kind of ethnographic fiction.

The temporal dimension of this book also involves dilemmas of representation. It focuses on a year of fieldwork, divided between 1991 (January to October) and 1992 (October to January), which through an ethnographic sleight of hand I treat as a single annual cycle of music and agriculture. Many subsequent visits to Kalankira, over more than a decade, have added an appreciation of the dynamics of continuity and change, a theme I briefly develop in Chapter 10.

The use of the ethnographic present has rightly come under scrutiny due to the way that it can create the impression that people's practices and traditions are somehow static or timeless, as if immune to the whims of history and fashion. As Ingold has observed, 'the ethnographic present is dead, but we do not know with what to replace it' (1996:201). My own concerns about this issue led to some attempts to describe Kalankira's practices using the past tense. But this seemed to convey the impression that these people, who I continue to visit whenever I can, are somehow consigned to the past as if denying their existence (and my ongoing relationship to them) in the present.[24] In this book I have opted to use the present tense to refer to practices and knowledge that I have every reason to believe are maintained at the time of writing. I also often use the past tense to refer to specific events or

---

[22] Nobody was sure about the meaning of the place name 'Wak'an Phukru', but some suggested that a *wak'a* (sacred place or spirit) had existed there and the Aymara *phukru* refers to a hole or pit in the ground (Bertonio 1984, II:280). The hamlets of Wak'an Phukru and Ura Kalankira joined forces, and differentiated themselves from the Pata Kalankira, in certain ceremonies (for example during Carnival).

[23] As most people head out to the fields or to pasture animals immediately after eating their cooked morning meal, I soon discovered that visits must usually take place very early in the morning.

[24] Bohlman describes this type of paradox particularly well: 'the present is … ongoing, but once inscribed in ethnography, it is marked by the syntax of pastness … The past, in contrast is frozen in a timelessness, from which it must be wrenched to be synthesized into the presentness of history' (1997:140).

Figure 1.1   The hamlet of Pata Kalankira (viewed from Wak'an Phukru), showing the church, tower and graveyard (foreground), homesteads with corrals (centre), and the rocky peak of *San Francisco Qala Walaychu* (top).

performances, or to evoke practices or knowledge that belong to the past. My hope is to achieve a balance between historical transformation and continuity. The musics of the Kalankiras are dynamic and constantly herald, respond to and create new contexts, but their repetition and continuity with the past is also critical to their (re)productive power. 'We have been playing and dancing like this ever since the time of *inka rey* ['Inka king']', people sometimes insisted, invoking a sense of ancestral power and emic authenticity. The production of musical sound in the present may be seen to articulate the tension between the past and the future, between continuity in form and dynamic transformation.

Environmental factors and harsh realities

In Bolivia, the forms and degree of environmental and ecological variation vary hugely according to geographical factors, such as altitude, latitude, or water-land mass relations. The highlands, while situated in the tropics, are extremely dry and cold largely because of altitude. In just a few hours walk, one can descend from the treeless landscape of Kalankira (c. 4100m) to a warmer ecological niche with abundant trees, where maize and peaches grow; a characteristic that has been critical to the Andean 'vertical economy' for millennia.[25] At the altitude of Kalankira, few crops grow besides potatoes, fodder barley, and small amounts of quinoa (*chenopodium*) and other Andean tubers.[26] Most families grow wheat (for grain) in various sheltered fields at slightly lower altitude, and some own irrigated plots (c. 3500m) where broad beans and peas also produce well. However, the key crop for people in Kalankira, as in much of the Bolivian *altiplano*, is the potato. Its cultivation represents a particularly long term historical continuity; serving to shape people's perceptions, sentiments and – as we shall see – aspects of the calendrical organization of Kalankira's evolving musical expressions (see Chapter 9).

My focus on music and expressive media might lead some to an excessively positive or even romanticized image of Kalankira. I certainly hope to convey something of the fascination, aesthetic pleasure, emotions and inspiration I experienced through living there. But, the harsh realities of life in this community and blatant inequalities, especially when compared to the opportunities, choices, expectations and physical comforts of my own world, are striking and in many respects shocking. Limited life expectancy and access to medicine, alongside depressingly high levels of maternal and infant mortality are obvious examples, yet without simple solutions. For example,

---

[25] See, for example, Murra 1979 [1956], Platt 1982, and Harris 1982b.

[26] For example, Isaña (*tropaeolum tuberosum*), Oca (*oxalis tuberosa*) and Lisa (*ullucus tuberosus*).

illness is usually attributed to spiritual offence, hospitals are places you go to die, and health workers – inevitably *mestizos* or outsiders – tend to be considered more dangerous than the disease (Stobart 2000). Daily life is immensely labour intensive and physically hard; all agricultural tasks, except ploughing with oxen, completed by hand, and the process of cooking – dominated by women – involves a staggering number of hours each day. Besides the trip to collect water from the stream or waterhole, arduous grinding of grain or peeling of potatoes (with delicacy that never ceases to amaze me), and the stoking and cleaning of the hearth, a constant supply of fuel must be provided. In Kalankira's case this is principally llama dung, which must be collected up, dried in the sun and stored.

It is tempting to assume, as do many development agencies in the region, that the 'pitiful productive levels' in such places as Kalankira simply reflect poor land quality. According to this logic, the best quality land was controlled by the *haciendas* (privately owned estates), forcing 'free Indians', such as the Kalankiras, to the margins – both in terms of land quality and participation in the market economy. However, according to Platt, around the 1850s the Indians of Chayanta (today's Northern Potosí) were considered 'amongst the richest Indians of Bolivia, and therefore those most able to support the burden of the tribute on which the state finances depended'. He suggests that the current low levels of production should not be attributed to some mythical condition of 'original poverty'. Rather, they should be seen as 'a particular "constellation" of articulatory mechanisms' resulting from recent history, such as the way 'state commercial policies have destroyed the favourable marketing conditions once enjoyed by the regions' ayllus' (1982:27–8, 62). Yet, it remains very hard to acquire any real sense of how people's quality of life in places such as Kalankira has fundamentally changed over the past few centuries. At the same time, in thinking about history and myth in such places, we must reject Lévi-Strauss' dichotomy between 'cold' mythic societies, resistant to historical change, and 'hot' societies 'that thrive upon irreversible cumulative change' (Hill 1988:4–5).

Imagined subjects

In many respects acquiring acceptance in Kalankira, although immensely traumatic, was probably easier for me than it would have been for a Bolivian ethnomusicologist. I am less directly implicated in the nation's class-ethnic hierarchy – the mass of complex, ambiguous and sometimes violent mutual imaginings derived from complex histories of power, inequality and exclusion, that police the boundaries of difference but also help people feel part of a group – an 'imagined community' (Anderson 1991) – and shape their musical practices. Instead, almost Martian-like, my looks, habits and attitudes

Figure 1.2   Kalankira's *siku* panpipe band, including the author (height 6' 3"), during the feast of Exultación in Wak'an Phukru. Note the earthenware pot of corn beer and bottle of cane alcohol supplied to musicians throughout the feast.

were so exotic and mysterious that I felt relatively free to construct a carefully edited identity and biography; one that stressed my background, interest and active participation in agriculture and music making, but tried to downplay my relative material affluence and privilege. When people exclaimed, as I toiled for countless hours in their fields, that I was different from the *cholos* of the town because I knew how to work, I felt the illusion was successful. Also, when I accompanied girls singing on the *charango* or perfomed with the men's various wind ensembles I felt a strong sense of integration – even though my attempts to fit in were vertically challenged (Figure 1.2).

The realization of just how little control I had over the imagined identity I had constructed and my integration struck me forcefully when, long after I had felt well accepted in Kalankira, doña Asunta (my host's mother) enquired in perfect seriousness whether I know how to speak with devils. People like me, she explained, come from the town of Potosí with *qullqi* ('silver, money') in their thighs. They just rub their hands and money appears. Such imaginings are revealing about local constructions of identity and alterity. They also reveal perspectives on class and ethnicity, invoking the 'myth of the conquest', as a 'primordial act of creative and clarifying violence', when terms such as Indian, *mestizo* ('mixed race') and white may have had actual racial meaning, rather than serving as metaphors for social hierarchy – almost independently of skin colour – as they do today (Gose 1994:19). The Kalankiras readily identified themselves as *indios* ('Indians') and *campesinos* ('peasants'), but unlike the urban *mestizos* and creoles of the towns, they did not invoke the 'myth of the conquest' to present social difference.[27]

Some of these social differences and productive processes were revealed in my own attempts to live with a peasant community. In early December 1990, I arrived in the sleepy colonial style town of Macha, rented a room and began to search for a *campesino* community with whom to live.[28] My task was complicated by the differences in identity and class between the *mestizo* town dwellers of Macha, usually referred to locally as *cholos* or *vecinos* ('residents'), and the peasants (*campesinos*) of outlying rural communities or *ayllus*, marked in particular by dress and music. The aspirations and social networks of Macha residents, many of whom are traders, are directed outwards towards the larger towns of the region, where many of them have family. Hearing of my intention to live with a *campesino* community, certain *vecinos* spoke with pride of the region's rich cultural heritage, whilst often expressing concern for my welfare: 'What will you eat? Won't you get ill? Where will you live? A few presented the peasants as dirty, uncivilized, lazy and unreliable; remarking how they are always getting drunk and fighting. It was often hard to see through this ambivalent and context sensitive discourse and to avoid internalizing some of the *vecinos'* fears, romanticizations and prejudices, which ensure that the peasants remain as violent imagined 'Others'. But the *vecino/campesino* distinction is by no means clearcut or static; many Macha residents are temporary or recent migrants from the *ayllus*, who – to varying degrees – work the land, maintain reciprocal relations, and participate in the ritual practices of their original communities.

Many *vecinos* develop relationships of *compadrazco* ('godparenthood') with peasant families, providing them, for example, with privileged access to cheap (or free) labour and to the peasants' animals and harvest products. In turn, peasants potentially acquire access to urban markets and products, as well as to lodgings in the town of Macha. Such accommodation is especially important during major feasts, such as at *cruz* (May 3), when a peasant feast sponsor may call upon his *vecino* godparent to accommodate up to fifty

---

[27] The term *campesino* ('peasant') was introduced following the 1952 national revolution to replace the derogatory connotations of the word *indio*. From a global and national perspective, such ethnic groups are also increasingly classified as 'indigenous' (a return to racial language); a powerful means by which to exert political leverage (Albo 2002, Van Cott 2002).

[28] I had decided to focus on *ayllu* Macha, both because they are Quechua speakers – a language I had studied over the previous year – and because I was particularly taken by the beauty of their distinctive local dress and weavings.

peasant musicians and dancers. It was through the introduction of a *vecino* friend, that her *ahijado* ('godson') Modesto Caballero escorted me on the long uphill journey from the warm climate of Macha (altitude 3000m) to the cold highland community of Titiri (4,100m). But my efforts to live in Titiri were abandoned after less than a month due to a series of difficult circumstances and unpleasant local jealousies. Despite the Caballero family's refusal to accept any contribution for board and lodging, rumours circulated that I was paying them huge sums of money and that I had photographed the community's llamas, causing them to die (presumably, I much later realized, by capturing their regenerative powers in my camera). This led me to try my luck in the hamlet of Pata Kalankira, which I had spotted from the footpath between Titiri and Macha. I had been struck by the beauty of its situation, nestling beneath Kanqali hill, and by how – unlike the scattered dwellings of Titiri – the homesteads of Pata Kalankira were built close together just across the gully from the church and cemetery (Figure 1.1).

I was received surprisingly warmly on my first exploratory visit to Kalankira and arranged to return a few days later following an invitation to stay with the elderly bachelor Lorenzo Mamani. Lorenzo was away when I arrived and later retracted his offer, but fortunately a young couple let me stay in one of their storage huts. This thatched adobe-mud hut became my home for nine months until I returned to Britain in October 1991, and again between November 1992 and January 1993. My 'hosts' were the young couple Paulino Jara Beltrán and Evangelia Anarata, both in their early twenties, who lived with Paulino's widowed mother Asunta Beltrán Gallego and their newborn son Mario.[29] Each morning and evening I shared cooked meals with the family in their tiny cooking hut, which also served as their sleeping quarters. As the only warm place, this was the social hub of the homestead, which consisted of four small huts built around a central mud 'patio'.[30] Some twenty metres down the hillside was the homestead of Asencio Jara Beltrán, Paulino's older brother. Asencio and his wife Bardolina Torres Qullqi had four children – Maria, Reneko, Daniel and the youngest Carlos – born during my first stay (see Character Glossary). The two brothers pooled resources and worked together on the majority of agricultural tasks, even though they each independently owned a number of fields and held separate entitlement to communal lands. The daily work of pasturing the herds of female and young llamas, and sheep,

---

[29] I stress the sense of visitation and dependency conveyed by the word 'host', which I use throughout this book and which I believe much better conveys the dynamics of my fieldwork relationship than terms such as 'informants' or 'consultants'. Here, I support Jeff Todd Titon's view of fieldwork as 'visiting' (2004).

[30] The two tiny glass windows and single perspex sheet in the thatch roof that Paulino subsequently helped me add to my hut, in order to have enough light to write when it was too cold outside, created a local sensation. No other local huts had windows; nor did anybody follow this example.

was to some extent shared out between the womenfolk and older children of the two households.[31] Asencio and his children were constantly around Paulino's homestead and the two households acted very much as a single extended family, no significant event passing without the close involvement of both families. As part of this extended family, I was regularly invited to meals in Asencio's homestead, and his children spent countless hours in my hut, playing, drawing with my pens, or just observing as I wrote my diary – whilst constantly on the look out for any exotic or discarded object I might have to offer.

My close and ongoing relationship with the family, which extends well beyond the pages of this book or so-called scholarly research, was formalized towards the end of my first stay when Paulino and Evangelia asked me to become *padrino* to their baby Mario. This meant entering a reciprocal relationship with the whole family who, since that time, refer to me as *compadre* ('co-parent'). During my stays in Kalankira, Paulino and Asencio became my closest friends and companions. We shared long hours together working in the fields, journeying, transcribing my recordings and in countless other activities; their voices, values, knowledge and opinions constantly weave through this book.[32] Through getting to know other families, I discovered that many of their views were representative of the community as a whole. However, despite these brothers' wealth of shared experience, knowledge and values, the contrast in their personalities, attitude and personal biography, deserves to be stressed.

Some ten years older than Paulino, Asencio is nearer my own age. Before marrying Bardolina, he had lived with a *chola* woman for several years in the mining encampment of Catavi (near Llallagua, Maps 1 and 3). In 1991 he was learning to become a *yatiri*, a ritual specialist (shaman) and healer, and was periodically called away to perform curing rituals. Asencio is an ebullient character: passionate, enthusiastic, earnest, imaginative, witty, confrontational and warm. He is immensely hard working but also somewhat chaotic, tending to lurch unpredictably from one crisis or disagreement to another. Despite occasionally becoming vindictive and insulting to me when drunk, we came to share a particularly close and deep bond of mutual understanding, friendship and trust.

In contrast, Paulino is by nature calmer, more equitable and reflective; generally keeping a low profile in public events, whilst also giving the

---

[31] In subsequent years the herds have tended to be pastured independently although the men have continued to work together.

[32] Some might consider that this type of approach relies excessively on a limited number of subjects, but it might also be argued that such close friendships and daily interactions provide a privileged context for reflection, comparison and developing understandings. The point seems to be that these approaches lead to rather different and mutually complementary forms of ethnography.

impression of quiet confidence. He was also surprisingly vain spending hours preening himself in preparation for major fiestas, a characteristic more associated with young men and women actively involved in courtship rather than those who have settled down. There was occasionally a brooding and remote aspect to his character, which was hard to fathom, yet overall Paulino was immensely positive, warm and companionable. I felt extremely relaxed and comfortable in his company, finding him easy going, whilst supportive and non-confrontational. For several local younger men, from whom we often received visits, he seemed to represent something of an idol and soul mate. From time to time he would hang-out with one these lads, chatting idly, strumming the mandolin-like *charango*, or even holding hands.[33] Whereas Asencio would typically assert strong opinions, for example when helping me transcribe tapes, Paulino tended to take a more considered approach, which sometimes seemed frustratingly non-committal. Despite the family's considerable material poverty, it was initially difficult to get Paulino to accept payment for my upkeep; this resulted I suspect from a combination of pride and nervousness about potential jealousies. Asencio, on the other hand, often borrowed money and his inability to repay often led to complex arrangements to ensure he was seen to pay his dues.[34]

It took several months before I felt genuinely accepted in Kalankira. At first women would pretend not to notice me when I passed and groups of girls would run away. Gradually people came to consider me fairly harmless, as well as a good source of photographs, high quality coca leaves (from La Paz) and medicines. Also, my strange looks, odd habits, curious stories and incompetence in their culture were clearly a considerable source of entertainment. As a guest I was on constant good behaviour. It was not until the return journey on a long and physically exhausting trip to the valleys (with doña Asunta, Asencio, his eight year old son Reneko and the family's male llama herd) that we all lost our tempers. This burst of ugly and unbridled emotion (talked about afterwards with great humour) overcame some of our many cultural differences, my relations with the family taking on a new warmth, honesty and sense of trust. From this cathartic turning point our bond of friendship increased dramatically as did my integration into the rest of the community. It was when people rushed to warn me to protect myself from a

---

[33] In the Andes, hand holding between young people of the same sex is quite common and should probably be interpreted in terms of affection and companionship, albeit intimate, rather than necessarily as sexual intention. Whilst people were generally prudish about public nakedness, they were relaxed about physical contact with persons of the same sex. (I certainly do not discount the possibility of certain forms of bisexuality or homosexuality, however I have no definitive evidence.)

[34] Whilst it was necessary to be seen as generous and to find ways to reciprocate the hospitality of individuals and the community as a whole, it was also necessary for people to be aware that surviving financially was also a critical issue for me.

vecino stranger who had arrived in the community, and was suspected of being a *llik'ichiri* ('fat stealer') – a terrifying being of the collective imagination that uses a special machine to steal human fat from sleeping Indian bodies, causing the victim to waste away and die – that I really felt that I had been accepted. Many had thought I was *llik'ichiri* when I first arrived.

Too many questions

> Ethnography often has more to do with what to leave out than with what to put in.
>
> (Friedson 1996:1).

Towards the end of my aborted attempt to carry out fieldwork in Titiri, Francisco Caballero turned to me and asked 'why do you keep asking so many questions?' His point hit its mark all too painfully; in my desperation for 'data' following several months trying to acquire access to a community, I had been treating my hosts as informants rather than as people. At home in England I would not dream of constantly pestering people with questions in this way, a realization that horrified me. As in other parts of native America, 'only the village idiot goes around asking questions', people are expected to learn by observation and imitation (Beaudry 1997:75, Diamond, Cronk and von Rosen 1994:9).[35] When I left Titiri and began to live in Kalankira I made a vow, and conscious effort, to avoid asking questions except of a practical nature. My plan was to let the ethnography reveal itself to me rather than setting the agenda with my questions. I was not entirely successful in resisting the temptation to enquire and did hold interviews with both Paulino and Asencio during the first week of my stay. Listening back to these tapes years later, it is evident that almost every question I posed led to a misunderstanding, false information, or for me to believe something that was later vehemently denied.[36] The unreliable nature of this information may in part be attributed to the ambivalence with which I was viewed at the time, as an exotic stranger, and my limited linguistic competence. But perhaps it reveals even more about the perennial danger of trying to direct ethnographic enquiry along our own research agendas (Titon 1997:88).

Fortunately, a few weeks after my arrival in Kalankira I was catapulted into the feast of Carnival. During these high-energy celebrations, in which I

---

[35] As if to prove the point, Titiri's one mentally handicapped inhabitant was known as *zingu*, from the Spanish *gringo* – the common and often derogatory Latin American term for white outsiders, especially north Americans.

[36] For example, Asencio gave a false name much to our amusement when we listened to the tape together years later. As names can be used in witchcraft and are often not revealed to strangers, I have used false names in previous accounts of Kalankira. However during discussions in 2002, in which we discussed the historical significance of this book, it was agreed that I should use true names.

tried to participate fully, I was left little chance to ask questions as I frantically attempted to record, document and keep track of events through an almost perpetual alcoholic haze – one that accompanies any festive music making in Kalankira (Stobart 2002a:107–109). On a few occasions, a precious recording was dubbed-over and lost when, in a state of intoxication, I turned the tape over more than once. Ethnography is a very imperfect, messy and unpredictable business; do not let the neatly presented pages of this book convince you otherwise!

The Organization of this Book

This book is organized into three main parts; the first three chapters (1–3) are dedicated to context and key themes, the next two (4–5) examine production through exploring guitars and song, and a third group (6–9) follows the cycle of the musical year, focusing on wind music. A final chapter (10) takes the form of an epilogue. Although these chapters very much belong together, most also stand independently and explore distinct sets of issues.

The first part, 'Creating Context'[37] introduces several key ideas and modes of organisation that underlie musical performance in Kalankira. Chapter 2 explores the concept of *animu*, the animating essence or soul substance of living things, which finds expression in musical sound, as well as in other forms. Music is intimately associated with metaphysics and I demonstrate how ideas of containment and circulation, found in the construction of dry season panpipes and rainy season *pinkillu* flutes, respectively evoke how *animu* enters bodies, infusing them with life, and emerges again at death, transforming into *alma* ('soul of the dead'). I argue that the 'weeping and feeding' relationship between offspring and guardian comes at the heart of understandings about the relationship between musical performance and production. All musical instruments 'cry' or 'weep' (*waqan*) and are explicitly played during feasts to console (spirit) guardians for their sacrifices, which bring nourishment and wellbeing into the human world. The chapter also discusses issues of identity and alterity and what it means to be *runa* ('human') and an *ayllu* ('ethnic group') member from the perspective of the Kalankiras. I argue that through the year, and often expressed through music or dress, this group 'produce' a range of different and sometimes contradictory identities according to shifting phases of production.

Chapter 3 introduces the calendrical and seasonal performance of music in Kalankira, and considers how ecology, history and politics have shaped as well as threatened such practices. The chapter ends with a local exegesis,

---

[37] In this title I warmly acknowledge inspiration from the volume *Creating Context in Andean Cultures* (1997), edited by Rosaleen Howard-Malverde.

which takes the form a story featuring the mouse and the coming of mortality, told to explain why the dry season *charango* attracts frost. This leads us to some remarkable ways of thinking about music and its centrality to ideas about human mortality and existence, whilst beautifully demonstrating how the production of music, food crops and identity (personhood) are intimately connected. When we begin to examine the production of sound in music, drawing on these ways of thinking about the world and its cycles of production, it begins to take on immense richness.

Chapters 4 and 5 are dedicated to 'Guitars and Song'. The first, chapter 4, considers guitar construction, decoration and performance techniques and examines how these contribute to the construction of Macha identity. The transfer of knowledge between music artisan and performer is given special consideration, leading to a discussion of the development of seasonally specific guitar decoration, and the meanings attributed to particular decorative conventions. It is argued that these seasonally specific decorative traditions should not be seen as cultural relics, but as the result of dynamic market forces and fashions, where modernity and the introduction of new materials through the twentieth century has contributed to an apparent indigenizing process. The second part of this chapter explores the rhythmic-harmonic feel, ergonomic sensations, and aesthetic language connected with the performance of *cruz* and *san pedro* courtship songs (*takis*) of the dry season, the most distinctive musical genres of *ayllu* Macha. I also develop the notion of *genre-technique-tuning* arguing that Kalankira *charango* technique does not tend to be flexible and extendable to other repertoires, but must be learnt anew with each tuning and genre, making the three a unity and closely linking the bodily sensations they involve with specific performance contexts.

Chapter 5, the second to focus on 'Guitars and Song', explores song performances and contexts: their aesthetics, poetic language, creative processes, and some of the multilayered and intertextual meanings their texts afford. The dichotomy between single life and marriage emerges as an important theme, where single life is often metaphorically connected with the dry season and married life with the rains. This is emphasized in a special ceremony accompanied by wedding songs, performed by older people, in which the mountain is married to the fields ('virgin'), in preparation for reproduction in the rainy growing season. Although courtship song genres are less explicitly connected with agricultural production, it is argued that participation in such music leads young people to develop understandings of broader productive processes, where sentiment and amorous relations play a key role, as well as to the forging of reproductive relationships.

The four chapters dedicated to 'The Music of a Year' begin with the harvest feast of the Holy Cross in May. I begin here because it is over the harvest period, following Carnival, that the new offspring foodcrops are gathered in and begin their life cycle which reaches its zenith and flowing at the following

Carnival. Music, I argue, follows a similar path from a period of inner maturation and accumulation of energies (a kind of inner growth) during the dry winter months, while harvested tubers and grains lie dormant, to one of external expression and circulation during the rains, when these tubers and grains are planted and grow towards Carnival and flowering.

Macha is known to outsiders and in a global context for just one thing: its violent ritual battles called *tinku*. Peasants, including the Kalankiras, converge on the town of Macha for the feast of the Holy Cross (*cruz*) in May, playing *julajula* panpipes. Chapter 6 explores the concept of *tinku* which surprisingly, given the violence of the fighting of the same name, means harmony, agreement or concord. Even though deaths sometimes occur in *tinku* battles, the discourse of male warriors and the structure of the *julajula* music and *wayli* dancing they perform, stresses life, its prolongation, and the maintenance of social harmony through imagery of balanced exchanges. *Tinku* is not about victory, but concerns personal courage, participation, exploring boundaries and travelling away from reproductive space; aspects central to the poetics of Macha manhood. In this dry season context, with its strong male focus, 'production' comes to mean exchange and growth through life from youth to the flowering of adulthood.

Chapter 7 is dedicated to the patronal feasts of the planting season during the month of September. In particular, it focuses on the *rinuwa* ('renewal') feasts when numerous *siku* panpipe groups, drums and other instruments are played side by side in cacophony. This music is interpreted in the context of a local musical exegesis, the story of a conflict over water, in which the devil has monopolized the water god requires for his children. This powerful imagery resonates vividly with local ideas about seasonal change, and the power struggle between the powers of darkness (devil) and light (god). Where the balanced exchanges of *tinku* and *julajula* panpipes in the previous chapter stressed life and continuity, *rinuwa* music concerns rebellion, destruction and overturning the existing order.

Invoking death and destruction, and putting the world out of balance in order to achieve new life remains an important theme with the onset of the rainy season in Chapter 8, which is closely connected with the feast of All Saints (1 November). *Pinkillu* flutes begin to be played, explicitly to call the rain and promote crop growth. The chapter explores two key cultural concepts reflected in Kalankira's music: *tara* refers to a powerful vibrant and highly 'productive' timbre, much sought after by players, while *q'iwa* describes a thin, clear and relatively 'unproductive' sound.

With the climax of the growing season, as the fields and hills become verdant and decked with flowers, we come to the feast of Carnival; the theme of Chapter 9 and the culmination of the musical year. Musical devils, called *sirinus*, begin to emerge from within the earth on the feast of their patron, St Sebastian (20 January), and continue to roam the hills at night until the end of

Carnival, their fatally seductive music potentially luring away anybody who strays out alone at night. They bring with them the new *wayñu* melodies of the year, and are said to emerge from the earth in the same way as new fruits, in particular potatoes. These *wayñus* herald the new generation of fruits, and evoke or represent the soul substance that will be embodied within them following the culmination of Carnival.

Rather than bringing together the book's disparate strands, to leave the reader with an excessively unified conclusion, chapter Chapter 10 takes the form of an epilogue. It explores a few developments over the subsequent decade, including tragedy and conflict, which bring the very notion of 'community' into question. Finally an ear is turned to the future.

Worlds of Sound

Energy, weeping and feeding: the background to music

One morning on the long journey back to the highlands with my host family's llama herd, loaded with sacks of maize from the temperate valleys, we stopped for a rest. While the llamas munched the coarse *ichhu* grass, the four of us sat and nibbled toasted broad beans; peeling the skin off each bean, before popping its delicious and tooth-shatteringly hard kernel into our mouths. Bean husks lay strewn around my feet, but – as I noticed with some embarassment – there were none visible close to my companions. Was I being greedy and eating more than my fair share? Then I observed Asencio pass a handful of empty husks to his mother, doña Asunta, who carefully packed them away, prompting me to enquire what she would do with these empty husks. 'If we leave them out here on the mountainside', she explained, 'they will weep like abandoned babies. They must be taken home and put on the fire or in the pot of potato peelings that is cooked up for the dog'.

The idea that these tiny empty bean husks were suffused with human-like sentiment, and that it was our responsibility to ensure their destiny and place in the order of things was a revelation. It also made me shamefully aware of the immense waste in my own society, and the gulf between our ways of approaching the world. I later learnt that all food crops are considered 'to weep' (*waqay*) if not cared for appropriately, highlighting peoples' emotional bond with the 'products' they bring into the world. Agricultural production was presented as a complex, shifting and interdependent web of relationships, where the wellbeing of humans depends upon productive relations with a multiplicity of beings, including the food crops they consume – whose cries powerfully express mutual dependence. The same verb *waqay* ('to weep/cry') is also used to refer to the production of sound by any musical instrument; sounds that are explicitly played to articulate relations with others – human and otherwise, whether serving to console, enchant or bring joy.

This chapter serves as an introduction and guide to several key themes in this book. It will explore the ontology of sound in Kalankira, as an expression of life energy and emotional power, and consider its place in producing and maintaining the relations that lie at the very heart of (human) existence and social life. This leads to a local story about human origins and a discussion of the *ayllu* (ethnic group), alterity and the production of identity.

Animu – Animating energy

Food crops weep in the same way as humans, it was explained, because they contain *animu*: the animating quality or essence of all living things, which is also found in certain types of rocks. The earth – with its body-like transformations, hydraulic movements and winds – is also considered to be full of *animu*, as are bright celestial bodies such as the sun, moon, stars and lightening. *Animu* is expressed as sound, movement, light, scent and autoresonance – its presence may be perceived through any of the sensory modalities.[1] Sound is equivalent to life and its shaping in music may, in certain respects, be seen as shaping life.

The word *animu* is a Quechua borrowing from the Spanish *ánimo*, which is typically translated into English as 'soul' or 'spirit'. However, the Kalankiras' use of the word *animu* suggests that it is a hybrid concept with roots in both Andean and European cultures (Stobart 2000:31). According to Paulino, each body is endowed with and contains a given amount of *animu*, which is expressed in multiples of three – a number with which it has a special association. This quantity of *animu* both denotes the character of the body and should not change through the course of its life. Thus, he asserted that men are physically stronger than women because they have six (identical) *animus* whereas women have only three.[2] Similarly, the immense power of the mountains (*jurq'us*) is related to their possession of twelve *animus*, a number used in ritual offerings (*despachos*) to convey a sense of 'abundance and fulfilment' (Armstong 1988:39). The number twelve (*chunka iskayniyuq*) is also related to the concept of *luriya* (Sp. *gloria* 'Glory'), which sometimes manifests itself as bright flashes of light in the night sky. Like other celestial bodies and phenomena, such as the sun, moon, stars and lightning, *luriya* is considered a particularly powerful source of *animu* – its relationship to humans compared to that between father and son. Perhaps reflecting this same association with the energy of light, the colour white is also especially linked with *animu*. For example, the white ruff of feathers on a condor's neck that stands out against its black body is referred to as *animu*.

With death, the energizing *animu* contained in the body is said to flow out and become *alma*; a Spanish loan word meaning 'soul' and exclusively associated with the dead.[3] 'The person's *animu* transforms to *alma*'

---

[1] The concept of *animu*, as described to me in Kalankira, has a number of similarities with Catherine Allen's account of the 'animating essence' *sami* of Sonqo, Peru (1988:49–54).

[2] He also pointed out that two *animus* can be seen in a person's shadow – for men and women alike.

[3] Rather different versions of the relationship between *animu* and *alma*, as well as the different aspects of the soul, are given in accounts from other parts of the Andes. See for example, Carter & Mamani 1982:348–9, Allen 1982, 1988:57–63 and Gose 1994:115–16.

(*animullataq almaman tukupun runaqta*) I was told. It is extremely dangerous for a living person to lose *animu* from the body, and many illnesses are attributed to its loss or corruption. 'Soul loss' is a well-documented category of illness in the Andes, where it is usually called *susto* (lit. 'fright, sudden terror') in Spanish, and attributed to unexpected shock (Joralemon & Sharon 1993:235–6). In Kalankira, the owl (*juqu*) and a small bird called the *ch'iki* (which ressembles a stonechat) were both claimed to steal people's *animu* and thus considered especially malevolent. In particular, the *ch'ik ch'ik* call of the *ch'iki* bird, which was seen quite regularly around my host family's homestead, was directly associated with 'cutting' or pecking away a person's *animu* from the body.

In other contexts, such as when Asencio was suddenly taken ill and collapsed following a wedding, this same percussive *ch'ik ch'ik* sound was associated with curses and sorcery; in this case of certain individuals known to be in dispute with Asencio.[4] In his survey of South American religions, Lawrence Sullivan suggestively observes that: 'Sound is always meaningful and whole. Speech threatens that integrity by fracturing the sound so that the meaning is parcelled out one syllable, one word, one sentence, or one spoken idea at a time' (1988:284). When the body is viewed as a vessel of *animu*, this contrast between resonant sounds, as whole, meaningful and healthy, literally 'as sound as a bell', and those that are fractured, impaired or foreshortened becomes highly relevant. The *ch'ik ch'ik* of sorcerers or the *ch'iki* bird, with its staccato and percussive ejective, and final velar stop (*'k'*), richly evokes a sense of fracturing or cutting, abruptly silencing the vowel sound. If we think of *animu* as sound that is musically orchestrated from the body's core, any threat to the integrity of this sound/*animu* might in turn be understood as a danger to the integrity of the body and the energies that animate it.

Musical instruments as bodies of *animu*

The link between musical sound and *animu* was made explicit in a multiplicity

---

[4] These sounds and curses were also referred to as *runa simi*, literally 'people mouth', which is often glossed as 'language' (that is, Quechua, from an indigenous perspective). Perhaps ironically, indigenous language activists have adopted the name *runa simi* in certain parts of the Andes as an indigenized alternative to the term 'Quechua', which according to Bruce Mannheim was adopted by the Spanish during the colonial period (1991:7). The term has now become disseminated in many parts of the Andes and, for example, appears in a number of Quechua language instruction manuals (for example, Grondin 1990). Thomas Solomon cites an example of the juxtaposition of '*runa simi*' and 'Quechua' in a song text sung by a peasant literacy campaign instructor in Northern Potosí, where the term *runa simi* has also begun to function 'as a means to re-establish the [language's] supposed native name' (1997:59). In the early 1990s at least the people of Kalankira clearly did not share these positive associations of *runa simi* with indigenous heritage; rather the term carried very negative connotations.

Figure 2.1   Two *Wislulu*: globular whistles used in healing practices.

of contexts and is perhaps best understood through considering the *wislulu*, a globular whistle commonly used in healing practices (Figure 2.1). *Wislulu* resemble hollowed-out oak apples (1–2 cm in diameter) and include a small orifice that may be blown across, panpipe-like, to produce a high-pitched whistling sound. Paulino claimed that *wislulu* grow on *q'ara ñanta* trees in the warmer valley regions of Northern Potosí and are sometimes blown up to the highlands during the windy month of August. They may also be purchased from market stalls specialising in ritual goods and are widely used in rituals to cure the loss or corruption of *animu*.[5]

Paulino also described how *wislulu* whistles, which are similar in form to the brass *wala* (Spanish *bala*) used by shamans to call down the mountain spirits, have the power to communicate with other people through the medium of dreams. If I were to sound a *wislulu* and think of somebody, he explained, this would lead me to appear in that person's dreams. Even if far away in England, he insisted, I could attract a person irresistibly towards me through sounding a *wislulu*. He compared this directness of communication to that of the telephone (despite, to my knowledge, having never actually used one).[6] It

---

[5] See Stobart 2000 for an account of the use of the *wislulu* in a healing ritual.

[6] Much daily importance and practical significance was attributed to dreams by my host family. Dreams from the previous night were sometimes discussed over our morning meal and, on the pretext of bad dreams, planned activities or journeys were occasionally cancelled (see also Mannheim 1987, Valladolid Rivera 1998:64, Howard 2002:28–9).

was made evident from various conversations and their use in curing rituals, that the containment of *animu* within a *wislulu* was related to its containment within a living (human) body (Stobart 2000:36–40). This was further highlighted when Paulino mentioned that the size of the *wislulu* should correspond to the size of the person who owns and sounds it. Thus, he explained, I would need an especially large *wislulu* because I was so tall. The idea of the *wislulu* as a container of *animu* and its association with body size provides us with some helpful perspectives on the construction and performance of musical instruments. For example, *julajula* panpipe construction and performance stresses the idea of a graduated sequence of receptacles – containing *animu* – where each represents a different stage or moment in the growth of a body. Indeed, it will be argued that this music and its associated dance are intimately associated with inner bodily growth and the prolongation of life. By contrast the *pinkillu* flutes of the rains are 'full of holes' and evoke the idea of *animu* emerging from within the instruments, in the same way as from a body, and transforming into *alma*. Accordingly, the performance of these duct flutes is intimately associated with death, but also regeneration.

Weeping and feeding: the 'heart' of production

Weeping (whether of a potato, infant or musical instrument) powerfully expresses the guardian-dependent relationship necessary for a dependent to live, develop and achieve its potential. In turn, the very act of 'hearing' (that is, responding to) such sounds, for example by providing food, comfort or care, confers status, responsibility and authority on the hearer. As Penny Harvey has remarked, the act of feeding is one of the principal means of creating kinship and facilitating relationships in the Andes. One makes oneself into an adult by starting to produce and feed others, and into a community elder by feeding the participants – especially the musicians and dancers – during feasts (1998:74). In turn, spirit and ancestral guardians are seen to feed the human community, by ensuring the (re)production of their herds and crops. The reciprocal nature of such feeding is sometimes made explicit, through ritual food offerings or social mechanisms such as *chuqu*, *ayni* or *mink'a*, where for example food is sometimes given in return for labour.[7] But Harvey

---

[7] Formalized forms of labour exchange are common in many parts of the Andes, but collective work in return for festive food (*chuqu*) – for example to help the elderly, infirm or widows with harvest – is not unusual (Harris 1982b:85). The best documented forms of exchange are *ayni*, where labour is reciprocated by labour in a similar branch of production, and *mink'a* where labour is remunerated with produce resulting from the work, such as part of the day's harvest (Harris 1982b:87). More generally, *ayni* refers to an obligation of reciprocity that may equally apply to revenge (Lucca 1987:32; Gonzalez Holguín 1989 [1608]: 40). Gose (1994:4–16) has developed a

observes that the provision of food by parents to children, alongside the hierarchy of responsibility and authority this entails, is 'uni-directional'. In other words 'kinship is the result of having been fed by others whom one has not fed oneself; it does not involve reciprocity' (1998:75).[8] Whereas food, authority and responsibility might be seen to pass uni-directionally from guardians to dependents, the cries of offspring or musical instruments (that is, sound) may be seen to move in the opposite direction – whether expressing desire, distress or youthful energy.

Sound initiates this process through communicating sentiment and literally *is* the energy or animating quality (*animu*) of living things or their potential. It is expressed from below or within (specifically from the *sunqu* 'heart' or inner earth) to 'produce' particular ends. For example young people are said to be *sunquyuq* ('possessing heart or sap'): a vitality that is thought to be lost or to dry-up in adulthood. They travel along, what might be called, the 'youth pathway', connected with *sonic production*, growth and accumulation of energies derived from others. In turn, guardians pass along the 'adult pathway', linked with *sonic reception* and the circulation and dissipation of energies through feeding others. From this perspective production and the workings of society and the cosmos are a kind of dual interdependent system. On the one hand, immature, unpredictable and demanding dependents – whose hunger, desires, anger and energy are especially vividly expressed through sound – bring energy, transformation, enchantment, joy and consolation. They are the future – that which has yet to be 'produced' and made visible. On the other hand, mature guardians/ancestors, associated with hearing and compassion, provide material sustenance, stability, moral values, control and authority. They are imbued with pastness – that which has been 'produced' and made visible. This imagery evokes the idea of a world that is in constant tension with itself – an ontological tension on which its very existence and continuity is founded.

---

particularly interesting analysis of the productive year in terms of the distinction between *ayni* (as symmetrical and egalitarian) and *mink'a* (as asymmetric and hierarchical) for the case of Huaquirca, Peru. It has some interesting similarities and differences with my own account of Kalankira.

[8] Alternatively the provision of food to offspring might be viewed as a 'gift' that must be repaid at a later date, for example, in the form of labour that young people are expected to contribute to their family. In this case, the cries made by offspring come to represent a kind of contract; indeed in Kalankira the ancestors are referred to as 'loan makers' (*mañaq ruway*) in libations, highlighting both their guardianship and contract with the living.

(behind/future)		(in front/past)
hidden (potential)		revealed ('produced')
Dependents (offpring)	→ crying/vitality →	**Guardians** (parents)
	←feeding/stability ←	
(youth)		**(adulthood)**

To appreciate such ideas it is also necessary to be aware of how the aural and visual senses are expressed in Quechua and Aymara time-space terminology (Miracle & Yapita 1981, Gifford 1986). In both languages the visible is related to coming first (before), being in front or ahead, and the past. In contrast, the future lies behind/after, comes later and is invisible. The Quechua *ñawpa* and Aymara *nayra* refer to events in the past and to space situated in front of ego. This concept relates to visibility and accordingly to the words for 'eye' (Que. *ñawi*, Aym. *nayra*). The Quechua and Aymara *qhipa* (*q'ipa, qhepa*) refers to space situated 'behind' ego and to 'future' events or those that come 'after'. From a human perceptual perspective, the ears are situated at the boundary between the essentially visual and aural realms; this may also be seen to define the point at which the past and future meet (Figure 2.2). The present might thus perhaps be seen to be represented by audition or hearing. To hear is to exist at a specific place and moment in time; it is the coming together of the creative, undefined latent aural future and the fabric of the visual past.

Ringing rocks and roosters: sound, cosmology and production

People in Kalankira regularly invoke this same dual ontological tension in stories about conflicts between god (*tiusninchis* 'god of us all')[9] and the devil (*supay, yawlu* from *diablo*). God is identified with the sun and is closely associated with 'hearing' and nourishing his children, moral values, revelation and the visible sphere of the past (he comes in front or ahead). The devil, by contrast, is connected with potential – that which has yet to be produced or revealed (coming behind and later) – and darkness. He is contained within the inner earth – kept down and in place through the constant 'trampling' of god's saints, his presence revealed by the voices of wild creatures (*khurus*). The names of these wild creatures were considered onomatopoeic; their names are literally their sounds (CD track 39). This sonic focus of the wild creatures of the devil's inner (*ukhu*) sphere was explicitly contrasted with the visual

---

[9] God is referred to in Kalankira as *tiusninchis*, 'god of all of us' using the Spanish *dios* 'god' and Quechua first person inclusive suffix *-nchis* (with the link *-ni*). I will usually translate *tiusninchis* simply as 'god'.

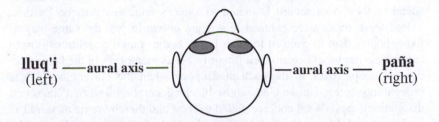

VISUAL
(in front, past, before)

Ñawpa

lluq'i —aural axis—   —aural axis— **paña**
(left)   (right)

Qhipa
(behind, future, follows)

AURAL
(latent sound)

Figure 2.2   Quechua time-space terminology and the aural axis

associations of the domestic animals of 'god's side' (*tiusninchis laru*), which are principally named according to the colours of their fleece (Flores 1986: 137–48).

The devil accumulates resources, especially water (that is metaphorically linked to sound), which he refuses to share with others (god's children). His relationship with god is in constant tension and flux, shifting with the seasonal alternation between the powers of light (god) and darkness (devil). This dual relationship and its connection with sound and light are vividly expressed in a story told by Asencio to explain the origin of the bell stones (*rumi kampana*) on Kanqali hill, a few minutes walk above Pata Kalankira. Like several other individuals, Asencio associated the derivation of the name 'Kalankira' (*Cayanquira*) with the bell-like *kalan kalan* sound emitted by these rocks when struck with a smaller stone (Figure 2.3, CD track 38). The ringing rocks also sound of their own accord on nights with a full moon (*jurt'a*) or dark of the moon (*wañun*), I was told, when they 'awaken' and 'walk around' together with other rocks, such as *illas* and *samiri*, which cry out like mating llamas or bulls and are linked with cattle reproduction. Asencio related the origin of the bell stones to a wager between god and *supay* ('devil'), represented respectively by black and red roosters. It was arranged that when god sent up the sun the owner of the first cockerel to crow would be the winner, but the loser would suddenly disappear '*kun!*' and be transformed to stone. In the story, god's black cockerel crowed first and 'right then *supay* entered inside the stone and became that bell. God had won'.[10] As if by chance, a new world order was created with god ruling the visible external sphere and *supay* ('devil') the invisible or dark inner one.

Asencio's tale highlights how the bell stones' resonance and ability to sound of their own accord is linked to *supay*'s animated presence within; indeed these rocks were claimed to contain *animu* in just the same way as living bodies. But in contrast to other living bodies that die and transform to earth, these hard rocks retain their integrity, act as memorials in the landscape, connect people back to the enchanted epoch when the current world was brought into being. Unlike God, whose black cockerel crowed first (its sound dissipating), *supay*'s red cockerel failed to crow and thereby remains stored as sonic potential. Many months later, Asencio invoked this same sonic potential in a libation for a *kitarra* (rainy season guitar) I had recently purchased. As we drank he exclaimed:

> It will crow like a cockerel. Let's drink to the Churikala cockerel. Let's drink for the cockerel rock so that [the *kitarra*] crows like a cockerel![11]

Discussing this later, he explained that *supay*'s red cockerel would make my *kitarra* sound well, but not god's black one. In the same way as *supay* is imprisoned in Kalankira's bell stones, he observed, the red cockerel of the libation is enclosed in a rock close to the village of Churikala, near the mining town of Colquechaka (Map 3). This suggests that its potential to crow remains stored up as *animu* within the rock, acting as a resource that may be invoked to enhance the sound of musical instruments. Indeed the practice of sacrificing a red cockerel and spilling a little blood on musical instruments in order to improve their sound quality is widespread in the Bolivian Andes.[12]

Asencio's story of the bell stones helps us appreciate why people invoke the red cockerel and the demonic forces of the inner earth as the creative source of powerful new musical sounds and melodies, which herald material

---

[10] *Supayqa ya listu ukhuman yaykupun rumiman tukupun a, chay kampanapis. Tiusninchis chayta kanan i.*

[11] *Gallo jina qhaparinqa. Churikala gallopaq tumarisunchis Gallo qaqapaq tomarisunchis gallo jina qhaparinanpaq.*

[12] Red roosters are sometimes sacrificed before important musical performances in other parts of Bolivia. I witnessed one such ritual in Walata Grande, an instrument-making village in La Paz department. As no red rooster was available, a red guinea pig was used instead, and the animal made to squeak moments before it was sacrificed. In her superb 1994 documentary film *The Devil's Horn* about Bolivian brass bands, the Dutch visual anthropologist Miranda van der Spek includes a sequence in which a red cockerel is sacrificed to the *sereno* [*sirinu*] and its blood dripped onto the instruments. INDICEP 1973:4 also notes the obligation to sacrifice a cockerel to the *sereno* [*sirinu*].

Figure 2.3   Asencio Jara and the author playing a bell stone on Kanqali hill

productions, such as potato harvest. Although surprisingly from an orthodox Catholic view, I was told that the devil (*supay*) transforms into god – as if the two are one and the same body at different phases in its life cycle (youth and adulthood) – the first connected with growth and accumulation and the second with nourishing others. In other words, the devil is 'unproductive' as far as others are concerned, whereas god embodies the apotheosis or victory of 'production' – (a point made especially clear in Chapters 7 and 9). Yet, the devil – in his very tendency to accumulate energies at the expense of others – embodies 'productive potential' – whilst god's energies are circulated and dwindle.

All devils are considered *q'iwa*, a word used to describe a thin 'unproductive' flute sound – suggestive of weeping or wailing – and also applied to individuals who are mean, selfish or cowardly, or small children who whinge and wail unnecessarily. People dubbed *q'iwa* accumulate resources for their own personal benefit, just as castrated male llamas (*q'iwas*) grow fat whereas their stud counterparts remain thin – their energies dedicated to reproduction. The word carries a multiplicity of negative connotations where lack of 'production' and cultural dissonance merge as one. *Q'iwa* musical timbre is contrasted with that of *tara*, which is vibrant and rich – that is, highly productive. *Tara* not only means 'harmonious' but is also applied to paired things that are productive through their reciprocation; such as the married couple at the heart of a productive family unit. In this sense *tara* is evocative of the local Quechua concept of *yanantin*, which is applied to paired things which belong together, such as arms, eyes or paired ritual drinking vessels, and which, according to Platt, may be strictly translated as 'helper and helped united to form a unique category' (1986:245).[13] *Tara* also evokes both a sense of sexual climax and death rattle, as if reaching the peak of 'youth pathway' or even life itself before embarking on the pathway of the ancestral guardians. The invocation, on the one hand, of personal accumulation as *q'iwa*, and on the other of release and circulation for the benefit of others as *tara*, would seem to underwrite many local understanding of relationships and musical organization. Indeed, I wish to suggest that the categories of *tara* and *q'iwa*, which are perhaps most vividly presented and juxtaposed in musical performance, are of critical importance to understanding conceptions of production in Kalankira – and may have considerable wider relevance to the study of production in the Andes.[14]

Balancing and consolation

Bringing *tara* and *q'iwa* into tune or equilibrium with one another in musical performance is often seen as an immense challenge. Not only does this refer to the practical problems of tuning two *pinkillu* flutes, pitched a fifth apart, together, but more generally of bringing *q'iwa*'s tendency for personal accumulation into dialogue or relation with *tara*'s association with productivity. The challenge is to match dependents (offspring) with guardians (nurturers), in order to initiate the uni-directional feeding process whereby kinship is created and life giving substances pass from one generation to the next. In this context, the notions of *tara* and *q'iwa* may usefully be seen as two extremes, stressing respectively the initiation of life (infancy) and its apotheosis (death/marriage), when accumulated energies are released. These ideas not only stress the dangerous extremes of life – its beginning and end – but also highlight disjunction, difference and hierarchy; the contrast in generation, size, power, knowledge and age between newly created and fully matured bodies. This disjunction and diachronic difference lies at the very heart of generating productive relations, powerfully expressed in the weeping and feeding relationship – and, as we shall see, is closely connected with the rainy growing season.

---

[13] The Quechua *yana* means help and the suffix – *tin* refers to a 'totality' or 'unity'.

[14] See Stobart 1996a for an overview of the concepts of *tara* and *q'iwa*. In this book I considerably develop the broader significance of these categories.

As offspring grow, become stronger and acquire independence their cries gradually lose the power to provoke compassion and the provision of nourishment. Young humans learn to shape these cries into speech and music, using these instead of weeping to achieve their needs and desires. Although still emotionally powerful, youthful voices and musical expressions must increasingly be accompanied by tangible contributions to the family's material production, such as pasturing animals and labouring in the fields. Gradually, as youths develop, their focus moves away from dependence to independence, where the provision of needs becomes associated with the reciprocity of mutual exchanges. The disjunction and uni-directional flow of nourishment across the generations gradually becomes balanced out and difference is downplayed. Dual relationships in music (for example between paired *julajula* panpipes) are instead characterized as 'elder' (*kuraq*) and 'younger' (*sullka*) brothers. The disjunction between generations (death and birth – as life's extremes) is negated, highlighting instead ideas of perpetual life – linked with the accumulation of fat – achieved through balanced and reciprocal exchanges. The exchanges between brothers are presented in terms of 'perfect equilibrium' (*puru iwalasqa*), but a degree of hierarchy is always present – indeed it is critical to generating exchanges and the flow of energies. As we shall see, these ideas of balancing, where cries across the generation gap – from offspring dependents to mature guardians – are transformed to 'enquiries' and exchanges between interdependent age mates, are closely associated with the dry winter months.

In a kind of nested hierarchy of nurturing, humans are responsible for the wellbeing of their foodcrops and domestic animals, adult humans for their children, and the spirit guardians for the human community. Indeed, spirit guardians are referred to as *tatas* ('fathers') and *mamas* ('mothers') and in stories, when these beings speak to their human charges, they refer to them as *wawas* ('children'/'offspring').

wawas ('offspring'/'children')	tatas/mamas ('fathers'/'mothers')
food crops	humans
human babies	human parents
human community	spirit guardians

In this nested hierarchy, *wawas* express their relationship to their respective *tatas* or *mamas* through sound. In the human community this takes the form of festive music, which in Kalankira is widely referred to as *kunswilu* ('consolation'). This music is intended to animate and bring *alegría* ('joy', 'merriment') to the spirit guardians, I was told, to console them for their sacrifices. Sometimes the recipients of this *kunswilu* were specified as the guardians or saints remembered in a particular feast, at others no specific guardians were invoked. It is notable that it is principally young people on the 'youth pathway' connected with aural expression, growth and accumulation who are expected to provide *kunswilu* (suggesting that community adults and elders are also, in part, recipients). Thus, through the process of human socialization the powerful and demanding cries of young helpless dependents are gradually transformed into musical expressions of consolation.

Pachakuti: time and transformation

During major feasts, it was often stressed that young people must play *kunswilu* ('consolation') continuously. On several occasions, when silence temporarily reasserted itself during a feast, I witnessed elders angrily insist that the musicians resume playing and continue dancing – despite being almost too exhausted and intoxicated to stand. This sense of sensory saturation during feasts contrasts vividly with the austerity of daily life, when most people rarely encounter music, or consume meat or alcohol (Stobart 2002a:100). As in many other parts of the high Andes, the overwhelming daily impression of Kalankira's soundscape is of silence, where sounds almost seem to be swallowed by the immensity of the open, barren and treeless landscape. Constance Classen suggests that the emphasis placed on sound by Andean people may be a way for compensating for the silence and the vast empty spaces of their highland environment (1991:252). To interpret the dynamic nature of much rural music of the high Andes as a form of acoustic compensation would be unduly functionalist, but the preference for strong and full sounds is striking. For the most part, the musical aesthetic is for strident and high-pitched women's vocal timbre, loud and piercing metal *charango* strings,[15] and registers that exploit the upper harmonics of wind instruments. Blowing a flute gently, in order to produce a soft, mellow and low-pitched timbre would be almost unthinkable for the people of Kalankira, who tend to aim for sounds that are dense, hoarse, vibrant or shrill.

It is as if Kalankira's feasts represent a sensory reversal or a *pachakuti* ('world turning') where the habitual silence and austerity is replaced by perpetual sound, abundant food and copious alcohol – transforming the hamlet and its inhabitants and invoking new forms, paths and trajectories. *Pachakuti* is well known in Andean ethnography and ethnohistory and is particularly associated with transformation from one order or 'epoch' (*timpu*) to another; such as the cataclysm that marked the end of primordial epoch of the *chullpas* and the start of the present period of culture and order (see below).[16]

---

[15] In urban contexts the *charango* is usually strung with nylon strings that create a mellower timbre than metal ones.

[16] *Pacha* implies both time and space, or the earth itself, and *kuti* suggests 'turning' or 'reversal'. See also Harris 1987:100–103; Bouysse-Cassagne & Harris 1987:28–35.

Such reversals are commonly associated with, or attributed to, the agency of musical sound. For example, according to the early chronicler Martín de Murúa, during his reign the ninth Inca king saw a man appear on a mountain pass near Cusco dressed in red and carrying a conch shell trumpet. The king earned himself the name Pachakuti Inca through persuading the man not to sound his trumpet, and thereby avoiding an *unu pachakuti* (apocalypse by water) (Zuidema 1985:215–17, Allen 1988:98). Catherine Allen relates a myth from Sonqo, Peru, in which a man sounded a (conch shell) trumpet causing a period plague (*pisti timpu*) and a reversal of the social order; domestic animals ate humans, and people consumed their children instead of nurturing them (1988:98). Similarly, in Kalankira, Asencio once sounded a *pututu* (ox-horn trumpet) during a lunar eclipse to revive the moon, which I was told had become 'ill' (*unqusqa*). I was amazed by the contagious terror that the eclipse inspired, with much wailing from women and children alongside strange unearthly noises from the chickens. Large stretches of dried grasses on the hillsides were set alight, and dozens of sticks of dynamite exploded. If the moon were to die, I was told, the 'earth would turn inside out' (*mundu tikrakamun*) – water would emerge from within to submerge its surface and we would all perish, highly reminiscent of Murúa's *unu pachakuti* (cataclysm by water). These examples highlight how through Andean history musical sound has continued to be identified with the articulation of shifts between distinct spatio-temporal orders, as well as with influencing hydraulic processes, so critical to life in the high Andes' arid environment.

Rather than serving as an accompaniment to productive tasks, as do 'work songs', music in Kalankira may be seen to operate at a more cosmological level as a means to transform time (and space) and to orchestrate cycles of production.[17] Indeed, we might think of the 'musical year' as a life cycle, which begins following Carnival (February/March); a single integrated performance that synthesises and creatively articulates the cycles of potatoes, llamas and humans, as well as the sun, moon and seasons.[18] This annual cycle of music is punctuated by *pachakuti*-like moments of radical change or reversal from one movement (phase in development, instrument, genre) to the next. In Kalankira's unfolding musical year these shifts sometimes take the form of ritual transitions called *kacharpaya* ('despatches'). People frequently connected these moments of radical transformation or transition, from one temporal order to the next, with the mythic catcalysm that brought the known world and moral humans (*runa*) into existence.

---

[17] Similarly, in his study of the northern Bolivian Callawaya, Oblitas Poblete has related the performance of *pincollo* flutes with *bombo* drums to attract rain to the 'transformation of time' (1978 [1960]:360).

[18] Anthony Seeger has also compared the Amazonian Suyá's year to a song (1987:140).

The coming of humans (*runa*)

The well-known story of the coming of humans (*runa*), reported in many parts of the Andes, was often recounted to me in Kalankira. According to Asencio's version, the earth was formerly inhabited by a prehuman race called the *chullpas* who were unable to speak and lived in half-light (*tuqra*), lit only by 'mother-moon, our mother the holiest Mary' (*killa mama*, *mamanchis Maria santisima*). The earth's soil was soft (*llamp' llamp'u*) and fecund, the stones buried deep inside. Don Adrian Chura, the oldest man in the district, referred to this primordial epoch of the *chullpas* as *amu timpu* or 'time of silence'. The word *amu*, which is common to both Quechua and Aymara, not only refers to silence, lack of speech or meditation, but also to the bud of a flower – it is an expectant silence, and suggests thoughts buried in memory.[19]

This primordial period of 'silence' ended when the *wirjin* ('virgin', or 'earth mother') gave birth to the sun, god the Holy Father. As he rose up, the *chullpa* race was roasted, 'totally burnt-up ... just like boiled potatoes'. In the words of Asencio:

> Well, *supay* [the devil] had appeared ... and god defeated him. If god had been beaten, then today there would have been no human beings. Perhaps there would have been *supay* beings ... throughout the world. As it happened, god won. So with god winning today we are human beings ... speaking and everything.
>
> Well then, he [*supay*] disappeared and entered somewhere in the earth ... that's why he's inside the earth, trampled-in, isn't he? That's why, because our god defeated him.[20]

Asencio told me that had god lost his fight with *supay* – as the world was being brought into being – the earth would have been populated by *supays*. The current world order and hierarchy, in which god comes first and is associated with revelation and the visual sphere, and *supay* comes later and is linked with containment, darkness and aural expression, would be reversed.

The violent and burning cataclysm of the sun's birth signalled the end of the soft and silent primordial era of the *chullpas* and announced the start of the Inka's epoch (*inka timpu*). In Kalankira the time of the 'Inka King' and of the

---

[19] The Aymara *amtasiña* 'act of remembering' and *amta* 'memory' also come from this same substantive root *amu* (Arnold 1988:380). This seems to contrast with the more negative associations of the *upa* (Quechua) which comes closer to the connotations of the English 'dumb', perhaps implying 'ignorance' and 'loss' rather than 'memory' and 'potential' (Howard-Malverde 1990a).

[20] *Supay chayñataq rikhurirqa ... intunsisqa tiusninchisñataq chay kanaykusqa. Tiusninchis kananman karqa, intunsis kunitan mana runa kashasunmanchu runa karqa. Supay kashanman karqa i? ... tukuy muntupi. Ya intunsis tiusninchis kanan. Ya intunsis tiusninchis kanaqtinqa kunanqa runa kashanchis a. Parlashanchis tukuy ima. Intunsis payqa chinkapun may jallp'a ukhu[man] yaykupun. Chayrayku jallp'a ukhupi, sarusqa i? Chayrayku tiusninchis kanasqanrayku.*

first enlightened humans (*runa*) was also referred to as *inkantu timpu* ('time of enchantment'), and *inkitu timpu* ('time of restlessness') because forms still remained fluid, ambiguous and undetermined. In this 'story time' (*kintu timpu*), as it is also known, wild animals (*khurus*) such as the condor, fox, partridge and toad freely transformed into humans, whilst for example pumas (*michi*) became rocks.

The Inka king, who appears to be thought of as a common ancestor (rather than related directly to the 'historical' Inkas), is said to have taught people how to speak and to play musical instruments. I was told that these same instruments are still played to this day and that people continue to perform his customs and dances. I encountered a considerable sense of nostalgia for the Inka's enchanted epoch when people were 'really together'.

> The Inka died, it seems the Inka ... was wiped out, completely. Then after that in the same way god was born. More and more the people multiplied. [The Inka] disappeared just like that, he was trampled down too. Then it was no longer the Inka's epoch in the way it had been with the toad and the wild animals [turning into humans]; no longer the era of the distant past (*ñawpa timpu*). In that time of the distant past ... in the same way the partridge was a woman, the toad was also a woman ... the [condor] was a man and carried girls off to [his] rock.[21]

Most people were a little vague about what happened following the death of the Inka and the somewhat surprising birth of god. Sometimes, usually following my suggestions, I was told about the 'Spanish' (*Ispañulis*) but as far as most people were concerned the story ends with the death of the Inka and the multiplication of the population. The critical part of the story, in every telling, was the cataclysmic transition from the silent moonlit epoch of the *chullpa* ancestors to the Christian solar age, which according to Tristan Platt in a study of childbirth practices in the Macha region is compared with the trauma of human birth (2002:128, 136). This analogy powerfully evokes the transition from expectant silence to sound – as the infant's demanding cries for comfort and nourishment. Platt characterizes the human foetus, within the mother's womb as aggressive and voracious; as if the woman is possessed by a 'small devil', and birth itself is likened to a battle (2002:132). This resembles Asencio's description of god's battle and defeat of the devil, after the 'virgin' (also a term for fields) had given birth to the sun – as if bringing the child into the solar Christian realm. In turn, the nostalgic epoch of enchantment, restlessness and transformations of the Inka king, and his teaching of speech, music and dance, are strikingly redolent of human childhood.

---

[21] *Inka wañupun, ya Inkachá yasta lliphunapun, ya tukuy ima. Ya tiusninchistaq chay jawaqa nasikullantaq. Astawan astawan ya runataq mirapun ya. Chinkapun a, chinkapun ya listu paypis sarusqallataq ari. Intunsis manaña Inka timpu jinañachu jampat'upis ya, khurusman nin manaña ñawpa timpuñachu a. Ñawpa timpu kaq nin a. Pisarqapis warmi karqa, jampat'upis warmillataq karqa nin [kuntur] qhari karqa, imillasta q'ipiq nin qaqaman.*

God's children

God and the devil feature prominently in Asencio's account of the creation of *runa*, as well as in many other stories I was told. So are the Kalankiras Catholics?[22] The saints are invoked daily when chewing coca before any agricultural work and almost constantly during libations, especially at feasts. As Abercrombie similarly observes among the nearby K'ulta, this devotion appears 'entirely heartfelt, betokening something other than a "thin veneer" of Christianity' (1998:110). Yet, in many cases the forms of these nominally Catholic saints and powers would horrify or be scarcely recognized by the Catholic Church itself.[23] For example, in Kalankira St Francis is known for his sexual prowess, St John is said to be the father of the devil, and St Sebastian is characterized as the patron of the *sirinus* or sirens (musical demons).

As also reported by other ethnographers, the sun is addressed as *tata santisimu* ('holiest father') in libations and is explicitly identified with god *tiusninchis* ('god of all of us'), whilst the moon *Maria, mama santisima* (Mary, holiest mother) is related to the virgin mother. The saints are viewed as immensely powerful and critical to particular or generalized aspects of, for example, agricultural production, health and fortune, but are also characterized as extremely jealous and potentially malevolent.[24] Some saints, I was told, belong to 'god's side' and others to *supay*'s (the devil's), although views about which belongs to who tend to vary according to context, individual knowledge or interpretation. Unsurprisingly, devotion to these less orthodox chthonic powers, which for the Kalankiras are in many respects just as Christian as any others, tends to take place in private – away from the eyes of the priest and outsiders likely to view them as 'a diabolic kind of antireligion' (Abercombie 1998:111). Participation in official public Church ceremony is limited, for the most part, to baptisms, weddings, and mass during certain feasts. Kalankira's own colonial adobe church was rarely unlocked, except for the patronal feasts in September, when the priest from Macha

---

[22] In the early 1990s, only one family in the Kalankira area was said to be *irmanus* ('brothers'); members of an evangelical church. They did not participate in feasts or other community activities and were clearly viewed with considerable ambivalence. The highly restrictive and moralistic attitude to participation in music making, dancing and drinking by certain evangelical Christian sects means that in some parts of the Andes traditional festive forms of music making have become very rare. However, local song genres are sometimes adapted to incorporate Christian words. For example, cassettes of evangelical songs in Carnival-style are widely available in the market centres of Northern Potosí.

[23] However, this is nothing new as is evident from William Christian's study of popular Catholicism in sixteenth-century Spain (1981).

[24] For example, when I travelled to the feast of St James at Bombori with Paulino, he was careful not to enter the church or to light a candle in honour of the saint (*tata pumpuri*). To do so, he explained, would provoke the jealousy of St Sebastian, for whom he lit candles some six months earlier, leading him to devastate the family's flocks.

visited the hamlet to say mass during the festival of Guadalupe. Identity as solar Christians – as god's children – and devotion to a range of nominal saints is critical to being *runa* and to bringing about production in Kalankira. So what does it mean to be, or not to be, *runa* in Kalankira?

Ayllus and alterity: identity, fat and production

The Kalankiras form part of *ayllu* Macha, one of several corporate descent groups of the region who share certain common resources, such as land, and are theoretically endogamous (that is, marry within the *ayllu*).[25] Macha territory comprises a continuous strip of about 100km from high altitude *puna* (rising above 4500m) to warm valley lands (dropping to 2000m). (Maps 2 and 3.) Although formerly Aymara speakers, Quechua has been the dominant language since at least the late nineteenth century. The group is clearly distinguishable from other *ayllus* of the region, such as the Laymis or Pukwatas by certain cultural traits, such as distinctive weaving patterns, style of dress, and forms of music – especially courtship song styles and guitar (*charango* and *kitarra*) construction (Chapter 4).[26] The principal wind instruments of the Machas (*julajula* panpipes, *siku* panpipes, *pinkillu* flutes) are similar to those played in other parts of Northern Potosí and bordering areas; although (with the exception of *siku* panpipes) these are not played in other parts of Bolivia.[27] As in other rural highland communities, the main (melodic) wind instruments are played in consorts or families and instruments from distinct families almost never mixed.[28]

---

[25] See Allen 1988:95–124. The word *ayllu* was used in Inka times to refer to the smallest landholding unit (100 tributaries), and is found widely in the Andes today having been interpreted variously as 'any group with a head' (Isbell 1978:105) or 'any social or political group with a boundary separating it from the outside' (Zuidema in Allen 1988:108).

[26] Walking through the bustling market town of Llallagua, in the heart of Northern Potosí, the peasant people from Macha *ayllu* are much more immediately recognizable than people from other *ayllus*. The men's woollen waistcoats, jackets and knitted hats (*ch'ulus*) and the women's embroidered woollen dresses (*almillas*), embroidered shawls (*rebosos*), and woven backcloths (*aksus*) with *ayllu* specific designs, immediately distinguish them. Among young unmarried women, in particular, *ayllu* Macha is notable for the continued use of the *almilla* and *aksu*. In many other *ayllus* embroidered skirts (*polleras*) have been the norm for at least a decade. The Machas are also distinguishable by their white felt hats, adorned with a black ribbon, which have a narrower brim and are more dimpled than their more northerly counterparts.

[27] For comparative examples from within the Northern Potosí region see Baumann 1982a, 1996, Stobart 1987, Sánchez 1989b, Calvo & Sánchez 1991, Harris 1988, Solomon 1997. For examples from bordering regions see Martínez 1994 on the Jalqas, and Arnold 1992 on the Qaqachakas.

[28] According to one individual, in the past the *kitarra* was sometimes tuned to play in combination with *pinkillus* flutes. As both instruments play rainy season *wayñus* this would be feasible, but I have not encountered this practice nor can I confirm that it was widespread.

The structure and history of *ayllu* Macha has been studied in depth by Tristan Platt, who has demonstrated that they are descendents of the pre-Hispanic federation of the Karakara (Qaraqara), who were yoked in dual organization with the neighbouring Charka federation (Platt 1986, 1982, 1987a). Politically and symbolically the Machas are organized into two moieties (*alasaya* 'upper half', and *majasaya* 'lower half), each of which is further subdivided into five 'minor *ayllus*', which in turn is divided into several *cabildos*. (Figure 6.1 in Chapter 6, shows Kalankira's place in *ayllu* Macha's structure.) The *cabildo* authorities have the most direct involvement with individual hamlets (patrilocal groups) and households, and are, for example, responsible for resolving disputes, distributing common land, and collecting *tasa* (land tax, now essentially symbolic). Selection for these positions of *alcalde*, *jilanqu* and *cobradores* ('tax collectors') is usually limited to those married (male) heads of household who have sponsored several major feasts. However, unlike certain other parts of Bolivia, *ayllu* authorities do not sponsor feasts (see Rasnake 1989:156–64). Indeed Kalankira's *alcalde* should not participate in music and dance during his year of office.

The *ayllu* is not simply a form of hierarchical ethno-political organization; it also refers to people's ongoing and reciprocal relationships with one another and the places they inhabit. These relationships are in turn closely bound up with what it means to be *runa* (plural *runakuna*), a Quechua word meaning 'person' or 'human being' (equivalent to the Aymara *jaqi*) 'culturally, an indigenous Andean person' (Allen 1988:262). In the words of Catherine Allen:

> An *ayllu* exists through the personal and intimate relationship that bonds the people and the place into a single unit. Only when *Runakuna* establish a relationship with a place by building houses out of its soil, by living there, and by giving it offerings of coca and alcohol is an *ayllu* established. The relationship is reciprocal, for the *Runakuna*'s indications of care and respect are returned by the place's guardianship. Mestizo schoolteachers do not make offerings of coca and alcohol, nor do they experience a personal bond with the place; therefore the school cannot be an *ayllu* (1988:106).

In this passage, it is striking how the notions of *ayllu* and *runa* exclude outsiders, such as (urban) *mestizos*, who instead are often referred to as *q'aras* (or *q'alas*) 'naked ones', denoting 'a fundamental lack of a kind of sociability that defines *runas* as human beings' (Gose 1994:22). As in many other parts of the Andes, any stranger who arrives in Kalankira and cannot readily be identified as an *ayllu* member will almost certainly be suspected of being a *llik'ichiri* ('fat stealer'). It is claimed that the fat they extract from *runa* is used in the urban and industrial world for anything from making communion wafers, candles or medicines, to lubricating trains, airplanes or moon rockets (Canessa 2000:713, Gose 1986). 'Body fat' (*llik'i* in Aymara), Andrew

Canessa observes, 'is a fundamental life source deemed to be given by the forces below. This gift defines the relationship of people with the spirit world and also accounts for the productivity of people on the surface of the earth' (2000:716). In stark contrast to the concerns with obesity in some societies, for people of the rural Andes human fat is a rare commodity and vividly expresses notions of accumulating energies, bodily growth, strength and productive potential; ideas that permeate Kalankira's music and dance during the dry winter months.

In much the same way as an *ayllu* is established through reciprocal exchanges between *runa* and spirit guardians, the circulation of fat – an important ingredient in many forms of ritual offering – is critical to ideas of bodily growth and development as a form of exchange process. In contrast, the *llik'ichiri*'s violent and illegitimate extraction of fat from *runa* might, according to Abercrombie, be seen as 'a terrible and antisocial manipulation of the logic of sacrifice', in which 'vital generative powers' are taken 'out of the proper form of circulation among gods, men, and animals, in order to produce an antisocial kind of wealth that cannot sustain itself' (1998:405). Thus, unlike the explicit violence of *tinku* fighting between *ayllu* members, which through balanced exchange – as a kind of 'violent harmony' – redefines boundaries and strengthens bodies enabling *runa* to achieve their life potential, the *llik'ichiri* uses clandestine violence to invade, weaken and potentially destroy the body.[29] Its corrupting power and violence polices the boundary between *runa* and *q'ara*, between identity and alterity, throwing into relief the processes by which identity and community are created, and thus who are insiders and who outsiders (Canessa 2000:717).

A point sometimes overlooked is that *runa* is just one aspect of the identity of peasant people such as the Kalankiras. *Runa* identity is 'produced', more or less consciously and collectively, in determined contexts to achieve particular 'productive' ends. Viewed from the perspective of the productive year there is good reason to argue that the Kalankiras only make themselves truly *runa* – 'produce' *runa* identity in its full glory or apotheosis – at Carnival, the zenith or flowering of the growing season. In other contexts or seasons, they tend to stress alternative elements of their identity linked with other 'imagined

---

[29] Despite well-documented histories of violence between *mestizos* and peasants in many parts of the Andes (Stern 1987), the Kalankiras rarely mention explicit violence in their encounters with *cholo* or *mestizo* townsfolk. In practice, opinions of *cholos* they know are selective, reflecting the treatment received from them; individual shopkeepers of Macha respectively considered *bueno* ('nice, good natured'), *sajra* ('evil, nasty') or imperious (*imperiakuq*). Yet, explicit violence often was invoked when talking about *ayllu* identity and affiliations, where groups from the opposing moiety or other minor *ayllus* – with whom common values and modes of cultural expression were shared – were referred to as 'enemies'. This suggests a kind of structural opposition, expressed most vividly in *tinku* ritual battles, seen to strengthen and reinforce both the physical body and the *ayllu* in a kind of 'violent harmony'.

communities', such as urban *mestizo* (*cholo* or *mozo*) or the Bolivian nation (Anderson 1991), each carrying its respective 'imagined' values, imagery, modes of production or collective power. For example, the Kalankiras often wear purchased *mestizo* style clothing on trading journeys outside the community to avoid discrimination, to present themselves as 'civilized' (*civilizado*) and to improve their bargaining power – thereby not only easing relations with *mestizos* but also potentially improving (economic) productivity.[30] In so doing, they are not simply adopting a false or 'inauthentic' identity, but producing a particular aspect of their '(in)dividuality'[31] – one that might appear to be violently contradicted in another context (such as in discourse about *llik'ichiris*).

An important point for this book is that the *q'ara* or *mestizo* association with individual accumulation at the expense of others (whether through balanced monetary exchange or corrupt means) becomes a trope for a particular aspect of the productive process. Through producing such forms of identity and behaviour the Kalankiras, both in individual encounters and collective festive performances, invoke ideas of (capitalist style) accumulation or bodily growth connected with particular phases in their cycles or routines of social, personal and agrarian production.

---

[30] In much the same way, I sometimes find myself invoking aspects of my rural background, which may include negative attitudes about perceived 'townie' values and ways of life, whereas in other contexts I may stress elements of an educated or cosmopolitan urban identity. These 'productions', which are part of basic social competence, are largely subconscious and the effects they 'produce' on others are directed to particular ends; such as smoothing over difference, protecting oneself from prejudice, and thereby enabling productive social or economic interactions. Although such processes can ring false or take the form of manipulation, the sensation of 'experiental authenticity' in given contexts is often much more important to us (Bigenho 2002:4).

[31] This allusion to the idea of a 'dividual', as different aspects of self, is informed by the work of Strathern (1981, 1991) and Harvey (1998).

Chapter 3

Orchestrating the Year

Seasonal alternation, calendars and power

> There can have been no time, since the human mind became capable of compassing abstract ideas at all, when man did not see in the passing of the seasons an image of himself. ('Dawn of the Year', *The Times*, Monday 6 April 1955.
>
> In A.S. Byatt ([1978] 1981), *The Virgin in the Garden*. Penguin Books)

In many rural communities of the southern and central Andes the economic and festive year is 'orchestrated' into seasonally distinct episodes, marked by a shifting array of musical instruments, genres, tunings and dances. But such calendars – musical and otherwise – are by no means simple, inert, ideology-free or apolitical reflections of 'natural' ecological and productive cycles. Historically, in the Andes – as in other parts of the world – they have functioned as a particularly important and powerful tool for invoking or controlling socio-economic, political and religious relations. Although the epistemologies and values that underlie and sustain musical calendars are open to ever increasing challenges, in many places this mode of orchestrating production and relations with the human and spirit community continues to serve as a potent medium for expressing identity, ethnicity, class, knowledge and political authority. In fact, modernity and the growth of market forces can contribute to the strengthening rather than weakening of calendrical musical practices, as I discuss in Chapter 4. Consequently, in this chapter I approach musical calendars as a dynamic mode of orchestrating relationships, expressing identities and understanding the world, rather than simply presenting them as vanishing relics.

Seasonal alternation

The vivid contrast in appearance, nature and experience of the landscape between Kalankira's two principal seasons almost gives the impression of two different worlds; a sense heightened by local discourse that describes the land of the ancestors as perpetually green (see Chapter 8). During the dry winter months the heavily grazed hillsides and harvested fields become yellowed, dried up and bare. By contrast, at the peak of the growing season in February the landscape is characterized by vivid green vegetation, most intense with the

fields of fodder barley around the church. Accordingly, people usually divided
the year into two main periods:

> **March – October**: cold, dry season. Local names: *chirawi* ('cold [epoch]') or
> *kusicha timpu* (Sp. *cosecha tiempo* 'harvest time')
> **November – February/March**: warmer rainy season. Local names: *paray
> timpu* ('rainy time') or *karnawal timpu* ('Carnival time'),

Figure 3.1 shows the main agricultural activities that accompany these two
principal divisions of the year. *Rinuwa timpu* ('renewal time') is closely linked
with planting crops and specific forms of music (see Chapter 7), whilst *lapaka*
is characterized as a lean and 'hungry' period when stores are low and pasture
scarce (see Chapter 8). In Kalankira the peak in the sun's annual cycle
(summer solstice) and period of heaviest rains is marked by the Christmas and
New Year llama mating ceremonies, whilst its nadir, the coldest and longest
night (winter solstice) in late June, is associated with *chuñu* (freeze-dried
potato) making and the feast of San Juan (St John, 24 June).

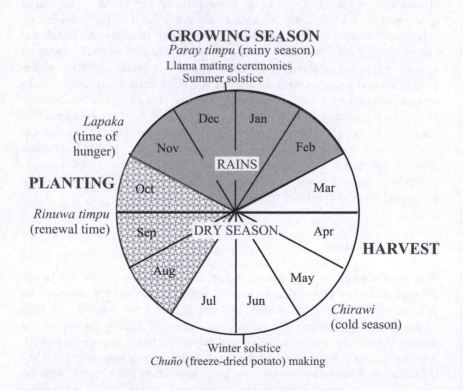

Figure 3.1   Classification of the seasons and principal activities

Fiestas and climatic uncertainty

In Kalankira, as in many other parts of Bolivia, the majority of seasonally rotating musical activities take place during feasts. Although accounting for no more than about forty days in the year, in many respects these festivities define, focus and give rhythm to people's lives. As Bourque observes, feasts also mark stages of development in the maturation of plants and people, assisting them to reach their full potential (1995:75). The unfolding year is not so much measured in weeks or months but referred to in terms of the festivals that punctuate it.[1] Outside festive contexts, young men sometimes strum a string instrument or sound a *pinkillu* flute as they walk to the fields or on a journey. But I have encountered very few 'work songs' or music played to accompany community labour comparable to that reported in contemporary and historical accounts from Peru (Romero 2001:43–50, Guaman Poma 1980:1050, Cobo 1990:214).[2] Nonetheless, festive music and dance are often explicitly related to the reproduction of animals and production of food crops, as evident from the words of Remejio Beltrán (c. 65 years) below. Our conversation was recorded in December – the peak of the rains – and his reference to 'Carnival' implies the entire rainy season (November–March).

> ... that's why we play. So as to make food grow for us here in this place, that's why. When we play at *cruz* [feast of the Holy Cross] we harvest the crops, the potatoes, we cut the barley. That's the time for *wayli* [dry season *julajula* panpipe music and dance]. Now it's Carnival season. The *pinkillu* – flute *wayñu* [dance-song] is for us to plant the crops, [for them] to sprout and grow – that's what it's for.[3]

In some of the year's main feasts (Figure 3.2) music is played constantly and is an integral aspect, while for others music is minimal and informal.[4] As the primary axes of seasonal transformation, the feasts of All Saints and Carnival are, as Harris observes, thought to be universal and 'celebrated worldwide', thereby serving to 'unify and transcend social boundaries'. By contrast, other feasts are subject to local variation and specific to particular

---

[1] People rarely referred to specific months, the only notable exception being August when offerings are made for the earth, which is 'mouth open' (*simi kichasqa*) at this time. Similar associations with feeding the earth and its sensitivity during August are found in several parts of the Andes, for example, see Sallnow 1987:131–2, Allen 1982:180, Isbell 1997:288.

[2] However, I did encounter examples of verses formerly sung (to wedding music) whilst trampling potatoes during the preparation of *chuñu* (freeze-dried potatoes).

[3] ... *chayrayku tukanchis, kay mikhuyta puquchipuwanchis kay lugarpi chayrayku. Chay kuruzta tukaqtinchis, kay puquy cosechakunchis, chay papas, siwaras rutukun. Chay timpu wayliqa. Kunanta kay karnawalta. Kay pinkillu wayñuta tarpukunanchispaq, puqunanpaq, wiñananpaq chayqa.*

[4] A few individuals visit other regional feasts, such as that of St James (Santiago, 25 July) associated with healing and held at the shrine of Tata Bombori. A little music making also takes place for Easter when the community authorities are rotated and at the school in August.

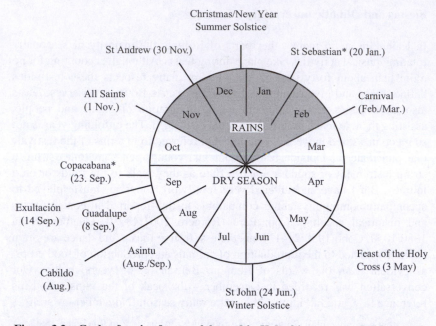

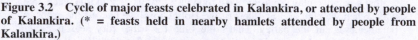

Figure 3.2   Cycle of major feasts celebrated in Kalankira, or attended by people of Kalankira. (* = feasts held in nearby hamlets attended by people from Kalankira.)

groups, thus serving as 'forms of individuation and differentiation' (1982a:59).

Although people widely identify the arrival of the rains with early November and their end with Carnival in February or March, on many occasions during the so-called 'rainy season', there are long periods of drought, leading crops to shrivel and die. When clouds do finally arrive, instead of rain they often bring hail, which people describe as 'punishment' (*kastiku*) from god or compare to an unruly 'wild animal' that devastates the fields.[5] To what extent, then, is the seasonal use of music and, for example, rain songs a means to 'impose system' on the 'inherently untidy experience' of seasonal climatic conditions? (Douglas 1994 [1966]:4). Are small-scale agriculturalists, in places where weather patterns and harvests are especially unpredictable, more likely to organize their music calendrically, or use it to influence atmospheric conditions? In Nigeria, where music is often linked to seasonal activities, Roger Blench observes that 'in the semi-arid regions it is common to find prohibitions on particular instruments during part of the year,

---

[5] Complex ceremonies to 'tame the hail' (*granizo jark'a*) are sometimes held in January and performed exclusively by men, who catch and consume a rodent, called a *viscacha* (*Lagidium Viscaccia*), and place a large number of specific offerings on various local mountain peaks.

for example when crops are growing' (2001:908). Such calendrical restrictions on music relating to crop growth, are also found in the Andes, and suggest both the precarious nature of 'production' and music's critical involvement. By contrast, in the Bosavi region of Papua New Guinea, home to the Kaluli, there is little sense that music is organized calendrically, despite much seasonal variation in climate and close links between music making and the environment. Is this because cycles of productions and sources of food are not such a critical issue? In contrast with Kalankira, or semi-arid parts of Nigeria, Steven Feld notes that 'the Kaluli diet is diverse and varied', and 'a low population density means that forest foods are never in danger of depletion' (1990 [1982]:5). Although it is important to be wary of 'ecological determinism', clearly the environmental dimension of calendrical musical practices and the different musical priorities that emerge as a result can be a significant aspect of the equation.

In many parts of the Bolivian Andes, where drought and failed harvests regularly lead to immense hardship, agricultural production is highly vulnerable – but this is not only due to ecological factors.[6] Evidence suggests that the organization of agriculture and modes of distribution were considerably more effective during prehispanic times than they are today (Murra 1979 [1955], Levine 1992). While some scholars have stressed the lack of productivity of contemporary peasant communities, characterizing them as 'subsistence' agriculturalists (Urioste 1987), other have stressed that Bolivian peasant farmers are the main providers of food for the towns (Yampara Huarachi 1992:145). This varies throughout the country, dependent on the quality of land, availability of irrigation, and access to markets – issues shaped by history and politics. Despite the relatively poor quality of their land and the small number of irrigated plots, most years the farmers of Kalankira are able to sell a small surplus. Nonetheless, they are highly dependent on harvests, some 60–70% of the food they consume being produced within the *ayllu*.[7] Most meals are prepared from home grown potatoes, *chuñu* (freeze-dried potatoes), wheat, barley, or broad beans, supplemented by bartered or purchased maize, rice, pasta, onions, garlic and (dried) chili peppers. Bread (rolls), sugar and fruit are rare luxuries, and proved an extremely popular gift when I brought them from the towns. In short, a good harvest with plenty of

---

6 The unpredictability and widespread anxiety surrounding both agricultural production and the availability of water, whether from rainfall or irrigation (Rösing 1996), is evident from much Andean ethnography and the book titles of Harris (2000) and Berg (1989). Also, control over water has been a matter of intense political importance and frequent conflict throughout Andean history (see Chapter 7).

7 A few individuals in Kalankira have very little entitlement to land, leading them to spend a large proportion of the year working as builders' labourers in the towns. I sometimes heard demonstrations of sympathy for such people for whom agricultural production could provide only very partially for their needs.

excess to sell is real reason for celebration and a source of extra cash, but a poor one can lead to the sale of llamas, sheep or oxen (a family's bank account) in order to acquire cash to purchase basic staples, or even permanent migration to towns.

Calling the rain and blowing away the clouds

While the seasonal rotation of song genres appears to be a widespread global phenomenon, the alternation of different types of instruments is less widely reported and might be seen as especially characteristic of the Central and Southern Andes and parts of Amazonia.[8] In Kalankira, both the *pinkillu* flute and the *kitarra* are for the most part restricted to the rainy season and explicitly said to 'call' or 'weep' rain and to cause the crops to grow. By contrast *julajula* and *siku* panpipes, and the *charango*, played during the dry, cold winter months, are claimed to attract the frosts and winds – which blow away the clouds, resulting in clear skies and cold nights. Whereas *julajula* panpipes are especially associated with harvest and the feast of the Holy Cross, the more fragile *siku* panpipes are linked with the planting season and *rinuwa* ('renewal').

Like Bourdieu's account of the Kybylia of Algeria, the 'passage from the wet season to the dry season' in Kalankira is 'effected ritually and collectively'. This transition is dramatically performed through music and dance: the rainy season instruments (*pinkillu*, *kitarra*) silenced, as the players burst from the dance circle enclosing them, and replaced a few moments later by the dry season *charango* (Figure 3.3) (see Chapter 9). However, unlike Bourdieu's Algerian example, where the date 'varies from region to region because of climatic differences' (1977:103), in Northern Potosí the date – the end of Carnival – is defined by the Catholic Church calendar. The transfer from the dry to the rainy season is in practice more gradual – *pinkillu* flutes making brief appearances at a few specific ceremonies during the planting season. Yet, if asked 'when do you begin to play *pinkillu* flutes?' without hesitation people said 'at All Saints' (1 November) – another feast from the Catholic Church calendar. Thus, not only are the seasons ordered musically, but the music is regulated by the Church.

The use of musical instruments to influence atmospheric phenomena was conceived at a highly practical level. As one man put it: 'with *pinkillu* flutes and *kitarras* it doesn't freeze or hail, the fields grow better'. In turn, Adrian Chura – the oldest man in the district – stated that the *charango* was

---

[8] See Ling 1997:65–74, Schneider 1949, Veiga de Oliviera 1995, Miller & Williams 1998:113. For example, the Amazonian Waiãpi play in excess of 65 different forms of wind instrument in seasonally orchestrated festivals (Fuks 1990:143).

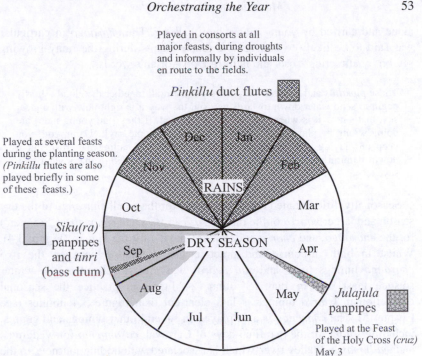

Played in consorts at all
major feasts, during droughts
and informally by individuals
en route to the fields.

Pinkillu duct flutes

Played at several feasts
during the planting season.
(Pinkillu flutes are also
played briefly in some
of these feasts.)

Siku(ra)
panpipes
and *tinri*
(bass drum)

RAINS

DRY SEASON

Julajula
panpipes

Played at the Feast
of the Holy Cross *(cruz)*
May 3

Figure 3.3   Seasonal alternation of wind ensemble instruments

necessary in order to attract the frost needed for making *chuño* (freeze-dried potatoes):[9]

> If you don't play the *charango* the frost won't won't come. Because this potato
> is given compassionate pain; with freezing frost it will be completely frozen in
> a single night. In two nights it will be made into beautiful dark black chuño.[10]

Many people impressed on me the importance of not playing the *pinkillu* flute,
or strummed *charango* or *kitarra* outside their prescribed seasons. These
instruments, which are especially associated with courtship, are often played

---

[9] Chuño (*chuñu*) is an important Andean mode of preserving potatoes. The potatoes are spread
outside over several nights during the coldest period of the year (June–July) to freeze. During the
sunny days they are trampled to squeeze out the moisture and desiccate in the sun. The resulting
freeze-dried potatoes will last for several years and are soaked overnight before use. This mode
of desiccation has been related to other Andean techniques, such as the processing of clay prior to
potting (Sillar 1994, 1996), and human mummification, where the freezing of potatoes is
metaphorically related to human death (Allen 1982:182, Isbell 1997:291–2).

[10] *Mana chay charankuta tukaqtiyki mana qasanmanchu. Porque es[ta] papita khuyayta lastan
qunan; qasa thaya sumaqta qasaqtin uj tutapi. Iskay tutapi chuñurqun chaypi kacha muraritu
ruwakun.*

alone and carried by young men when walking. The *charango* in particular was said to be likely to damage the tender plants during the rainy growing season by attracting frosts and hail. In Don Adrian's words:

> Those *pinkillus* and *kitarras*[11] when we get them all together the clouds shortly begin to send water down towards us. And the way it is right now with a clear sky, that's how it is when the *charango*'s played. If they [the young men] are doing wrong by playing the *qhaliyu charango*, [people say]: 'Damn you! you keep on playing that [*charango*]. Damn you! you're calling the frost. Put it down! dammit! Pick up the big guitar! Where's the *pinkillu*', that's what they say.[12]

Seasonally differentiated tunings are used for the small *charango* of the dry season and larger *kitarra* of the rains: *cruz* ('cross') and *san pedro* ('St Peter') for the *charango*, and *charka* and *yawlu* ('devil') for the *kitarra* (Figure 3.4). Whilst in both discourse and practice the alternation between the two *charango* tunings (*cruz* and *san pedro*) was clearly related to the winter solstice feast of San Juan (St John, 24 June), in practice the seasonal distinction in *kitarra* tunings is less clear-cut than Figure 3.4 implies (see Chapter 5). The *charango* is also played in several other tunings and genres, including *salaki* for the two final days of Carnival, *casamiento* for weddings, and *walli mayun* 'valley river'which is associated with trading journeys to the valleys with llamas.[13] In the early 1990s only a few older men could remember how to play *qhaliyu*, which was said to be the most important *charango* genre before the 1950s. Several men also know how to play certain *cholo* or urban styles (*layku-layku*) in *natural* tuning – genres that are unconstrained by seasonal considerations.

Immense regional and sometimes local diversity exists in the calendrical organization of musical instruments, song genres, tunings and related dances, as repeatedly documented in accounts of the music of highland Bolivia and certain other parts of the Andes.[14] It is common to find at least four types of

---

[11] The word *charango* is sometimes used to refer any type of strummed string instrument including rainy season guitars. To avoid confusion I shall only use the word *charango* to refer to the small dry season mandolin-like instrument and the word *kitarra* for the larger rainy season type.

[12] *Chay pinkillusta charankus [= kitarras] qututuqtinchisqa phuyuqa recien lamarkamun. Kunanrí kayjina lijitu kashan, chaymanta charanku tukaqkunata. Kay qhaliyu charankutaqa juchashanku 'karaju! chaylla tukashanki karaju! Qasallata waqashanki karaju! chuqay karaju! Jatun kitarray ayarikuy, pinkillu maytaq' ninku a.*

[13] However, my host family considered that a *charango* should not be taken on these journeys as it was sure to be broken.

[14] For example, Vellard & Merino (1954), d'Harcourt & d'Harcourt (1959), INDICEP (1973), Oblitas Poblete (1978 [1960]), Baumann (1979, 1981, 1982a, 1982b), Paredes-Candia (1980), Buechler (1980), Grebe Vicuña (1980), Carter & Mamani (1982), Stobart (1987, 1994, 1998b), Mamani (1987), Diaz Gainza (1988), Harris (1988), Sánchez (1989b, 2001), JAYMA (1989),

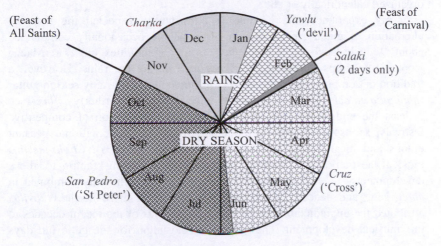

CHARANGO TUNINGS

Other dry season *charango* tunings
Walli Mayun ('valley river')
Kasamintu ('wedding')
Qhaliyu - known by old men only

Figure 3.4   Annual sequence of *charango* and *kitarra* tunings

instruments, many of which are seasonally rotated, played by the same individuals in a single community. A spectacular example is that noted by Hans Buechler in Irpa Chico, near Lake Titicaca, where some 12 types of instruments are played through the course of the year, each linked with a specific calendrical activity, period or feast (1980:358–9). A few general patterns exist, such as the widespread performance of (*pinkillu*) duct flutes and larger forms of guitars during the rains, and of panpipes, the *charango*, notch flutes and the pipe and tabor during the dry winter months.[15] But there are

---

Berg (1989), Flety & Martínez (1992), Martínez (1994), Calvo & Sánchez (1991), Cavour (1994), Solomon (1997). Although calendrical music and dance performance is widespread in parts of Peru and Ecuador, most existing ethnography indicates that music is less integral to agricultural production than I discovered in Kalankira and other parts of Bolivia. However, this may well reflect the interests and focus of the researchers rather than the characteristics of the specific groups studied. (See for example Turino 1993, den Otter 1985, Coba 1992, Schechter 1992.)

[15] Raimund Schramm and Thomas Solomon have both developed hypotheses to explain why wind instruments of the Bolivian Andes are connected respectively with the dry winter months or rains. According to Schramm, the bamboo and cane used to construct panpipes and notch flutes (*quena*) grows on riverbanks in the tropical lowlands making these dry season instruments both

numerous exceptions to these patterns, and many places where music is not organized calendrically at all.[16]

In my experience, the Kalankiras consistently respected the seasonal alternation of guitars, even though older people occasionally complained about 'loutish lads' (*machu machus*) from communities close to Macha jeopardizing crops by playing the *charango* during the rains. However, a tradition of combining the dry season *charango* and large rainy season guitar (*qhunquta*, *talachi*, *guitarilla*) has been widespead in the northerly *ayllus* since at least the mid 1980s, apparently due to the introduction of competitive festivals, sponsored by the Catholic-run Radio Pio XII, national peasant unions and local non-governmental organizations (NGOs). *Cholo-mestizo* musical aesthetics are another important contributing factor to these developments, as *charango* and Spanish guitar are commonly combined in *cholo* song and dance.[17] Several older people from these northerly *ayllus* attributed the unpredictable weather and poor yields of the recent decades to this music development. They expressed nostalgia for the good old days

---

conceptually 'low' and 'damp'. By contrast, he relates the *tarka* and *pinkillu* (recorder-like) duct flutes of the rains to materials from higher altitudes, characterizing them as conceptually 'high' and 'dry' (1992:327–8). Taking a slightly different approach, Solomon observes that the cane or bamboo instruments of the dry season are naturally hollow, and this 'lack of internal substance in the material of the instruments seems to be iconic of the inability of the land to produce during the dry season'. By contrast he sees the pithy centre the *sauco* [*sawku*] branches used to construct *pinkillu* flutes, as 'iconic of the moist conditions and plant growth of the rainy season' (1997:185–6). While these interpretations are thought provoking, as soon as we move outside Northern Potosí the neat seasonal distinction between construction materials becomes problematic (Schramm's study encompasses the entire Aymara region). For example, the *musiñu* flutes and numerous other forms of *pinkillu* of La Paz and Oruro Departments – all associated with attracting rain – are made from cane or bamboo. Given the diversity and unequal distribution of knowledge, people's creativity in finding new meanings, and the ways identity is marked by cultural difference we should hardly expect seasonal music and dance performance to conform to some kind of widely accepted and contradiction-free system.

[16] This latter point has been stressed by Isabelle Verstraete who has conducted research in South Western Bolivia (personal communication).

[17] Thomas Solomon has observed how among the Chayantakas, the *charango* is now played all year round (1997:174). However, I am not convinced by his intriguing argument that the introduction of the *anzaldo* – which he describes as a medium sized *charango* (originally from Anzaldo, Cochabamba Department) – stimulated the abandonment of the seasonal distinction between the *charango* and *qunquta* (guitar). He argues that because the *anzaldo* is 'intermediate in size between the *qhunquta* and *juch'uy* ['little'] *charango*', it presented a problem for the rainy and dry season classification of instruments (ibid.: 174). However, in the late 1980s, the *anzaldo* was a tiny, high-pitched *charango* and only in the 1990s did the fashion for larger *anzaldos* develop in the region. Solomon evidently encountered this large sized instrument during his fieldwork in 1993, by which time the small *anzaldos* had all but disappeared. Furthermore, the practice of playing the small *anzaldo charango* alongside the rainy season *qhunquta* (that is, all year round) was already widespread in central and northern parts of the Northern Potosí region as early as 1986. This example highlights the rapidity of changing fashions in the dynamic musical traditions of the region.

when crops grew well and people respected the authority of the *ayllu*. In the past, this 'prohibition' against playing the *charango* during the rains even led to young men who persisted in playing sometimes being thrown in jail in the town of Chayanta.[18]

Today in the North of Potosí, it is principally in *ayllu* Macha, with its distinctive, smaller and shallower form of *kitarra*, that this combination has not become widespread. But in both Kalankira and the region's northerly *ayllus*, the musical ordering of the seasons is intimately connected with the *ayllu*'s political order and authority, and calendrical performance is often imbued with ancestral authority.

Calendars and power

A calendar can be characterized as a temporal framework to live by, through which collective action, economic activities, socio-political relations and belief systems are coordinated, ordered, controlled and maintained. According to Bourdieu, the coherent, contradiction-free calendars that anthropologists are tempted to construct, based on the most frequently attested features provided by informants, represent a form of 'synoptic illusion'. They represent, he argues, 'a sort of *unwritten score* of which all the calendars derived from informants are then regarded as imperfect, impoverished performances' (1977:98). This point, which is highly relevant to the practice of ethnography in general, also highlights how calendars constructed, committed to writing and enforced by those in positions of power or authority are a potent means of social control. Although subjects required to perform from this *unwritten score* (calendar) may come to endow its performance with heartfelt sentiment, embodying and claiming it as their own, their agency may have been usurped in particular ways by the 'composer'. For example, in ancient China, inhabitants of regions newly incorporated into the empire would be said to have 'received the calendar' (Gell 1992:313, after Pelliot 1929:208).

The Inca calendar has been subject to considerable scholarly attention; its immense importance as a mode of socio-political and religious organization notably revealed through the work of R. Tom Zuidema (1977, 1985, 1992). He demonstrates how it served to orchestrate social hierarchies, movements of subjects through the empire, the timing of agricultural tasks, and a complex series of religious rituals, sacrifices and festivities. Each month one hundred llamas were sacrificed, their colour and quality of wool were chosen according to the need for rain or the growth cycle of the crops, and the responsibility for

---

[18] Buechler (1980:358) also observes that in La Paz department playing musical instruments outside their specific season was liable to punishment by community authorities.

raising them rotated between specific groups.[19] A sequence of distinct dances, song genres and instruments were performed as part of each month's ceremonies. For example, during the festivities of the tenth month of *Coya Raymi* (approximately October) a 'special dance' was performed in honour of the gods and Inca ancestors accompanied by panpipes – 'long and short tubes that were placed like organ pipes' – in which the participants wore 'red tunics that reached down to their feet and feather diadems on their heads' (Cobo 1990:147).

Competing calendars: potatoes and maize

Maize and its cultivation cycle were of central importance to Inca religion, economy, ideology and political organization. The Inca himself ceremonially initiated the digging of the maize fields, priests cultivated a plot of maize within the temple of the Sun, and small buns (*bollos*) made from ground maize and llama blood – signs of the Sun and his veneration – were offered to all those visiting Cusco from the provinces and sent to all the principal *huacas* (sacred shrines) of the empire.[20] In many respects the Inca calendar was a 'maize calendar'. However, in much of the *Collasuyu* – the southerly quarter of the Inca Empire, corresponding in part with today's highland Bolivia – which was dominated by a network of Aymara kingdoms that only came under Inca control after a long period of resistance, the potato was the principal crop. Thérèse Bousse-Cassagne has observed that the Aymara calendar was measured exclusively according to the rhythm of highland tubers and grains (quinoa), and did not take valley crops into account (1987:277). She interprets the circulation of *bollo* (maize and blood buns) throughout the Inca Empire, following a period in which all outsiders were excluded from Cusco, as a mechanism to subordinate outlying parts of the empire to Inca values and cosmogony (1987:288–9). During this same festival, music, dance and dress assisted this process of subordination. The way that integration and unity, as joint participation in an Inca dance, is contrasted with difference, as each nation performs its own pre-Incan songs and dances in the Inca capital, is remarkable in the following description of the festivities by Cobo.

> All of the nations that obeyed the Inca, each dressed in the style of their region, participated in this dance. ... During the rest of this day, each nation performed the dances and songs that were done before they had become subjects of the Inca (Cobo 1990:148).

On the one hand, the Inca's subjects must participate and coordinate their movements in his dance, and on the other, the diversity of dress, music and

---

[19] See also Murra 1978 [1955]:47, Sullivan 1988:172.
[20] Bouysse-Cassagne 1987:290, Cobo 1990:148, Murra 1978:40–41.

choreography emphasize the Inca's power and the enormity of his dominion. In addition, as in today's Andes, these forms of dress, music and dance also undoubtedly served to place his subjects within hierarchies of power and exclusion (Femenías 2003, Zorn 2004). As Bouysse-Cassagne has suggested, the calendrical sequences of Inca rituals would also have enabled an understanding of the difference between the Inca imperial conception of time and that of Aymara communities, based on potato cultivation. Indeed, she argues these two temporalities could coexist within a single individual – much as I have noted for the case of music and dance. In short, a conception of time derived from his or her own land – making that person an Aymara – and one from the state calendar, making that person a tributary of the Inca State (1987:290–91). This suggests that, for Aymara communities, calendars and their juxtaposition – articulated through festive performance – may have functioned as a particularly potent medium through which to negotiate power relations and express different forms of identity.

Continued colonialism: the Catholic calendar

With the arrival of the Spanish in the Andes (1532) came another calendrical layer, with its own cosmogony and values, which continues to dominate the timing of festive performance to this day. Despite most people's very elementary reading ability, many families in Kalankira purchase an annually published calendar (*almanaque*) of Catholic saints days and moveable feasts, which are widely available in bookstalls or grocery stores. Not only is this critical for knowing the dates of feasts, but also to understandings of the calendrical dimension of individual identity. For example, to determine his newborn son's name, Asencio asked me to help him consult the family's *almanaque*. I read out the list of saints whose feast fell on the day of the baby's birth, including the name finally chosen for him: Carlos.[21]

Like that of the Incas, the Catholic calendar clearly served as a powerful ideological tool and mode of control in the colonial period. Although this calendar's orientation to northern hemisphere Europe would seem at odds with the seasonal cycles and ecological realities of southern hemisphere Bolivia, people in Kalankira considered its relationship with their own productive activities and identities as extremely natural. The associations of European Catholic saints days and feasts sometimes coincided or fused with the prehispanic festivals, such as All Saints as the feast of the dead (see Chapter 8).[22]

---

[21] Saints and their feast days have also been very important to defining identity as members of confraternity organizations (Saignes 1995:187, Platt 1987b).

[22] See, for example, Sallnow 1987:156, Urton 1986:45–64, Zuidema 1997:143–60.

How much the Catholic calendar and observance dominates seasonal music, lives and productive activity in Kalankira is debatable. On the one hand, the annual feast calendar published by the Church provides the framework governing the temporal organization of music making, much of which is played explicitly to honour particular saints, who are attributed power over human fortunes. The festivals also act as primary points of reference in people's temporal landscapes. On the other hand, it can be argued that this system, although nominally Catholic, largely operates outside the Church's sphere of control. Indeed, for the Kalankiras, the Church may represent a potent and ambiguous source of external power, which – like the 'demonic' spirits of the inner earth – must be respected, consoled, fed with offerings, appealed to at particular moments, but avoided at others.[23] However, the Church's power and people's ambivalence to it (and its priests) must also be understood in the context of its close association with *mestizos*, creoles and the world beyond. As Abercrombie has argued, we discover not so much a 'syncretic blend of two religions' or cultural systems, but an 'interculture', the dynamics of which are:

> ... profoundly historicized in the consciousness of all Bolivians, whether from the city or the countryside and whether self-identified as campesinos, mestizos or criollos. Both urban-national and rural-'indigenous' cultural formations have come to presuppose one another's presence, producing in each a kind of class- and ethnicity-marked position on the Bolivian scene as a means of positive identity through contrast with culturally distinct others (Abercrombie 1998:111).

As we shall see, these kinds of dynamics – where identities are produced through contrast with culturally distinct others – are especially vividly expressed in festive performance involving music and dance. In certain respects the seasonal cycle of music in Kalankira might be characterized as the invocation of a shifting sequence of relations to culturally distinct others and mythic histories. The Catholic Church is critical to seasonal musical performance in Kalankira, not simply as the institution that defines the calendar of feasts, but as one implicated in long, complex and often violent histories of asymmetrical power relations with other groups.

Calendar music, class and competing knowledge

Calendrically organized music and dance performance, alongside devotion to specific saints, are important markers of ethnic, territorial and class identity,

---

[23] This parallelism was clearly identified in Kalankira. A large rock face beside the well-worn footpath to nearby Apacheta was said to date from the epoch of the primordial *chullpas* and was known as *yawlu iglesia* ('devil's church').

often simultaneously expressing both local and regional characteristics. For the most part, the more agriculturally orientated of such musical practices are the preserve of rural peasant communities, distinguishing them from *cholo* and *mestizo* townspeople and villagers, whose performance practices are rarely considered to influence atmospheric conditions or agricultural production.[24] For example, villagers from Macha and from larger towns of the region perform local, regional or national dance-song genres on the *charango* throughout the year, often in conjunction with a Spanish guitar. Their identification with more urban orientated expressions, values and 'Western-style' epistemologies, often leads them to perceive local rural knowledge and beliefs about music's power as 'ignorance' or symptomatic of a primitive mentality; in short the superstition of backward and uncivilized peasants.[25]

These attitudes, based on the 'dominating knowledge' of 'Western' (secular) science and disseminated via, for example, schools, development projects, unions (*sindicatos*) and radio stations, have contributed to the gradual decline of calendrical music traditions in many parts of the Southern Andes. Such local knowledge is rarely taken seriously by *mestizo* teachers in rural schools, whose attitudes are shaped by a dominant metropolitan model of modernity in which each step from hamlet, to village, to town, to city is construed as 'more civilised' (Howard-Malverde & Canessa 1995:234).[26] Almost inescapably, the aims of school education – shaped by this modernist national project – constitute a direct threat to calendrical musical traditions, which serve as a mode of peasant resistance and powerful identity marker:

> on the one hand, formal schooling and Spanish language acquisition are seen as essential for social betterment; on the other hand, their pursuit entails the inevitable abandonment of values and patterns of life that have served indigenous people well in their resistance to total colonisation over time (ibid: 241).

Within this class-knowledge hierarchy, radio broadcasts and festivals of peasant music, sponsored by unions or development agencies, rarely respect,

---

[24] However, associations with agriculture are not entirely absent from the calendrical festive performances of the *cholo* townspeople of the small towns and villages of Northern Potosí (such as Macha or Pocoata), many of whom also rely on the land. Also, the inhabitants of towns such as Lahuachaka (Aroma Province, Oruro Department), situated on the main road between La Paz and Oruro, coordinate performance according to the seasons.

[25] See Hobart (ed.) 1993, Howard et al 2002:2.

[26] The ways in which teachers use music, media, space and dress to mark class distinctions was forcibly brought home to me during a community meeting at Kalankira's recently opened school in 1996. The *mestizo* teachers all wore track suits, placed themselves on raised seats and kept a radio playing music throughout the meeting, conveying the sense that the schoolyard spatially belonged to the teacher's urban sphere rather than the rural community in which it was actually situated. Howard-Malverde & Canessa have characterized the Andean rural school as an alien and colonizing cultural institution 'at the heart of the indigenous community' (1995:237), whilst Soto describes it as 'a strange organism' or 'island within the community' (1996:141, Plaza 2002:142).

acknowledge or prioritize seasonal distinctions, and are sometimes unaware that they even exist. In addition, widespread urban migration and the introduction of brass bands into many parts of the countryside have further weakened connections between music and agricultural production.[27]

When a young peasant of Northern Potosí plays the *charango* during the rains, thereby potentially attracting frost and endangering crops, his action might express youthful rebellion or contempt for traditional *ayllu* knowledge, values and authority. But it is also likely to reflect a complex cluster of class-related aspirations, including a desire to be perceived as *civilizado* ('civilized') – like the *cholos* and *mestizos*, whose *charango* performance is not subject to seasonal constraints.[28] Yet, such musical expression is also a marker of alterity, as illustrated above when don Adrian referred to peasant *charango* players who contravene calendrical patterns as *mozos* – a term applied to young *mestizo* men from the towns. *Ayllu* identity, knowledge and values are intimately connected with, and subtly interwoven into, the seasonal performance of music. In this way, music linked to the agricultural calendar emerges as a powerful medium through which to express both social inclusion and exclusion within the Bolivian social hierarchy.

In the final part of this chapter, the connection between *ayllu* identity and seasonal transformation emerges once again in a local exegesis told to explain why instrumental performance influences atmospheric conditions. This thought-provoking account, which has been very influential to my approach in this book, takes us in unexpected directions.

Mortality and the mouse *charango*

In a conversation about the how are young men (*mozos*) are claimed to endanger the crops by playing the *charango* during the rainy growing season,

[27] For example, in many rural communities of departments Oruro and La Paz the performance of traditional instruments is now largely restricted to elderly men; younger men usually preferring to dedicate themselves to brass bands. Feasts are also sometimes dominated by returning migrants from the cities who may express their status though hiring costly brass bands and urban-style dance costumes, such as the *morenada*. In such contexts, I have sometimes seen the appearance of elderly players of traditional instruments ridiculed. However, many migrant clubs have sprung up in La Paz in which the players perform music from their rural area of origin. Authenticity is often an important issue for members of these groups who are sometimes critical of the 'impoverished' performance practices maintained in the countryside, and present themselves as custodians of the tradition (see Turino 1993 on comparable dynamics for the case of migration to Lima, Peru). However, these migrant ensembles, whose public performances typically include musics from different times of year, rarely respect seasonal performance practices.

[28] The form of the *charango*, material used for its strings (nylon or metal), type of tuning, genres performed and techniques utilized are also important markers of respectively peasant, *cholo* or *mestizo* forms of identity, which are often subject to subtle contextual distinctions (see also Turino 1984).

I asked Asencio: 'why does the *charango* attract frost'. As the question slipped out, I found myself half expecting him to say something like 'it's our custom', 'the ancestors know' or 'don Adrian [Chura] knows' – the usual dead-end answer to this sort of question (Turino 1989:1, Solomon 1997:32, 91). Instead, to my surprise, he launched into an extended exegesis:

> [The frost] comes when *qhaliyu* is played. The *qhaliyu* song [is when] the mouse's song is played on the *charango*.
> Long ago this [current] epoch didn't exist. Nor did the *qhaliyu charango* exist long ago … things were different.

> [You know] the way the [people of *ayllu*] Laymi play now? It was just the same [here] long ago, it's said. That's the way it was in that era. It was a good time, the potatoes were good; they grew well …

> The mouse brought [the *charango*] here. Probably saying 'I'm going to sing', the mouse sang and there it was. From then till now there have been *qhaliyu* verses. They haven't disappeared. Now we're in the epoch of the mouse's *qhaliyu* verses, that's why it's a bad time. It brings ill. Things are no longer fine and beautiful, are they?

> HS. Don't things grow well these days?

> AJ. Things don't grow any more in the era of the mouse. In the epoch of the distant past the Laymis existed. [You know] how those Laymis play? It was the same here. Those grandfathers [played] just like the Laymis. And Adrian can still play that way.[29]

In this account, Asencio contrasts the epoch of the distant past (*unay*), when the potatoes grew well, with the present 'bad' time initiated by the mouse's *charango*. In other words, this instrument and its music transformed time, where the rupture between the distant past and the present is equivalent to that between the rainy season (when potatoes grow well) and the dry winter months. The reference to the mouse suggests the kind of fantastical story usually associated with *inkantu timpu*, when wild animals and humans are said to have freely exchanged forms (Chapter 2). But Asencio also relates the

---

[29] *Chay qhaliyu kaqtin jina. Qhaliyu chay … wayñu nin, juk'uchaq wayñun nin chay charanku.*

Unay mana karqachu nin kay timpu. Chay qhaliyu charanku mana kaqtin unay. Karqa nin … chay uj jina.

Kunan kay Laymis tukan? Kikin karqa nin unayqa. Ajina karqa nin chay timpupi. Sumaq kay timpupi, sumaq kaqtin papasta, sumaq puqun nin…

Juk'ucha chayta churasqa nin a. Entonces nuqa takirisaq nispacha takirin juk'ucha ya listu. Chaymanta hasta kunitan qhaliyu wirsuqa ari. Mana chinkapuñachu. Kunan qhaliyu juk'uchaq wirsu timpunpi kashan, entonces timpu mal ari. Mal ruwan manaña sumaq waliqchu, i?

(HS. Kunan timpu mana sumaq puqunchu i?)

Mana puqushanña juk'uchaq timpunpi. Ñawpaq timpu karqa nin, kay Laymi. Laymi runas tukan i? Kikin kaq nin a kaypi. Chay awilitus awilitus Laymis ajinata. Chay Adrianpis chaypiraq takiq nin a.

mouse's arrival to a musical transformation within living memory, contrasting the dry season song style of his own ethnic group, the Machas, with that of a nearby Laymis. Many other people also told me that the development of the dry season *charango* songs or *takis* (*cruz*, *san pedro*) played in much of *ayllu* Macha dated from around the 1950s. Before this time Macha *takis* had apparently resembled those played today by the Laymis and certain other ethnic groups of the region, such as the Pukwatas (CD track 44). Several older people in the community could just remember how to play in this genre (CD track 43),[30] but I also encountered a lively and very intoxicated group from San Lazaro performing in a reminiscent style in Macha during the feast of the Holy Cross – a song with striking tonality (CD track 3) (Example 3.1).

Ch'aki jawasita (*hiyaway*) *karaju!*	Dry broad beans (*hiyaway*) dammit!
Juqu jawasita	Moist broad beans
Sapallay puñusaq (*hiyaway*) *karaju!*	I will sleep alone (*hiyaway*) dammit!
Jamunki wasita!	Come to the house!

It seems likely that this shift in musical style resulted from the political upheavals surrounding the 1952 national revolution and subsequent land reforms. Does the mouse represent a political figure of the period? – much as the MNR leader Paz Estensorro was dubbed *mono* ('monkey'). Might people look back to the time before the revolution with nostalgia as a period when the potatoes grew well? To date nobody has been able to provide me with satisfactory answers to these intriguing questions.

However, Asencio placed the mouse's arrival in the context of an even more fundamental transformation; the coming of human mortality. Before the mouse *charango* people did not die but simply disappeared for a few days, weeks or months or even years.[31] With the coming of the mouse and his song, people began to die for good. They fall to the ground "'*q'irr!!*'" dead, dry, never to return!' and are eaten by wild creatures and transformed into earth, evoking Kalankira's harsh desiccated environment during the cold dry winter months when the *charango* is played. When I discussed this story with don Adrian – the only other person I found to whom it was familiar – he highlighted the close association of mice with both consumption and reproduction, observing that they reproduce in the cornfields, beneath stacks of straw, and chew their way through stored food crops and clothes. In turn, cats and foxes consume them; or as he put it, mice are these predators' 'snack' or 'mutton', which enable them to eat and live. More surprisingly he told me

---

[30] Rather confusingly most people referred to this near obsolete style as *qhaliyu* – the genre that, according to Asencio, was introduced by the mouse. It is also widely used as a generic term for any dry season *charango* music. *Qhaluyu* is also the name of a popular dance, involving stamping (*zapateo*), from the Cochabamba valleys, which has acquired national popularity.

[31] He compared this to my own absences as I disappear from the hamlet for long periods but then turn up again without warning.

Example 3.1   Song from the region of San Lazaro, performed in Macha during the feast of the Holy Cross in May. Transposed down about one semitone. (CD track 3)

that it was due to the mouse that I also eat and am alive![32] The point here seems to be that the mouse set off the process of consumption, destruction and reproduction in the world. It brought not only mortality, where bodies were consumed and returned to earth, but also the need to eat and reproduce: the mouse with its *charango* music set time in motion, initiating cycles of life, and the very rotation of the seasons – at the same time marking a disjunction between the living and the ancestors, who were formerly undifferentiated.

This account not only places music at the very heart of human existence, but also reveals important things about storytelling and local exegeses. How do we account for the apparent temporal contradiction between events from 'mythic' time and living memory? I suggest that this exegesis demonstrates how stories of paradigmatic events from the 'first times' or 'mythic' past – connected with the creation of order in the world – serve as a means to make sense of values, orders or events in the present or from more recent living memory.[33] From this perspective, the repeated passage of the seasons is iconic of the cycle of human birth, life and death; the transformation from the rains to the dry season, at the end of Carnival, evokes the separation of things formerly unified, such as the dry season songs of the Laymis and Machas. The end of Carnival, when *charango* playing begins, is also when the new crops of the year begin to be consumed; consumption necessarily involving mortality (Chapter 9). The *charango* causes a *pachakuti* ('world turning') and transforms time from a period of rain and vegetative (external) growth to one of frosts, desiccation and bodily (internal) growth.

So what is the connection between the mouse and the 'little' *charango*, as it is often known? Clearly, both are diminutive and initiate a process of consumption, involving both (internal bodily) growth and destruction, where the living and the ancestors become separated from one another, just as the Laymis become separated from the Machas. It is noteworthy in this context that the Kalankira's often claim to copy their *pinkillu* flute *wayñu* melodies of the rains from the Laymis, perhaps suggesting that during the rainy growing season, there is a symbolic musical reunification of the Machas and Laymis, as well as of the dead and the living (Chapter 8). Asencio's thought-provoking exegesis draws us into particular ways of thinking about the relationship

---

[32] Among the Brazilian Suyá, it is also the mouse that, according to myth, taught humans to gather and consume food crops. The mouse is closely connected with boys' rites of passage into manhood (Seeger 1987:2, 25–9).

[33] In her analysis of Peruvian oral historical narrative, Howard-Malverde has argued that 'meaning is constituted in the act of performance, as it unfolds in the here-and-now', where 'the speaking of history is found to be an activity that breaks down the barriers between an objectual past and a present praxis' (1990b:81). On similar lines, Abercrombie has discussed how 'foundational "first time" events' shape understandings of other spheres of life (1998:113), and Platt observes how each human birth is seen to replay the solar cataclysm from Andean myth-history (2002:128).

between music, productive processes and the seasons, ones that have powerfully shaped my approach in this book.

In this chapter I have provided an initial sense about why the performance of music, according to an unfolding seasonal calendar, is such an important aspect of what it means to be a Kalankira and how this relates to broader socio-political relations. Performing this annual cycle of music and dance is a powerful means to express active participation in the productive life of the human and spirit community, as well as to express what it means to be a Kalankira.

Part II
Guitars and Song

Chapter 4

Fabricating Tradition and the Macha Groove

Guitars, artisans, seasonality and performance

Charankituy tiyan pinu pinumanta	I have a *charango* made of pine
Kurtasitan tiyan chulaq chuqchamanta	It has strings of girl's hair
Llavisitan tiyan yawluq kirunmanta	It has tuning pegs of devil's teeth
(dry season song verse, Kalankira)	

Even without the markers of distinctive local dress, the ethnic identity of a young Macha man is immediately apparent from the sounds of his inseparable companion, a dry season *charango* or rainy season *kitarra*. To play the *charango* and *kitarra* are taken-for-granted male skills in Kalankira, although the competence to tune an instrument accurately, make major shifts between the various tunings, and to animate dancing and singing varies considerably between individuals. My host Paulino, a particularly fluent and expressive *charango* player, attributed such musical skills to dedication, rejecting the notion of inherited talent. Indeed, the technique of younger teenagers is usually rather elementary, that of older men rusty, and the most visible and dedicated players are young men of courting age, who carry an instrument almost constantly. Not only does this assist them in developing technique and individual style but also identifies their status as a lad on the look out for a girl. A *charango* or *kitarra* is a critical courtship tool and typically one of the first purchases a young man makes when, in a major rite of passage, he makes his first solo trip to town for work.[1] These instruments are also important fashion accessories, and youths often go to great lengths to acquire up to date, sought after models, which to a surprising degree conform to accepted ethnically specific forms of construction and decoration. For lads involved in courtship, a *charango* or *kitarra* is often the focus of immense emotional, creative and financial investment.

A quick glance at the form and decoration of instrument itself also indicates ethnic affiliation. This clear demarcation of dress, instrument construction and musical style tends to be much more difficult if not impossible to discern with other *ayllus*. Guitar construction and song style emerge as especially critical to the musical construction of Macha regional and ethnic identity and these

---

[1] In recent years certain young men have alternatively or additionally purchased a radio-cassette player and recordings of *cumbia* music.

differences are most marked in the courtship songs accompanied by the *charango* or *kitarra*.

In this chapter I explore these musical constructions, focusing not only on ethnicity but also seasonality and performance. I shall look closely at the instruments themselves and consider the role of guitar makers, fashion and market forces in shaping both Macha ethnicity and calendrical performance practices. I contend that through much of the twentieth century the guitar construction, innovation and marketing centred on the village of Pocoata developed, strengthened and consolidated calendrical performance practices. Although not fully part of the performance tradition, these specialist instrument makers emerge as key players in the reproduction, development and indigenization of seasonal performance and therefore of the construction of Macha identity. But how much should their agency be seen as 'fabrication', as suggested by the Spanish term *fabricante* ('maker') and with the English implications of 'invention' or even 'falsehood', and how much as simply 'manufacture'?

As noted in the previous chapter, people in Kalankira insist that the *cruz* and *san pedro charango* genres which so vividly express Macha identity date from no earlier than around the 1950s. People used to play like the Laymis, it was claimed, whose principal (highland) dry season song style is similar to that of many other *ayllus* of the region.[2] Such recent genesis of traits, traditions or artifacts considered characteristic of a particular group is widespread around the world (Hobsbawm 1983:1, Romero 2001:85). The second part of this chapter examines how this distinctive 'Macha groove' – as I dub the rhythmic-harmonic-kinaesthetic feel of this music – is realized in performance and involved in the process of constructing Macha bodies.

Construction and performance

Although most players don't tend to think of them in this way, musical instruments are 'commodities'. Like other commodities, they are subject to often-complex journeys between producers and consumers, which can be likened to 'life histories' or 'biographies' (Kopytoff 1986:66). To analyse the 'complex social forms and distributions of knowledge' that commodities represent, Appadurai makes what he recognizes as a somewhat crude, but still useful, differentiation between 'production knowledge' and 'consumption knowledge' (1986:41). Here I adapt this model to differentiate between the

---

[2] In more northerly parts of the region the differences in dry season song styles often appear to relate more to highland (*puna*) – valley distinctions, rather than *ayllu* affiliation. See Solomon 1994b, 1997:341. For further discussion of these genres see Stobart 1987 and Stobart & Cross 2000.

knowledges associated with musical instrument 'construction' and 'performance' in order to explore how artisans impact on performance practice. In some traditions, when the instrument maker and player is the same person, these two types of knowledge closely overlap, with the construction process emerging as integral to the instrument's role, meaning and aesthetic power in performance (see Feld 1991:98). But when specialists make instruments, varying degrees of social, physical, temporal or cultural distance exist between makers and players. Sometimes highly effective feedback mechanisms exist between them where innovation in construction both enable and respond to shifting performance possibilities and expectations – as evidenced by the innovations of, for example, Hotteterre, Böhm and Sax. However, the innovations of performers and makers by no means always move in tandem, and clearly always unfold within the context of wider social, political, economic and cultural dynamics.

While this distance can be seen as a barrier to communication and to the transformation of performance traditions, it also may heighten the desirability and kudos that players (and listeners) attach to instruments, where particular artisans are sometimes attributed mysterious esoteric knowledge, legendary craftmanship or magical powers (Becker 1988). For example, instrument maker Pedro Azatia from the village of Pocoata, who died in about 1970, is reputed to have developed the *talachi* – a form of rainy season guitar. He was well known for having a double thumb (*tarañu*) on one hand, which I was told led to the *talachi*'s name, linking it with magical powers and notions of abundance.[3] The fetishization of particular instruments and makers, and the kudos attached to them, can potentially add meaning or potency to performance and influence a player's social standing (see Nercessian 2001:10).[4]

Instrument makers are by no means always players and their clients may come from a different ethnic, social, cultural or class group from their own, with few shared aspects of musical culture or values.[5] For example, the Kalankira's *julajula* panpipes and *pinkillu* flutes are typically purchased from peasant artisans who live in the valleys, work on a small scale, and participate

---

[3] Personal communication, Evaristo Kaysana (born 1922) – guitar maker, Pocoata. The word *tarañu* incorporates the word *tara* which both refers to 'doubleness' and to energy and abundance (see Chapter 8 and Stobart 1996a).

[4] For example, knowledge that a violinist is playing a Stradivarius or Amati instrument may well influence both the performer's and listeners' reception of the sounds, as well as defining the player's social position.

[5] The only remaining maker of certain duct flutes played in much of Southern Bolivia belonged to an Evangelical sect who strongly disapprove of the drinking and dancing which accompanies the fiestas when these flutes are almost exclusively played. This flute maker explicitly stated that he did not know how to play the instruments he makes, which are highly sought after and, by local standards, extremely expensive (Stobart 1988:31, 44).

in similar calendrical performance traditions. By contrast, their guitars and *siku* panpipes are mostly made by specialists who tend to identify more closely as *cholos* and have less seasonally constrained and agriculturally orientated performance practices. Most of these latter artisans are also more economically reliant on instrument construction, more widely integrated into markets, and their 'commodities' tend to be more susceptible to 'fads and fashions'.

In their study of the 'arts' of the Maroons of Surinam, Richard and Sally Price differentiate between the 'fads and fashions' and 'style changes'. They suggest that, although innovative and surprising on the micro-level, fads and fashions 'do not reflect fundamental changes in aesthetic ideas', whereas style changes are 'genuine *developments*, in a directional, generally non-reversible sense' (1980:200–201). This distinction is useful when considering developments in instrument construction and decoration, as well as the innovation of styles. Christopher Page has related some of the most fundamental sound shifts in Western music to developments in musical instrument technology, mapping these onto the transformation of the medieval psaltery, via the harpsichord, to the piano (2000:141–7). The multiple fads and fashions in the design and decoration of the harpsichord and piano are well known, but at the time it would have been hard to predict which would ultimately lead to long term transformation of the instruments. In other words, only history can ultimately reveal which innovations are fads and which lead to long-term developments. According to Richard and Sally Price, the latter become 'institutionalized ideologically, that is, they involve shifts in generally accepted concepts of form', which can be 'broadly enough defined to permit significant internal experimentation and developments' (1980:201).

We need to be careful how we read musical instruments and mindful that they are 'entangled in webs' of social, cultural and historical processes (Dawe 2003:278). Aspects of their construction and decoration may derive more from a particular maker's cultural values, knowledge and expectations than the performance culture in which they are played. Maker's motivations and specific innovations may have more to do with economics and market forces than with performance concerns. The most successful makers are often those who combine a good commercial sense, including individual style and innovation, with high quality craftmanship and a knowledge of the cultural context and fashions of the players. Such artisans emerge as important figures in shaping musical cultures and 'traditions', even though – from the perspective of performance and identity – they are outsiders. Musical artisans, and their relationships with players, are a crucial, if often overlooked, aspect of ethnomusicological enquiry, as they function as 'agents setting a variety of social practices in motion' (Dawe & Dawe 2001:63; Dawe 2001:226).

(A) MARKETS AND MEANING: HISTORY IN THE MAKING

One morning, before setting off on a trip to town, I told Paulino that I was planning to purchase a new *charango*. My existing instrument was made in Betanzos, near Potosí and had been bought by Asencio to replace one he had lost. Like other players from Kalankira, Asencio had doubtless purchased this instrument in the town of Macha, from one of some ten general stores that stock *charangos* and *kitarras* of variable quality and price, which are traded from Pocoata and Betanzos (Map 1). This small and evidently rather cheap Betanzos *charango* was hopeless; a view clearly shared by Paulino who, in intense frustration and annoyance – as he struggled in vain to tune it – had described it as *q'iwa*, a word meaning not only 'impossible to tune' but redolent with negative associations (see Chapter 8). Paulino advised me to make sure that my new *charango* was decorated with two parrots (*luritus*). With these, he insisted, it would 'weep beautifully' (*kachitu waqan*), but without them it would be *luqt'u*, a word applied to people who are 'deaf' or who lack understanding. This type of parrot decoration immediately identifies a *charango* constructed in the hamlets around the small colonial town of Pocoata, home to many respected makers (see Maps 1 and 3).

Pocoata is just half an hour's lorry ride away from Macha, on the road to Llallagua, and until recently held an unparalleled position as the primary producer of guitar-type instruments for the Northern Potosí region.[6] It supplies locally, seasonally and ethnically differentiated instruments for both peasant and *cholo* markets, including the deep bellied rainy season guitars decorated with plant imagery (*qhunquta*, *guitarilla*, *talachi*), played in most of the northerly *ayllus* of Northern Potosí.[7] The slimmer rainy season *kitarra* (or *p'allta*) and *panti* (or *samba*, *tabla*) *charango* are constructed primarily for the Macha market.

Over 20 makers work around Pocoata, but according to one artisan, Bonifacio Ojeda (born 1929), very few existed in the nineteenth century. Bonifacio, who learnt the trade from his father and grandfather, put the number at two or three, explaining that in his youth there were about ten. This raises the question of how long the various local guitars, which are so ubiquitous today and undoubtedly based on Spanish prototypes introduced in

---

[6] Since the late 1980s, Pocoata's fiercest competition has come from the makers of the village of Qalaqala near Uncia. However, Qalaqala *charangos* are based on a prototype originally traded from Anzaldo (department Cochabamba), ressembling a miniature Spanish guitar; a style of instrument that I have never seen played by the Machas. Similarly, the large rainy-season guitars called *qhunqutas* made in Qalaqala (which are based on Pocoata instruments) are not played by the Machas (Stobart 1987, Solomon 1997, Lyèvre 1990, Laime 2002). In the early 1990s a few individual makers worked in the towns of Macha and Ocuri.

[7] See Stobart 1987, Lyèvre 1990, Sánchez 1989b, Calvo and Sánchez 1991, and Laime 2002 for more detailed discussion and images of these instruments.

the sixteenth century, have been so integral to the region's rural soundscape. The widespread representations of guitar-type instruments in colonial iconography suggest that, at least by the seventeenth century, such instruments had become widely disseminated in the central Andes (Gisbert 1980). Legal records from Cusco, Peru, uncovered by Geoffrey Baker, reveal that the Indian 'master carpenter' Miguel Poma was contracted in 1629 to make three dozen small guitars (*discantes medianos*), a dozen *vihuelas* and six harps (2001:57). Seventy guitars and strings are also listed in the 1659 inventory of a Cusco clothing and merchandise shop, implying – as Baker suggests – that guitars 'were not regarded, or priced as a luxury', nor sold in specialist music shops (2001:57). Guitars were evidently bought off the shelf in large numbers, just as they are today. Further evidence from nearer Macha is provided from the 1683 census in which nine guitar makers are documented for the mining town of Oruro (Zulawski 1995:122). Compared to the figures for other specialist craftsmen working in Oruro at the time, such as blacksmiths (five), barbers (five), hat makers (eight), and candle makers (eleven), guitar production emerges as extremely significant.[8] Again this high number suggests that guitar-type instruments may have been quite widely disseminated among the rural communities of the region for several centuries. This also seems likely given the high level of market participation and commercial ingenuity by peasants of the region dating back to the sixteenth century (Larson 1995:20). But, when guitars found their way to Kalankira – with its close proximity to the colonial mines of Titiri – remains unclear.

Another question is how the guitars of the central Bolivian highlands and valleys became so closely associated with agricultural production and calendrical performance practices. As we have already seen, there is evidence that seasonally regulated music existed in prehispanic times (Chapter 3), but how quickly and how widely did the guitar come to be seasonally organized? Although widely played in the rural communities of Southern Peru, accounts of the *charango*'s influence on atmospheric conditions and performance restriction during the rains appear absent from the ethnography (Turino 1983).[9] In part, this might be explained by the absence of an equivalent rainy season guitar that alternates with the *charango*. It should also be stressed that guitar-type instruments are rare in many parts of the Bolivian Andes, especially on the *altiplano* where a wide range of wind instruments are alternated calendrically. This suggests that the calendrical use of guitars – especially the

---

[8] According to the census, seven of the guitar makers of Oruro were *forasteros*, Indians who had left their native communities to take up residence elsewhere, and two *yanaconas*, Indians who were not identified with any particular *ayllu* (Zulawski 1995:122). This implies that these makers, especially the *foresteros*, probably maintained close links with rural communities who may have been an extremely important market for instruments, as they are today.

[9] For example Parejo-Coudert (2001:237) shows the *charango* played during both rainy and dry season feasts in Southern Peru.

existence of distinct dry and rainy season forms – may be quite a localized phenomenon, largely confined to the central Bolivian highlands and valleys.

The parrot *charango*

Following Paulino's instructions as closely as possible, I returned to Kalankira a few days later clutching an instrument decorated with a single parrot – as none were available with a pair (Figure 4.1b).[10] However, the sound of this large black laminated *panti charango* was excellent and Paulino very much approved.[11] Our ensuing conversations suggested that his insistence on parrot decoration was not merely a form of quality assurance, but that the parrot was itself significant, its image and the sound of the *charango* intrinsically linked. Other people also told me that parrots are diviners (Sp. *adivino*), 'they know the names of everybody', they are curious, attract the girls and talk constantly.[12] Parrots are 'intact' or 'untouched' (Sp. *intacto*) and 'cannot be killed' people declared; so a *charango* decorated with them would last 'the whole time, up until the next year' – an important consideration as instruments are often broken during feasts.[13] The image of the parakeet or parrot, projected onto the *charango* thus suggests invincibility, special knowledge, uninterrupted utterances, command of sound and control over names, implying a somewhat ambiguous power over people. These various associations may be seen to be highly relevant to the instrument's primary performance context – the highly competitive sphere of courtship songs. However, parrots also evoke certain negative and undesirable connotations and were sometimes said to be bad or *malos* (Sp.).

The parrot's bad temper is important in a well-known story, sure to be known by guitar makers in Pocoata, about the origin of food crops (Urton 1985:262, Paredes-Candia 1988: 69–74, Platt 1987b:161). The other key protagonist is the fox (*atuq*), sometimes called Antonio, who is famed for his appetite – both for food and sex. In the story, the fox hears about a feast being held in *janaqpacha*, god's celestial sphere, and asks the condor to fly him there. After gorging himself at the feast, the fox discovers that the condor has flown off without him. To descend back to earth, he starts climbing down 'god's beard' – a rope of *ichhu* grass. But part way down the fox sees a parrot

---

[10] The seasonally differentiated decoration and forms found in the dry season *charangos* and rainy season *kitarras* played in Kalankira in the early 1990s are by no means fixed as innovation and developments in guitar making are highly dynamic.

[11] The word *panti* is used to refer to a number of highly saturated colours including dark reds, black or deep purple. Other names for this style of *charango* include *tabla charango* and *samba*.

[12] Once when Asunta wanted me to speak continuously, so as to hear the sound of English, she asked me to speak 'like a parrot' (*lurujina*).

[13] Broken instruments are commonly referred to as *wañusqa* ('dead').

Figure 4.1   Photographs of a large Pocoata style *panti charango* and a small Betanzos style *charango*; and a close up of parrot decoration on a *panti charango*

and can't resist mocking him, shouting out *mat'i simi* 'gourd beak'. The enraged parrot has his revenge by pecking through the *ichhu* grass rope so that the fox tumbles to earth – shouting out to his children to catch him as he falls. But to no avail. The fox hits the earth with an almighty *TIN!* and his stomach bursts open scattering the various food crops and seeds now grown and consumed by humans.

Several people in Kalankira correlated this story directly with the image of the parrot on the *charango*. One friend even associated the idea of the old-style *charangos*, made from gourds (*mat'i*), with the fox's mocking description of the parrot as 'gourd beak' (*mat'i simi*). Interpreting this story within a seasonal context, the parrot and the playing of the *charango* emerge as important actors in enabling the harvest to begin each year. These associations were invoked on the Friday night of Carnival, following the despatch of the rainy season instruments, when I heard a man shout *luru, luru* ('parrot, parrot'). This was a request that the *charango* be played – the first time since the end of the dry season in October – so that the new foodcrops of the year could begin to be eaten (Chapter 9). For people in Kalankira, the *charango*'s parrot decoration was closely identified with the function and seasonal significance of the instrument – the identities of the spiteful parrot and frost-attracting *charango* merging as one. Close parallels are also evident with the story of the mouse's *charango*, which introduced consumption and mortality into the world (Chapter 3).

The painted *kitarra* (*p'allta*)

The decoration of the brightly coloured Macha *kitarra* is even more obviously connected to the rainy season. Sometimes people would point to the ring of alternating green leaves and pink-red flowers, or *planta* ('plant'), typically painted around the bridge, and say that this was 'for calling the rain' (Figure 4.2). This ring of green and pink also evokes the three wreaths (*pillus*) of green willow and roses that are placed on graves in the cemetery for the feast of St Andrew on 30th November, highlighting how the souls of the dead play a critical role in the growth of crops (Chapters 8 and 9). Sometimes, in place of the wreath image, two plants with leaves (and sometimes flowers) stand symmetrically on either end of the bridge, curving towards the soundhole. Similar plant imagery (in red and green, or black) is found on most other forms of rainy season guitars made in Pocoata, which the makers variously termed 'flower' (*t'ika*) or 'wild cherry tree' (*ginda sach'a*).[14]

On the *kitarra's* soundboard (Que. *uya* 'face') three further concentric rings of rays radiate from the sound hole (Que. *jusq'u* 'hole', or Sp. *voz* 'voice'), typically two of green enclosing one of red. Paulino described this motif as 'like the sun' (*intijina*), which he described as 'big' at the time of the summer solstice and peak of the rains around Christmas.[15] Other people described this motif as *ch'unka* ('beard'), which can also suggest the sun's maturity and power. Interestingly, Guaman Poma's (c. 1615) depiction of the sun during the month of December shows an especially large, bearded face surrounded by

---

14 See Sánchez 1989b:30, Lyèvre 1990:193, 210 and Laime 2002 for illustrations. According to a player interviewed on Radio Pio XII, the black flower decoration is associated with performance at All Saints (November) and the red flower with Carnival (personal communication Vimar Chire).

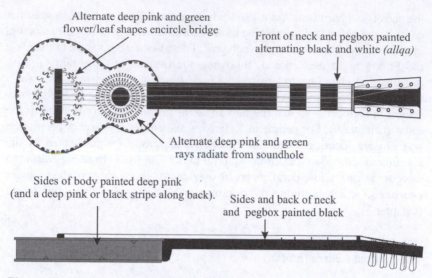

Figure 4.2   **Diagram showing *kitarra* decoration**

rays (1980:232). However, makers in Pocoata variously described these concentric rings as 'mountain peaks' (*cordilleras*) or *kantuta*, the red (and yellow) Bolivian national flower, demonstrating an interesting disparity between 'production' and 'consumption' knowledge (Appadurai 1986:41).

Alongside their decorative motifs, Macha *kitarra's* are usually very colourful; the sides of the 'body' (*kwirpu*) are typically painted deep pink[16] and a pink or black stripe is painted along the 'back' (*wasa*). The neck (*braso* 'arm') is painted mainly black, except around the tuning pegs and a few alternating spaces between frets. Those areas that are left unpainted – as white poplar (*alamo*) wood – create an *allqa* colour contrast, between black and white (Figure 4.2). According to Verónica Cereceda, colour contrast of this type is associated with fortune (1990:62).[17] The fact that three frets are left unpainted (that is, white) is also perhaps significant as this number is especially associated with *animu* (Chapter 2). In the early 1990's, I witnessed a new vogue develop, especially in the Ocuri area of Macha territory, for a larger shallow-bodied Macha *kitarra* called a *quinze* ('fifteen'), so called after its fifteen strings (five courses of three strings). Apparently, Feliz Ramirez from Pocoata developed this instrument, which was decorated in precisely the same way as the standard *kitarra* except for the sides and body of which were

---

[16] Occasionally I have seen instruments painted green.

[17] On other forms of rainy season guitars made in Pocoata it is common to find a red-green *allqa* colour contrast between alternate frets. This same red-green contrast is also found between the concentric circles around the soundhole of the *kitarra*.

often painted green or brick red. Subsequently, this instrument, which was almost double the price of the standard model, lost popularity and seems to have disappeared.

Comparing bodies: *charangos* and *kitarras*

The Quechua (and sometimes Spanish) terminology for the parts of the *charango* and *kitarra* are for the most part derived from the human body. These include: *uya* 'face', *jusq'u* 'hole' (or Sp. *voz* 'voice'), *wasa* 'back', *kwirpu* (Sp. *cuerpo*) 'body', and *maki* (or Sp. *braso*) 'arm'. This is common worldwide, but the body metaphor seems especially significant when we compare the *charango* and *kitarra*. In terms of size, the difference between the two instruments is obvious and leads to a focus on growth, with these instruments representing different stages of development. A few individuals connected the diminutive size of the *charango*, often termed *juch'uy charango* ('little *charango*'), with youth and immaturity, a sense further emphasized by the distinctive green colour used to paint the bodies of Pocoata *k'ullu* ('wooden') *charangos*, which several people related to the idea of 'unripeness'. In contrast, the larger size and deep pink colour of the *jatun kitarra* ('big guitar'), as it was often dubbed, would seem to evoke maturity; perhaps even a ripe fruit that is ready to pick.

A further decorative convention also appears to emphasize this distinction between mature and immature bodies, and to suggest seasonal associations. Whereas *allqa* colour contrast (white-black) is found between alternate frets on the *kitarra*, the fretboards of *charangos* are monochrome, either coffee coloured (natural wood) or painted black (Figure 4.3). In a fascinating

Figure 4.3   Photograph of a small *k'ullu* ('wooden') *charango* and *kitarra* made in Pocoata

semiotic analysis of colour contrast, Verónica Cereceda observes that in many parts of the southern and central Andes travellers interpret sighting an adult *allqamari* bird, with its contrasted black and white (*allqa*) plumage, as a good omen. However, no such positive values are associated with seeing the *suwamari* – the name for the juvenile bird of the same species – that has monochrome coffee-coloured plumage (1990:57–8) (Figure 4.4).

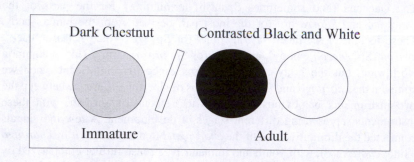

Figure 4.4   Colour distinction between young and adult *allqamari* bird (adapted from Cereceda 1990:62)

Through linguistic analysis of the Aymara root *suwa*, Cereceda identifies lines of association linking the *suwamari*'s immature state of development and monochrome colour with the wilting of crops, due to lack of water (1990:70–71). In approaching the relationship between *allqa* (mature bird, colour contrast) and *suwa* (immature bird, monochrome) she hypothesizes the following opposition:

[ALLQA]	[SUWA]
(*agricultura abundante*)	*naturaleza marchita, escasez* (1990:71)
(agricultural abundance)	withered natural world, scarcity [of water])

As Omar Laime has observed, this suggestion seems to correlate precisely with the dual seasonal roles of the *charango* and *kitarra* (Laime 2002:77, 81). The connection of (a) the growth of crops during the rains with the *allqa* colour contrast (black–white) of the *kitarra* fretboard, and (b) the withering of crops and shortage of water during the dry winter months with the monochrome fretboard of the *charango*, seems to engage with a series of widely shared cultural values and aesthetic categories. Although people in both Kalankira and Pocoata are well aware of – and even reproduce – this particular decorative convention, it should be stressed that nobody actually identified or articulated its somewhat abstract connection with the state of crop growth.

Clearly the form and decoration of these guitar type instruments is far from arbitrary. Indeed, in the early 1990s many people in Kalankira had clear ideas about how aspects of their construction and decoration related to seasonal performance and music's contribution to agricultural production. This raises a number of critical questions concerning agency – who are the innovators of such forms and decoration?

Making history

I spent several days visiting seven different instrument makers living in the dispersed homesteads around the Pocoata valley all of whom combine agriculture with instrument making. Most of them are unlikely to consider themselves *campesinos* ('peasants'), identifying instead with the *cholo* townsfolk of Pocoata. Many of these artisans supply *charangos*, generally of higher quality and often including intricate wooden or mother of pearl inlay, for the *cholo* market. But, like instruments for the *campesino* market, these *cholo* instruments tend to include wooden tuning pegs and metal strings. Whilst in the early 1990s a peasant-style *charango* was likely to cost between 35 and 80 pesos (US$5–10), a *cholo* style instrument would cost between 100 and 300 pesos (US$15–40). In turn, an urban-style *charango* with machine heads for tuning and nylon strings, as played by most Andean folk groups that tour internationally, could cost between 350 pesos (US$50) and several hundred US dollars. These contrasts should be understood primarily in terms of class, identity and ethnicity. Whilst the *charango*, as the fusion of European technology with Andean creativity is 'by its very nature a hybrid', which 'may be defined as mestizo', its forms reflect a complex and shifting series of social relations and hierarchies (Turino 1984:255).[18]

Pocoata's artisans told varying stories about the development of guitar-making traditions for the peasant market over the twentieth century, but what emerged was a sense of dynamic change, innovation, fashion, and lively market forces. A very approximate chronology of parts of this process relevant to the forms and decoration of (peasant-style) guitar-type instruments played in Kalankira is:

1920   First drawings on soundboards of rainy season guitars.
                Pulu or *mat'i* ('gourd') *charangos*, mainly traded from Sucre[19]

---

[18] Turino 1984 gives an excellent account of the social history of the urban-mestizo *charango* in Southern Peru.

[19] According to Bonifacio Ojeda *charangos* with a gourd sound box, which were widespread at this time, were also made in Pocoata – the gourds were collected from the valleys of Umerika, Aceroma, and Carasi.

1940/50	First use of parrot motif to decorate rural *charangos*[20]
1960	First use of analine dyes to decorate rainy season guitars
	Disappearance of gourd (*pulu* or *mat'i*) *charangos*
1960/70	Gut strings (*chunchuli*) replaced by steel (*acero*) and nylon
1965	First carved wooden armadillo-shaped *charangos*
1970	First black laminated *medio cuadrado* ('half-squared') instruments
1970/80	First use of green paint for backs of armadillo-shaped *charangos*

General consensus held that instruments were not decorated in the early part of the twentieth century,[21] and many of these *charangos* were made from gourds and traded from Sucre. The first drawings on rainy season guitars were dated to the 1920s and depicted plant images, similar to those drawn today. However, the bright colours used to decorate, for example, today's *kitarra* only became available with the arrival of analine dyes in the 1960s. It is unclear when northern Potosí style rainy season guitars, such as the Macha *kitarra*, developed. However, I suspect that the variety of five fret instruments played today do not date from much before the twentieth century.[22] According to Bonificio Ojeda, the parrot image was introduced by Agapo Mollenedo in the 1940s, and copied from school textbooks. Others dated it to the 1950s and one instrument maker claimed it was as late as 1960. The arrival of metal strings between the 1960s and 1970s had an immense impact on the musical aesthetics of the region as steel strings are much louder and can be tuned at considerably higher tension. Replacing gut strings with steel and nylon also meant that strings do not go out of tune in the rain – which, as a few villagers were amused to recount, had often damped performance.[23] Agapo Mollenedo, who introduced parrot decoration, was clearly identified as one of the most innovative makers as he also was the first to carve *charangos* from a solid piece of wood in the shape of an armadillo, the most standard Pocoata model today.[24] He is further credited with initiating the use of the distinctive green

---

[20] However, Celestino Tumuri dated this to approximately 1960.

[21] This is supported by images of large undecorated guitars from departments Oruro and La Paz depicted by Melchor María Mercado in watercolours dating from 1858 and 1859 (Mercado 1991:105, 112).

[22] The fact that the *charango* usually includes some 10–12 frets (even though the rustic construction means that these are redundant above the fifth fret) suggests considerable continuity with *cholo-mestizo* traditions and performance practice in which higher frets are regularly used in melodic *punteado* technique. By contrast the five frets of rainy season guitars imply that these instruments were developed later with a peasant market specifically in mind.

[23] According to Evaristo Kaysana (born 1922) gut strings were of sheep or goat. They were not made in Pocoata, but traded from Sucre. *Charangos* tended to use four strings, two narrow and two wider gauge.

[24] Flat (*liso*) *charangos* with ox-bone frets, often referred to as *llawaqasa* and perhaps resembling Anzaldo-style instruments, were mentioned by several makers and seem to have been common for about thirty years before this innovation. It is likely that the idea of carving wooden *charangos* in the shape of an armadillo, an animal often used to form the body of the instrument,

(*sapolin*) paint for the back of the body – a feature that was also to become strongly identified with Pocoata. The larger black laminated *charangos* favoured in the Macha region for the feast of the Holy Cross (3 May), variously known as *panti*, *bombo*, *samba* or *tabla charango*, also seems to have developed as recently as the 1970s.[25]

The makers presented these various innovations to me as an economic strategy 'to sell more instruments'. Yet these developments are far from arbitrary, suggesting a close fit between Appadurai's 'production knowledge' and 'consumer knowledge', where the key innovators clearly held a deep knowledge of 'the market, the consumer and the destination of the commodity' (1986:41–2). While the instrument makers of Pocoata usually express their identity with *cholo*-style instruments and repertoires, they share much cultural and agricultural knowledge, and a range of continuities in musical practices, with their peasant clients.[26] But, even if aware that certain types of music have been traditionally associated with attracting the rain and stimulating plant growth (such as *pinkillu* flutes), it is doubtful whether these artisans would actively participate in such agriculturally orientated musical practices, which are so closely connected with *ayllu* identity. It is unclear whether a Pocoata maker originally initiated the decoration of rainy season guitars with plant imagery or whether he simply adopted an existing rural practice of adorning instruments.

Even if the stimulus for such forms of decoration originally came from peasant players, the development, dissemination and marketing of such innovations must be attributed to the makers. Decoration does not simply 'reflect' links between these guitars and the rainy growing season, but rather consolidates and strengthens these associations, thereby heightening the importance of the instrument's role in agriculture. If we continue this line of

---

was in part borrowed from the major *charango* making centre of Aiquile, in the Cochabamba region, where this is the standard model (Cavour 1988:94–100).

[25] Ernesto Cavour identifies this form of construction with the Mizque region (department Cochabamba) where he notes that it is known as *rankha charango*, *tabla charango* or *ronco charango*. The use of a high-pitched drone string (*uñita*), half the length of the other strings, on instruments from both regions suggests that the Macha instrument was probably modelled on that of Mizque. However, Cavour notes that the performance of the Mizque instrument (which uses mainly nylon strings and incorporates tall bamboo or wooden frets, unlike the mainly metal strings and frets of the Macha type) is restricted to the rainy growing season (1994: 266–7) while the Macha *panti charango* is played only during the dry winter months. A recording (CD2:10) of the rainy season *tabla charango* from Raqaypampa (department Cochabamba) may be heard in Sánchez et al. (2001), who suggest that this instrument was introduced in the nineteenth century by Avelino Lopez Zurita, the founder of a string instrument workshop in Aiquile (2001:83).

[26] Many of the small towns of Northern Potosí are home to rich musical traditions that involve repertoires linked to calendrical festivals. For example, according to Zulema Arce, during All Saints (1 November) in Pocoata, *tonadas* are traditionally sung to the *quena* (notched-flute) and *lata caja* ('tin drum' – an empty alcohol tin beaten with a drum). Similarly, during Carnival a sequence of different *tonadas* and other genres are sung to the *charango* in *diablo* ('devil') tuning.

reasoning, the seasonal differentiation between the dry season *charango* and rainy season *kitarra* might also be attributed to the agency of *cholo* instrument makers. Creating (or capitalizing upon) a requirement for two instruments emerges as a superb marketing strategy – enabling artisans to sell twice as many guitars. Tailoring instruments to particular ethnic-regional markets, such as the Macha *kitarra* or *panti charango*, enables individual makers to carve out niche markets for themselves. Approached from such perspectives, the association between rural guitars and agricultural practices emerges not so much as a cultural relic but as a dynamic ongoing process, deeply interwoven with market forces and a demand for shifting fashions. Paradoxically, market forces and the introduction of new materials, such as analine dyes and oil-based paints, seem to have fuelled, rather than threatened, this process. It might be argued that market forces and the trappings of modernity, such as analine paints, have actually contributed to an apparent indigenizing process.

Some might interpret these market strategies as forms of manipulation or exploitation, where subaltern groups (the *ayllus*) literally play into the hands of a dominant *cholo* class (the instrument makers), in a music that reproduces asymmetries of power (Bourdieu 1977:192–5). According to such a view the *fabricantes* (Sp. 'makers'), are involved in 'fabricating' *ayllu* traditions and identity, with the English implications of fabrication as 'falsehood'. However, the socio-cultural distance and power imbalance between guitar makers and their peasant clients should not be overstated; indeed since colonial times trade specialization has often represented an economic strategy to compensate for lack of access to land (Saignes 1995:184). My own approach is thus less cynical; it stresses the superb craftsmanship of these guitar makers, their ingenuity and the pragmatics of economic survival. Their instruments continue to foster immense musical creativity and diversity, giving distinctive expression to the *ayllu* and motivating its reproduction – both by bringing couples together in song and through regulating agricultural production.

(B) THE MACHA GROOVE

Instantly perceived, and often attended by pleasurable sensations ranging from arousal to relaxation, 'getting into the groove' describes how a socialised listener anticipates patterns in a style, and feelingfully participates by momentarily tracking and appreciating subtleties vis-à-vis overt regularities. It also describes how a seasoned perfomer structures and maintains a perceptible coherence (Feld 1994:111).

... physical grooving ... being together and tuning up to somebody else's sense of time is what we're here on the planet for (Keil, in Keil & Feld 1994:24).

While string instruments and their dissemination are highly subject to market forces, shifting fashions and aspects of modernity, this does not hinder their ability to articulate deeply held ideas about seasonal transformation and identity. The introduction of mortality and consumption by the mouse *charango*, as described by Asencio in Chapter 3, was linked with a well known historical musical disjunction between the Laymis and Machas, dated to around the 1950s and identified with the arrival of *cruz* and *san pedro* genres – the most distinctive musical expressions of Macha ethnicity and regional identity which are constructed both musically and in the body.

The 'Macha groove', which finds its most paradigmatic expression in the *cruz* genre, involves a particular rhythmic-harmonic feel and cluster of ergonomic sensations in the motions of the dance and guitar players' hands. In other words, being Macha is not only about the way you look and sound, but also the way you move – embodied, for example, in both the feeling of unrushed connectedness (*link'un*) in the flow of performers' movements and the energetic bouts of *zapateo* ('stamping') dancing that punctuate sequences of sung verses. Learning to enter the Macha groove involves internalizing a vocabulary of movements, constructing a specific type of body and aesthetic vision, and fashioning an expressive self in relation to this body (Foster 1997:241). Although the various string genres played in Kalankira are, by many standards, technically undemanding and might theoretically be reduced to a few simple movements, the ways in which these are realized by individual players often demonstrates immense subtlety, creativity and expressive range. *Charango* technique represents an important sphere of individual male expression and personal style, which is comparable to the dry-season song poetry and weaving of women. But, rather than valuing complex technique or virtuosity, the focus is upon economy of movement and flow, where the right hand strums and the left hand remains in the same position, rarely moving more than one finger at a time (Figure 4.5).[27]

Macha bodies in motion: strumming, stamping and dancing

In the peasant communities of Northern Potosí and many other parts of the Andes, guitar-type instruments are almost always strummed, rather than plucked.[28] Alongside the metal strings favoured for the *charango* (and increasingly adopted for rainy season guitars),[29] strumming ensures maximum

---

[27] One left-handed player in Kalankira strummed guitars with the left hand, reversing the orientation of instrument (left to right, upside-down) and tuning the strings in reverse order. This was described as *lluqtu* (Quechua) or *sordo* (Sp.), literally meaning 'deaf' or lacking in understanding.

[28] The melodic and harmonic plucking techniques found in certain *charango* styles of the region, especially by recording artists such Los Pocoateños and Gregorio Mamani, reflect urban *mestizo* or *cholo* identity or aspirations (see Turino 1984: 259–63, Leichtmann 1987:93, 1989).

[29] Metal strings have been the norm on Macha *kitarras* since the 1980s, usually with one low-

Figure 4.5   Photograph of *charango* players during the feast of the Holy Cross (May)

volume – an important consideration in outdoor fiesta contexts or in noisy bars where plucked strings would be almost inaudible. While the *charango* is usually strummed with the index finger alone, the *kitarra* is typically played with three fingers, thereby creating a heavier and somewhat denser sound. The basic strumming pattern for both these instruments in Kalankira and many other parts of *ayllu* Macha consists of a long downstroke followed by a faster down/up stroke (long – short – short).[30]

For the sake of clarity I usually present these movements in the ratio 2:1:1 in my transcriptions, but their precise ratios vary immensely according to context and personal style, and represent an important expressive resource (Example 4.1). Although a few players make the three strokes seem almost even in length (1:1:1), asymmetrical ratios are more common and are often sustained extremely precisely. For example, an analysis of Paulino strumming the *charango* in *san pedro* for over 30 seconds (using a computer to measure

---

pitched nylon *bordón* string included on the central course. However, in the 1980s the majority of *guitarillas* and *talachis* played in northerly *ayllus* of Northern Potosí used nylon strings, occasionally doubled at the octave with metal strings. Today it is common to find instruments with all-metal strings, including some with wide gauge.

[30] This contrasts with the alternated up and down strokes of, for example, the Easter songs of certain more northerly *ayllus* of Northern Potosí (Stobart & Cross 2000:72–7).

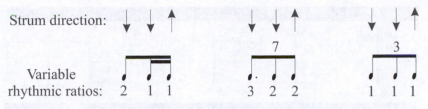

Example 4.1   Rhythmic flexibility in *charango* (and *kitarra*) strumming. (CD track 45)

events in milliseconds) demonstrated that he sustained an astonishingly regular asymmetical ratio of almost precisely 3:2:2. (CD track 45) While *kitarra* players sometimes depart from this pattern in order to follow the rhythm of the *wayñu* melody, in *charango* genres this pattern is periodically interspersed with syncopations or brief rapidly strummed figures, especially during instrumental interludes or *zapateo* dancing sections between verses.

However, rapidly strummed figures tended to be used sparingly, in contrast to the 'virtuosic' pretensions of high speed strumming sometimes encountered in the towns. On one occasion, Paulino wittily parodied a local man, whose style included frequent fast strummed figures, clearly conveying the idea that this was 'bad taste'. Some years earlier, when helping me to develop my own *charango* technique, Paulino had similarly criticized the fast 'flashy' and uneven strumming patterns that I had picked up from listening to urban players. He described these as *turpiyu* (Sp. *turbio* 'muddy, troubled') and encouraged me to play in a 'smooth' (Sp. *suave*) and more regular way. This regular and controlled sense of rhythm was referred to as *sumaq link'un* ('it flows/connects well'). The verb stem *link'u-* is widely used to refer to the act of fingering the frets of a guitar or holes of a flute, to bring a change in pitch, and more generally to refer to melodic movement (even resulting from interlocking panpipes). *Link'u* also refers to the 'zigzag' or 'meandering' image, found in dry season dance choreography (Chapter 6), and which is one of the most characteristic motifs in men's knitting and women's weaving of *ayllu* Macha. This image beautifully conveys the sense of repetition and rhythmic balancing between the 'straight/true' (*chiqan*) and the divergent/crooked (*link'un*), so critical to the unhurried flow of music, life and the seasons. It is notable that flowers, evoking moments of heightened sensory and aesthetic release, occur at the turning points – where death and new life meet, as they do at Carnival (Chapter 9).

Much as the snaking *link'u* pattern is among the most characteristic motifs of Macha knitting and weavings (Figure 4.6), the guitar strumming figure in Example 4.1 above are among the *ayllu's* most salient musical markers. This (long, short, short) rhythmic pattern is identical to the rhythmic sequence of an intensely energetic *zapateo* ('stamping dance') performed by men for *cruz*, the

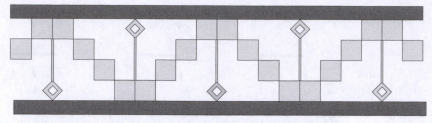

(a) *Link'u link'u* ('zigzag, meander') or *Mayu* ('river')

(b) *T'ipalaqi* (T'ipa leaf) design. T'ipa is an evergreen tree

Figure 4.6   Two common patterns used in the men's woolen *ch'ulu* hats. Men knit these hats typically using old bicycle spokes as needles

Feast of the Holy Cross (3 May), accompanied by the *charango* in *cruz* ('Cross') tuning.[31] This aggressive dance, consisting of fast synchronized stamping, is often performed in alternation with *julajula* panpipe music as men key-up for ritual battles (*tinku*) or alternatively used as a means to release aggression when encountering rival groups (Chapter 6).[32] CD track 1 features the sounds of men trotting in a snaking dance file (*link'u link'u*), accompanied by a *panti charango* in *cruz* tuning, and an extended burst of *zapateo*. This recording was made at about midnight on the eve (*vispira*) of the feast of *cruz*, just before the cross was removed from its sanctuary on a high promontory overlooking the fields for many miles around. The basic *zapateo* figure consists of a six beat sequence in which the left (L) foot marks the strong beat, followed by two fast stamps with the right (rr) foot on the offbeat. A single powerful stamp (L) is performed on the sixth beat marking the end of the phrase, which in some cases is preceded on the fifth beat by a slow (LR) or fast (lrlr) alternation of feet (Example 4.2).

---

[31] This dance is also performed at other dry season feasts in Macha territory, such as at Easter in Chayrapata, which, like the feast of *Cruz* in Macha, is noted for its ritual fighting (*tinku*).

[32] Platt suggests that this dance invokes the power of an earthquake, as one of the most devastating disasters that the divine powers can inflict on the inhabitants of the Andes (1987a:88). He bases this idea on Bertonio's gloss of the Aymara *apal apaltatha* (1984 [1612], II:23) as many dancing together stamping the ground, trembling trees or other things, including the earth from earthquakes.

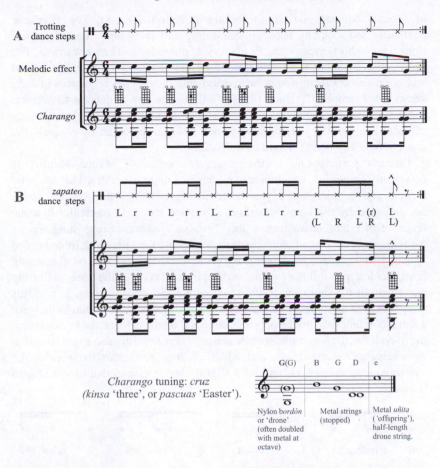

Example 4.2   Cruz *zapateo* sequence and *panti charango* motif. Excerpt A shows the trotting dance and *charango* phrase of the first part of the recording. Excerpt B highlights the coordination between the *charango* strumming pattern and stamping dance (*zapateo*) later in the recording. (CD track 1)[33]

This stamped and strummed motif is among the most distinctive expressions of *ayllu* Macha identity, and – in the context of men's dancing to accompany the cross – was a particularly salient expression of Macha notions of masculinity. As I also found, the rhythmic synchronization, immense energy and control involved in the *zapateo* also invoked a particularly powerful sense

---

[33] The use of the low-pitched *bordón* ('drone') string and high-pitched *uñita* drone is characteristic of the larger laminated forms of *charango* (*panti*, *madera* or *bombo*) favoured for the feast of *cruz*. The half-length *uñita* is often created by placing a nail half way down the fingerboard as a bridge.

of 'connectedness' and group feeling (Clayton 2001:8). The rhythmic continuity and iconicity between strumming and stamping, where the motif (long, short, short) evokes Macha identity as powerful and brave warriors. The same *zapateo* pattern is also performed by men and women together in *cruz* and *san pedro* courtship songs, and periodically punctuates sequences of sung verses (for example, CD track 12). The call for the ring of dancers to perform a *zapateo* is often announced by a singer shouting *usshh!!* In a highly characteristic posture – that I have sometimes seen parodied by *cholos* – the dancers typically bend forward as they stamp.

Through participating in the *zapateo* a sense of Macha identity is powerfully embodied, which in turn relates to a more generalized kinaesthetic feeling you acquire when you enter the 'groove' of the various songs accompanied by the long-short-short strummed motif. In particular it is the sense of lift that characterizes this 'groove', where during sung verses participants in the ring of dancers (most noticeably the girls, with folded arms) typically make a gentle stepping movement, alternating feet on the strong beats. Each step is followed on the offbeat by a relaxing of the knee and lifting movement of the same leg, leading to a gentle sway of the body. In turn this sway serves as anticipation to the next step, with the other foot, and in its wake a corresponding sway in the opposite direction on the offbeat. As I discovered, the overall feeling was a pleasurable sense of constant lift, also experienced in the energetic *zapateo* itself, and which in turn permeates the feel of the *charango* strumming style and, to a slightly lesser extent, that of the *kitarra* (Example 4.3).

R   relax/lift   L   relax/lift   R   relax/lift   L   relax/lift

Example 4.3   Diagrammatic representation of step and sway in *taki* dancing

Economies of movement: flexibility of expression

Whilst the characteristic Macha (right hand) strumming rhythm is common to various *charango* and *kitarra* genres, the (left hand) fingering techniques of the various tunings-genres are differentiated according to song form, season and context. For all the local genres of Kalankira, the player's left hand remains in first position, where maximum expression and volume is sought through minimum movement. This is facilitated by high resonance, resulting from lightness of the instrument's construction, and the use of metal strings. Strings are usually depressed lightly, especially those at low tension, as excessive pressure tends to push them out of tune (a common problem for outsiders accustomed to playing the standardized Spanish guitar).

Rather than actively moving the hand up and down the fingerboard, the left hand is kept in first position, with no string stopped above the fifth fret (see Baily 1985:244). This facilitates certain types of subtler finger movements (such as damping), permitting players to avoid dedicating much attention to technique, and ensures a secure grip of the instrument.[34] In the context of courtship song performance, these latter considerations are priorities. Indeed, *charango* and *kitarra* players usually dance alongside the singers they accompany, which may also entail sprinting or leaping from boulder to boulder as high-spirited and intoxicated groups of youths roam wildly between bars and homesteads. These instruments and their associated techniques are superbly adapted to this musical context, where a 'fussy' technique, which involves shifting left hand positions, would be highly impractical. Although in other cultural contexts, fast fingerwork or other feats of virtuosity might be foregrounded and carry considerable cultural capital, in Kalankira's participatory courtship songs such expressions are seen to disturb the conviviality of the performance. It is tempting to contrast this relative invisibility and subservience of technique with the obsession for it found in certain other musical cultures, where immense discipline and numerous hours of daily practice are dedicated to developing instrumental technique (Neuman 1990 [1980]:32–7). However, for many young men of *ayllu* Macha, the *charango* is an almost constant companion – a musical prosthesis – with which, often alongside peers, they acquire immense familiarity and often play out amorous obsessions. Through these countless hours, players gradually develop their own individual style, where technique is directed towards achieving maximum motivation for singers and dancers from minimum movement. One of the ways such economy of movement is achieved is through the use of damping (*ch'inlla*- 'silencing') – subtle movements that are scarcely perceptible from watching a player's fingers. This means that the musical resources available from a single finger position are greatly enlarged, where a string may alternatively be:

(1) unstopped – allowing the string's full length to sound,
(2) stopped – altering the pitch by depressing a string behind a fret, or
(3) damped – silencing the string by touching it lightly.

The use of damping is particularly characteristic of the two seasonally alternated *charango* genres *cruz* and *san pedro*.[35] In the case of *cruz*, the player's index finger remains constantly positioned behind the first fret on the

---

[34] The rustic construction and low string tension of many of the instruments produced for the peasant market, means that chords played above the fourth fret are often very out of tune and lacking in resonance.

[35] Damping is less common in the other Macha string genres and in other parts of Northern Potosí.

third string, alternatively stopping, unstopping or damping the string. This hand position, where the little finger is typically poised near the fifth fret and the middle and ring fingers held in readiness to play the second and third frets, is a defining feature of the *cruz* genre (Figure 4.7). Several variant tunings are common for *cruz* (see Appendix 3) using this same hand position, and it might be argued that, in the experience of many if not most players, it is the position of the hand, more than the tuning itself, which defines the genre.[36]

Besides issues of economy of movement and spatial perception, the tendency to play in first position should be seen, as Peter Manuel also observes for the case of Flamenco guitar, 'not as a limitation, but rather as a means of exploiting the potentialities of using open strings in harmonies' (1988:56). The role of open strings is highlighted in the following examples that feature Paulino playing *cruz* and *san pedro* consecutively on the same large laminated *panti charango* (Example 4.4). At my request, in the interests of comparison, the low-pitched nylon drone string (*bordón*) is tuned at the same pitch in both examples.

A constant drone effect on 'G' and 'e' is found in both these examples, created by the open nylon *bordón* string (G) and metal 'e' string, which are never fretted.[37] As in the case of Flamenco guitar harmony, the 'nontriadic notes in the altered chords are almost exclusively rendered on [these] open strings', whereas the 'fretted notes provide the triadic intervals' (Manuel 1988:56). In *cruz*, the 'home' position and principal tonality of the genre is achieved by stopping the middle ('b') string on the first fret (typically whilst either damping or stopping the bottom string on the fifth fret). This raises the string's pitch by a semitone to 'c', the tonal centre, which is also the pitch on which the singers' voices settle. This C major harmony, supported by the (G, e) drones, is alternated with an implied dominant (G), incorporating a sixth ('e') rather than the triadic notes (b and d). In *san pedro*, the voices define the tonal centre as G, but the constant 'e' in the *charango* drone also implies the relative minor (E minor) as do the A minor implications in the final chord before the phrase is repeated. 'Altered chords' incorporating a sixth seem to be particularly characteristic of guitar harmony of rural Northern Potosí, evoking a rich sense of pentatonic bitonality, which also characterizes certain wind genres. This also demonstrates some of the limitations of using Western harmonic language to categorize such forms of guitar harmony, which often appears to be shaped more by technical and melodic considerations than strictly abstract harmonic ones.

---

[36] This would seem to be a good example of how the layout of a guitar type instrument 'provides a framework for musical conceptualization', where more generally the guitar 'lends itself rather well to spatial thinking' (Baily 1991:151).

[37] Note that the (unstopped) e string is in a different position in these tunings.

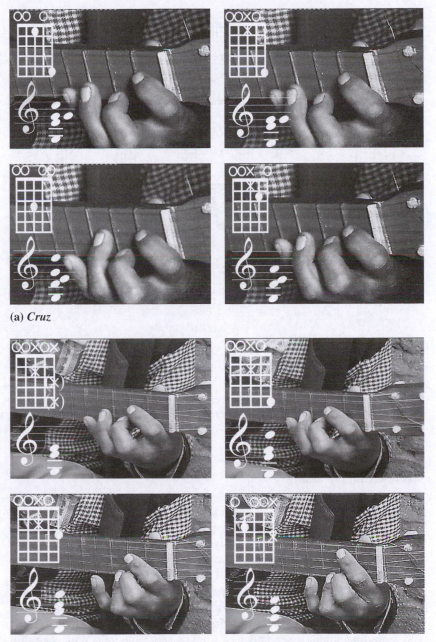

(a) *Cruz*

(b) *San Pedro*

Figure 4.7   Left hand position when playing the *charango* in *cruz* and *san pedro* tunings/genres. For key to left hand fingering see Example 4.4

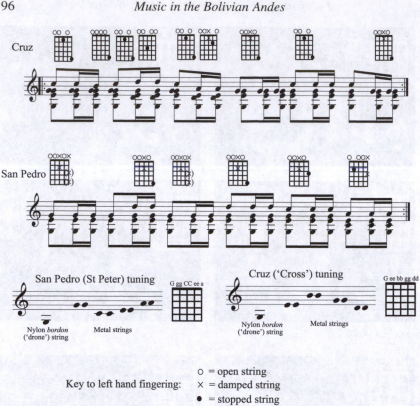

Example 4.4   Comparison of the basic repeated motif, fingerings and tunings of the *cruz* and *san pedro* dry season *charango* genres. Transposed up about one semitone. (CD tracks 40 and 41)

Genre-technique-tuning

One notable aspect of left hand *charango* techniques is that each technique – or hand position – is restricted to a single specific tuning and genre and with each shift in tuning and genre, the player is required to learn an entirely new relationship with his instrument. Indeed, I often encountered players who were competent in certain genres-tunings but entirely unable to play in others. Thus, rather than learning a flexible technique – in the same way as practising scales or chord sequences in different keys for a jazz improvisor – Kalankira's *charango* players must learn *the* technique of the genre, with technique, tuning and genre functioning essentially as a single inseparable unit. With each shift of *genre-technique-tuning* comes a corresponding transformation of the player's body, which might be seen to enter a different phase, mode of being or 'bodyscape'. This bodily experience of particular musical genres can

Example 4.5 Melodic variation on the *charango* in *cruz* genre. Transposed up about one semitone. (CD track 40)

clearly be extended to the various other instruments and genres played through the course of the year.[38]

Theme and variations

It is the repeated six beat melodic-harmonic motif which defines the *cruz* and *san pedro* genres and underlies the young women's voices in courtship song. In performance these motifs are characterized by much subtle variation, as evident from Paulino's demonstration of *cruz* genre (CD track 40, Example 4.5). For the sake of clarity this is reduced to a single melodic line (see Example 4.4 for the chords). In line 5 in following a melodic idea Paulino includes a seven beat phrase (instead of the usual six). In song performance this would confuse singers but extending phrases is quite common when *charango* players extemporize between verses.

Although *cruz* and *san pedro* were presented to me as fixed genres – played the same each year since the 1950s, they have been subject to constantly shifting fashions and stylistic innovation. While these genres powerfully evoke Macha identity as an endogenous – and, in some respects, imagined – political group, they also serve as important vehicles through which to express shifting local and individual stylistic differences. No two *charango* players in Kalankira expressed these genres in precisely the same way, yet – like the young women's vocal gestures and texts – a considerable amount of local coherence was maintained, distinguishing the Kalankiras, in more or less recognizable ways, from other communities. For example, the *cruz* style of nearby Tumaykuri (CD track 5, Example 4.6) – its verses full of word play – is markedly different in style from that of Kalankira (CD track 7, Example 5.4).

Awirintitachu Muskatilatachu	Any cane alcohol? Any Muscatel?
Kay llajtayjuntachu foresteratachu	Is this village crowded? with strangers?
Kay llajtayjamanta forestera valen	From this village strangers are expensive
Tini, tinisitu pampa tinisitu	Got some, got some flat land
Fiesta rikushayku pata kunisitus	We're off to party with acquaintances above
Pata kunispata sullka churisitun	We know the youngest son above/on top
Sullkaman qhawasqa chawpi churisitun	Checked-out the youngest, middle son
Si chawpi churinchun kuraq churisitun	Let the middle son, then the eldest

Some of these local styles become sub-genres in themselves. For example, one of the most popular variants of the *cruz* genre, played on small *charangos*, is called *San Lazaro* – named after the village where this style developed. This

---

[38] While this unity of tuning-technique-genre applies to all Kalankira's *charango* music, it does not affect the *kitarra* of the rains in quite the same way, which plays a range of different *wayñu* melodies using similar technique (Chapter 5).

Example 4.6 *Cruz* **song from P'uytukuri community, near Tumaykuri. (CD track 5)**

style is technically more challenging, requiring more flexibility of left hand movement, than the style played on the larger *panti charango* (Example 4.7).

Given the virilocal nature of residence in this part of the Andes, where women leave their kin to marry into the man's community, the primary motivation of these songs is to bring together men and women from different communites of *ayllu* Macha (for which endogamous marriage rules apply). In other words, within a single performance these genres need to absorb local stylistic differences from diverse parts of the *ayllu* if they are to be effective as a medium for courtship. Indeed these stylistic and potentially erotic juxtapositions – between voices and guitars – add to the piquancy and dynamism of performances, where the genre is stretched and its expressive potential explored. We consider the dynamics of song performances in the next chapter.

Conclusion: construction in progress

Like guitars and guitar music in many other parts of Latin America, those of Kalankira emerge as especially potent expressions of regional, ethnic and class identity, as well as crucial to courtship. Entering the Macha groove involves particular types of rhythmic feel and other sensations, most notably embodied in the rhythm of the *ayllu's* warlike stamping dance (*zapateo*) and distinctive *charango* strumming rhythm (in the *cruz* genre), which are connected with the ritual battles of the feast of the Holy Cross (*cruz*) (Chapter 6). The development of this most vivid musical marker of Macha ethnicity is dated to the turbulent 1950s, and in one local exegesis is related to a radical disjunction in both ethnic relations and mythic time (Chapter 3).

Based on Spanish technology introduced in the sixteenth century, Kalankira's guitars are deeply integrated into the productive cycles of the

Example 4.7   *San Lazaro* style; melodic characteristics and fingerings. (CD track 42)

ayllu, their forms, decoration, tuning and performance practice closely connected with the unfolding seasons. This seasonal size distinction is suggestive of the dual and balancing phases of a life cycle, where small, immature and growing bodies, on the 'youth pathway', consume and accumulate the energies of others, in the same way as the diminutive mouse *charango* (Chapter 3). In contrast, fully-grown bodies, on the 'adult pathway', are principally associated with nurturing the young and giving their energies for the benefit of others – the bright red *kitarra* suggestive of a mature, sweet fruit ready to be eaten. However, guitar form and decoration are important sites for innovation and shifting fashions, where meanings are not fixed. For example, around 2001 a very large model of *panti charango*, termed *Villalta* after its maker from Pocoata, became extremely fashionable around Macha. Approximately the same size as the standard *kitarra*, this new *charango* potentially renders the size typology relating to seasonal performance redundant. Will this lead to the erosion of seasonal performance practice? Might larger *kitarras* begin to be constructed to compensate? Or, are large *Villalta charangos* simply a passing fad? This cannot be easily predicted, but serves to highlight the unstable nature of symbolic meanings and how these are influenced by innovations that capture the imagination of players.

What is notable is how, through much of the twentieth century, the developing forms and decoration of the peasant-style guitars constructed in Pocoata seem to have consolidated and strengthened music's connection with agricultural production and seasonal performance practices. Even if not all these innovations can be attributed to the agency of the Pocoata's luthiers, these artisans' critical role cannot be doubted. The success and persistence of certain instrument forms and types of decoration may also be attributed to market forces, capturing players' imagination and coming to represent *ayllu* identification. What may have begun as 'fads and fashions', closely connected with marketing strategies, may sometimes lead to longer term 'style changes', resonating with wider cultural developments to become 'instutionalized ideologically' by the performers, as 'generally accepted concepts of form' (Price & Price 1980:201). Some of the conventions of guitar form, decoration and performance described, which have been reproduced in subtly shifting forms for well over fifty years, would seem to be good examples of this process – contributing to the strengthening of ethnic identity and music's association with agricultural production.

Marrying the Mountain and the Production of People

Songs of courtship and marriage

Camisay planchados kurtas igualados	Ironed shirts, tuned strings
Chayqa chayamuyku joven igualados	That comes to us, paired with a lad
	(*san pedro* song verses)

Many aspects of Kalankira's landscape are personified as a kind of extra-human community, who like their human counterparts 'walk around' and express emotions, such as desire, hunger or anger (Chapter 2). In this chapter we see how the agricultural land known as *wirjin* ('virgin') is made ready for planting through ritual marriage to the mountain in the *asintu* ceremony, which features singing by mature women. Through this ceremonial activity and the song texts, the cycles of human and agricultural production are explicitly and consciously brought together by community adults. Such singing by adult women is in many respects exceptional as most forms of women's song performance cease after cohabitation or marriage. Young unmarried people involved in courtship dominate Kalankira's music making, especially the various song genres accompanied by the dry season *charango* and rainy season *kitarra* that form the focus of this chapter.[1]

By evoking the contexts of specific song performances, I explore relations between social, musical and agricultural production. The texts sung by young unmarried women tend to focus on courtship, lovemaking and anxieties about marriage, rather than explicitly invoking agricultural production. Nonetheless, these songs vividly express the fertility embodied in young single people. Also, because these courtship genres and their respective instrumental accompaniment and tunings are organized seasonally, they turn out to be the most pervasive markers of the unfolding musical year. Unlike wind music that is restricted to a few festive contexts (except the *pinkillu*), the *charango* or *kitarra* accompaniment to these genres is heard on a regular basis, as lads strum an instrument while, for example, hanging out with friends, pasturing

---

[1] Adults periodically participate in music making, especially wind music, and sometimes specialize in certain instruments (such as *siku* panpipes). See also Martínez 1998:10. In other parts of the Bolivian and Peruvian Andes, sometimes due to urban migration by the young, certain local musical genres have become the preserve of older people (Stobart 1988:76).

oxen, walking to the fields or heading for an amorous rendezvous in the mountain peaks.

Thomas Solomon observes that young men of *ayllu* Chayantaka say they play rainy season guitars in order to 'get girls' or to invoke *kustumbri* ('custom') rather than to make it rain. He argues that 'as Chayantaka grow older and through experience come to better understand the symbolism of the agricultural cycle, they get the "bigger picture" about how musical performance and the fertility of the fields are related' (1997:182). For the Kalankiras, while individuals undoubtedly acquire a broader understanding of productive and musical processes as they age, learning to play a musical instrument or sing is not somehow divorced from the broader productive activities in which music is embedded and necessarily involves engaging with wider productive and social processes, contexts and sets of relations. To suggest that a 14-year-old lad from Kalankira might be ignorant of the *kitarra*'s association with attracting rain and promoting plant growth would be an insult to his knowledge. Through musical participation young people not only develop cognitive and other competences, such as coordination, social skills, verbal dexterity and the manipulation of metaphor, but also learn how particular genres, tunings, melodic forms and gestures, poetic metres, verbal imagery and vocabulary, dance styles, rhythmic feels, bodily sensations, timbres and techniques relate to particular contexts. From this perspective, musical participation emerges as a powerful force in the 'production of people'. By this I mean the diverse processes by which an 'unsocialized creature', associated with the wild and ambiguous mountain sphere, gradually becomes 'fully human' through increasing integration into the human and ultimately ancestral community (Canessa 1998:240).[2]

For the Bolivian Jalq'as and Tarabucos, Rosalia Martínez (1998) has charted the journey from childhood to adulthood through women's song. She identifies three main phases: childhood, young-bachelorhood and marriage. Young girls initially learn to sing whilst outside on the mountains pasturing animals, an ambiguous and marginal space that according to Martínez 'embodies the imaginary idea of the non-social', and only present their voices in public before the community from about the age of 16, which signifies their integration into the life of the group.[3] From this age on, young women's mastery over words, in singing and creating (dry season) song poetry,

---

[2] See Isbell & Roncalla 1985 and Harris 1980. Also, in a study of Macha childbirth practices, Platt characterizes the human fetus as an aggressive devil-like being, which is immensely dangerous and painful to the mother and exorcised in childbirth (2002:132). He also relates birth to the first mythic rise of the sun when the primordial *chullpas* were destroyed in the solar conflagration (Chapter 2).

[3] In Kalankira, as a group of some eight of us danced from house to house, I witnessed girls, aged around 13 or 14, singing in public for the first time. Like some kind of formal audition, the

highlights their increasing expression through language, which is fundamental to what it means to be human (Martínez 1998:10, Harris 2000 [1980]:182–3).[4] But it is only when joined to 'their other half' – made two in marriage – that people are considered whole (Isbell 1978:23).[5]

Single life and married life

Besides birth and death, the most critical transition in the human life cycle is cohabitation or marriage: the creation of a *qhariwarmi* ('man-woman') unit or household, as the basic economic and (re)productive building block of a community. Marriage is virilocal, so for a woman in particular it represents a radical disjunction in social relations and way of life, as she must leave her community. Like many couples in Kalankira, my hosts Paulino and Evangelia first met and got to know one another through singing courtship songs together, and apparently Paulino was drawn to Evangelia's beautiful singing. In many respects young single women dominate the symbolic discourse and performance of song and enjoy considerable liberty, but following cohabitation their singing and dancing is immediately restricted and their sexuality and fertility come under social control (Isbell 1997:281) (Figure 5.1).

Martínez contrasts the 'excess' and eroticism of unmarried women's singing with the *mesure* ('moderation') of married women, citing examples of how when they are inebriated they nostalgically sing the courting songs of their youth (1998:16–17). However, my experience in Kalankira was rather different, perhaps reflecting local variation and/or my gender: I was told that married women are only permitted to sing wedding songs, *wayñus* during certain Carnival rites and laments. The only married woman not to respect these local restictions was my *comadre* Leonarda Mamani, from nearby Ura Kalankira (Lower Kalankira) who sang a variety of *takis* for me to record, accompanied on the *charango* by her husband Octavio Suyo. In many respects Leonarda, whose mother was a *chola* from a mining family of Lipez (near Ocuri), considered herself superior to other local women, and her forthright attitudes were often unpopular – regularly leading her into disputes. Exceptionally among local woman, she had been married before, had travelled

---

older singers insisted these younger peers sing alone and commented critically on their shy performances.

[4] Although married men act as the voice of individual households in community meetings, in the sphere of courtship song, women are considered to have greater command over words than men (Harris 2000:182–3).

[5] The symbolic importance of this 'dual' aspect acquired through marriage and associated with achieving 'fully human' identity is highlighted in Laymi rites for the dead, where an unmarried man or woman was buried with a hen or cockerel respectively (Harris 2000:195).

Figure 5.1 Young women of Kalankira singing songs (*takis*) to *charango* accompaniment (foreground from left: Sebasta, Gregoria and Margara Beltrán)

widely and worked in the tropical region of Chapare. Her brother, Gregorio Mamani, is also one of the best-known and most prolific recording artists of the Northern Potosí region, and Leonarda has appeared on at least one of his recordings of *ayllu* Macha music, as part of the group *Zura zura*. In many respects, Leonarda threatened and contravened local expectation about how a woman should behave, despite the popularity of her husband.

For other married women the restrictions sometimes seemed tantamount to a prohibition. For example, Paulino with uncharacteristic harshness immediately vetoed my request to record Evangelia singing, even though he and many other local men continued to play music to accompany courtship songs after marriage.[6] The sexual connotations of a girl singing to a man were also vividly brought home when I encountered Cenovia Beltrán, about a month after she had been 'stolen' away to live with a man in his community.

---

[6] Nonetheless, on one occasion, I did hear Evangelia sing a song she had learnt at school. This suggests that, as in the case of wedding songs, it may not be so much the act of singing that is frowned upon as the implications of particular genres. For example, Paulino's mother Asunta – who had been widowed since Paulino's infancy – sang for me several times, although I never saw her sing during a fiesta.

I had often recorded her singing in the past and she had expressed some frustrated amorous interest in me. When I enquired whether her new living situation meant she would no longer sing for me, she looked at me saucily and chuckled 'that depends on you'. The implications were blatantly obvious.

The courtship song texts of the dry winter months often contrast single and married life as distinct phases or 'pathways', characterized by very different experiences, expectations and modes of expression. These songs commonly present marriage as a form of death, while during weddings newlyweds are called *wawa* ('babies'), emphasizing the sharp separation between these two life pathways. Whereas youthful unmarried (post-adolescent) bodies are associated with mobility, independence, seduction, growth and accumulation, the dual bodies of married adults are connected with stability, restricted movement, reproduction, nurturing and the redistribution of energies. This distinction is of great importance to the mapping of music onto the productive year, where the associations of the 'youth pathway' tend to be connected with the dry winter months and those of the 'adult/married pathway' with the rains; a contrast also evident from comparing the bodies of the *charango* and *kitarra* (Chapter 4). Courtship song lies at the intersection of these two pathways and serves as a powerful force in establishing settled social relations and (re)production. However, jealousies and extra-marital affairs resulting from its ambiguous seductive powers may also be destructive to marriages (Turino 1983:95, Martínez 1996:18) or, as we shall see in Chapter 10, lead to the complete breakdown of community relations.

The importance of the dichotomy between single ('youth pathway') and married life ('adult pathway') as a way of understanding production is highlighted when we consider how marriage influences peoples' lives. Only married couples are usually eligible (or in practice are economically able) to sponsor major feasts; an important means of acquiring prestige and a prerequisite to assuming positions of authority in the community. Unmarried adults are excluded from these social mechanisms and alternative strategies are necessary for them to acquire prestige or integrate into the community.[7] Kalankira's only spinster, Santosa Beltrán, never married I was told because a nearby mountain peak (Figure 1.1), known as *Qala Walaychu* (literally 'rock lout'), impregnated her when she was a girl.[8] No man had dared incur the mountain's jealousy by marrying Santosa and subsequently the local *yatiris* ritually married her to the mountain. In this way she was made 'dual' and integrated into the community, her mountain husband – on whose peak llamas

---

[7] Kalankira's two most notable bachelors – Adrian Chura and Lorenzo Mamani – both held positions in the *sindicato*, the peasant union that has been seen to undermine the autonomy of the *ayllu* (Rivera Cusicanqui 1990:116, 1992:123). Don Adrian also acquired considerable reputation as a healer (*paqu*) and storyteller, while Lorenzo led the community's *siku* panpipe band and was the church sacristan.

[8] Cf. Isbell and Roncalla (1985:24).

are mated each year (Chapter 8) – ensuring the fecundity of the community's herds. Santosa's special relationship with the mountain was also used to explain why her brother Victor Beltrán, with whom she lived, was favoured with the district's largest herd.

Taki and *wayñu:* Kalankira's song genres

Sharp contrasts in form, creative processes and gendered roles underlie the distinction between Kalankira's *charango* song genres, or *takis* ('songs'), of the dry winter months and its *kitarra* songs, or *wayñus*, of the rains. Whilst *takiy* is the common Quechua verb 'to sing', and the verb *wayñuy* is sometimes heard in reference to dry season songs, a seasonal-genre distinction is widely maintained between these terms (see Solomon 1997:100–101). Most dry season *takis* consist of a short repeated vocal phrase of paired couplets, with a set number of syllables, accompanied by a repeated *charango* figure of fixed length – both parts incorporating subtle variations. The poetry is the central focus, usually including a combination of improvised, locally composed and widely known sequences of verses. These various genres and their associated tunings and *charango* techniques are closely linked to specific contexts or seasons (Example 5.1).

As the principal courtship genres, *cruz* and *san pedro* are played respectively from the end of Carnival until late June and from late June until October (Figure 3.4). *Salaki* is also associated with young unmarried people, and is sung and danced by couples on the final two days of Carnival (Chapter 9), and, although rarely heard today, *walli mayun* was associated with journeys to the valleys and mostly sung by men. Men characterize themselves in the words of this genre as foxes, which are known for their sexual appetite and lack of discrimination. The best-known verses are:

Walli mayun qhincha, chhalla chapapayuq	River valley beer bar, hut of dry maize stalks
Maypi aqha tiyan? – ususin yapayuq	Where's the corn beer? – daughter as a bonus
Walli mayun qhincha, atuqjina qhincha	Valley river fornicator, fornicator like a fox

Matrimonio (*kasamintu*) is performed at weddings, which are usually celebrated during the dry season, and sometimes incorporates *takipayanaku*, the witty trading of insults, especially between male kin and female affines.[9]

By contrast the *wayñu* songs of the rains do not follow any set poetic metre or phrase length, and melodies tend to be more extended and follow fixed

---

[9] Flety & Martínez 1992: Track 17, Solomon 1994a, Arnold & Yapita 1998a:552.

Charango song genres (*takis*): dry winter season (March–October)

genre	*charango* phrase	syllable count[10]
cruz	3 + 3 = 6 beats	6 + 6 = 12
san pedro	3 + 3 = 6 beats	6 + 6 = 12
salaki	4 + 4 = 8 beats	6 + 3 + 6 = 15
matrimonio ('wedding)	5 + 5 = 10 beat	8 + 8 = 16
walli mayun ('valley river')		6 + 6 = 12

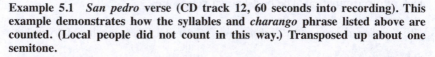

Example 5.1 *San pedro* **verse (CD track 12, 60 seconds into recording). This example demonstrates how the syllables and *charango* phrase listed above are counted. (Local people did not count in this way.) Transposed up about one semitone.**

texts. This means that each *wayñu* is a unique entity with its own individual melodic and poetic identity. Although *wayñus* played on *pinkillu* flutes are highly formulaic, almost always following the form AABB- (Chapter 8), those accompanied by the *kitarra* tend to be variable in form. Unlike many guitar *wayñus* from other parts of Northern Potosí, those of *ayllu* Macha often consist of a single melodic phrase repeated in its entirety (rather than several sections with internal repeats). Example 5.2 was recorded in Kalankira during

---

[10] In practice, singers often drop the final syllable of each line – especially in *matrimonio*, where 7 + 7 = 14 is usually heard. However, people helping me transcribe always automatically included the final syllable.

Carnival; note the invocation of flowers, the lower river, death and the 'siren' (*sirina/sirinu*) as important symbols of the rains, which appear in many *wayñus*, and the widespread metaphorical assocation of a girl's weeping with rain (CD track 32).

Uray mayunta rishani	I'm going along the lower river
Jawas t'ikasta pallaspa	To pick broad bean flowers
Sirinay rosasa x 2	My siren rose
Sima jawas t'ikastachu	If there are no broad bean flowers
Wañuy kawsayta maskaspa	I shall search for life in death
Sirinay rosasa x 2	My siren rose
Ima phuyu, jaqay phuyu	What cloud? that cloud
Yanayaspa wasaykamun	Blackening, from behind
Sirinay rosasa x 2	My siren rose
Chulaypaq waqayninchari	My girl's tears
Paraman tukuspa jamun	Come turning into rain
Sirinay rosasa x 2	My siren rose

Example 5.2 *Wayñu* **song with** *kitarra*. *Uray mayunta rishani*. **Transposed up about one semitone. (CD track 32)**

Despite subtle local and individual variation, people presented the musical aspect of dry season *takis* as static. Indeed these songs have remained recognizably the same since I first visited Macha territory in 1987. Within this relative fixed musical form, young women constantly invent and improvise new sets of verses, which are often juxtaposed with classic ones dating back many decades. When I enquired why dry season songs have such a regular structure and poetic form, whereas those of the rains do not, Asencio related the variability and unique identity of *wayñus* to the way they are taught to people by the *satanas* ('satans').

> It's like they're from the *satanas*. Probably the *satanas*. Just like that they deliver a different *wayñu* tune. Another, another, and now another, they teach. They are singing, some with another *wayñu*, and some with another one. And another, now another in the same way comes to be known. That's why it's like that.[11]

This highlights how musical inspiration is often attributed to powers associated with demonic beings, such as *sirinus* ('sirens') and *satanas*, rather than the creativity or genius of an individual (Chapter 9). By contrast the texts of dry season *takis* were closely identified with human expression, although older men sometimes downplay the immense verbal artistry involved, as in the words of Hilarion Gallego from nearby Titiri:

> They just sing about anything [in *takis*], the people just speak [...] it just comes out, it just comes out of the people ... Right now we are drinking, when we get tanked up now, right now, see? We're just talking now, aren't we? That's all it is.[12]

While dry season *takis* (especially *cruz* and *san pedro*) are created by young unmarried women and reflect their concerns, the texts of *wayñu* are usually sung by women from a male perspective; women in these songs representing objects of (male) desire. Like most other music, the acquisition (or composition) of *wayñu* is associated with and largely controlled by men, as the instrumentalists (Harris 2000 [1980]:183, Martínez 1998:6). Whereas the texts of dry season *takis* focus on the preoccupations of young women, especially anxiety about marriage, and regularly refer to *wira* ('life/fat'), those of the rains evoke flowers, *siway* or 'sweetness' (Chapter 9) and sometimes refer to male conquest or even to giving birth. The contrasts between the two song types are summarized below:

---

[11] *Paykuna satanasmantajina. Ichari satanas. Wak wayñu ya esta chayachin. Wakin wakin waktaña, yachachinankutaq. Wakin wak wayñu, wakin wakwan kay takishanku ya. Wakin waktaña yachallantaq. Chayrayku jina chayqa*

[12] *Taki nomas de cualquiera, hablan nomas la gente [...] sale nomas, de la gente nomas sale eso ...Ahorita nosotros estamos chupando, cuando tankamos kunitan, ahorita, nove? Estamos ya, estamos hablando no? Eso nomas.*

Taki	*Wayñu*
dry season, 'little' *charango*	rains, 'big' *kitarra*
static musical form, unchanged each year	new each year, attributed to *satanas/sirinus*
short regular musical phrase/syllable number	extended form, irregular syllable number
text independent from music	unity between melody and text
poetry composed by women	acquisiti/composition by men
text: female perspective (subject)	text: male perspective (woman as object)
wira ('life/fat'), female anxiety about marriage	*siwa* ('sweetness'), flowers, male conquest

Over the remainder of this chapter I shall examine four songs and their performance contexts, where each song belongs to a distinct genre and takes its place within the seasonal cycle. We begin with the harvest season in May, the time of *takis* in *cruz* ('cross') tuning/genre.

(1) *Cruz* – youthful pleasures and the tears of marriage

Track 7 on the CD transports us to the llama corral beside Asencio's house and into a circle of about ten dancers, whose faces and expressions are scarcely visible in the darkness. It is about 9pm and our bodies are numb from exhaustion, having just danced up the steep path from Macha – a homeward journey of over six hours. Nonetheless, the girls' voices – and the *charango* that sustains them – draw us into the dance, and our bodies into the groove; our endurance and stamina fuelled by corn beer and watered-down cane alcohol. It is the feast of the Holy Cross (*cruz*) on 5 May, and there has been almost constant music and dancing for three days. Plenty else is going on in the corral besides our circle, and from time to time other rings of singers and dancers strike up, or competing *charangos* are strummed nearby, distorting the sound of our own accompanist. These duelling *charangos* remind us that in many contexts 'playing music is an overtly aggressive act' (Harris 2000 [1980]:183).

The young women are the primary focus of our ring of dancers, and congregate together on one side, dominating the proceedings. Two sisters are the clear leaders; they initiate new sets of verses from their huge repertoire, their voices ringing out confidently above those of several younger, more timid and less experienced girls, some of whom have arrived from other hamlets. The two sisters, Sabasta and Margara Beltrán, are in their early twenties, and like their younger sisters are considered very good-looking. Even day-to-day, when herding their llamas up to the peaks for pasturing or collecting water from the stream, they are always immaculately dressed. Tonight they are striking in distinctive black woollen dresses (*almillas*), hitched-up provocatively above their knees,[13] and beautiful home woven backcloths (*aksus*) of *ayllu* Macha. Sabasta, the elder of the two, has a flirtatious and jaunty way of wearing her white felt hat, enabling her to peer out coyly as she sings. Aside from these attractions, they are also daughters of Victor Beltrán who has the largest llama herd in the community. No feast goes by in Kalankira without the visitation of a good number of young lads armed with their *charangos*, and a predatory glint in their eyes.[14] Can they 'steal' one of these girls away to their hamlet? they wonder. A few of these young men are dancing in the circle, and the *charango* player, with his small Betanzos-style instrument in a variant of *cruz* tuning, is himself a visitor I scarcely recognize.

Even if not all the multiple interactions within the circle are of an amorous nature, the idea of courtship and the implications of marriage are omnipresent in the repeated verses that the girls sing:

1	*Cantan cantaremos bailan bailaremos*	Sing, let's sing dance, let's dance
2	*Kay watitatawan wira pasaremos*	With this year let's pass life/fat
3	*Watamanta wata ya no hay noticias*	From year to year still no news
4	*Nutishallanqanqa pero nutishallan*	There will be news but just news
5	*Sumbriruy patapi sumbriritullataq*	On top of my hat there is another hat
6	*Wata kunanjina sultiritullataq*	This time next year and still single
7	*Intirun makipi anillusllapuni*	On every hand rings for sure
8	*Hasta al wayñunaypis sultirallapuni*	Until my death/*wayñu* single for sure
9	*Kasarupi tunay que tal mulistuta?*	Dance in marriage; is it tiresome?
10	*Sultirapi tunay que tal tunantita?*	Dance when single; how's the player?
11	*Kasarachu kani waqas purinaypaq?*	Am I married to walk weeping?
12	*Sultirallaq kani wiray pasanaypaq*	I'm just single to pass my life/fat away
13	*Kasaruchá ari waqaspapis purin*	Then, married perhaps to walk weeping

The high-pitched, piercing quality and rhythmic enunciation of the voices is immediately striking. These qualities are likely to be appreciatively described by my transcription assistants with words such as *jatunmanta* ('loud'), *ch'uya* ('clear') and *ñañumanta* ('high-pitched'). By contrast girls who mumble or sing quietly (*pisimanta*) are often criticized, demonstrating an aesthetic for a dynamic and clearly articulated performance style. In this particular rendering

---

[13] Married women wear their *almillas* below the knee.

[14] Playing the *charango* is often linked with predators in local stories. For example, the condor is said to be like a *charango* because, it 'carries off girls' to the rock where it lives; its flapping wings make the sound *chilin chilin*, 'just like a *charango*'. Antonio, the trickster fox, is especially associated with playing the *charango* and even referred to as *charanguero* ('charango player'). In one story he visits a group of girls on several nights, playing a *charango* made from a *q'iwayllu* cactus, with strings of the roots of mountain grasses (*ichhu*) and tuning pegs of dog's teeth. He appears to the girls as a handsome young stranger and superb *charango* player, and accompanies their singing all night. But each night, just before dawn, he creeps off – taking one of the girls' sheep with him. On his final visit the girls discover he is a fox when he departs without saying farewell and growling *kuwarr* 'like a dog'.

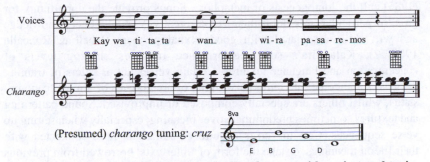

Example 5.3 *Cruz* **verses accompanied by the** *charango* **with conjectured tuning and fingerings. Transposed down about one semitone. (CD track 7)**

of *cruz*, the singers focus on just two pitches, about a tone apart (Example 5.3). On the stressed fourth syllable of each line, the voices descend a tone to the 'tonic' on which they then remain – as though resolving a dissonance in the manner of an appoggiatura. However, neither the transcription nor this description does justice to the immense timbral richness of the voices. For example syllables 4–6, notated as repeated pitches, consistently involve a gradual and highly expressive microtonal rise alongside a shift in harmonic spectrum. Standard music notation is also unable to reflect the fluidity in the voices' rhythm as they respond to the shifting poetic gestures; these subtle forms of variation being critical to these songs' expressivity.

This song leads us into unfamiliar aesthetic territory and its economy of musical resources belies the immense richness in texture, poetic device and allusion. The lines are organized in pairs connected by various types of semantic or syntactic features or word play, where – according to Bruce Mannheim – rhyme carries little or no aesthetic weight (1986:55). For instance, the juxaposition of *sumbriritullataq* and *sultiritullataq* in lines 5–6, is an example of syntactic coupling – where the words share almost identical sound patterns but unrelated meanings. Another common device is 'semantic coupling', where paired lines may include synonyms for the same idea, or juxtapose opposing or complementary ideas or concepts (Mannheim 1986:56, Lienhard 1992:355–7). For example, in lines 11–12 the Quechua *purinaypaq* ('so as to walk') and Spanish derived *pasanaypaq* ('so as to pass by') convey the same idea with contrasted vocabulary. We also find opposing or complimentary juxtapositions in *kasarupi* ('in marriage') and *sultirapi* ('in single [life]') lines 9–10, or between *anilluspuni* ('rings for sure' that is, 'married') and *sultirallapuni* ('single for sure').

Quechua verbal art, in songs and riddles, has been interpreted as critical to the 'acquisition of the cognitive skills required for social interaction and more generally in the reproduction of cultural systems' (Mannheim 1986:69), including learning to articulate metaphoric relations; what Isbell & Roncalla

(1985) call the 'ontogenesis of metaphor'. Songs provide the opportunity for girls, in particular, to exhibit their verbal creativity, intelligence, knowledge and wit; skills associated with good sexual partners (Isbell & Roncalla 1985:22). Kalankira's song performance involves shifting levels of concentration and language textures. Certain verses act as fillers or framing devices, some come into temporary vogue or are classics of almost 'canonic' status, whilst others are specially composed or improvised. Sound patterning and textures sometimes predominate over meaning, especially when setting up verse sequences. Certain verses acquire connotations little connected with their literal meanings, or take the form of 'intertexts' borrowed from previous speech or song events, carrying ideological baggage. When re-articulated in the here-and-now, these words allow for the opening up of new meaning as well as the preservation of existing ones (Howard-Malverde 1990b:5, Mannheim & van Vleet 1998:332).

While numerous other verses were sung during the course of this 'performance', which lasted several hours and was accompanied by a series of different *charango* players, these particular lines express the anxieties of young women and their perspectives on marriage rather well. They also evoke certain parallels between the human life cycle and seasonal transformation. The first line, with its Spanish words, immediately locates us in the act of dancing and singing – an activity with strong erotic overtones. This is an especially common line, frequently used to start a singing session or as a filler between sequences of verses. It is paired with line 2 that conveys a sense of savouring single life while it lasts, because after cohabitation or marriage it is no longer acceptable for women to seductively open their mouths and express themselves in *takis*. The important word *wira* (line 2) seems to be a compound concept resulting from a fortuitous union between the Spanish *vida* ('life') and Quechua *wira* ('fat'). People in Kalankira pronounced the two words identically and insisted they were essentially the same idea. The Quechua *wira* ('fat'), judging from its use in song, specifically implies unmarried life and is associated with ideas of bodily development and accumulation of fat; one the most potent expressions of life force and vitality in Andean cultures (Canessa 2000:709–11).[15] Moreover, as *wira* is among the most ubiquitous elements in the vocabulary of dry season *takis*, but almost entirely absent from the *wayñus* of the rains, it reinforces the connection between unmarried life, accumulation and the dry winter season.[16]

---

[15] To describe a person as *wirayuq* (literally 'fatty'), usually implies a 'strong' and well-developed physique, rather than excess fat.

[16] The refrains of dry season song genres from other parts of Northern Potosí often include the word *wirita* or *wiritay*. Several local people related this to the Spanish *vida* ('life') in its diminutive form *vidita*. Thomas Solomon, however, translates *wirita* as 'dear', presumably the Spanish *querida* (1997:369).

Verses 3–6 continue to focus on the idea of remaining single and the years passing, evoking the anxiety of not finding a partner alongside the awareness that doing so will bring the pleasures of single life to an end. Asencio explained that line 5 referred to the girl carrying off a boy's hat and placing it on top of her own; a clear expression of amorous interest (see Harris 2000 [1980]:186). He maintained that this was really a *machu machu* ('crude' or 'sexually explicit') verse, as the implications are that sexual relations will take place 'in some out of the way corner, like mating llamas' when the boy came to reclaim his hat. The idea of indulging in sexual relations without any immediate expectation of marriage is conveyed by the pairing with line 6. Sexual experimentation is an accepted part of young people's lives, but such encounters are associated with 'wild' places, such as mountainsides or by rivers or streams, whilst married sexual relations are linked with domestic space (ibid. 186).

With verses 7 and 8, the idea of resisting marriage – rings on fingers – is made even more explicit; the singer will stay single until death. Here, the word for death (*wañu-*) is pronounced *wayñu;* the rainy season music linked with the souls of the dead (Chapter 8). Lines 9–10 juxtapose the associations of married and single life, focusing on the restrictions on singing and dancing following marriage. Paired with the question 'is it tiresome?' (line 9) is the enquiry 'how's the [*charango*] player' (line 10), which brims with sexual innuendo; prowess in sex and music go together.[17] When discussing these lines, Asencio explained that for married women 'it is like being tied up and locked inside' the house, contrasting the freedom and mobility of young single women with the enclosing domestic space of marriage, evoking images of 'planting' and 'placement' (which dominate the *asintu* wedding songs discussed below). Line 13 goes on to connect the lives of married women with perpetual weeping – a common metaphor for rain, evoking the rainy growing season.

In departing her community to live with a man, a woman metaphorically 'dies', leaving her family, community, and former life behind. Indeed, early one July morning a group of young men arrived at a neighbouring homestead with their *charangos*, to ceremonially 'steal away' (*suwanakuy*) Cenovia Beltrán, one of the girls of the hamlet. Together with Paulino and several other neighbours, I walked down to the house to watch her departure. As she and her mother prepared her clothing, placed food crops inside a blanket and she set off, the pair of them wept and wailed. Another set of *cruz* verses from the same feast highlight this sense of sorrow, loss and metaphorical death, as the man – in a discourse of predatorial theft – 'steals' (*suwa-*) a woman away from her home:

---

17 See Harris 1980:73, Isbell & Roncalla 1985:22.

Pacha sut'iyayta inti kananayt[a]	Now with dawn the sun is victorious
Kunanmá ripusaq uj sunqu nanayta	Now I really will go, bringing pain to a heart
Qharita, qharita risqaypi wañusaq	The man, the man, I will die where I go
Wañunallaypaqpis iskaychá kapusaq	And in dying perhaps I will be two
Wañunay ratusta kinsaman tukusaq	To die suddenly I will transform to three
Kinsaman tukuspa chaywan wañupusaq	Becoming three with that I will die

Asencio explained that, the two final lines associate death with the couple giving birth ('becoming 'three'). Alongside these associations of death with departure and sorrow, a metaphoric and erotic analogy exists between death and sexual union, leading to reproduction (Chapter 8).

These various *cruz* verses vividly evoke the anxieties of young unmarried women contemplating marriage. But this language also presents them as enjoying their freedom, playing 'hard to get', and in no hurry to settle down. They can be seen to dominate the symbolic discourse – taunting the boys and asserting 'girl power'. Although, agricultural production and the broader context (a harvest feast) are not alluded to directly, undoubtedly they underlie many aspects of the experience of the performance and the metaphorical language of the girls' poetry. For example, married life is associated with death, weeping (rain) and *wayñu* music, powerful imagery tied to the rainy growing season, when energies are directed to the creation of new life. In contrast single life emerges as a time of independence and sensual pleasures, such as singing and dancing, and is linked with notions of 'life' and the accumulation of fat. These ideas – expressed in a variety of different ways – underpin local approaches to musical and agricultural production in Kalankira.

(2) *San Pedro*: young Empire builders

Leaving behind the feast of *cruz* in May, we now move on through the year and pass the winter solstice (24 June). From late June men begin to tune their *charangos* from *cruz* into *san pedro* ('St Peter'), named after the feast of St Peter that was formerly celebrated in Macha on 29 June. Most people did not consider that this shift in genre-tuning had a direct influence on day-to-day weather conditions. However, it coincides precisely with the time that toads are said to transform to doves, a metaphor for the way water is thought to start to rise and fill the atmosphere as clouds (doves) in anticipation of the rainy season. With the summer solstice and peak of the rains in December, this hydraulic movement reverses; doves are claimed to revert to toads as water begins to accumulate in the lower places (Chapter 7). In addition, St Peter is said to sleep in the gullies together with *wintura* ('venture') the wind, suggesting communication with inner places, and to be the 'keyholder' (*llavero*) who keeps the rainy season *wayñu* music and *sirinus* (aqueous musical devils) locked inside the inner earth during the dry winter months.

San pedro music had been heard for several months by the time I recorded the next song on 17 August in the dried-mud patio of Luis's Beltrán's homestead (Example 5.4). It is about 10pm and a burble of drunken conversation emerges from the kitchen hut, where libations continue among a few older people. After much music and dancing, just a handful of young people remain. Sabasta and Margara are singing *san pedro* verses accompanied by Paulino who, although a married man, is a popular accompanist. He is strumming my new parrot-decorated *panti charango* (Chapter 4), his attention and the singers sometimes distracted by a drunken passer by (CD track 15).

Example 5.4 ***San Pedro*** **song verses with** ***charango*** **accompaniment.** *Punta Walaychitu.* **Transposed up about one semitone. (CD track 15)**

Punta walaychitu lluqsirikushayman x 2	Lads of the peaks should be emerging
Walaychuchus kanman malientechari x 2	I wonder if these lads are wicked?
Jinamá nuqayku takiq tusuq kayku x 2	That's how we are, we're singers and dancers

Wawa masistapis imperiachiq kayku x 2	Babies all together, we're empire builders
Sullka wiñastapis trasunachiq kayku x 2	Youngsters growing up, we're just behind
Juch'uyta jatunta trasunachiq kayku x 2	The small, the big, we're just behind
Runaq wawasninta imperiachiq kayku x 2	Via infancy to humanity, we're empire builders

This set of verses evokes the idea of rebellious young people rising up to replace the previous generation and highlights the tension between the youth and adulthood. As mentioned above, youth seems to be presented as a kind of 'pre-social' phase in the life cycle where young people emerge from the wild, mountain world, and full personhood is only achieved through marriage. The idea of bringing productivity through domestication and marriage had permeated this particular day, in which the mountain peaks (*qullus*) had been ritually married to the fields (*wirjin*) in preparation for planting and the growing season. Having briefly glimpsed the courtship singing of young people at the end of the day, let us now turn the clock back a few hours to the main ritual events of 17 August, which include a rare opportunity to hear the singing of older women.

(3) *Kasamintu* ('Marriage'): the fields marry the mountain

It is now about midday and I find myself crammed into a small hut belonging to Santosa Beltrán with over twenty local men. We are just reaching the climax of an elaborate series of ritual preparations for the exceptional form of marriage known as *asintu*, a word presumably derived from the Spanish *asentar* 'to seat' or 'to place'. The marriage takes place in August, the month when the earth (*wirjin* 'virgin') is said to be 'open mouthed', awaiting food offerings in preparation for the planting season, and when the 'mountains arise' (*qullus jatarisqa*), as if from a long sleep. The *asintu* ceremony explicitly concerns the marriage of the 'fields' (*wirjin*) to the mountain peaks (*qullus*); the verses of its wedding songs invoking the fertility of the earth in the forthcoming growing season.

The two principal sponsors of the event, Victor Beltrán (*alferéz* 'lieutenant') and his younger cousin Luis (*mayura* 'major'), are seated on the ground on either side of a special altar, the *siñura misa* ('lady altar'), which has been set up in honour of *wirijin* ('virgin'), who represents the fields of the community. Muttering incantations, Victor places ritual ingredients on the skull of a ram that was sacrificed earlier in the day. The whole animal was later eaten communally as an offering to *wirjin*, having been cooked without salt – which would be harmful to her. After the meal, all the bones were collected up and buried together with the skull and horns at *Q'illu-q'illu* ('Yellow-yellow') on nearby *Paqullu* mountain.

At a climactic moment in the ceremony, Victor turns to Asencio and asks him to play the *charango* as *kunswilu* ('consolation'). To my surprise Asencio starts to strum in *kasamintu* (Sp. *casamiento*), the genre performed at weddings. I turn to Paulino and enquire 'why wedding music?' He replies, 'it is for the marriage of the *wirjin* ('fields') to the *jurq'us* ('mountains').[18] After the ritual and meal, we all move outside. Asencio continues playing the *charango*, accompanying a few older women singing wedding verses. As they dance, the married couples face one another with arms straight ahead, right arm in left, and left in right. However, as I join the dancing, as an unmarried man at the time, I am told that I should hold hands with my partner in a figure of eight, right hand in right, left in left. This results in a crossing of arms (Sp. *cruzado* 'crossed' or *simp'a* 'plaited'), rather than creating the enclosing nest-like space of married couples (Figure 5.2). This idea of a nest (*thapa*), or uterine embrace, powerfully evokes local ideas about reproduction, where the homestead in which a married couple are 'seated', and which becomes their locus of productive and reproductive activity, is referred to in ritual as *thapa* ('nest') or *silla* (Sp. 'seat').[19]

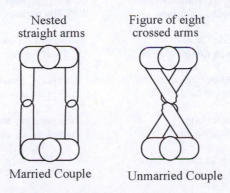

	Nested straight arms	Figure of eight crossed arms
	Married Couple	Unmarried Couple

Figure 5.2   Wedding dancing: married and single couples

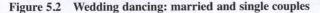

The singing of the *asintu* wedding verses is dominated by the spinster Santosa Beltrán, who is heard alone on CD Track 9 accompanied by Asencio. It is tempting to characterize the *charango's* regular harmonic shift on the seventh vocal syllable as 'tonic' (B flat) to 'dominant' (F), whilst highlighting

---

[18] Although I have encountered occasional references to female mountains, more often the *jurq'us* ('mountains') were presented as the male consort of the female fields, or *wirjin* ('virgin'). Harris also observes that the 'Pachamama is the "wife" of the mountains' 2000:208).

[19] The use of the 'nest' as a name of endearment for the house is widespread. See for example Arnold, Jiménez & Yapita 1991:128.

a melodic drop of a semitone. However, as there is little sense of 'coming home' to the tonic, it is probably more appropriate to think of the harmony as 'bitonal', and thus avoid the hierarchical tonic/dominant implications of functional harmony. In each line the voice enters on or slides up to the 'tonic' and periodically leaps up approximately a fifth (or down a fourth) on the seventh (or third) syllable. The disjointed and almost humorous way the voice is 'thrown' upwards, alongside a strong accent and microtonal sliding, is particularly characteristic of the *kasamintu* genre. It is also notable that these upward leaps usually occur on strong consonants, thereby heightening the rhythm of the words (Example 5.5). In the verses themselves, we discover constant references to planting the *wirjin* ('fields'), alongside powerful evocations of human marriage (CD track 9).

1	*[Ananay] kacha t'ikit[a]*,[20]	Ah! beautiful flower
	Ananay pantis t'ikit[a]	Ah! Panti flower
2	*Lantaykusaq, lantaykus[aq]*	I shall plant,[21] I shall plant
	Wirjiniyta lantaykus[aq] (x 2)	I shall plant into my virgin
3	*Chaywantaqchá chillchirinqa*	With this perhaps sprouting
	Chaywantaqchá iqharinqa	With this perhaps bursting
4	*Ananay kacha t'ikita*	Ah! beautiful flower
	Ananay pantis t'ikita	Ah! Panti flower
5	*Lantaykusaq mallkiykusaq*	I shall plant, I shall plant[22]
	Wirjiniyta lantaykusaq	I shall plant into my virgin
6	*Uwijayta lantaykusaq*	I shall plant my sheep
	Luritayta lantaykusaq	I shall plant my gloria
7	*Chaywantaqchá chillchirinqa*	With this perhaps sprouting
	Chaywantaqchá iqharinqa	With this perhaps bursting
8	*Ni kaypichu, mayllapichu*	Not here, I wonder where?
	Anki thapitallaypi	Even just in my nest

---

[20] In performance the final syllable of each line is not enunciated.

[21] The 'yku' suffix in *lantaykusaq* and *mallkiykusaq* refers to performing the action towards the interior; hence I shall plant into. This suffix also suggests that the action is performed with especial care.

[22] In Northern Potosí *mallki-* refers to both 'small, tender plants' (Pedro Plaza pers. comm.) and to the act of 'planting' (Rosaleen Howard pers. comm.). Indeed, evergreen *molle* twigs were planted on the mountain peak following the *asintu* ceremony. The word *mallki* also refers to the 'eternal tree', depicted, for example, in the famous drawing from the wall of the *Quri kancha* in Cuzco by Santacruz Pachacuti Yamqui [1613] (Harrison 1989: 82) and to the mummies of the past Inkas which were placed inside a room with golden walls (also see Garcilaso 1989 [1966]: 180–81).

9	*Lantaykusaq mallkiykusaq* *Thapitayta lantaykusaq*	I shall plant, I shall plant I shall plant my nest

10	*Wirjiniyta lantaykusaq*	I shall plant my virgin

— — — — — —

11	*Juch'uy wirjin, jatun wirjin* *Chaywantaqchá chillchirinqa*	Little 'virgin' [field], big 'virgin' [field] With this perhaps sprouting

12	*Juch'uy qullu, jatun qullu* *Chaywantaqchá iqharinqa*	Little mountain, big mountain With this perhaps bursting

13	*Juch'uy qullu, jatun qullu* *Chaywantaqchá chillchirinqa*	Little mountain, big mountain With this perhaps sprouting

14	*Chaywantaqchá mallkirinqa....*	With this perhaps it will plant

15	*Ananay kacha t'ikita* *Ananay pantis t'ikita*	Ah! beautiful flower Ah! Panti flower

16	*Lantaykusaq mallkiykusaq* *Thapaypi sillaypi*	I shall plant, I shall plant In my nest, in my seat

Selected couplets (repeated themes excluded)
NOT INCLUDED ON THE CD RECORDING

17	*Chuqi sintay, quri sintay* *Thapaypi sillaypi*	Golden ribbon, golden ribbon In my nest, in my seat

18	*Chuqi sintay, quri sintay* *Kawisayta lantaykusaq*	Golden ribbon, golden ribbon I will plant my head

19	*Chaywantaqchá majarinqa* *Kay irapis, kay thapapis*	With this perhaps will come aid And this corral, and this nest

20	*China uña, urqu uña* *Chaywantaqchá majarinqa*	Female young, male young With this perhaps will come aid

21	*Chuqi simintu, simintu* *Quri simintu, simintu*	Golden foundation, foundation Golden foundation, foundation

22	*Lantaykusaq mallkiykusaq* *Paqullita Sapirita*	I shall plant, I shall plant Paqullu mountain *Sapiri*

23	*Lantaykusaq mallkiykusaq* *T'ika pampa t'allanchista*[23]	I shall plant, I shall plant Our [llama] corral of flowers

---

[23] *T'alla* is the Aymara word for a female deity, the consort of *Mallku*. In this context *t'alla* was said to refer to the llama corral, whilst *t'ika pampa* is a flat place covered with flowers.

24	*Chaywantaqchá iqharinqa*	With this perhaps bursting
	Chay lantas qhawantaqchari	To watch the plants, perhaps

25	*Pulurisa, pulurisa*	Flowers, flowers
	Thapaypichá muyurisaq (x 2)	Perhaps in my nest I will circle

26	*Lantaykusaq mallkikusaq*	I shall plant, I shall plant
	Q'illu-q'illu kawisayta (x 4)	*Q'illu-q'illu* my head

27	*Lantaykusaq mallkiykusaq*	I shall plant, I shall plant
	Paqullita kawisayta (x 2)	*Paqullu* (mountain) my head

28	*Kay thapapi, kay sillaypi*	In this nest, in my seat
	Lantaykusaq mallkikusaq	I shall plant, I shall plant

The verses vividly evoke the forthcoming growing season where, in the same way as marrying human couples, the earth is ritually prepared for reproduction and renewal. Marriage is strongly associated with ideas of 'flowering' and the refrain-like *Ananay kacha t'ikita*, *Ananay pantis t'ikita* ('Ah! beautiful flower, Ah! *panti* flower') regularly punctuates the verses sung at any local wedding, as the single most defining poetic image of the *kasamintu* genre.[24] The imagery

Example 5.5 *Asintu* wedding song accompanied by the *charango* in *kasamintu* style and tuning. A second vocal line highlights the sliding gestures of the voice. **(CD track 9)**

[24] See Arnold and Yapita 1998a for discussion of wedding music of the nearby Qaqachakas.

of *panti* seems to draw together notions of female fecundity, both as dark fertile fields and menstrual blood as, contrary to 'Western' reproductive knowledge, a woman is thought to be most fertile during menstruation (Harris 2000 [1980]:186).[25]

In these verses Quechua poetic conventions, as discussed above, actively contribute to forging metaphorical connections as images of human, animal and agricultural reproduction are brought together, and draw creatively from one another, in a rich and common language; a powerful poetics of (re)production.[26] For example, animal corrals and nests are planted with flowers (line 23), and sheep and *gloria* are planted as if seeds (line 6); presumably also a reference to the actual burial of the skull and bones of the sacrificed ram at *Q'illu-q'illu* ('Yellow-yellow') on *Paqullu* mountain (lines 26–27) as part of the *asintu* ceremony. A desire to nurture new life is also evoked by references to caring for female and male offspring (line 20). With the image of a 'corral of flowers' (line 23) or 'circling in a nest' (line 25), the idea of reproductive space is again highlighted, in turn evoking that created by the *qhata* dancing of the rains, when male instrumentalists are 'grasped' in a corral-like ring of dancers and compared to growing plants (Chapter 8). Finally, the *sapiri* of *Paqullu* mountain (lines 22, 27) refers to the most powerful local spirit guardian of the community, who is sometimes called down to shamanic sessions in the form of a condor. It is the *sapiri*, as the 'head' (*kawiza*), which oversees the fortunes and annual renewal of the community and its productivity.

These verses, performed by a mature adult woman (albeit a spinster) who was at least forty years old at the time, demonstrate an impressive grasp of the metaphoric language of agricultural production. By contrast, such direct invocation of agricultural production and the spirit world (such as the *sapiri*) is never found in the *takis* of young unmarried people (see Harris 2000 [1980]:198). However, an important implication of this ritual marriage

---

25 According to Bertonio (1984 [1612], II:248) the flowers of the *Panti* (*Cosmos Argentus*, see Lucca & Zalles1992:110) resemble Camomile and are white, red or purple. However, a more immediate association of the word *panti*, for the people of Kalankira is with a dark, deeply saturated colour. For example, the *panti* charango is so-called due to the black colour it is painted, and the most distinctive colour used in men's knitted hats (*ch'ulus*) is a deep purple, known as *panti*. Furthermore, deep crimson wool, referred to as *panti* and later compared to blood, was carefully placed on the ram's skull during the *asintu* ceremony. Several people also used this word in reference to fertile soils (*panti jallp'as*), mentioning that good soils are black (*yana*) whilst poor unproductive ones are yellow (*q'illu*). Finally don Adrian observed that the *panti* charango is especially favoured during the feast of *cruz*, which celebrates the fields (*chaqras*) and harvest, as it 'makes the potatoes grow large'.

26 Here we find resonances with the unaccompanied songs sung for the food crops and animals by older women among the Qaqachakas and certain other *ayllus* (Arnold, Jiménez & Yapita 1991, Arnold & Yapita 1998b). However, in Kalankira I found no equivalent unaccompanied songs, and those considered by Arnold, Jiménez & Yapita do not appear to be related to wedding music.

between the *wirjin* (fields) and *jurq'us* (mountains) is that these personifications of the landscape are conceived as single and in need of marriage. Just like humans, these youthful, independent and mobile bodies must be settled in place (*asintu*) and brought under social control ('cultivation') if they are to be made reproductive and give birth to food crops.

For the final song in this chapter we move to the start of the rainy season proper, with the feast of All Saints in November. *Wayñu* music now begins to be performed and accompanies an explosion of ritual activity explicitly dedicated to promoting crop growth and animal reproduction (Chapter 8).

(4) *Wayñu:* harnessing girl power and confused creation

Among the many rituals dedicated to the dead and to the fertility of each family's crops and animals during the feast All Saints was an elaborate community ceremony called *waka ñakaku* ('ox slaughter'). This was held on the afternoon of 6 November and dedicated to Mama Copacabana, a powerful local saint (Chapter 7), and to the *lumpris* (Sp. *cumbres* 'mountain summits') a ritual epithet for 'bulls'. The sponsor (*alférez* 'lieutenant'), who it was specified should be an 'unmarried woman' (*sultira*), was Sabasta, Victor Beltrán's eldest daughter – even though her parents had clearly provided the food and drink. A black sheep was slaughtered and cooked for the ceremony, but the sacrificed ox was symbolized by special breads broken by Sabasta and Victor. Over the breads was poured the red blood-like juice of wild *ayrampu* berries, which was said to be Mama Copacabana and related to unmarried women (*sultira*). Sabasta handed the red stained bread around the assembled company, which people described as 'ox strength' (*waka kallpa*), as though recirculating the force of this most powerful creature. Notions of (male) bodily destruction and intense female fertility, evoking menstrual blood, permeated this ceremony at the start of the rainy growing season.

In the evening, a party of us set off to perform *wayñu* at various local homesteads; three girls sang and Paulino and Kaytano Chura took turns on the *kitarra*. Our lively music was seen to bring *kunswilu* ('consolation') and fortune wherever we visited; each family welcoming us with a bucket or earthenware *yuru* of corn beer that was placed in the centre of the patio, around which we danced. After some eight houses, many different *wayñus* and much corn beer it was approaching 10pm. At this point the girls asked Paulino to play a song called *Macha Cholita* ('girl from Macha'). Evidently Paulino, now married for two years and no longer up to date with the latest fashions and hits among the young, was unfamiliar with this song. As can be heard (CD track 27), he attempts to accompany, his *kitarra* tuned in *charka*, but after a few verses stops and to the girls' amusement Kaytano takes over on a different *kitarra* in *yawlu* tuning (CD track 28). This, like other *kitarra wayñus*, was evidently viewed as a composed song with a set sequence of verses, each of which is repeated. In practice singers often confuse or reverse couplets (as in this recording), sometimes commenting on their 'mistakes' afterwards or even during the song itself.

Kaychu chay Macha plazita	Is this the square of Macha?
Kaychu chay Macha chulita	Is this the girl from Macha?
Imaynallapitaq suwasqayki x 2	How can I steal you away?
Tutallachu yaykumusaq	Might I come by night?
P'unchayllachu yaykumusaq	Might I come by day?
Imaynallapitaq suwasqayki x 2	How can I steal you away?
Paramanchu tukupusaq	Shall I become rain?
P'isqumanchu tukupusaq	Shall I become a bird?
Imaynallapitaq suwasqayki x 2	How can I steal you away?
Paramanchu tukupusaq	Shall I become rain?
Phuyumanchu tukupusaq	Shall I become a cloud?
Imaynallapitaq suwasqayki x 2	How can I steal you away?
Kunturman avionininchis	To the condor in our airplane
Cha[ya]muchun ripunanchispaq	Let it arrive, for us to go away,
Imaynallapitaq suwasqayki x 2	How can I steal you away?

Charka and *yawlu* ('devil') tunings are identical except for string (IV) that for *yawlu* is tuned one octave higher (Example 5.6). Musically this means that in *charka* tuning the melody sounds relatively muddy and low in pitch, as it merges with the other strings. By contrast, in *yawlu*, the melody sounds out brightly, one octave higher in pitch, clearly distinguishing itself from the lower pitches of the other strings. Indeed Paulino described *charka* tuning as 'mixed up tuning' (*chakru telmasqa*), as all the strings are loose (*llawqa*). During the dry winter months several people told me that *charka* tuning is used for the first part of the rains, up until the feast of St Sebastian (20 January), when it is replaced by *yawlu* ('devil') tuning to perform the year's new Carnival *wayñus* (Chapter 9). However, when I enquired about this practice during the rains (when the instrument is actually played) some of the same individuals insisted that either tuning could be used, according to preference. Associating the muddy sound of *charka* tuning with All Saints and the high clear melody of *yawlu* with the new *wayñus* and food crops of Carnival seems very logical in terms of the 'bigger picture' (Figure 3.5). However, from a pragmatic performance perspective, the 'bigger picture' may become irrelevant or be seen to restrict individual expression.

The girls' request for the song *Macha Cholita*, and Paulino's unfamiliarity with it, suggests that it may have been quite new to their repertoire. However, Gregorio Mamani, who lived in nearby Tomaykuri until around 1990, released a version of this song on a commercial cassette in the

Example 5.6 *Wayñu* song with *kitarra* accompaniment: *Macha Cholita*. Shows contrast between *yawlu* and *charka* tuning on the *kitarra*. The *bordón* pitch is shown as the same to ease comparison. Transposed down about one semitone. (CD track 28)

late 1980s.[27] He performs the song in *cholo* style, accompanied by *charango* and Spanish guitar. Three of the Quechua verses are almost identical to those performed in Kalankira, whilst the melody, which is different in tonality, is similar in shape – especially in the refrain *Imaynallapitaq suwasqayki*. Although Mamani claims authorship, it is possible that the song is partly based on existing local rural repertoire. His insertion of verses in Spanish ruptures the coherence of the song's performance in Kalankira, in which the 'condor airplane' is the witty answer to the riddle 'how can I steal you away'. This 'punch-line' charmingly integrates this image of modernity with the traditional tale of the condor carrying a girl off to its nest.[28]

[27] *Mi gatito miau miau: Gregorio Mamani y su fantasico charango* ('My kitten *miau miau*: Gregorio Mamani and his fantasic charango'), Producciones Musicales: Borda, Cochabamba C-1048.

[28] See Harris 2000:156.

My suggestion that Gregorio Mamani may have based his recording of this song on existing local repertory highlights the unpredictable journeys often made by songs transmitted orally and those transmitted through recorded media. An 'old' song can potentially become a 'new' song again once it leaves recorded media and enters (or re-enters) the oral mode, where it becomes 'resignified' (Manuel 1993:141). This is particularly interesting in the local context, in which new *wayñu* songs must be acquired each year (Chapter 9). People did not appear unduly discriminating about how they actually acquired these 'new' songs or even whether they were already 'oldies'. Reworkings of popular urban genres 'originally' featuring electronic instruments (such as *cumbia* or Peruvian *chicha*) are commonly heard played on 'traditional' instruments.[29]

While people in Kalankira may have been aware of Gregorio Mamani's recording of *Macha plazita*, especially as his sister Leonarda lives there, I suspect that due to lack of cash to purchase commercial cassettes or batteries for radio-tape players, this song was learned orally. People often asserted that *wayñus* are ultimately derived from the *sirinus* or *satanas*, but it was rare for songs or melodies to be attributed to an individual 'composer'. I sense that the mysterious or confused origins of *wayñu* songs and melodies are actively maintained in Kalankira – perhaps to ascribe greater power to them – whereas in other areas of Bolivia, I found people happy to volunteer the composer's name. Music, such as that of Kalankira, which outsiders and ethnographic recordings often label 'autochthonous', 'indigenous' or 'authentic' is often the product of complex journeys, borrowings and transformations, which encompass different social groups, musical technologies and forms of resignification. The 'authenticity police', to borrow Michelle Bigenho's apt expression, might be tempted to critique such variegated origins as evidence of 'inauthenticity' (2002:4). However, for the participants, such borrowings and musical interactions seem integral to the dynamism of living musical performance and contribute in important ways to their 'experiential authenticity' (Bigenho 2002:17). Bigenho explains this in terms of the sensory feeling in music performances that establishes relations between physical places and people (ibid.). Whatever the origins of the song, this performance of *Macha plazita* during the feast of All Saints powerfully connected people and places, as the 'Macha girls' articulated themselves, through sung poetry, as objects of male desire.

---

[29] This phenomenon is even more widespread in other parts of Bolivia and the world (Manuel 1993). For literature on Peruvian *chicha* music (a blend of Peruvian *huayno* melody with Columbian cumbia rhythms) see Romero 2002.

Conclusion: song and the production of people

In the wedding music of the *asintu* ritual, the ritual language and song texts of the adult performers are explicitly directed to agricultural production. The productive year emerges as a microcosm of the human life cycle, where the loutish mountain peaks are ritually married to the *wirjin* ('virgin'), in order to make her reproduce during the rainy growing season. But singing by older women is unusual, and it is young unmarried people involved in courtship who dominate Kalankira's song genres, which are in turn the most salient markers of the unfolding musical year. Why do young people maintain these seasonal genres if their interests in courtship eclipse those of agriculture? Calendrical feasts provide the primary context through which friends and members of the opposite sex meet in song performance, their interactions lubricated by corn beer, cane alcohol and meals provided by the sponsors. In addition, local ideas about courtship, sexuality and the human life cycle in general are closely connected with young people's daily participation in agriculture and competence in such activities are seen as important elements in a potential partner's desirability.

For the most part, young singers and dancers remain on the sidelines of the long sequences of ritual libations made by adult sponsors and hosts during feasts, and their song words rarely invoke the spirit world these rituals address (see Harris 2000:198). Nonetheless, musicians are regularly acknowledged as a critical part of the action and are a focus of interest. Sometimes youths are in the centre of complex ritual activities, as happened with Sebasta as the *sultira* ('unmarried') sponsor, who embodied the idea of fertility. Young people involved in the performance and creation of Kalankira's seasonally and contextually distinct song genres cannot easily avoid embodying aspects of the music's broader associations and contexts, as well as developing cognitive, motor and social skills. This does not so much contradict, but is driven by, their principal motivations for music making: courting, partying and self-expression. The performance of these genres is not only critical to the production of people, but also weaves young people's emotions, anxieties, gender identities and creativity into the very fabric of the year.

This is most evident when we compare the practices and discourses surrounding the performance of dry season *takis* and rainy season *wayñu*. Among the most remarkable differences concern musical form and approaches to composition. The constraints of the short regular phrase and syllable number of *takis* evokes a sense of containment and definition, which contrast vividly with the *wayñu*'s undefined form, requirement for annual renewal and mysterious origins connected with the inner earth. Although there is much room for creativity in *takis*, the performers are shaped by these genres' closely defined parameters that remain essentially unchanged from year to year and which, in the case of *cruz* and *san pedro*, are the most salient musical markers of Macha identity (Chapter 4). In other words, these *takis* may be seen to represent a powerful force in the 'production of people', shaping unsocialized creatures connected with the ambiguous mountain sphere into Machas. At the same time, the unchanging form of these genres from year to year, their constant references to *wira* ('life/fat'), and expressions of ambivalence to marriage – evoke continuity or prolongation of life. Strikingly similar ideas emerge in men's *julajula* panpipe performance (Chapter 6), which is connected with the same time of year and linked with male development, containment and prolongation of life.

By contrast, *wayñu* tunes must be new each year, suggesting radical transformation or death and regeneration, metaphorically comparable with human reproduction or the growth of crops. Whereas women dominate the composition of *taki* poetry and sing from a female perspective, it is largely men who control the acquisition or composition of *wayñus* (melody + text). This seasonal shift in gender roles, related to musical creativity and expression, reflects how men come to dominate public discourse following marriage.

Although young unmarried people dominate the performance of both these genres, the *takis* of the dry season (especially *cruz* and *san pedro*) are especially closely connected with youth and development, whilst *wayñu* suggests marriage and reproduction. For young women, singing *takis* is a powerful expression of independence, freedom and sexuality whilst at the same time a critical force in shaping and defining their identity, as well as potentially securing a marriage partner. From a different angle, Martínez characterizes song and the voice as a 'state of inner liberty', constituting the person, speculating that it is 'a necessarily non-social manner of living within the constraints of the social' (1998:18–19). Although *wayñu* is an important courtship genre, its associated discourses and metaphorical language evoke marriage, death, weeping rain, reproduction and male control. When young people perform these songs, as Turino rightly warns us, the image of 'fertility' [of the fields] is unlikely to be 'uppermost in their minds' (1993:105). But nor are musical, social and agricultural production neatly separated spheres of activity; rather they are deeply interwoven and draw creatively from one another.

Part III
The Music of a Year

Chapter 6

May–June
Violent Harmony and
the Making of Men
Julajula panpipes and harvest time

Kalankira's musical year, with its seasonally alternated genres and instruments, might be thought of as a single integrated performance (Chapter 3). But where does the musical year begin? Paulino was unequivocal about this; the 'new year' (*musuq wata*) starts after the dramatic apotheosis of Carnival, while Asencio insisted that the feast of the Holy Cross is 'number one'; it is the first feast of the year (following Carnival). Accordingly, this section dedicated to 'The Music of a Year' begins with the feast of the Holy Cross (*cruz*) in May. So why are the months between Carnival and *cruz* not accorded their own chapter? The principal reason is that no feasts with communal music making take place in Kalankira over this period. Lent commences immediately after Carnival, and although this did not seem to restrict informal playing by Kalankira's young *charango* players, in nearby *ayllus* music is sometimes explicitly prohibited (Solomon 1997:99). Following the exuberance of Carnival, music making passes though a lax time until May.

In this, the first of four chapters focusing on the main 'musical' seasons of the year, I demonstrate how *julajula* panpipe music and *wayli* dancing associated with the feast of *cruz* are connected with broader ideas relating to *kusicha timpu* ('harvest time') – a term widely used to refer to the entire dry winter season (April–October). People in Kalankira characterized *cruz* as the feast of the 'fields' (*chajras*), relating it to harvest and autumn ploughing, when men become the warriors of *tata wila cruz* ('Father True Cross'), embodied in the community's cross, dancing and playing *julajula* panpipes to honour and console him. This seasonally specific conquest over the earth, leads the men of the *ayllu* away from (female gendered) points or places of origin and notions of an ancestral or uterine past, and into exchanges and new trajectories well beyond the boundaries of their fields and communities. In many respects the musical and choreographic expressions of *cruz* concern the 'poetics of manhood' (Herzfeld 1985), as men come to confront the wider world and its inherent dangers in this rite of passage.

Macha's place on the world map

> *Tinku* is the name of the ritual battles in which two opposing [*bandas*] meet one
> another, often called Alasaya (upper side) and Majasaya (lower half). It
> resembles a combat between warriors, but in reality it concerns a rite: which
> unifies rather than separates. ... It does not mean then, that one of the two
> elements crushes and destroys the other, the confrontation is not 'to the death',
> but rather 'to life'. From the confrontation is born life, [which] is the realm of
> fertility and reproduction.[1]

For most of the year the small sleepy town of Macha, of some 600 inhabitants,
is a seemingly deserted backwater. But in early May, for the feast of the Holy
Cross (*cruz*), it suddenly fills to overflowing with thousands of peasants
dancing into town playing *julajula* (*wauku* or *suqusu*) panpipes, and scores of
traders, police, tourists and usually several film crews. Macha's fame and
notoriety hangs on just one aspect of this annual feast: the *tinku* or 'ritual
fighting' which is sometimes presented as the 'fiercest and most authentic' of
the Bolivian Andes.[2]

Tinku fighting is a widespread Andean phenomenon that is well documented
in both historical and contemporary ethnographic literature. In some parts of
the Andes, ritual fighting has been abolished by state authorities, or
transformed into a dance. For example, in Southern Peru *sargento* dancers
now perform the *tinkuy* dance during Carnival, replacing the annual territorial
battle banned in 1952 (Allen 1988:183). But in the North of Potosí, regular
tinku battles, staged during calendrical feasts, remain common, and the
casualties or fatalities which result are typically interpreted as blood sacrifices
to the mountain spirits or mother earth (*pachamama*) that ensure agricultural
fertility.[3]

As I write in the year 2003, the 'Macha *tinku*' finds itself at an interesting
historical juncture. Failed efforts to control the more violent aspects of the
tinku through heavy police presence, the use of tear gas, and the banning of
montera fighting helmets, led in 2002 to an alternative proposal. Tito Burgoa,
who was born in Macha but has lived much of his life in La Paz, has initiated
a 'Tinku-Macha' project, which seems to have won the support of Macha's
townsfolk, to promote *tinku* as a tourist attraction in this desperately poor part
of the Andes. Through the Tinku-Macha Foundation, the town is close to

---

[1] Webpage of the dance association: *Fraternidad Taller Cultural Tinkus Wist'us*. (La Paz,
Bolivia). http://www.wistus.8m.com/cgi-bin/framed/2176/eltinku.html (accessed: 5.3.2003). My
translation.

[2] See for example Revista Gatopardo http://www.gatopardo.com/noticia.php3?nt=680
(accessed 5.3.2003).

[3] For example, Catherine Allen writes that 'the encountering *ayllus* "feed" the source of their
vitality and well-being, with an outpouring of their own blood and energy, liberated through *tinku*
(Allen 1988:206). See also Sallnow 1987:138.

acquiring official recognition as a cultural heritage site and capital of *tinku*. In this new vision for a 'Macha Festival of Tinku', an annual craft market is combined with a competition during the local peasants' annual pilgrimage to Macha. Not only do individuals compete in the traditional one-to-one ritual fighting, but groups will also vie for prizes awarded for their presentation, choreography and musical interpretation (Burgoa 2002:22). The more violent aspects of the *tinku*, such as stone throwing, will be outlawed and each year's winning troupe will act as the official representatives for the 'Tinku-Macha' organization at national and international events. These recent efforts to tame the *tinku* and fashion it for global consumption stand in stark contrast to local discourse about this feast as told to me by people in Kalankira, and to my own impressions when I participated in a Macha tinku in 1991.

Violence and the marks of manhood

> Dancing soon turns to violence and erupts like liquid from a blender.
>
> Dust rises from a thousand scuttling feet as hundreds of fists thud against cheekbones. Bloodied faces puff beneath the Andean sun. An Indian woman with a baby sleeping in cloths slung from her back drags her tattered husband from the scrum.
>
> The visitors stare silently, and migrate to the balcony of the mayor's residence to watch the mayhem from a safer distance. Disbelief creeps into their faces.
>
> 'This is barbarous and I don't know whether it is a good or bad thing', says Justin Hall, a cartoonist from San Francisco.
>
> An Indian woman screams and struggles to save her husband from six men kicking his head. The odor of grain alcohol is heavy in the air.
>
> 'It's like watching a car accident. Now it's all pure emotion,' says Jerry Tal from Israel. 'I don't know if I should be watching this.'
>
> A police officer appears. A warning shot cracks. Tear gas billows. The fighters scatter, leaving the plaza empty save for one woman choking on the gas and men sprawled unconscious from alcohol and beatings (Gori 2003).

The sensational language of this journalistic account conjures up how outsiders almost universally find the violence of *tinku* ugly and deeply disturbing. But to justify it in terms of its role in agriculture or symbolic meanings, might equally fail to confront what the violence means to the individuals who participate in it?[4] Despite the widespread interpretation of *tinku* and the periodic deaths that result from it as a blood sacrifice to 'feed the earth', nobody I spoke to in Kalankira confirmed this, and in fact, several men actively denied it. Instead they compared *tinku* to a 'sport' or game, which they

---

4 See Harris (2000 [1994]: 142) for a pithy discussion of this ethnographic dilemma.

evidently anticipated with an eagerness and excitement reminiscent of the emotions surrounding an important football match in the UK.[5] For most of the people I spoke to, *tinku* is about expressing courage, strength, manhood and *ayllu* (team!) identity. This focus on life, potential and invincibility, which also emerges from *julajula* music, might explain why people disputed its widely reported connection with blood sacrifice and death. Men charge into battle shouting *su chacha karaju!* ('I'm a man dammit!')[6] or *su Macha karaju!* ('I'm [a] Macha dammit!'), bellowing and pawing the ground like powerful crazed bulls, which are among the most potent models for the 'poetics of manhood' in the region (Herzfeld 1985, Harris 2000:152). I encountered a strong moral imperative to participate; those who fail to fight are dubbed *q'iwa*, a word applied to people who are mean, miserly or cowardly. According to some accounts, these individuals are sometimes beaten up for failing to participate.[7]

Most men expressed confidence about the hand-to-hand fighting, with punches and kicks, between paired combatants, but the dangerous *chuqay rumi* ('stone throwing') which the town authorities and police have tried so hard to abolish, is clearly the real challenge to their bravery and a primary medium through which they express their courage and manhood. The following *cruz* song verses, which were sung on 2 May, the eve of the feast, evoke the danger and fear associated with *chuqay rumi*.

Chayqa kurus chamun tusurikuy nispa	Here *cruz* arrives saying 'dance!'
Pataras, pataras muchu jichu kani	Kicking, kicking, I'm really tough[8]
Rumi parapis waqarikuq kani	In the rain of stones I'm a cry baby
Pataras, pataras muchu jichu kani	Kicking, kicking, I'm really tough

These verses also highlight the sense of obligation for men to 'dance' for *tata wila cruz*, with the fighting emerging as a climax in the dance's choreography, rather than as a separate activity. After the *tinku* was over, I encountered little talk of defeating others, instead men proudly paraded the evidence of their bravery and resistance – such as black eyes, broken noses, torn lips.[9] Asencio told me that the feast of *cruz* in Macha is a *marka fiesta*, which I understood

---

[5] Several other writers have noted how *tinku* fighting is sometimes classified as a 'game' – Quechua *pujllay* or Aymara *anata* (Platt 1987:84a, Cereceda 1987:212).

[6] In this context men often used the Aymara *chacha* ('man') as well as the Quechua *qhari* ('man'). It is unclear whether this is in imitation of other Aymara speaking *ayllus* or has remained in the collective memory since the nineteenth century when Aymara was the dominant language of *ayllu* Macha.

[7] See Harris 1988:3, Solomon 1997:504.

[8] Presumably a reference to both fighting and stamping the ground in *zapateo* dancing (Chapter 4).

[9] My friend Ben Kohl once expressed his surprise that more developed fighting techniques, such as Kung fu, had not – up to that time – been adopted in *tinku*. This may yet happen, but such innovation would suggest a focus on objectively 'winning', rather than an ethos of expressing personal endurance and bravery.

to refer to an annual pilgrimage to the *marka* (Aymara: 'capital town') – a practice with apparent prehispanic roots (Solomon 1997:422). However, instead of this expected association, Asencio explicitly linked the word *marka* to cattle 'branding' (Spanish *marca*). 'In the feast of *cruz*', he explained, 'we brand one another' (*markanakunchis*), miming the moves of *tinku* fighting, as he spoke. From this perspective, the fighting at *cruz* emerges as a rite of passage in which the injuries signify 'brands', marking quality and identity as brave, male warriors of the *ayllu*.[10]

According to Tristan Platt, today's *ayllu* Macha are descendents of the dominant ethnic group of a prehispanic federation called the Qharaqhara [Karakara], whose capital was on the site of the present town of Macha (Platt 1986:229, Harris 1986:261). The Qharaqhara and Charka federation to the north, whose capital was Sacaca, were yoked in dual organization to form the Charka confederation (Harris 1986:261, Solomon 1997:429–30). This powerful political entity was famed for the skill of its warriors, who successfully resisted Inka conquest for several hundred years. When finally incorporated into the Inka Empire, in recognition of their prowess as warriors, the Charka paid their tribute in blood, rather than with agricultural products, by forming part of the Inka standing army (Solomon 1997:430–32).

Drawing on these historical associations, Thomas Solomon has suggested that the ritual complex surrounding *julajula* panpipe performance today 'is a vehicle for the collective memory of the contemporary indigenous population of Northern Potosí, providing a basis for people's continuing self image as proud warriors' (1997:462). Solomon draws attention to the similarity in organology, construction, style and choreography between *julajulas* and another form of panpipe played on the Bolivian and Peruvian *altiplano* called *chiriguanos*, which accompany dances representing fierce 'savage' tribes of the tropical lowlands.[11] Solomon suggests that:

> ... what was originally a pan-central Andean musical representation of warlike jungle tribes like the Chirguanos became a more generalized musical representation of bellicosity, adopted by warriors of Charka for their own ritual battles between moieties (1997:465).

This is a compelling hypothesis which resonates with the continued articulation of identities and political relations through musical, choreographic

---

[10] I have witnessed women fight in *tinku* in other parts of Northern Potosí (see Harris 2000:147–8), but have the impression that this is rarer in the Macha region. Exceptionally, children and women fight in the town of Macha on Good Friday as a representation of chaos. Christ has died, I was told, so the world spins out of control.

[11] Historically, the Chiriguanos were a warlike tribe from the Amazonian forest region who made continued attacks into highland regions up until the sixteenth century, and against whom the Charka warriors protected both the Inka Empire and their own territory (Solomon 1997:462–4). See, for example, Oblitas Poblete 1978 [1960]:356, Bellenger 1986 [1983]:18–19, Baumann 1982a:29, Parejo 1991:6, Cavour 1994:46–9.

and costumed representations or parodies of other social groups; one of the most characteristic aspects of festive performance in the Andes.[12] Whilst mocking 'others', the complex of *julajula* panpipes, dancing and *tinku* fighting emerges as an especially privileged medium for the expression and maintenance of *ayllu* structure, identity and territory. The disparate elements of the *ayllu* are ritually brought into relation with one another at its capital (*marka*)-Macha, thereby reaffirming its framework of connected parts or harmonic relations.

Indeed, the bellicosity of *tinku* has come to be re-represented and exoticized in urban contexts as a major national folkloric dance-music genre called 'Tinku'; a heavy stomping dance which parodies *tinku* fighting.[13] Taken abroad by urban folklore groups 'Tinku' sometimes serves as a powerful medium for evoking deep, powerful and indigenous aspects of Bolivian national identity.

Harmony through violence?

The feast of *cruz* is notable as one of the few regular occasions that the *ayllu* is revealed as an entity, the various alignments of its structure played out through music, dance and fighting (Stokes 1994:12). In particular the *Alasaya* and *Majasaya*, between which the principal fighting and maximum violence traditionally takes place (Platt 1987a:84). The Kalankiras explained that as members of the minor *ayllu* Tapunata (Alasaya), their *rumi tinku* ('stone fighting') during *cruz* in 1991 was principally directed against members of a different minor *ayllu* Ala Qullana (Majasaya), who they considered 'enemies' due to longstanding territorial disputes. When a member of this rival *ayllu* was killed during the stone throwing (*chuqay rumi*), fear of reprisals led us to abandon a trip a few months later to the mines of Salinas Baja with the family's llama caravans to collect rock salt for exchanges in the valleys.[14]

During *cruz* 1991 several other levels of *ayllu* structure were also expressed musically, through less formal encounters between troupes of *julajula* panpipe playing warrior dancers termed *wayli* (Sp. *baile* 'dance'). Kalankira, along with Palqa Uyu and Iru Pampa, was one of three local *wayli* troupes from the higher altitude district of Cabildo Palqa Uyu – each carrying their own cross

---

[12] This is evident from almost any ethnographic account or collection of recordings. See, for example, Baumann 1982a, Paredes-Candia 1991 [1966], Romero (ed.) 1993, Cánepa Koch (ed.) 2001.

[13] Although imitations of 'authentic' peasant dress are worn by Tinku dancers in urban festivals, the heavy repetitive and 'stomping' duple metre of the music usually evokes and exoticizes the idea of peasant music rather than attempting to recreate it.

[14] According to the Macha police, a man from Chuqi Qayara (minor ayllu Majapicha, moiety Majasaya) was also killed this year.

to be blessed in Macha.[15] On the footpath, each group's music sponsor (*mayura*) and his assistants used whips to keep these and other troupes using the same path apart. However, after our formal arrival in Macha and the deposit of our *julajula* panpipes in the house of a *mestizo* resident (our main sponsor's godfather), we joined forces in a stamping dance (*zapateo*) accompanied by a *charango*. I was surprised to find myself dancing in good-humoured solidarity side by side with men who, a few hours earlier, had been expressing intense aggression towards my host *wayli* group. Hostilities again erupted on the journey home and a full-scale battle was only avoided when, on the insistence of the women, the Kalankira and Palqa Uyu *wayli* troupes formed into two circles and released their aggression through *zapateo* ('stamping') dancing, accompanied by their respective *charango* players. We later briefly stopped at Iru Pampa, which is home to Asencio and Paulino's paternal family, and were invited to drink corn beer. However, when it was announced that Iru Pampa's own *wayli* troupe was about to arrive from Macha we quickly departed in order to avoid confrontation. Later that same evening, taunts were exchanged between men from Pata Kalankira hamlet and Wak'an Phukru, who only a few hours earlier had been dancing together as members of the same *wayli* troupe.

This journey to Macha represented one of the most vivid expressions of 'branching' (or 'nested') levels of *ayllu* structure I have encountered (Platt 1986:231, 236) (Figure 6.1). It is significant that much of this political structure was expressed musically, music and dance serving sometimes to taunt opposing groups and at other moments to sublimate aggression.

While ongoing territorial disputes are often expressed in *tinku*, major territorial battles may also erupt at any time of year. *Ch'axwa*, the usual term for such battles in the North of Potosí, tend to take place on the disputed territory itself, rather than at predetermined ritual sites associated with *tinku*, and slingshots (*warak'a*) and other weapons are used. For example, some 40 men from cabildo Palqa Uyu, including Paulino and many others from Kalankira, participated in a *ch'axwa* battle near Ocuri in October 1992. They fought in support of the neighbouring Tomaykuris in a territorial dispute against the Maraguas, who were supported by the nearby Q'illu Q'asas (who became particularly bitter opponents in the *tinku* in Macha a few weeks later for All Saints). According to Paulino, some 200 men fought on each side, using long sticks (*waruti k'aspis*) and slings (*warak'as*) as weapons. Many goat horn trumpets (*cornetas*) were sounded to give the fighters 'strength' (*kallpa*) and 'fortune' (*surti*), as their sound is 'rich in *animu*'. Paulino also specified that 'we won' (*nuqayku gañayku*), a claim rarely made following *tinku* which, by contrast, involves one-to-one fighting, between combatants of

---

[15] Troupes also travelled from the larger lower altitude communities of Puka Mayu and Katiriri, which also form part of Cabildo Palqa Uyu.

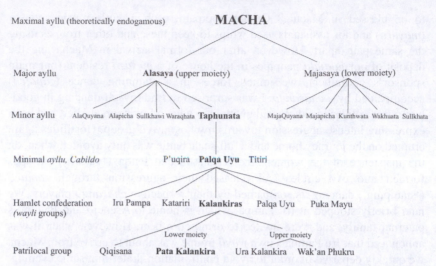

Figure 6.1   **Place of Kalankira within the institutional structure of *ayllu* Macha (partially based on Platt 1986:231 and Mendoza & Patzi 1997)**

similar sex, age and physique – where 'like fights like', and 'the idea of balance is firmly maintained' (Harris 2000 [1978]:177). Thus, unlike the more destructive and asymmetrical nature of *ch'axwa* battles, *tinku* has been widely associated with the definition and maintenance of balanced relations, especially the dialectical dualism or 'charged diametricality' of the *ayllu* (Sallnow 1987:145).[16] In this context the word *tinku* emerges as a form of 'violent harmony', leading us to look in more detail at the word *tinku* itself, which is common to both Quechua and Aymara, and by no means exclusively associated with violence.

Tinku as Harmony?

The most common daily use of the Quechua verb stem *tinku* in Kalankira is in reference to 'meetings' or 'encounters', such as between two people on a footpath or even between lovers (Platt 1987a:97, Bouysse-Cassagne & Harris 1987:31). Bertonio's 1612 Aymara dictionary includes entries for the verb stem *tincu* that convey symmetry, equilibrium, agreement or concord between (paired) things (Bertonio [1612] 1984, II:351, Platt 1987a:83). This idea of the pairing and 'balancing' of equivalent things, or reciprocal exchange, is common to many analyses of *tinku*, in both historical and modern

---

[16] See Platt 1987 for a detailed discussion of the differences between *ch'axwa* and *tinku* (1987a:94–5).

contexts.[17] In his Quechua–Spanish dictionary of 1608, González Holguín describes the root *tinku* (*tincu*) as conveying the idea of bringing voices together in a concordant or harmonious way or of tuning voices together, as well as more generally to convey the idea of 'agreement' or 'concord' (the Spanish *concordancia* often implying musical harmony). This direct correlation between *tinku* and musical concord or agreement, is particularly notable because the other word for battle in Quechua, *ch'axwa* (destructive or asymmetrical battles) is also widely used to refer to an unpleasant 'noise' or 'din' (Chapter 7).

Many of these associations of the word *tinku* have striking resonances with the fundamental meanings of the Greco–European concept of 'harmony' (ἁρμονία), as (a) the 'joining' of parts which would otherwise be separate, (b) 'agreement', (c) 'concord' and – by extension – the idea of a framework of connected parts, or unification of dissimilar components into an ordered whole, such as that of the universe or of settled government (Little et al. 1973:928, Rowell 1983:40–41).

Although this comes close to the varied etymology of *tinku*, the focus in *tinku* tends to be upon balance or equilibrium between paired components – almost as mirror images of one another – rather than dissimilar ones, resulting in a sense of dialectical tension or in Sallnow's words 'charged diametricality' (1987:145). In his volume *Musical Thought in Ancient Greece*, Edward Lippman invokes precisely this sense of dialectical tension:

> … harmony shows the inevitable relation of opposites, the holding in balance of forces at odds with one another; in a word, the central connection of permanence with transience (Lippman 1964:10–11).

Indeed the concepts of both harmony and *tinku* can be seen to embody a sense of inner tension and contradiction – of beauty and violence.[18] For example, the Greek goddess *Harmonia*, who personified harmony and order, was sometimes presented in myth as the daughter of Aphrodite (goddess of love) and Ares (god of war), thereby representing 'both harmony and harmony in disagreement' (Schueller 1988:1–3, Lippman 1964:4).[19] While such an interpretation of 'harmony' runs counter to most modern Western sensibilities and 'common sense', harmonic relations – such as the 'harmony of the spheres' or Western functional harmony – tend to be intensely hierarchical.

---

[17] See, for example, Bouysse-Cassagne & Harris 1987:30–31, Allen 1988:207, Sallnow 1987:145.

[18] In a fascinating exploration of Andean aesthetics, subtitled *de la belleza al tinku* ('from beauty to tinku') and drawing principally on plastic language and myth, Verónica Cereceda argues that beauty never appears alone as if of value in itself, but rather is always involved in connecting or mediating between opposing principles, such as illness and health, life and death (1987:217).

[19] Somewhat surprisingly, given modern sensibilities, Horace presented harmony as the 'discordant union which binds together the world and regulates the heavenly spheres' (Schueller 1988:1–3).

Unlike the feast of *cruz* where the inherent violence underlying harmonic relations is made explicit, in most Western contexts it often tends to be hidden, or as Bourdieu would have it 'symbolic' (1977:196). More generally, Jacques Attali has argued that music is used 'strategically by power to make people *forget* the general violence' and to '*believe* in the harmony of the world' (1985:19). Tristan Platt argues that the balance found in *tinku* might be best understood as a means to legitimate and maintain political stability – to create 'harmony' – in the wake of the establishment of a hierarchy (Alasaya over Majasaya) through military victory in *ch'axwa* (1987a:94–95).[20] From this perspective, *tinku* can be viewed as a means to transform unpleasant noise (*ch'axwa*) into (musical) concord. In *tinku* we find violence invoked as inherent to the harmony of the world, serving in part to make people *forget* hierarchy and to *believe* in the possibility of balanced and harmonious relations.

The harvest season

The festival of *cruz*, when the year's principal *tinku* erupts, takes place in May, the onset of the coldest period of the year, when the high Andes are characterized by gradual desiccation and death. Water descends to the lower and 'inner' places where, according to local stories, it is hoarded up and monopolized by *supay* (Chapter 7). During this season, the eye is greeted by dry and barren earth, shrivelling vegetation and dried-up streambeds, with any remaining water often paralysed into ice by the intense cold of the long winter nights. But in many respects this season is far more associated with life, fat and health, than with death for at no other time of the year are the stores of each homestead better stocked or are people less likely to go hungry. There is even plenty of food for the mice and parrots, I was told. Although the visual impression of the landscape is one of scarcity, it is the time of inner abundance, suggesting bodily growth and maturation; imagery that I suggest, is evoked in the structure of the *julajula* music and *wayli* dancing of the feast of *cruz*.

The harvest season might thus be characterized as a period of optimism and celebration. Yet, my own experience of helping my hosts and other families with their harvest tempers this image of plenty. The months of intense care and labour dedicated to ploughing, planting, fertilizing, weeding, ridging, and

---

[20] Platt interprets *tinku* battles as a means 'to manage violence to social ends, to subject it to rules and ideas, to *fashion it* as a force which – if not recognized and channelled – constantly threatens the social "order", in order thereby to extract from the confusion and disagreement the basis for a new affirmation of the possibility of harmonious coexistence' (1987a:85). My translation.

Figure 6.2   Harvesting potatoes

finally harvesting the fields was often greeted by miserable yields – largely resulting from poor weather. On many occasions, after carefully burning offerings of an aromatic herb called *q'uwa* and chewing coca leaves to the 'virgin' (*wirjin*) of the fields, we would sink our *lluqanas* ('picks') into the earth only to discover tiny, marble sized potatoes (Figure 6.2). Sometimes, overwhelmed by a sense of hopelessness, I would be astonished by my hosts' patience, resilience and almost unquestioning acceptance of these meagre rewards for their huge efforts. At these times my mind would race back to my own childhood on a farm in Cornwall and my father's similar fortitude, but also humility, in the face of disastrous harvests. Over several millennia, Andean farmers have developed a wide repertory of strategies for coping with the unpredictability of weather conditions, which include planting crops of genetically diverse 'association-mixtures' in a range of different places, at different altitudes, and at different times, as well as developing freeze-drying techniques to enable tubers to be stored for many years (Berg 1989, Valladolid Rivera 1998:72, Harrison 1989:172).

Besides harvest and storing crops, the principal activities between Carnival (February/March) and late June are the ploughing of fallow land (*barbecho*) while the earth is still soft from the rains, trading journeys to the valleys, and the preparation of *chuñu* (freeze-dried potatoes), which is dependent on both intensely cold nights and sunny days. Both the *charangos* and *julajula* (or *wauku*) panpipes played during this season were explicitly claimed to call the frosts necessary for *chuño* making. Indeed I was told that 'if you don't play the *charango* it doesn't freeze'.

The feast of *Cruz*

Asencio explained to me that *cruz* is the feast of the 'fields' (*chaqras*), a point made especially explicit during *barbecho* ploughing in late February when we drank libations to *tata pachaqa* ('father one hundred') and *kinsa milagro* ('three miracles'). When I enquired about these patrons, Victor Beltrán hummed a *julajula* panpipe melody associated with *cruz* to highlight their identification with *tata wila cruz* and the feast of the Holy Cross.[21] For the Kalankiras, *tata wila cruz* and his feast were intimately associated with the realization of a new generation of offspring from the fields, resulting from joint labours with his consort *mama candelaria*, whose feast is celebrated on 1 February (Candlemas).

Asencio was the principal sponsor or *alférez* ('lieutenant') for *cruz* in 1991, one of the most onerous and prestigious sponsorship roles of the year. In addition to feasting the community for nearly a week, he was responsible for carrying its cross to Macha. With Asencio as *alférez* I could hardly avoid becoming deeply involved in the preparations, which began several months in advance as food crops were set aside and extended family and neighbours were called upon to help. These months of preparation and accumulation of scarce resources, which would then be consumed within a matter of days, represented an immense personal commitment on the part of Asencio and Bardolina, his wife, but clearly perceived as an important and worthwhile investment. Paulino often told me of his own ambition to sponsor this feast, and his conviction that such sacrifice or investment would ensure the future abundance of his family's herds and crops, as well as improving his standing in the community.[22]

As we helped Asencio prepare for *cruz* in Kalankira, a second sponsor, the *mayura* or 'captain', was also making ready for the feast in Qullpa Quchi, a lower altitude hamlet some ninety minutes walk away. Asencio explained that

---

[21] *Cruz* is often referred to locally *tres de mayo* (Sp. 'third of May'), stressing the number three, which is also evoked in the idea of *kinsa milagro* ('three miracles') and *kinsa temble* ('three tuning'), an alternative name for *cruz* tuning on the *charango*. See Chapter 4.

[22] Paulino did indeed sponsor the feast of *cruz*, as *alférez*, several years later – inviting me to serve as *mayura*, a role that I was sadly unable to fulfil due to commitments at home.

his own sponsorship position, as *alferéz*, was 'greater' (*aswan jatun*) than that of the *mayura*; comparing the two positions to a pair of oxen, where he was the 'right' (*paña*) and the *mayura* the 'left' (*lluq'i*). Together these two sponsors represented a confederation of some seven or eight hamlets and a number of dispersed homesteads that are affiliated to a particular cross that, for most of the year, lives in a shrine (*calvario*) just below Qullpa Quchi. Traditionally the complementary roles of *alferéz* and *mayura* were alternated annually between the upper (*pata*) and lower (*ura*) moieties of this confederation, where in theory the *mayura* of one year would automatically become the *alferéz* for the next.[23]

The role of the *mayura* is of special interest from a musical perspective, as with this position comes the responsibility to acquire a new set of *julajula* panpipes, provide and teach a new melody to the players, and ensure that dancing during the feast is lively and well disciplined. Throughout the feast, as in many others in the North of Potosí, the *mayura* carried a whip and periodically lashed the legs of any dancers who fell out of line or failed to dance energetically. Two unmarried girls carrying white flags, called *imilla wawas* ('girl babies') also used whips to energize the dancing and quell violent scuffles with other *wayli* groups.

Elsewhere in Macha territory I have attended a *julajula* rehearsal called by the *mayura* and involving a small core group of the male players on the evening before embarking on the pilgrimage. Following a ritual for the new set of instruments, the *mayura* played the complete melody repeatedly while a bottle of watered down cane alcohol circulated. We gradually joined in, moving to increasingly larger instruments as we acquired confidence. The principal concern was that we would be able to play with adequate volume to compete with other groups. According to past *mayuras* I spoke with in Kalankira, a rehearsal staged in advance of the feast seems to be the exception rather than the norm.[24] Also, any preparatory rehearsal was unlikely to have involved more than a small minority of the players who actually performed during the feast.[25] In practice, so long as a small core of men can play the new melody reliably, others are able to quickly learn it.[26] Indeed, the limited

---

[23] Although the *mayura* was important in 1991, in subsequent years, this position has sometimes been abandoned adding further to the burden of the *alferéz*. This may simply be because the role of *mayura* is less prestigious.

[24] Asking a member of my host family to accompany me to the mayura's house 90 minutes walk away on the pretext of a possible rehearsal was unthinkable. As on many other occasions, my research interests were forced to take second place to my social obligations.

[25] Zegarra & Puma note that the lead *wauqö* players in Tinkipaya were termed *wayñu wayaqa* ('melody bag') and were considered to have special aptitude for music (c. 1997:22). No such specific individuals were identified for the case of *julajula* performance in Kalankira.

[26] Turino presents the rehearsals and composition sessions in Conima, Peru as 'the fountainhead of the whole creative chain of musical performance' (1993:73). By contrast, things tended to be considerably more ad hoc in Kalankira. During the feasts themselves players would offer melodies

technique required for *julajula* performance, alongside the structural similarity of melodies from year to year, made these instruments especially conducive to general participation – where all men accompanying the cross, besides the sponsors, are expected to play. The number of participants in the Kalankira *wayli* troupe varied through the course of the feast, some thirty men participating for the entrance into Macha.

The appearance of the *julajula*

For the Kalankiras, *julajula* panpipe performance was linked exclusively and intimately with *kusicha timpu* ('harvest season') and the feast of *cruz*, an association that is common in many other parts of the Northern Potosí region. But these instruments are also heard at several other dry season feasts, especially those associated with harvest or planting and are often played at patronal festivals.[27] In Kalankira these instruments were widely claimed to blow away the clouds, and to attract frost and hail.[28] Whilst an especially close connection undoubtedly exists between *julajula* panpipes and *tinku*, it is not rare to encounter combatants arriving for *tinku* playing other instruments, such as the *pinkillu* flutes played at All Saints in Macha. However, whereas rainy season instruments tended to be connected with the inner earth (*ukhu pacha*), *julajula* panpipes were especially associated with 'order' and the sky gods.[29] Indeed, following the long cold night of the winter solstice in a rural community near Sacaca, I once knelt facing East with a group of *julajula* players to welcome the sun's return or rebirth.[30] As the sun popped over the horizon we played a *kuwla* (*kulwa, copla*) in its honour (CD track 4) (Example 6.1).

My initial encounter with *julajulas* in Kalankira was late at night, following a day of collective beer brewing for *cruz* at Asencio's house. As we boiled up

---

they claimed to have heard elsewhere, had 'invented', or which came to them on the spur of the moment. I also participated in this process as a player; melodies that I offered or which literally fell under my fingers were sometimes, but not always, taken up by the whole ensemble. The idea that a rehearsal was necessary in advance of playing together continually for several days often seemed redundant, unless public competition with other ensembles was likely to take place early in the feast.

[27] For example, Easter (April), Asencion, San Juan (June), San Lazaro, San Francisco and Rosario (October). Exceptionally, *julajulas* are played during the rains in a few places, such as for the feast of Santa Catalina (November) in Tacopaya (Cochabamba department) and, according to Arnaud Gerard, for Christmas in Ocuri (personal communication).

[28] See also Zegarra & Puma (c. 1997:22).

[29] See also Rosalía Martínez (1994).

[30] In Northern Potosí, as in many other parts of Bolivia, the winter solstice is identified with the feast of St John (*San Juan*), 24 June. Harris also includes a photograph of kneeling *julajula* players playing 'to ask pardon of Father Sun' (2000:52).

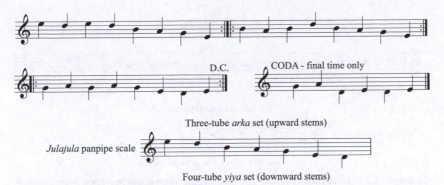

Three-tube *arka* set (upward stems)

Julajula panpipe scale

Four-tube *yiya* set (downward stems)

Example 6.1 *Kuwla* (*kulwa*) on *julajula* **panpipes, played to the sun at dawn after the night of the winter solstice (Ch'uslonkari, near Sacaca, Map 3). Transposed up about one tone. (CD track 4)**

the treacly sweet *tiqti* syrup needed to hasten the beer's fermentation, the previous year's *mayura* handed around the few surviving *julajula* panpipes from his turn as music sponsor. Together we played the *suna* melody from the previous year into the darkness, to the dramatic backdrop of flames leaping around the boiling drums of *tiqti*, as if enacting the final despatch (*kacharpaya*) of the melody and instruments, both of which are acquired new each year (Example 6.2).[31] It was an appropriately ragged performance for a melody destined for oblivion, which – for me at least – powerfully invoked a sense of departure, potential renewal and paradoxically continuity (CD track 48).

The first public context in which the new *julajula* panpipes and *suna* melody, provided by the new *mayura* for 1991, were heard was late on the evening of the 2 May. Past *mayuras* mentioned 'inventing' the *suna* melody, or acquiring it from the valleys, nearby towns or communities when they purchased the new set of instruments.[32] This was the start of the feast proper, the *vispira* ('vespers'), when the community cross (*tata wila cruz*) was brought out of the *calvario* and dressed ready for its journey to Macha. The *calvario* is a small hut enclosed in a walled compound with a commanding position over Palqa Uyu valley. In a constant kaleidoscope of sound and movement, *julajula* panpipes alternated with *zapateo* dancing to a *panti charango*, as the all-male musician-dancers formed a long single file, led by the man with the largest 4-tube panpipe, and circled the hut tracing snaking patterns across the enclosure (CD tracks 1 and 2). These serpentine formations, called *link'u link'u* or *q'iwi q'iwi* are a particularly distinctive

---

[31] The despatch of this melody seemed to parallel the brewing process in which we were also involved, where decay was hastened leading to a process of rebirth.

[32] An elderly man told me that formerly *julajula* melodies used to be acquired from a special *yuraq qaqa* ('white rock') in the highlands, but now they tend to come from valley *sirinus*.

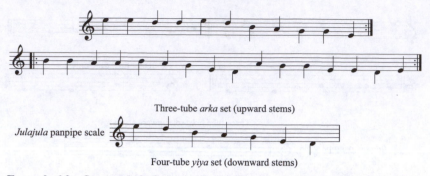

Three-tube *arka* set (upward stems)

Julajula panpipe scale

Four-tube *yiya* set (downward stems)

Example 6.2   *Suna* melody from previous year, played during corn beer making. (CD track 48)

feature of *wayli* dancing, and were interspersed with circles (*muyu*, *rueda*) moving alternately anticlockwise ('right' *paña*) and clockwise ('left' *lluq'i*).

I was invited to squeeze into the tiny hut, alongside the new and old sponsors, to help dress the cross for its journey. It was as if, through these careful preparations, *tata wila cruz* was awakened to become a living presence in our midst. Finally at about 2am, after a communal meal and several more hours of music, dancing and libations, Asencio brought the dressed cross out of its hut, and I joined the *julajula* panpipe ensemble to kneel before it and perform a *kupla*. Unlike the *suna* melodies, which are renewed annually and performed while dancing, the *kupla* melody is usually unchanged from year to year and played kneeling. In other parts of the region *kupla* (*kulwa*) are played kneeling facing the door or altar of the church in a pilgrimage site, and are sounded as the group arrives, departs and sometimes at dawn on feast days. However, in Kalankira the emergence of the cross from its *calvario* for *cruz* was the only time that I encountered a *kupla* performance. Perhaps reflecting their infrequency, the performance was shambolic – the first two sections following the form that I knew well from other regions, but the last section essentially falling to pieces (Example 6.3). I expected the musicians and sponsors to be critical of this poor performance at such a ritually potent moment. Would this been seen as disrespectful to *tata wila cruz*? Would we repeat the piece?[33] No, the performance was passed over without comment. The players had completed the appropriate moves, expended effort – whatever the resultant sounds.

Over the following week the *wayli* troupe played its single *suna* melody for many hours each day to provide *kunswilu* ('consolation') and 'honour' (*honor*) for the cross on all its movements, including the long journey to Macha and back – taking some seven hours each way. When the cross 'rested', standing

---

[33] I once witnessed Asencio repeat an entire series of ritual libations, having become too drunk to continue on the previous day.

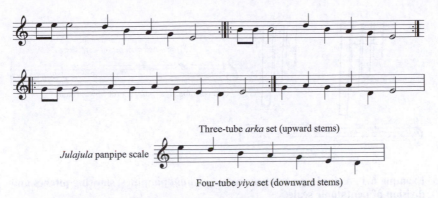

Example 6.3 *Kupla* **melody of** *julajula* **panpipes, as heard in several other parts of Northern Potosí (see Stobart 1998b, CD track 6)**

on a cloth to avoid contact with ground, the *panti charango* would usually strike up and we would go into a strenuous trotting and stamping dance. The llama corrals adjoining the homesteads of the *alferéz* (Asencio) and *mayura* were the two, widely separated foci of most of the ceremonial activity, the *wayli* troupe accompanying the cross on the many journeys between them, circling important rocks en route. The *suna* was always played as 'consolation' when llamas and sheep were ritually slaughtered for consumption during the feast.

Julajula panpipes, harmony and the making of men

Compared to most other genres, the music of *julajula* panpipes – also known in Kalankira as *wauku* or *suqusu* ('bamboo') – seems serious and austere in nature. This impression is heightened by the fact that, unusually, they are played without drum accompaniment. The sombre timbre also stems from the use of bamboo (*Arundo donax*) in construction, which grows in the warm valleys of Northern Potosí and is thicker and stronger than the thin, fragile and more resonant canes of the tropical lowlands used in most panpipe making. Although Kalankira's *mayuras* usually purchase the new *julajulas* from a maker based in the valleys, elsewhere in Northern Potosí they are often made within the community, reflecting the simplicity of construction. In common with many other Andean panpipes, *julajula* are constructed in pairs so that the notes of the scale are divided between two (half) instruments, played using 'hocket' or 'interlocking' technique. For the case of *julajulas*, a seven-note anhemitonic pentatonic scale is divided between a four-tube *yiya* (Spanish *guia* 'guide') and three-tube *arka* (Aymara/Quechua 'follower') pair (Example 6.4).

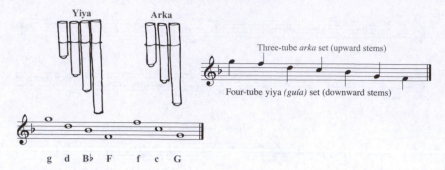

Example 6.4   Paired *yiya* and *arka* set of *julajula* panpipes, showing pitches and division of pentatonic scale

Troupes of *julajula* usually consist of twenty-five to thirty men playing pairs of *yiya* and *arka* instruments in five (or six) sizes, tuned in parallel octaves (Figure 6.3). For the larger sizes the melody is divided between two players, but for the smaller *ch'ili* and *wiswi* sizes players sometimes hold the *yiya* and *arka* pair together and play the complete melody. When the pair of instruments is played in this way it is described as *iraskillu*.

In Kalankira the paired *yiya* and *arka* instruments were compared to 'elder' and 'younger' brothers, suggesting a temporal distinction where the elder brother (*kuraq*) leads and takes his turn first, while the younger brother (*sullka*) follows.[34] *Julajula* melodies begin with the four-tube *yiya* and end with the three-tube *arka*; similarly, the file of players is led by a man with the largest (*machu*) four-tube *yiya*, and immediately followed by the player of the largest three-tube *arka*.

Interlocking: to die without the other

According to Baumann, the dialogic ('hocket' or 'interlocking') technique, by which paired *julajula* players alternate their notes to create a melody, is sometimes referred to as *tinku* (1996:32) – tying the instruments in yet another way to the theme of 'violent harmony'. However, don Adrian also described this playing technique as *watanakunku* and *qhespinakunku*; both of which incorporate the suffix – *naku*- to express reciprocal action.[35] *Watanakunku* may be literally translated as 'they tie one another', suggesting that through their mutual action, the paired players are bound into an interdependent unit. This

---

[34] A male/female gender distinction between paired panpipes has been recorded in certain parts of the Andes (Grebe 1980:332, Baumann 1981, Valencia Chacón 1981:12, Harris 1988:4), however this was not recognized in Kalankira.

[35] See Stobart 2002b for more detailed discussion.

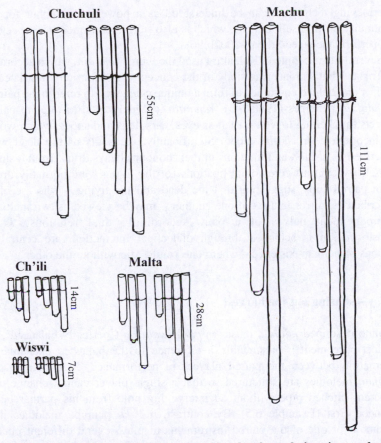

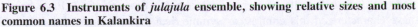

Figure 6.3 **Instruments of** *julajula* **ensemble, showing relative sizes and most common names in Kalankira**

has parallels with the *malta kuchuy* ceremony, a rite of passage when 'adolescent' male llamas leave the reproductive herd of female and young llamas to join the adult males, and are briefly tied together in pairs. Both of these cases suggest that entry into male adulthood does not only involve leaving behind immaturity and dependence but specifically the setting up of interdependent relations. That this is expressed as paired males, rather than as the male and female unit which forms the basis of household and family, is notable.[36] Pedro Plaza proposes that don Adrian's other word, *qhespinakunku*, is best translated as 'one without the other would die out'. This suggests that the continuity of sounds in a melody, achieved through this form of

_____

[36] See Platt 1986 for other ethnographic examples of rituals practices from *ayllu* Macha involving paired men.

interlocking technique, can be understood as a powerful metaphor for the continuity of life itself, a theme which is also suggested from other aspects of the performance (see Stobart 2002b:96).

Several other people in Kalankira used the word *yanantin*, which according to Tristan Platt's pioneering study of the concept may be strictly translated as 'helper and helped combined to form a unique category', to refer to the pairing of *julajula* panpipes (1986:245). *Yanantin* is widely used to refer to paired objects that belong together, such as eyes, ears, legs and shoes, which would be incomplete or *ch'ulla* alone. Significantly, the souls of the dead were described as *ch'ulla* and libations in their honour always drunk from a single vessel. By contrast ceremonial libations for the living were normally drunk from paired cups, suggesting that the dead and the living – who are often described as mirror images of one another – may be viewed as two mutually interdependent halves of a pair. Accordingly dual relations, where transformation is achieved through dialectical interaction, are central to notions of human existence – where one would 'die without the other'.

Julay – sharing out the harvest

Paulino described *julajula* music as *puru iwalasqa* ('perfectly balanced', 'in perfect agreement'); presumably a reference to the balanced exchange or alternation between the paired players in performance. It is notable that *julajula* melodies are structured so that a single player cannot change to a different pitched pipe without an intervening note from his partner being sounded first (Example 6.5). By contrast, in *siku* panpipe melodies it is common for one of the paired instruments to play several different pitches consecutively before its partner sounds a note (Example 6.6). Elsewhere I have characterized this contrast as symmetrical and asymmetrical forms of dialogue (Stobart 2002b:94).

Julajula panpipe performance can be interpreted as an especially vivid musical expression of balanced exchange or perhaps a form of diachronic 'harmony'.[37] Indeed the very name *julajula* suggests the idea of distributing resources in a balanced way, or according to individual capacity and strength. Several people connected the name of these instruments with the verbs *julay* or *julaqay*, which refer to emptying the contents from one (overfilled)

---

[37] In Western music theory, 'harmony' tends to be associated with the combination of simultaneous notes to create chords, and is distinguished from 'melody' as a succession of notes (Little et al. 1973:928). However, for the ancient Greeks 'harmony meant successive, not simultaneous tones', and referred to the ways that these notes related to one another (James 1995 [1993] 79–80). In the case of *julajula* music the sense of 'harmony' is not so much implied through the intervallic relationships between successive notes as the diachronic relationship between the two players.

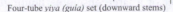

Example 6.5 *Suna* **melody played on** *julajula* **panpipes at the calvario near Qullpa Quchi. Each change in pitch involves alternation between players. Transposed up about one semitone. (CD track 2)**

Example 6.6 *Huayño* **melody played on** *siku* **panpipes (see Chapter 7). Shows how players may move between pitches without intervening notes from their partner (as in the opening phrase). The numbers refer to the tube on which a given pitch is played, number 1 is the shortest tube. (CD track 18)**

container into another, until the goods or weight is divided according to the receptacles' respective capacities. The example most often used was of sacks (*kustalas*) of maize or potatoes; where the redistribution of products was not only related to the capacity of the sacks, but also the respective strengths of the llamas that would carry them, suggesting the notion of measure.[38]

Growing bodies of sound

Unlike, for example, *pinkillu* flutes that are said to have 'many holes', *julajula* tubes consist of a graduated sequence of bamboo tubes and take the form of

---

[38] This aspect of measure in the word *julay* was further highlighted by Ciprian Beltrán's example of cutting a piece of wood to length. He expressed this as *sumaq iwalananpaq* ('in order to equalize/match nicely').

vessels or receptacles – also suggested by their connection with the verb *julay*. They can be seen as a graduated sequence of receptacles – containing *animu* – where each represents a different stage or moment in the growth of a body.[39] This idea of growth was not only vividly expressed in the structure of *julajula* music, but also – as we shall see – in the zigzag (*link'u-link'u*) form of the players' dancing.

Julajula panpipes consist of a single row of tubes that can potentially be played from either side. In practice however, the short tubes are held on the player's left and the longest tubes to his right. The consistency of this orientation was striking, and on one occasion I was embarrassed to discover that I was the only member of a large ensemble holding my instrument the 'wrong way around'. This way of playing is consistent with many other types of Bolivian panpipes, such as *sikus*, where the player is forced to play with the shorter tubes to his left and longer to the right, due to the inclusion of a second parallel row of open tubes that cannot be sounded (Bellenger 1987:123). Several people remarked that *julajula* melodies always 'play from the left to the right' (*lluq'imanta pañaman tukukun*). Indeed, the melodies I encountered in Kalankira and many other parts of Macha territory consistently began on the shortest pipe of the four-tube *yiya* instrument and literally moved 'to the right', to end one octave lower on the longest pipe of the three-tube *arka*.[40] This orientation was very significant and in numerous contexts I was told that the living travel 'to the right' (*pañaman*) and the souls of the dead 'to the left' (*lluq'iman*). Similarly, I discovered – both from local discourse and practice – that rings of dancers almost always begin and end their dances by circling to the right, thereby ensuring that movements to the right framed those to the left.[41] In short, the movement of *julajula* melodies from left (short, high-pitched tubes) to right (long, low-pitched tubes) vividly invokes ideas of bodily growth, as individual development and accumulation. Each rendition of the tune – a descent of an octave and corresponding doubling in size – might be seen to chart a melodic journey from childhood to adulthood – a point made explicit in the accompanying dance. In addition, the balanced alternation between paired instruments, described above, suggests that an offspring may

---

[39] Each body is endowed with a given amount of *animu*, I was told, which remains constant throughout life. Thus this growth sequence would seem to concern the increase of bodily mass. See Chapter 2 for a discussion of *animu* and Stobart 2000:34 and 42 concerning analogies between the containment of *animu* in globular whistles (*wislulu*) used in healing practices and in living bodies.

[40] *Julajula* melodies in other parts of Northern Potosí sometimes begin on a larger tube of the *yiya*, but consistently end on the longest tube of the *arka*.

[41] Asencio observed that circling right and left were both *surti* (Spanish *suerte* 'fortune'), implying general 'wellbeing' and 'health'. He explained that circling to the left was for the *surti* of the souls of the dead (*almas*) and that to the right for our own *surti*, and in addition was related to the flow of *animu*.

only grow and become culturally mature through participation in social interaction and reciprocal exchanges.

The gradual nature of this transformation is evoked by the stepwise movement characteristic of *julajula* melodies; intervals of more than one step (within the pentatonic scale) are extremely rare, except on repeats and between sections. Progressive growth is also often invoked in other aspects of the musical structure. *Suna* melodies usually consist of two or three repeated sections, sometimes with an unrepeated final section acting as a coda (AABB, AABBCC or AABBC). The four-tube *yiya* ('elder brother') initiates each section, and it is common for each of these sections to begin with a progressively larger *yiya* tube (A = tube 1, B = tube 2, C = tube 3). Finally, the ends of melodies, and sometimes of individual sections, are characterized by a distinctive cadential gesture played between the longest tubes of the *yiya* and *arka* pair (Examples 6.2, 6.5 and 6.7). In this cadential formula, which is passed over quickly when the melody repeats, the *yiya* note almost suggests a brief moment of hubris – a stretching of the melody – before return to the 'tonal centre' played by the three-tube *arka* ('younger brother').[42]

In sharp contrast with the feeling of arrival evoked by the final cadences of *pinkillu* flute *wayñu* melodies of the rains (when the dancers literally stand in place for a moment before the tune is repeated CD tracks 22, 33 and 35), the meandering contours of *julajula* melodies are characterized by the impression of almost seamless continuity. Melodies tend to be repeated many times, so that without considerable familiarity it is often hard to identify their precise structure and repeat scheme. A sense of continuity and ambiguous structure is also sometimes heightened by variation in tempo and rhythmic unpredictability. Although the *suna* melodies I heard in Kalankira were of unusually regular rhythm, suggesting a local stylistic feature, those from many other parts of Macha territory and Northern Potosí typically defy assimilation into a regular pulse or metre. See CD track 8 and Example 6.7, recorded in Chayrapata in Macha territory.

In this latter example from Chayrapata, the alternation between the *yiya* and *arka* pair tends to be smooth and quite regular, but the characteristic manner in which players breathe between repeated pitches results in a slight delay. In a superb account of this rhythmic phenomenon in *ayllu* Chayantaka, Thomas Solomon has interpreted the groups of alternated notes between these repeated pitches as variable length 'phrases' (1997:450–51). Whether players actually perceive the melodies in this way is hard to ascertain, but this approach helps highlight the sense of irregularity. For example, the numbers of notes in groups from Example 6.7 would be:

‖: 5 + 5 + 2 + 4 + 2 + 3 :‖: 4 + 6 + 2 + 3 :‖: 5 + 2 + 3 :‖

---

[42] I use the term 'tonal centre' reservedly.

Three-tube *arka* set (upward stems)

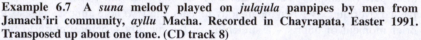

Four-tube *yiya (guía)* set (downward stems)

Example 6.7   A *suna* melody played on *julajula* panpipes by men from Jamach'iri community, *ayllu* Macha. Recorded in Chayrapata, Easter 1991. Transposed up about one tone. (CD track 8)

Julajula music seems to evoke powerful notions of inner growth and accumulation, a sense of seamless continuity, and unpredictability – ideas that also seem to find expression in the players' dancing.

The immortal snake

As they enter the towns of Northern Potosí accompanying their community cross, each troupe of *julajula* panpipes plays its own individual new *suna* melody for the feast, the players dancing in a long snaking file (*link'u link'u*) (Figure 6.4). Periodically circles (*rueda, muyun*) punctuate this serpentine choreography, the group tracing its unique cartography of the town, the square, and its approach to the church. As they sound their *suna* the group is in constant movement; the melody often merging with the noises of *tinku* fighting (CD track 6). On arrival, the players kneel in front of the church door, or inside before the altar, to perform a *kupla* (*kuwla, kulwa copla*) melody in 'adoration of the sanctuary'.[43]

The snaking *link'u link'u* is the most paradigmatic of the dances performed by *julajula* players. It usually consists of a file (*fila*) of between twenty and fifty players, led by an adult man, called the *punta* ('tip', 'peak'), who plays the largest (*machu*) four-tube *yiya* instrument. He should be 'strong' (*wirayuq*, literally 'fatty'), courageous and 'good at fighting', I was told, and is flanked

---

[43] However, for the entry into Macha during the feast of the Holy Cross, *wayli* groups tend to form into a tight group, rather than a snaking file, and rarely perform a *kupla* at the church. The *link'u link'u* is nonetheless performed on many other occasions during the week of festivities.

Figure 6.4   The snaking *link'u link'u* dance during ceremonies at the *alferéces* home during the feast of *cruz*. The dance is led by the player of the largest four-tube *yiya* panpipe

by the *imilla wawas* ('girl babies'); unmarried girls with white flags and whips – the only female participants in the *wayli*.[44] Immediately behind the *punta* comes another adult man playing the largest (*machu*) three-tube *arka* instrument, the *yiya*'s partner. In theory, instruments are played in progressively smaller sizes along the length of the file of dancers, although in practice precise size hierarchy was not observed. However, smaller instruments, such as *ch'ilis*, did tend to congregate near the tail – the players often holding both the *yiya* and *arka* pair together (*iraskillu*) enabling them to play the complete melody. I was told that a 'boy' should come at the very end of the file of *wayli* dancers – the *qhipa punta* ('back/behind tip'). He plays the smallest *wiswi* (or *chili*) paired set and initiates the melody (Figures 6.5 and 6.6).[45]

In practice this boy rarely played with the *wayli* group – presumably due to his tender age. However, I noticed his presence at the *calvario* and the

---

[44] The most common formation is two *imilla wawas*, one on each side of the lead dancer. However, I have also sometimes seen three or one.

[45] The role of this boy is not reported in other accounts of *wayli* performance that I have read. Paulino contrasted the boy as the *qhipa punta* ('behind tip') with the man at the dance's head, the *ñaypaq punta* ('front tip').

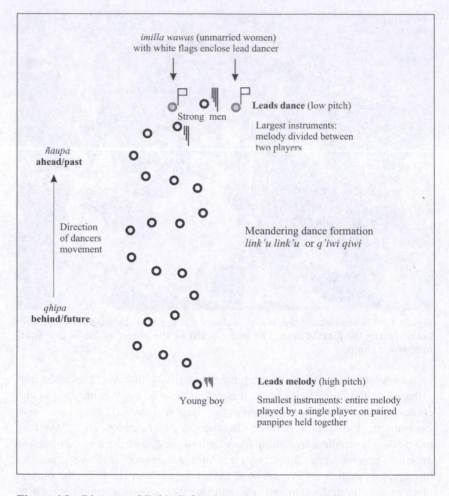

Figure 6.5   Diagram of *link'u link'u* dance

mayura's house on the eve of the feast and was struck by the way that he was requested to start the melody, following a break in playing. The boy initiated the melody playing his high-pitched *yiya* and *arka* set (*iraskillu*), and was gradually joined by the rest of the ensemble fitting lower pitched interlocking parts (This boy's high-pitched *wiswi* instrument is clearly audible on CD track 2.) According to Asencio, the boy and his role in the ensemble are referred to as *ch'ili* ('quite small'),[46] *irpita* (*irpa*) or *ira*, both the latter of which are

---

[46] According to Herrero and Sánchez, the Quechua *ch'ili* refers to objects that are relatively small but not the smallest category (1983:66).

common Aymara terms for the leader of a musical ensemble.[47] This suggests an interesting double hierarchy where the dance is lead by a mature adult man (*punta*) but the boy at the back of the line leads the music – which ultimately impels the dancers forward into battle.[48] According to Paulino, this youth should be some 10 years of age; on the cusp of adolescence yet still 'like a woman' (*warmijina*) – reminding us of the *malta kuchuy* ceremony described above. In this rite of passage, paired 'adolescent' (*malta*) male llamas depart the herd of female and young animals, which is tended by women and children and returned to a corral beside the family's homestead each evening. Following the ceremony, the *malta* llamas join the male herd that roams freely on the mountain peaks, occasionally overseen by the men. Periodically the male herd is rounded up, loaded with sacks of harvest or exchange products, to journey along meandering footpaths and dried-up river courses to the valleys or elsewhere, led – often in a long file – by the *delantero*, an outstanding animal chosen for its leadership, intelligence, knowledge and strength.[49] The male llama herd and its association with travel during the dry winter months would appear to serve as an important model for the organization of the *wayli* troupe and more generally for local constructions of gender.

With his immaturity, feminine associations and maximum distance from being a man, it is as though the boy at the end of the line symbolically remains on the cusp of dependency and the boundary of the female dominated sphere of the home (corral, field). Starting the melody on the smallest size instrument, and playing the entire tune – by uniting the *yiya* and *arka* instruments – is also evocative of the high-pitched, continuous and sentiment-laden weeping of an infant or for the dead (see Chapters 2 and 8). The other players are emotionally and morally bound to respond to this call, leading them to action and to advance through the dance, socially shaping this creative impulse into the independence and dialogic harmony of manhood. Each graduated step forward brings increase in size, descent in pitch, and – in the very separation and interlocking of the paired panpipes – the assertion of life.

Paulino compared the *link'u link'u* dance with a snake (*katari*) and went on

---

[47] It is evident from several studies that *ira* and *yiya* (Spanish *guia* 'guide') are used interchangeably to refer to the four-tube *yiya* instrument (Baumann 1979:38, 1996:32, Calvo & Sánchez 1991:10). See Sánchez 1996:87–95 for a detailed etymological discussion of the *ira* and *arka* principle.

[48] Similarly, Alberto Camaqui from *ayllu* Laymi compared the sound of the small high-pitched *julajula* that leads the *suna* melody to 'whistling' to bring the warriors into 'order'.

[49] I acknowledge inspiration from the work of Zegarra & Puma (c. 1997:16–17) concerning the parallel between the form of the *link'u–link'u* dance and that of a file of llamas. They also suggest associations of this choreographic motif with meandering rivers, intestines, footpaths and weaving motifs. These various metaphorical associations are also highly relevant for the case of Kalankira, although there is not space to develop them in depth here (see Stobart 1998a).

Figure 6.6 *Link'u link'u* **dance, showing the leader (*punta*) enclosed by unmarried girls waving white flags. (Photograph taken during the feast of *cruz* in Chayanta, where a similar dance formation is common, but different style dress is worn.)**

to mention that snakes do not die, but simply shed their skins periodically.[50] Besides close associations with devils, the inner earth, aggression and danger, snake imagery highlights ideas of length or prolongation – rather than ends. Indeed, Paulino's association of snakes with immortality should perhaps be interpreted as the privileging of life and its prolongation over death and birth. Certainly, compared to other dances of the year, the very length of the line of dancers is remarkable – especially when performed by large numbers. The way that each man dances singly (*sapallan*) is also notable especially when compared to *qhata*, the principal dance of the rains in which the dancers weave alternate arms in a circle enclosing the male musicians (Chapter 8). The relationship between these dances was highlighted when a circle of dancers holding hands was dramatically broken at the final climax of Carnival and moments later followed by *link'u link'u* dancing (Chapter 9). This vividly brought to mind several of the associations of the harvest season: the separation of offspring potato tubers from the earth (parent plant, and one another) at harvest, or young men setting out on independent journeys away

---

[50] Zegarra & Puma (c. 1997:15–16) also note an association between the meandering form of this dance and the snake, observing that the snake is the guardian of the mother earth.

from their parental home to work in the towns. In addition, the file of separate dancers is strikingly similar to the discrete tubes and pitches of *julajula* panpipes, and to the structure and orientation of the melodies they play.

The organization of the *link'u link'u* dance, where a boy plays the smallest instrument at the 'tail', and a fully-grown man, at the peak of his powers, plays the largest *yiya* instrument at the 'head', is highly suggestive of a progressive growth cycle from youth to adulthood. In this context, the unmarried *imilla wawas* ('girl babies'), who accompany the lead dancer, evoke not only their procreative potential and that of the personified 'fields' (*wirjin* literally 'virgin'), but with their white flags the very flowering or zenith of the man's life cycle.[51] Several people related these flags to 'potato flowers' (*papa t'ika*), and Paulino identified their connection with the use of white flags in Carnival, especially to mark the despatch of the souls of recently deceased men (see Chapter 9). In short, the mature, strong and courageous lead dancer, who sounds his large, deep and breathy *machu* ('ancestor', 'elder') panpipe, may be seen to embody notions of arrival, flowering, death, and regeneration (or procreation). Having literally reached the end of the line, with no further position to adopt, the player must confront his destiny. This idea of arrival, confrontation and realization is nicely conveyed in the following *cruz* song verses, in which *julajula* panpipes are compared to barley straw and referred to with the name *suqusu* ('bamboo'):

Suqusu suqusu siwara suqusu	Bamboo, bamboo, barley bamboo[52]
Ñawpis chamuniña maypitaq quykusun	Now I arrive in front, where will we give?

The verb stem *quyku-* ('give') in this context carries implications of (a) hitting an opponent (b) sexual intercourse, (c) understanding or realization and (d) generosity or self-destruction ('giving way'). It is as though, with his arrival, this man releases his pent up energies as a form of sacrifice for the benefit of others. As we shall see in Chapters 8 and 9, this is precisely how the powers of recently deceased men are harnessed during the rains to encourage the growth and fruiting of crops. However, as I noted above, the focus of the *wayli* dance is not on the extremities (head and tail) with their implications of death and childhood, but on its length – suggesting prolongation of life, as implied

---

[51] A more widespread term for these girls, in other parts of Northern Potosí and neighbouring areas, is *mit'ani*. Sparked by this name, Thomas Abercrombie has suggested that, alongside the military associations of *wayli* dance groups (with roots in sixteenth century *confradía* organization), such groupings may have been related to the local contingents of *mita* labourers which, until the nineteenth century, were taken to Potosí by appointed *mita* 'captains' (*mayuras*). Making this connection more explicit, Abercrombie cites the example of a custom linked to the *mita* and involving the year's *julajula* players that was performed in Kult'a until 1977 (1986:243–4, n.39).

[52] *Siwara* specifically refers to green fodder barley rather than grain barley (*grano*).

by Paulino's immortal snake analogy.[53] Thus, it would seem that the types of production associated with *julajula* panpipes and the *wayli* concern exchange rather than regenerative processes. It is as though the head and tail of the dance are located on the boundary or within the rainy season, whilst the rest of the dance – the growth cycle from youth to the flowering of manhood – stretches over the cold dry season. Once more the year comes to symbolize a microcosm of the human life cycle.

In the imagery of *julajula* music and *wayli* dancing we discover that regenerative processes are downplayed in favour of exchanges, which may involve monetary transactions. For example, Paulino declared that *ranti p'acha* ('bought clothes') – machine produced jumpers, jeans and scarves – should be worn for the pilgrimage to Macha at *cruz*, and contrasted this with Carnival when 'woven clothes' (*away p'acha*) or 'Indian clothes' (*indio p'acha*) of the *ayllu* are worn (Figure 6.7). Ideally the traditional dress for Carnival should be new and home woven, he insisted, reflecting a parallel between the growth and flowering of vegetation, which clothes the *ayllu* during Carnival season, and the weaving of new textiles to clothe its inhabitants, marking them as *runa*. In other words, for Carnival the production of clothing should take place within the *ayllu*, reflecting ancestral powers and traditions, and the community and its land as a locus of production, whereas for *cruz* the clothing should be produced outside the *ayllu* thereby invoking ideas of exchange, markets, money and journeys away from home community.[54] In addition, the wearing of bought clothing by the dancers at *cruz* was related to urban mestizo or *cholo* identity; men should go as *mozos* and women as *cholitas* I was told, terms used to refer to young lads or girls from the towns who wear urban-style dress. In short, through the dress respectively worn at *cruz* and Carnival, people 'produce' distinct forms of identity connected with particular modes of production.

---

[53] According to Harris (1988:4) *julajulas* are also played to expel epidemics, again highlighting their associations with life and health.

[54] Accounts of exchange journeys to the valleys often stress the bartering of local or subsistance products and notions of use-value, rather than the use of money. On my own journey to the valleys, it was principally salt and sugar (the latter purchased en route in the town of Ocuri) that were bartered for maize, squashes and wooden tool handles. Such forms of barter are the norm because, as Olivia Harris observes, products are generally more useful than money for valley dwellers living far away from markets. However, money is sometimes accepted from kin or members of the same *ayllu*, almost as a favour to avoid the need to carry huge loads of produce (1989:243). Although it might be tempting to associate bartering with nostalgic notions of a 'natural' economy, and the use of money with capitalist notions of accumulation and individual gain, Harris argues that in these contexts there is no systematic difference between monetary transactions and barter (1989:236, 243). In other words, the expressions of exchange surrounding the feast of *cruz*, and transactions it heralds, can and clearly do involve monetary transactions.

Figure 6.7 Left: *Away p'acha* **('woven clothes'). Right:** *ranti p'acha* **('bought clothes'). Modelled by Emiliano and Crispin Beltrán**

Left (a) Men's traditional Macha style dress, worn daily by most men and renewed at Carnival: woollen waistcoat, jacket and two pairs of trousers (white and black) tailored and traditionally woven (by men) in the *ayllu*. A white felt hat is worn over a woollen *ch'ulu* hat with earpieces, knitted by the men, and car-tyre sandals are typical.

Right (b) Purchased dress worn for *tinku* fighting at the feast of *cruz:* a *montera* fighting helmet (often with with large brightly coloured feather), a mass-produced patterned jumper, crossed brown (vicuña coloured) scarves, a manufactured carrying cloth tied at the waist, jeans or trousers, woven leggings (not shown here) and heavy boots or shoes.

Conclusions

Tinku continues to be treated by local civil authorities as brutal, savage, and uncivilized, while anthropological analysis has led to the idea of *tinku* as symbolic of balanced and creative intercultural exchange and dialogue. In the mid 1980s Tristan Platt invoked the 'balanced symmetry' of *tinku* in his call for an 'Aymara anthropology' which could engage on an equal footing with other global intellectual traditions and serve as a tool to break the hegemonic communicative circle (1987a:124). In recent years, this notion of *tinku*, as balanced intercultural dialogue and exchange, has acquired increasing global currency. The '*Tinku* Intercultural Network' (*Red Intercultural – Tinku*), which promotes relations between Andean and Nordic countries, presents the *tinku* as 'a confrontation of antagonistic and complementary powers; a dialogue of personalities, emotions, forces, experiences and concepts'.[55] The Bolivian 'Tinku-Macha' foundation has responded to these global interpretations of *tinku* as the 'search for a space for exchange, debate and the creation of new proposals to strengthen the project of native peoples in order to achieve a society which is more just, mutually supportive, free and equal, as an expression of the cosmovision of interculturality of native peoples' (Burgoa 2002:21). Alongside the local reality of *tinku*, a global network has identified its aspirations with the perceived values of *tinku*. It is as though the concept of *tinku* has taken on a life of its own, journeying outwards to find new contexts and meanings in a range of national and global settings.

The way that the concept of *tinku* has itself journeyed out into the world has striking resonances with some of the local approaches to this phenomenon and its associated music and dance at the feast of *cruz*. Connections with travel outside the community, dialogic harmony and male development, as a kind of rite of passage, permeate this music and dance. The insistence on wearing purchased, industrially produced clothing, evoking *mozo* or *cholo* (*mestizo*) identity, also harmonizes with this focus on places well outside the ancestral reproductive heart of the *ayllu*. But for the *mestizo* organizers of Tinku Macha Foundation, who aim to 'recuperate' the feast, return it to an imagined pure ethnic past and promote it as a tourist attraction, the wearing of manufactured clothing is interpreted as the corruption of tradition. In short, the dynamics surrounding *cruz* expressed to me in Kalankira suggest centrifugal movement away from the community, and entry into wider networks of exchange and accumulation – as a seasonally specific mode of production. By contrast, those invoked by the heritage perspective of the Tinku-Macha Foundation, suggest centripetal movement – a desire to return the 'Folk' to a pure idealized ancestral tradition, purged of modern corruptions such as purchased clothing. However, paradoxically this same notion of centripetal movement, as a return

---

[55] My translation (http://tinku.nativeweb.org/ftsearch.php) – accessed 10.3.2003.

to ancestral traditions and modes of (re)production within the *ayllu*, resonates well with the associations of the rainy season and especially Carnival, when people in Kalankira insist that home woven traditional *ayllu* dress should be worn. Here we discover that ideas about authenticity, whether 'cultural historical' or 'experiential', are underscored by the poetics of seasonally contrasted modes of production.[56]

Although it is common for one or two people to die in *tinku* each year, the musical and choreographic expressions of *cruz* precisely concern life. Both the long snaking *link'u link'u* dance and the seamless *julajula* melodies stress continuity and the prolongation of life. Perhaps this focus on prolongation – where the more male dancers included means the longer the snake – partly explains the widespread insistence on participation in the dancing and the fighting. In other words, participation is critical if life is to be sustained, as also evident in the term *qhespinakunku* ('one without the other would die out') to describe the dialogic performance technique of *julajula* panpipes. In turn, this helps us gain a better grasp of the approaches to production that underlie the troubling violence of *tinku*. I have suggested that the harvest season (*kusicha timpu*), a term often applied to the entire dry season, concerns life and bodily health, as powerfully expressed though the 'perfectly balanced' exchanges, or diachronic harmony, of *julajula* panpipe performance. How long can this symmetry and balancing act of life be maintained, as expressed by dancing along the immortal snake (one of the devil's creatures)? How long can the cycle of exchange and consumption, initiated by the mouse *charango* (Chapter 3), continue before the fruits of harvest start to run out and renewal becomes necessary? This will be the theme of the next chapter.

---

[56] See Bigenho (2002:18) on the distinction between 'cultural-historical' and 'experiential' forms of authenticity.

June–October
Cacophony, Community and the Water War

Saints, *siku* panpipes, and miraculous 'renewal'

> I would argue … that music is socially meaningful not entirely but largely because it provides means by which people recognise identities and places, and the boundaries which separate them (Stokes 1994:5).

From a scientific perspective seasonal transformation results from the annual rotation of the earth, which causes shifts in day length, temperature and precipitation. But through history and across cultures such alternation is often metaphorically related to power struggles between forces of darkness and light. The ancient Greeks connected winter with Persephone's sixth monthly sojourn in Hades, a period when darkness, cold and images of withering death characterized the visual realm of the living. With her annual return to the sphere of the living, came spring, bursting new plant life and the sovereignty of light.

This chapter is dedicated to Kalankira's expression of this seasonal metaphor, focusing on a local story of seasonal transformation. The tale focuses on a violent disagreement over access to water between the 'devil' (*yawlu*) – ruler of darkness and the inner earth who accumulates water for his own purposes, and god (*tiusninchis* – 'god of us all'), explicitly identified with the sun (*inti*) and known as *tata santisimu* ('holiest father') in libations, who seeks control over water for the good of humans. Although the elderly storyteller, don Adrian Chura, does not directly relate his account to seasonal transformation but rather to dispute over water, a common theme in the arid Andean environment, this dimension immediately occurred to my local transcription assistants. Unlike some other parts of the world, in this Andean context the circulation of water is intimately associated with solar transformation: the peak of the rains coincides with the summer solstice (December), and the greatest scarcity occurs around the winter solstice (June). This solstice/water connection is encapsulated in the widespread local belief that following the winter solstice, toads (*jamp'atu*) transform into doves (*urpi*), which are metaphorically related to clouds, suggesting transevaporation. Musically, this coincides with the shift in *charango* tuning and song genres from *cruz* to *san pedro* (Chapter 5). After the summer solstice in December the doves revert to toads, which are closely associated with the female gendered earth *wirjin* ('virgin') and the build up of water in damp, low places and water sources, suggesting downward hydraulic flow and accumulation in lower-inner places (see Torrico 1988).[1]

God's eventual defeat of the devil in don Adrian's story is only achieved through the combined actions of a group of local and regional saints. Their arrival – one by one – gradually shifts the balance of power in favour of god, bringing violent victory and 'renewal', seen in the miraculous circulation of water and new life for god's children. Their unity of purpose against a common enemy transcends the usual jealousies and regional identities with which these saints are normally associated and creates a kind of 'imagined community' (Anderson 1991). This chapter explores how a similar sense of transcending local boundaries, to invoke a broader musically imagined community, is expressed in *siku* panpipe performance. *Siku* panpipes are played during these same saints' feasts, which are celebrated through the dry winter months between late June and October, as the sun's power grows from its nadir at the June solstice through the spring equinox in late September. It is particularly remarkable that this equinox – the shift in power between the forces of darkness and light – is marked by a group of patronal feasts in which cacophonous *rinuwa* ('renewal') music is played. Significantly, don Adrian told me his fascinating story about god and the devil's conflict over water precisely to explain the need for performing wind music as 'consolation' (*kunswilu*) during saints feasts, and in particular the necessity for the cacophonous *rinuwa* music of late September.

Preparing the earth

The months before the winter solstice in June are a time of plenty, with the storerooms filled to maximum capacity from the year's harvest. But as the months after the harvest pass, people start to parcel out their supplies more carefully so that they will last through the rains. However, the pressure on human food seems minor compared to that on grazing land, which becomes increasingly scarce and a growing source of conflict. During my stay in Kalankira at this time of the year, ever more frequently Paulino and Asencio's families stayed at their lower altitude huts at Janq'u Loma, where there was less pressure on pastureland. There was no space for me in these tiny herding huts, so I sometimes found myself alone in Pata Kalankira hamlet, which for much of the time was silent and deserted. This isolation was heightened because many men spent the months between harvest and the start of planting as migrant labourers in the large towns, especially Cochabamba or Sucre, typically working in construction. But in late August people began to prepare for planting, and the momentum of community activity gradually grew, first

---

[1] For connections between toads, water and rainmaking in the Andes see, for example, Platt 1986:243, Berg 1989:109, and Rösing 1996:162.

with the *asintu* ceremony on 17 August (Chapter 5), shortly followed by the *kawiltu*. At *asintu*, the *siku* panpipes – which will be discussed in detail below – appeared for the first time that year.

On 28 August, I accompanied Paulino and Asencio to the *kawiltu* (Sp. *cabildo*) in nearby Ura Kalankira, an annual ceremony dating from the colonial period, where men from each household pay *tasa* ('land tax') for entitlement to plots of community land (see Platt 1982: 36–43). Even though each contributor's name was carefully ticked off in an exercise book, and the money was apparently taken to Potosí by one of the *cobradores* (Indian tax collectors) these payments had become almost purely symbolic and ceremonial – each household paying just 1 peso Boliviano, the price of a handful of sweets.[2]

The ceremony was overseen by the *alcalde* ('mayor') in whose presence, I was warned, music must not be played.[3] To ensure I had understood this, Asencio placed my *charango* on the ground and dramatically mimed jumping on it, whilst repeating the word *orden*, *orden* ('order, order'). This, he warned me severely is what would happen if I played in the *alcalde*'s presence, a vivid contrast to the usual requirement for music as 'consolation'.[4] It is tempting to imagine Spanish colonial policy lurking somewhere behind this tradition of musical prohibition, which evokes the smashing of instruments and suppression of music making of the seventeenth century Extirpation of Idolatry campaign (Arriaga [1621] 1999: 81–4, 169–71).

In the evening, after the *alcalde* had departed, music making began in earnest and continued for another day. Following the suppression of music, people's behaviour seemed considerably more riotous than usual with many drunken brawls and humorous parodies of other social groups. On the second day, several men dressed up in tattered old clothes, daubed green paint on their faces to represent bruises, and staged mock fights, in imitation of valley dwellers, who they presented as uncivilized and 'backward' (*lluq'i* which means both 'left', as in orientation, and 'left behind').[5] Alongside the riot of other music making, the mock 'valley dwellers' also made chaotic sounds on

---

[2] During the patronal feasts in September men took turns to run around astride a long pole, evoking a hobby horse-like mule referred to as *samba*. This hilarious buffoonery, I was told, represented the *cobrador* journeying to Potosí with the year's *tasa* payments.

[3] Similar restrictions also, apparently, apply for the case of the *jilanku* – another leading local position of authority.

[4] Paulino explained, that the *alcalde* and his wife are also the only people who do not participate in the entire community's final despatch (*kacharpaya*) of Carnival. Neither, he added, should they indulge in drinking alcohol or sexual intercourse during their year of office. However, this *alcalde* did not seem restrained by this restriction on alcohol. It was evident, as he sat on an upturned crate beside the *iskina misa* ('corner altar') making lewd comments, that he had already exceeded his capacity.

[5] This parody was referred to as *walli katuta*, ('valley walking sticks). The word *katu* was applied to the wooden handles for digging tools, such as the *lluqana*, that highland herders

pinkillu flutes, an instrument closely associated with the valleys, where they are made. Playing the *pinkillus*, both badly and in the wrong season, was also perhaps intended to invoke highland (*puna*) cultural superiority and relative cosmopolitanism.[6] While the *asintu* ceremony reflects preparations for the forthcoming growing season, as the gendered powers of the earth are brought into formal union, the *kawiltu* highlights the now symbolic payments made to the state for entitlement to communal land.[7] In particular, the *kawiltu* ceremony – with its suppression of music – inserts Kalankira into the historic workings, power and magic of the state. The final critical ingredient necessary to bring 'renewal', as the growth of crops and arrival of new life, is water. This resource is not only vital to life but also, as we hear in the following story, to understanding the music of the planting season.

(A) THE BATTLE FOR WATER – A STORY (Adrian Chura) [8]

A full translation of this story with the Quechua text is found in Appendix 1. To emphasise don Adrian's verbal artistry and dramatic style a recording of the first part of the tale is included on CD track 46. The English translation below is divided between narrative and dialogue sections in accordance with don Adrian's presentation.

[HS. Where do all the different instruments come from? For example, the *jula-jula* panpipes. From where? From what epoch do they come – those *wauku* [*julajula*] panpipes?]

1

Oh? Those *julajulas*? [HS. The *wayli* dance.] Oh that, our-god's feast, you want to know about that, with all that dancing, is that the question? Well, now then I'll tell you the story. Well, this is the way it is with those *wauku* [*jula jula*] panpipes.

2

Then god just like that, all by himself, watched and said:

[God] 'dammit! those devils are wanting to pester my children on

---

brought home on their exchange trips to the valleys. According to Paulino, people used to hobble around in old clothes imitating old men and using *katus* as walking sticks. This tradition is reminiscent of many Andean dances that parody old men with walking sticks (Turino 1993:95–9, Paredes-Candia 1991 [1960]:123).

  [6] Ironically, when I travelled to the valleys with my host family, several valley dwellers characterized highlanders as backward and claimed to provide maize for them to exchange because they felt sorry for them.

  [7] Platt observes that six-monthly meetings, known as St John and Christmas *cabildos*, approximately coincide with the religious festivals of 24 June and 25 December (1982:38–9).

  [8] I am most grateful to Pedro Plaza for his help in the translation.

every mountain. What will become of us? Well, damn it! What can I do?

3

'Well, my son.[9] Why don't you go out onto the mountains and look after my children. This damn devil wants to control the children; he always wants to dominate ['trample'] them.'

4

'Well then, as the miracles are being performed we will go and watch them, that's it.'

5

And then it's said that [Saint] Killakas led the lake from the sea [*lamar*].[10] And this lake went to the mountain of Potosí, right there. Right to that place.

6

[God to Devil] 'Dammit, my children go to the valleys, so then why are you holding back this lake? I'm going to make the watermill work – that's why I'm leading the water there.'

7

It is said that the hill spread-out of its own accord. The peaks flattened themselves down. In this way the mountains brought their respective rivers intimately together to make water capable of carrying sediments.

8

Then god [said]

'Damn and shit! Where will my children be able to go now that you've held up the water? What matters is the mill, not your children. When your children have wallowed in filth[11] they will crawl along there anyway. [The watermill] won't go damn and shit! All that stuff [building, hardening] you are doing deep inside is [just making work] for the millstone damn it! We shall have to come face to face over this, damn you!'

9

It is said they met with determination.

10

[God] 'Who do you think you are? – making enemies with my children and holding up the water like that. It will not be like that! All right, let's fight! All right that's it!'

11

Father Saint Killakas appeared first and was beaten up by the devil who carried him just by himself.

12

---

9 Presumably god is addressing one of his saints.

10 Although derived from the Spanish word for 'sea' (*la mar*), the local concept of *lamar* also implies water contained within the body of the earth (without implications that this is saline).

11 Literally, 'done that messy thing'.

[Killakas] 'Well, he held me up all by myself'
complained that *paruma* [saint] to god.
13

> [God] 'It must not be like this! He grabbed you?'
> [Killakas] 'Yes, he grabbed hold of me'.
> [God] 'There are four or five of you, go and live in [take over] all the
> mountains. It's not going to be like this!'

14

Well, then my master, father Mankiri, did something.
15

> [Mankiri] 'I will go and stand in the narrow *watul* place (*watulk'ulku*)
> father. You can recruit me for that.'
> [God] 'Alright go there my child.'

16

Well then there's Panakachi. Father Panakachi came here – as three brothers.
Then Panakachi [said]:
17

> 'Those devils always cause us losses.[12] Also when people fight we
> hurt one another. Damn it! I will be a healer and relieve the pain
> through curing', he said.

18

So then there was the great mama Copacabana and she lived in the lake it's
said, that mama Copacabana.
19

> 'Well, I will hit [the devil] with a golden staff damn it! Let's see damn
> it! Now he'll see' she said, saying 'give me a golden staff father'.

20

> [God] 'Alright, I shall bring it to you my child dammit! Who's going
> to guard dammit? You have to safeguard the children'. Saying, 'You
> will strike with the stick, hit with the golden staff'.

21

> [Copacabana] 'Alright father, 'she said, 'that's it'.

22

And then father Turaqhari also said:
> 'Forge me a silver helmet, a good quality silver helmet, and also
> make me knuckle-dusters, good quality silver knuckle-dusters. Forge
> knuckle-dusters for me, bring them to me father.'

23

> [God] 'Alright, with those you will fight ['give'].'

24

---

12 In Kalankira the word *susuri* used here was applied to illness or loss of animals when, for
example, correct offerings had not been made.

So it was that in this way god brought together father Mankiri, then father Killakas, father Panakachi, father Exaltación, and then father Turaqhari it is said.[13] Along with father Exaltación they all got together and approached the devil.

25

> [Saints] 'All right, you bastard, still no water? Are you still not going to liberate the water?'

26

> [Devil] 'I still need to drive it, damn you! There's more work to be done. Your children are not important.'

27

> [Saints] 'So you are not going to let the water out? That's it then, we'll fight.'

28

The devil also stood up [and faced them] it is said. Well, then they had an encounter with the devil it is said. Then father Turaqhari, the one with the silver knuckle-dusters, gave the devil a blow here on his twisted nose *k'iq umm!!* knocking him to the ground. Then mama Copacabana hit the devil with her staff.

29

> [Copacabana] 'What do you want to do? What do you want? Release this water, damn you! Give it for the children; we are the owners of the children. You'll see! Do it, do it!'

30

The devil was completely smashed up, his nose and horns completely destroyed, it's said. That's the way it was dammit. They all grabbed him [saying] 'You're like a lout damn you', and all tied the bastard up. They beat him as they tied him. Those fathers Killakas and Mankiri [said] 'We'll puncture him, that bastard.' He was trampled down *'pum puuw'*. Right then the water disappeared into the depths – *KUM!*

31

They tied him up, and from then to this day it is said that father Killakas treads down the devil. Like that, horribly tied-up he's trodden down. Because of this Killakas exists and those sanctuaries, and thus god and those guardians.

32

> [God] 'Well, how are the children going to console us? Now my child, you will be taken and such miracles will be given. I will give you all these miracles and with that you will be looked after with great respect, taking special care, with great respect.'

33

---

[13] Clearly, don Adrian misses several saints from this list.

[Mankiri] 'Well father, you will determine a place for me to reside. Well, I father Mankiri, will stand in a ravine and bridge it with the arms of my cross. There I will trample on him [the devil].'

34

So they scattered about in the Killakas place, dividing themselves. Because of that, in every hill there are mother and father from that time; if not there would not have been any [parents] for you. And then there is the father saint of the True Cross (*tata santa wila kurus*) and there is god.

35

[God?] 'Well I'm placing you [saint of the True Cross] to be a miracle. Well, now you will pass this on to all the children. When they give you this news, let us have it told as if to their mothers and fathers.'

36

So I've told you all this, said like that. Well, there it is! That's why *waukus* [*jula jula* panpipes], *sikus* [panpipes], brass bands, and those *ch'unchu's* quenas [notch flutes] go passing on this message of consolation. Because of 'renewal' it's said.

The context of the water war

Water is a central component in the Inka history of human origins. The god Wiracocha sent the various peoples he created along subterranean waterways to their specific places of emergence (*pacarinas*), where they could claim rights to lands and waters for their descendents (Sherbondy 1992:54). The various peoples and 'nations' emerged from springs, rivers or caves with their own distinctive dress, languages and songs, their common origins transformed to locally differentiated markers of identity according to the quality of water (Betanzos 1968:9; Molina 1943:8). As he drank water collected from one of Kalankira's springs, Paulino remarked that the language we speak depends on the water of the place that we come from, which explains why he speaks Quechua, others speak Spanish or Aymara, and I speak English. On other occasions I was told how the aqueous *sirinus*, musical devils who bring the new *wayñu* melodies each year and wear the distinctive local dress of the *ayllu* during Carnival, emerge 'like water' along little tubes through the earth (Chapter 9).[14] This highlights a close equivalence between the distinctive local 'flavour' of water and music, and a parallel between the flow of water and (musical) sound.[15] Here, I simply wish to stress the centrality of water to

---

[14] *Sirinus* and their enchanting musical powers are especially associated with 'clear' (*ch'uwa*) spring water, a clarity, quality and taste acquired on its underground journey from the great celestial and inner sea (*lamar*).

ethnogenesis, and its critical importance as both a source of life and to seasonal transformation. Hardly surprisingly it is also one of the most politically charged and contested resources in the Andean region.[16]

The initial image evoked by don Adrian's story suggests that God is in a weak position in relation to the devil(s). In a seasonal context, its opening is suggestive of the winter solstice, the time when the sun's (God's) strength is at its annual nadir, and the devil's power at its zenith. According to Asencio, the devil was fathered by San Juan (24 June) thus highlighting his association with the winter solstice.[17] He was born on *papa santa loma* ('sacred potato hill'), mothered by *doña flojita* ('lazy lady'), the consort of the wind (*wintura* 'venture').

The imagery of the lake being led from the sea by the saint Tata Killakas is made even more powerful by the use of the verb *pusay*, which exclusively refers to leading people or animals.[18] The lake's destination – the famous mountain of Potosí – is indeed surrounded by many man-made lakes, that have historically been used to process Potosí's extraordinarily rich mountain of silver, which has brought immense wealth to some and hardship for most (Baptista Gumucio 1988:29). *Supay* (the devil) hoards all the water for himself, behaving in a way that all 'devils' (*yawlus*) do: *q'iwa*, or mean and selfish, a word that is of immense importance in music (Chapter 8). God wants the water in order to run his watermill at Guadalupe (story paragraph 6) and to create *wawas*, a word meaning both human 'babies' and used metaphorically to refer to new food crops. The reference to Guadalupe has a multitude of local resonances for Kalankira. It is a village with several watermills in the *chawpirana*, the region midway between the highlands and warm valleys (Map 3), where we stopped on our winter journey to the valleys. Guadalupe is also the female patron saint of Kalankira, referred to as *mamanchis* 'our mother', whose feast is celebrated in early September. Does don Adrian's story imply that the 'mother' of the community is seen to grind down and

---

[15] Classen highlights this parallel observing that 'sound, like water, vivifies the cosmos (1991:241), where music is often played explicitly to imitate the sound of running water (Zuidema 1986a:185).

[16] See Mitchell & Guillet (1994). The recent 'water wars' of Cochabamba, over control of the city's water by a foreign multinational company, highlight the volatility surrounding access to water in Bolivia (Laurie, Andolina & Radcliffe 2002). Access to the sea, following Bolivia's loss of its coastline to Chile in the war of the Pacific, also remains a running sore in the nation's psyche – marked by the display of national flags each year on the 'day of the sea'. Several researchers have noted hydraulic approaches to the division of space (Urton 1981:43, Sherbondy 1992, Zuidema 1986a, Arguedas 1985 [1956]) and the concept of the 'hydraulic mountain', which is equated with the circulatory system of the human body (Bastien 1978, Arnold 1988).

[17] The feast of San Juan was identified with the winter solstice, when the sun is 'small' (*juch'uy*).

[18] Asencio related this part of the story to our own upward journey with llamas a few months earlier, carrying valley products for deposit in highland storerooms.

transform old embodied forms (like grains) to bring renewal – evoking the process of cooking?

God's orientation to redistribution stands in vivid contrast with the devil's tendency to accumulate. Transformation and redistribution is also evoked in God's plan to circulate water as though hills are mating with one another, and their rivers flow 'intimately' together (paragraph 7). Such metaphorical language has many resonances with local concepts of reproduction in humans and animals. But god's works of renewal are hindered by the devil, suggesting that the devil makes his children hard, strong and resistant so that they cannot be easily crushed by the millstone (paragraph 8), recalling the devil's association with the bell stones and other rocks around the landscape of Kalankira (Chapter 2).

Only through the active participation and sacrifices of the saints is the devil finally defeated, the water released and 'renewal' realized in the miraculous birth of new offspring. Their collective action is reminiscent of social practices in Kalankira which ensure that no individual acquires excessive resources or power (see Turino 1989:4). The saints are all referred to as 'fathers' (*tatas*) and 'mothers' (*mamas*), general terms of respect used for any adults. These titles confer adult status, with the responsibility to care, protect and provide for children, and contrast with the more youthful devil, who is referred to as *machu machu* (paragraph 30), a word also applied to loutish young men. This permits speculation that the devil's relationship to god parallels that of young people to adults; an idea supported by several local people. Both represent definable phases in the transformation of a single body through time, even if they are manifested as distinct in the story.

The gradual coming together of saints in this tale also suggests the passing of various patronal festivals leading up to All Saints, the start of the rains. (However, their order of appearance in the story does not precisely match the sequence of their feast days.) People from Kalankira actively participate in their own patronal feasts of Mama Guadalupe and Tata Exultación in early September, and many attend the *rinuwa* feast of Mama Copacabana in nearby Tomaykuri later in the month. The name for the feast of All Saints (*todos santos*) acquires a new localized relevance, where 'all the saints' – through their joint participation – realize this seasonally specific Andean miracle: the provision of water and rain.[19]

The Saints and their Feast Days (in order of appearance in the story)
24 September   Tata Killakas
late June[20]   Tata Mankiri (September: procession through Potosí)
14 September   Tata Panakachi (Feast of Exultación in Panakachi, prov. Bustillos)

---

[19] The saints' violent destruction of the devil may be reflected in the large, and particularly brutal, *tinku* battle traditionally held in the town of Macha for All Saints. Asencio and Paulino told me that this particular *tinku* was much more dangerous than the one for *cruz* in May.

[20] A moveable feast.

23 September   Mama Qupaqhawana (Copacabana) (golden staff)
8 October   Tata Turaqhari (silver knuckle dusters, helmet)
14 September   Tata Exultación – mentioned later when saints attack

Following their victory the saints scatter about the hills, creating a sacred landscape as a memorial to new generations of children, where the miraculous *tata wila kurus* with his special association with harvest takes pride of place (Chapter 6). The saints continue to 'trample' the devil, suggesting that, like the shifting character of the seasons, their encounter with the devil is an ongoing struggle, and they must be continuously consoled with music, which serves to pass on the message of this miraculous story of *rinuwa* ('renewal'). The direct references to music only at the very beginning and end of don Adrian's story highlights how music's significance goes well beyond the purely 'musical' and is intimately connected with the most fundamental transformations in life cycles.

It is in the patronal feasts that these saints are commemorated and consoled, both through the performance of *siku* panpipes in Kalankira's own feasts and of cacophonous *rinuwa* music in late September. This *siku* music is, in many respects, exceptional with much closer links to urban-national genres and repertoires than any of the other musics performed in Kalankira. This close identification with the music of other powerful social groups means that connections with agricultural practices are less explicit, but it is striking how this more nationally orientated music, alongside an apparent obsession with skins and drums, is restricted to this particular time of year.

(B) THE PATRONAL FEASTS – *SIKU* PANPIPES

Most of the saints' feasts in the Macha area are celebrated between July and September; a relatively slack time between the completion of harvest and the most intensive planting.[21] This period is known as *muyu fiesta* ('round and round feast') as the local priest is constantly on the move, travelling from one small church to the next. Before acquiring a jeep he was unable to return home for many weeks. For most small outlying churches, like that of Kalankira, this is the only mass of the year and these feasts one of the few occasions that the church is unlocked. In 1991, this was also almost the only time that a motorized vehicle drove into Kalankira, requiring community members to spend several days preparing the road for the priest's jeep. Kalankira's two patronal feasts, Mama Guadalupe and Tata Exultación (Guadalupe's consort), are both held in September. In contrast to other feasts, much of the ritual

---

[21] This pattern is common elsewhere in the Central-Southern Andes. See, for example, Sallnow 1987:179. However, Harris notes a decline in the number of saints' day feasts celebrated among the Laymis (1982b:93), which also also seems to hold true for the Macha region.

focused on the church and the procession of its saint icons to and from the sponsors' homesteads. Aside from the presence of the priest at the feast of Guadalupe (1 September), the intensive festivities and elaborate range of customs (*kustumbri*) for these two feasts were in most respects identical. Both were divided into four days:

1   *Uywa wañun* (animal slaughter) – eve of feast day
2   *Pasante* (main feast day)
3   *Ch'iwu* (parodies of domestic animals) [22]
4   *Servicio mikhuchiku* (feeding of the helpers)

While my role in Guadalupe was balanced between active participation and observation of the huge array of events and customs, in Exultación I participated fully as a member of the *siku* panpipe band (*tropa*). In both feasts, paired eight tube (*primero*) and seven-tube (*segunda*) *siku* panpipes were played throughout, using interlocking technique between paired players, and accompanied by a large bass drum (*tinri* or *bombo*). The ensemble usually consisted of six members, led by Lorenzo and Nicolas Mamani, two elderly brothers, who played the pair of larger *sanqa* instruments (Example 7.1, Figure 1.2). Four less competent players (myself included), played the two pairs of smaller instruments (*ch'ilas*), pitched one octave higher (Figure 7.1).[23]

Unlike Kalankira's two other principal wind genres, *siku* panpipes are always accompanied by a double-skin bass drum (*bombo*, *tinri*), on this occasion played and owned by Nicolas, the eight-tube *sanqa* player.[24] The *bombo* skin was kept highly tensioned and care was taken to keep it dry and supple. For example, performances were halted periodically while a fire was made to dry and tighten the drum skin, and in hot weather the skin was regularly smeared with *trago* (cane alcohol).

Sikus are strongly associated with patronal festivals and, despite the

---

[22] See Platt 1987b:156–63 and Abercrombie 1998:377, 388–92 for accounts of similar customs.

[23] *Sikus* usually incorporate two parallel rows of tubes of equal lengths, an open-ended row placed behind the set closed at the lower ends (from the player's perspective). The function of these open tubes, which are not blown directly, has been the subject of considerable debate, the two most usual explanations are that they (1) add strength to the instruments – so that they do not fall apart or crack so easily – and (2) reinforce the upper octave or harmonics (Langevin 1987:104). Another consequence of the addition of this second row of open tubes, which do not sound if played directly (only resonating in sympathy with the respective blocked tube, to produce a sound one octave higher), is that the player is forced to hold the instrument with the (a) short high-pitched tubes to his left, and (b) long, low-pitched ones to his right. This is obviously the reverse to, for example, the piano (Bellenger 1987:122). I have already discussed the significance of this orientation for the case of *julajula* performance (Chapter 6).

[24] Thomas Solomon notes that in *ayllu* Chayantaka playing the *bombo* and *sikus* occupy separate roles, where the *bombo* player stands in the centre of the circle of *sikus* (1997:141). In Kalankira and many other parts of Northern Potosí that I have visited the *bombo* has always been played by one of the *siku* players.

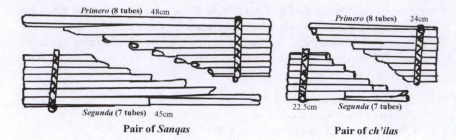

Figure 7.1   Diagram of *siku* panpipes showing relative instrument sizes

Kalankiras' insistence that they are dry season instruments which attract frost
and wind, I have encountered them in saint feasts during the rains in several
other parts of Northern Potosí.[25] Their primary role was 'to make the sponsors
dance' I was told, but they also provided music for processions and special
pieces to honour the saints. Compared to *julajulas* and *pinkillus*, playing *sikus*
was considered the realm of specialists, in part due to the large repertoire and
oral adeptness needed to rapidly work out one's part in a melody. Feast
sponsors from communities without their own ensemble often contract outside
siku bands, paying them with, for example, sacks of maize or potatoes.[26] It is
perhaps significant that Lorenzo, the leader of Kalankira's ensemble, owned
very little land, few animals and spent much of the year working in Sucre.[27]
This suggests that the semi-professional aspect of *siku* performance may have
served as a strategy to improve his economic situation and somewhat
ambiguous social standing in the community. *Siku* bands do not expect to
receive economic rewards for playing in their own communities, but are
treated with immense respect and consideration during the patronal feasts.
Special plates of food were brought to the ensemble by the *alférez* himself, and
great care was taken to ensure that we had a constant supply of corn beer and
cane alcohol. The goodwill and participation of the *siku* players was seen as
paramount to the success of the feast.

    Thomas Solomon has suggested that *siku* panpipe performance is a recent
introduction to the Northern Potosí region and that the impetus for playing

---

[25] For example, the feast of Santa Barbara in Salinas in January.

[26] The hiring of musical ensembles for saints' feasts is widespread; see for example Sallnow
1987:182.

[27] Lorenzo, who died in about 1994 (around the same time as his brother Nicolas), was a
bachelor, the church sacristan, a healer (*paqu*), and the *subcentral* – the local representative for
the peasant union (*sindicato*). He was an outrageous, complex and often irascible character, with
great ability as a *siku* player. He shared a homestead with his other brothers Nicolas and Nolberto,
who had been widowed several years earlier.

Example 7.1 *Siku* **panpipe** *huayño* **played during the feast of Guadalupe. Lorenzo Mamani can be heard whistling the melody through his teeth before the panpipes commence. (CD track 10)**

came from school teachers, beginning in the 1960s or early 1970s (1997: 143–4). Like Solomon, I have encountered conflicting views about the antiquity of *siku* performance (Stobart 1987), although in the case of Kalankira their introduction seems to be somewhat earlier. Don Adrian, who claimed to be about eighty, assured me that he had played in a *siku* band in his teens, which suggests that these instruments had been played locally since at least the 1940s.[28] Whatever their history, *sikus* continue to have strong associations with other regions and other social groups. *Mestizo* or *cholo* specialists usually construct them, whereas peasant artisans living in the valleys make the other local wind instruments.[29] Alongside the instruments themselves, the repertoire and genres played on *sikus* are associated with and acquired from towns or other regions. Several of the melodies we played were claimed to have come from Challapata or Yamparaez, near Tarabuco, and the principal dance genre was the urban/national style *huayño* (Example 7.1), which is markedly different in style, rhythm, and choreography from the

---

[28] Adrian's younger brother Siciliano, who also played in this *siku* band, mentioned that their father had taught them to play and that there had been another local group at the time.

[29] The two sets of instruments played in Kalankira in 1991 were made respectively in Condo (near Challapata, department Oruro) and in the market town of Llallagua (Map 1). I often encountered makers from Condo on trading trips to Macha and other parts of Northern Potosí.

identically pronounced rainy season *wayñu*.[30] While all the other genres of
Kalankira are pentatonic, *sikus* are constructed to play a seven-note diatonic
scale, which is more common in urban contexts. However, many *siku*
melodies are essentially pentatonic in character. Also, the tuning of this
diatonic scale, the precise intervals of which vary considerably between
individual *tropas* (sets of instruments), has a tendency for neutral intervals
(such as a rather flat leading note).

The *siku* band played four main genres connected with specific activities:
huayños, *dianas*, *coplas* and a *marcha*. For the most part we stood in circle
around a pot of corn beer and a bottle of diluted cane alcohol (Figure 1.2) and
played an almost constant stream of *huayños*, to provide 'consolation'
(*consuelo*) or merriment (*alegría*). Unlike *pinkillu* or *julajula* music, where a
single new melody acquired for the feast was often repeated constantly for
several days, the *sikus* performed a large repertoire of old and new tunes. Also
in contrast with *pinkillu* flute *wayñus* or the *suna* melodies of *julajula*
panpipes, I encountered no sense that new *siku* melodies should be acquired
annually (see Chapter 9). Most melodies were repeated five or six times and
then, after a brief drink of corn beer or cane alcohol, a different melody began.
Sometimes Nicolas and the *ch'ila* players would have scarcely grasped the
tune before Lorenzo, who claimed to know 120 *huayños*, instigated yet
another – often a previously unheard melody.[31] Periodically, the stream of
huayños would be punctuated by a *diana* ('fanfare'), played to mark the
reception of a gift (*arku*) by the sponsors, such as a bank note placed in their
hats.[32]

At dawn on the first day of the feast (*pasante*) the *siku* band entered the
church, removing their hats and, with an immense sense of devotion and
seriousness, knelt facing the altar to play a series of *copla* (*kuwla*) in honour
of the saints and church (CD track 14). *Coplas* were played on several other
days, usually in sets of three – each one repeated three times. After playing,
the musicians always walked backwards to exit the church, facing the altar as
a mark of respect. Whenever the saint icons were carried in a procession
between the church and sponsors' home, the same slow and stately *marcha*
('march') was always played (CD track 13) (Example 7.2).

A common feature of many of the *huayños* we played was a rising stepwise

---

[30] To differentiate these genres I use Spanish (*huayño*) and Quechua (*wayñu*) orthography
respectively. For further background on the Bolivian *huayño/wayño* see Paredes-Candia 1991
[1966]:70–87, Thorrez Lopez 1977, Leichtman 1987 and Wara Céspedes 1993:52.

[31] According to Ramiro Gutierrez, in parts of department Oruro, *siku* bands sometimes compete
to play the largest number of melodies (personal communication).

[32] It is also common practice in other parts of Bolivia for brass bands or, for example, *musiñu*
duct ensembles (Stobart 1998b:286–87), to play a *diana* to mark the reception of a gift by the
sponsor or crate of beer for the musicians.

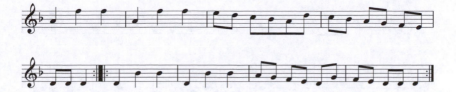

Example 7.2 *Marcha* **played on** *siku* **panpipes (main melody) during the feast of Exultácion. Transposed down about one semitone. (CD track 13) Some listeners may hear this melody as anacrustic (that is, starting with a crotchet upbeat). However, the perception of an anacrusis would probably not be shared by people in Kalankira (see Stobart & Cross 2000)**

motif that initiated the third and final repeated section of the melody. This appeared to function both as an emblem or musical marker of the ensemble, and as a means to easily extend melodies from two to three sections (Examples 7.3, 7.4 and 7.5). The distinction between *siku* and *julajula* construction, performance practice and repertoire is notable, as summarized below, and highlights the contrast between notions of the local (or regional) and the national.

Jula-jula panpipes (May)	*Siku* panpipes (August-October)
bamboo (*suqusu*) from valleys	thin cane from tropical zones (see Chapter 6)
4 + 3-tube pairs (single raft)	8 + 7 (or 7 + 6)-tube pairs (usually double raft)
strictly symmetrical interlocking	asymmetrical interlocking (see Chapter 6)
rural makers (mainly)	specialist makers, often *cholos* or *mestizos*
played without percussion	played with bass drum (and sometimes side drum)
local/rural genres	*cholo*/urban (national) genres
small repertoire (*suna*, *kulwa*)	large repertoire (*huayños*, *marchas*, *dianas*, *coplas*)
new *suna* melody each year	new and old repertoire (technique/memory)
non-specialist performers	specialist semi-professional performers
dance in file, separate (men only)	accompany dancers in lines, holding hands (m/f)

In some areas *sikus* are increasingly substituted for the more prestigious, expensive, and louder option of brass bands. Indeed, Lorenzo and Nicolas sometimes fantasized about following the precedent of a village some five hours walk away, Castilluma, and forming their own brass band. From their perspective, *sikus* and brass bands were in most respects equivalents; both perform an essentially national repertoire and are hired, in a semi-professional capacity, by the sponsors of patronal feasts. Significantly, don Adrian ends his story of the saints by listing *siku* panpipes alongside brass bands as instruments that should be played to console the saints; the two fulfilling essentially the same function. Although various other local instruments may also perform, the specific requirement for patronal feasts in Kalankira – and elsewhere in Northern Potosí – is for the *siku* (or brass band), both closely linked with outside social groups.

It is fitting that *sikus*, the instruments played for the saints' feasts focused

Example 7.3

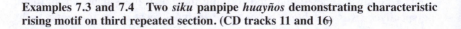

Primeros (8 tube set) upward stems

Segundas (7 tube set) downward stems

Example 7.4

Examples 7.3 and 7.4   Two *siku* panpipe *huayños* demonstrating characteristic rising motif on third repeated section. (CD tracks 11 and 16)

around churches, should – like the church and the priest, who often attends such feasts – have such strong exogenous associations. Harris has differentiated between, on the one hand, 'locally based, bounded and secret' knowledge of the inner world, connected with local mountains, shamanism, fertility and remote ancestors, and on the other, that of 'priests who communicate with the deities of the upper world, come from outside, speak foreign languages, and are part of a global organization and hierarchy'. As

Harris stresses, this correlation is far from complete, but identification of the inner world with the local, and the upper world with the exogenous, has considerable salience (1995b:115). As Seeger suggests for the case of the Amazonian Suyá, the performance of music derived from other social groups may be seen as a means to 'incorporate the power and material resources of the outsider into the reproduction of their own society and simultaneously establish the otherness of the others and the changing, growing selfness of themselves' (1993:33). Perhaps, the association of patronal saints with exogenous music, like Andean pilgrimage in general, is a means to 'recharge' local sources of power – as if inserting them into a cosmic or national grid (Sallnow 1987:180).

The performance of regional and urban-national derived genres, which in certain respects transcend distinctions of class and ethnicity, can be seen as a way to invoke a wider 'imagined community' or (emic) notion of 'nation' (Anderson 1991). *Siku* music emerges as a medium through which the Kalankiras are united with fellow Bolivians – a form of musical lingua franca or 'interculture', divided from their other local musics or 'micromusics' (Slobin 1993, Blacking 1987:96). The pairs of (hand-made) paper national flags worn in the sponsors' hats (for both feasts in 1991) evoked this sense of a broader imagined community, and the idea of insertion into the exogenous power networks symbolized by, for example, the nation, and institutions of the state or church.[33] Anderson's notion of 'pilgrimage', as a growing consciousness of connectedness to some wider 'imagined community', may also be helpful here (1991:54–65). The role of *alferéz* – Kalankira's most prestigious and onerous sponsorship role – suggests not only deeper integration into the community but also increasing consciousness of and connectedness with powers, people and places from well beyond its boundaries. A similar sense was evoked by the collaboration of the various regional saints in don Adrian's story: a disparate group forced to come together to achieve a common goal. This is also reminiscent of the national draft for the disastrous 1932 Chaco war against Paraguay, which generated mutual awareness between different levels of Bolivian society, and led indirectly to the 1952 national revolution (Klein 1992:194, Dunkerley 2003:144). Indeed, don Adrian's words are suggestive of the local honouring of heroes who fought for the nation and patronal feasts can in some sense be seen as expressions of remembrance.

In contrast to the circulation and reciprocal encounters evoked during the

---

[33] The national flag, familiar from schools and the police station (and in towns) immediately conjures up associations with state institutions and associated forms of knowledge, power and control. Asencio associated it with the rainbow, a potent symbol of power Andeans link with the *amaru* serpent and sometimes the local distribution of water. Allen notes that in Southern Peru the rainbow serpent is said to siphon water from one spring to another as he arches his body across sky following rain (1988:53).

harvest feast of *cruz* in May (Chapter 6) suggesting entry into exchange networks and markets, the *siku* music and imagery of the patronal feasts of September invoke wider spheres of power – perhaps extending to the very boundaries of the nation as a form of conceptual body.[34]

Dancing around the skins

On the eve of both feasts people congregated in the sponsors' llama corral where, following several hours of libations to almost constant *siku* music, the llamas and sheep to be slaughtered were selected from the herd (Figure 7.2). The *siku* band followed the remaining animals out of the corral, playing constantly while the *alférez* sprayed them with corn beer. The musicians continued some way up the mountainside to the *chisiraya*, a stone associated with the herd's fertility, which was circled before returning to the corral. As we arrived back in the corral during the feast of Guadalupe, a player turned to me and explained that this music had been to encourage 'llama mating' (*llama arqinapaq*). Music continued, or *kunswilu* 'consolation' as it was termed, as beautiful home woven cloths were laid out over the selected animals, as if clothing them. Their throats were swiftly slit and a little blood daubed on each person's cheeks and the instruments as a blessing (*bendición*). As in other similar ceremonies, I was overcome by the immense respect shown for the animals rather than the horror of slaughter. After the animals had been skinned, their pelts were carefully laid out on the ground and the *alferéces* were led around them in a dance called the *pusariq* ('leader').

The four dancers held hands in a line, with the *alféreces* in the centre, the male *aysiriq* ('puller') to the right and the female leader to the left (Figure 7.3). Followed by the *siku* band walking behind in single file, the *aysariq* led the dancers around the entire group of skins a few times. Then circling one or two skins at a time, starting from the smallest (number 5) he led them up the dance to the stud llama (*lantiru* number 1). Having reached the top of the dance, the female leader then led them back in the opposite direction, moving clockwise around the skins. A few days later the *aysariq* explained to me that the *pusariq* dance was 'to make a reversal to take place' (*kutichimpunapaq*), thereby causing the domestic animals to multiply.

Only during the two patronal festivals in September did I see the skins of animals slaughtered for feasts laid out on the ground and the *pusariq* dance performed. The focus on skins occurred again in the final ceremonies when, just before the *siku kacharpaya* ('despatch of the *sikus*'), the *alferéz* placed the

---

[34] The metaphor of the body as a means to understand political, territorial and cosmological units and their boundaries has deep historical roots in the Andes (Classen 1993) as elsewhere (Douglas 1994 [1966]).

Figure 7.2   Kalankira's *siku* panpipe band during the *uywa ñakakun* ('animal slaughter'). Feast of Guadalupe

Example 7.5   *Siku* panpipe *huayño* played to accompany *pusariq* dance. (CD track 17)

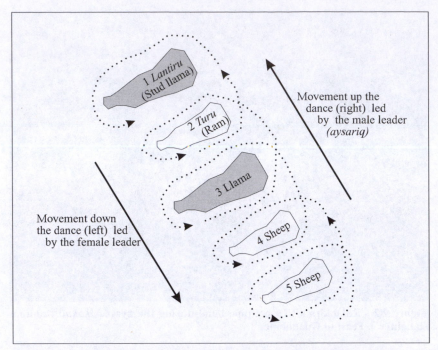

Figure 7.3   Diagram of the *pusariq* dance around the llama and sheep skins

gift of a llama pelt on the bass drum, evoking a connection with the drum skin.[35] The *sikus* then began to play and departed the *alferézes'* homestead, accompanied by a long line of dancers holding hands. As the *siku* band headed out of sight, a consort of *pinkillu* flutes – instruments of the rains – struck up at the *alferézes'* house and played for a few hours, as if heralding the start of the growing season proper in November.[36] *Pinkillu* playing alternated with *siku* performance throughout the final day of each feast, but after these brief outings *pinkillus* were not heard again or played regularly until the feast of All Saints at the beginning of November.

---

[35] In the feast of Guadalupe the llama skin was then handed to the owner of the panpipes (who played one of the smaller instruments and was not a resident of Kalankira). For Exultación, both a llama and sheep skin were placed on the drum, one for each of the two leading *sanja* players.

[36] At the moment this happened during the feast of Guadalupe it suddenly began to hail very heavily, covering the hamlet and its immediate surrounds with a deep layer of hailstones, whilst leaving the surrounding hills entirely untouched. This could scarcely have been a more vivid demonstration of the local claim that *sikus* attract frost and *pinkillu* flutes bring rain. My host family treated the idea that this musical confrontation could have such a dramatic, and to my mind astonishing, effect on atmospheric conditions as quite unsurprising.

(C) THE *RINUWA* FEASTS

The story of god and his saints' defeat of the devil leading to the release of water and the creation of new life, as recounted by don Adrian, ends referring to *rinuwa* or renewal. Whilst the word *rinuwa* is presumably derived from the Spanish *renovar* ('to renew'),[37] it carries immediate musical associations of drumming and cacophony for the people of Kalankira. For example, when I asked one elderly man the meaning of this word he simply made the onomatopoeic sound *tin tin tin* to represent drums.[38] Paulino explained that when a single band of *sikus* plays, the ensemble is referred to as *sikus*. However, when many *siku* ensembles come together in cacophony, they are termed *rinuwa*.

Numerous rural musicians from around the Macha area attended the two so-called *rinuwa* feasts of San Lazaro (21 September) six hours walk away and Mama Copacabana (23 September) in rural Tomaykuri, only about 30 minutes walk from Kalankira (Map 3). Although well known and locally important, only one man from Kalankira travelled to the first fiesta, but Paulino and many other neighbours attended the feast in Tumaykuri. Among the multiplicity of instrumentalists at San Lazaro were *siku* bands and *julajula* ensembles,[39] as well as several individual side drum (*tambora*) and notched-flute (*quena*) players, and one pipe and tabor (*kuntur pinkillu* 'condor flute') player.[40] Many young men, referred to as *monos* ('monkeys') or *ch'unchus* ('jungle Indians'), spoke in falsetto voices and played constant pranks. Through the late morning, groups of musicians swarmed into the village and assembled around the church, the sounds of their diverse musics constantly growing in volume and cacophony. With the priest's arrival, all instruments were hushed for mass. But as soon as the service was over, and people began to spill out of the church, the multitude of instruments struck up again in even wilder and more chaotic cacophony (CD track 21).

For the feast of Mama Copacabana in Tomaykuri, many *siku* ensembles arrived with young women carrying colourful flags; some having walked for at least eight hours from the *chawpirana* ('middle altitude region', Map 3). The ensembles congregated just outside the church door and at least seven

---

[37] Alberto Camaqui of *ayllu* Laymi supported this derivation and also translated *rinuwa* as *cambio* ('change'). However, he observed that the planting season is not called *rinuwa* by the Laymis.

[38] This would seem to be a widespread and ancient ideophone for expressing percussive sounds among Quechua speakers. For example, it is found in the stem of the common Quechua word for 'drum' *tinya* (Gonzalez Holguín 1989 [1608]:343) and in Kalankira is the common ideophone used to refer to exploding dynamite.

[39] Several large *julajula* (*wauku*) ensembles played for this feast but no *julajulas* were present for the feast of Mama Copacabana.

[40] Plenty of *charangos* accompanying courtship songs in the bars were also in evidence, but these did not seem to be connected with the cult of the saints.

Figure 7.4 Cacophonous procession following mass during the feast of Copacabana

ensembles played their own melodies simultaneously and in complete cacophony for the final hour before mass (CD track 18; see Example 6.6, Chapter 6). Once again the instruments were silenced for mass, but as soon as it was over, the *siku* ensembles began to play joining a huge procession, headed by the *monos* and priest. In jubilant cacophony it included a pipe and tabor player, the *quena* notched-flutes of the *monos*, and several lone drummers, as well as the *siku* ensembles (Figure 7.4).

The *monos* or *ch'unchus*

The *monos* or *ch'unchus* are young men – usually commited to dancing at the feast for three consecutive years – who constantly fool around, stealing objects and playing tricks. They wear jester-like trousers with legs of contrasted colours (*allqa*), llama fleece wigs *t'aka uma* ('dishevelled head') and monkey masks.[41] The Spanish *mono* means 'monkey', while *ch'unchu* is commonly used in the high Andes to refer to dances that imitate Indian tribes from the tropical lowlands (Cánepa Koch 1993, Van Kessel 1981:38, 158). Various people identified *monos* with *satanas colorados* (Sp. 'coloured satans'), which appear at the end of Carnival, and are said to be 'from inside' (*ukhumanta*).

---

41 Paulino danced as a *mono* for three consecutive years prior to his marriage.

Paulino mentioned that in the past *satanas colorados* used to dance at the feast of Copacabana, but this made god 'angry' (*phiñakun*) so more recently *monos* dance instead. Like all 'devils', *monos* were said to be *q'iwa*, which is sometimes glossed as 'half-male, half-female' and linked to their use of falsetto voices (CD tracks 19 and 20). Sometimes groups of *monos* dance together to *siku* panpipe music using lassos (*chicotes*), with metal rattles on the handles, which they interlace (Figure 7.5, CD track 19).[42] Several *monos* also carried a *quena* notched-flute, which few could actually play, and a side-drum player sometimes followed them. Indeed, when I asked a *mono* dancer to play his *quena* to me, an elderly man nearby immediately pointed out that the *mono* didn't know how to make the *quena* sound and took the young man's instrument to play a *kupla*. (CD track 20).

The condor flute

Several pipe and tabors, called *kuntur pinkillu* ('condor flute') or *quri pinkillu* ('golden flute') were also played at the *rinuwa* feasts. These small duct-flutes,

Figure 7.5 *Monos* **dancing during the feast of San Lazaro**

---

[42] Unlike the Peruvian devotional dances documented by Deborah Poole (1991), no choreographed dances were performed at the *rinuwa* feasts.

made from a condor wingbone, are played with their left hand – using four fingers – while a drum hung from the left wrist is beaten with the right hand (Figure 7.6).[43] The 'condor flute' is the only form of pipe and tabor played in this region of Bolivia and is explicitly associated with *rinuwa timpu* ('renewal time'). Unfortunately, although well known to people in Kalankira, nobody there actually possessed or played a *kuntur pinkillu*, so my information on performance practice is limited to a few brief words with a player in San Lazaro. On CD track 21 he is heard performing beside the church door, alongside several other ensembles and *mono* dancers, as the congregation emerges following mass.[44] The timbre of the 'condor flute's' high-pitched sound is particularly dense and vibrant, and its slow and exceptionally meditative melody contrasts with other local genres. The name *quri pinkillu* ('golden flute') also suggests sacred associations, like the 'golden ribbons' (*quri sintay*) of the *asintu* songs (Chapter 5), which Paulino described as 'pathways' between the generations, linking the living with the ancestors.

When I asked don Remejio Beltrán why the 'condor flute' is played in *rinuwa timpu*, he explained:

> [Because of] that god of ours, all those little devils dance there to the bone [flute]. They do it as they come out. That's why [the condor flute] is played *wish ish ish...* so that they dance, as fast as their legs will allow them them.[45]

An equivalence between dancing devils, especially 'colourful satans' (*satanos colorados*), and the sprouting of seeds at this time of year, where the word *chillchi* (from the *asintu* songs in Chapter 5) was said to mean both 'dance' and 'sprout', is especially relevant here.[46] From around late September early-planted crops, such as broad beans, begin to sprout and stored seed potatoes begin to chit prior to planting. Might this connection with bursting skins or husks, as the shoots of green plants force their way out of seeds or tubers, in part explain the obsession with animal skins during the patronal feasts and the widespread association of drums with the planting season in this

---

[43] In Juncal, Cañar (highland Ecuador), *Táita Carnaval* is said to play a condor bone flute and small drum, which is a chest 'filled with gold and precious gems'. With this music he is said to open the mountains one by one, allowing access to the riches contained within them (Krener & Fock 1977–8:153–5, cited in Sullivan 1988:214).

[44] This performance has resonances with an image by Guaman Poma that depicts dancing before the altar accompanied by a similar sized pipe and tabor (1980 [c. 1615]:f.783). Andean pipe and tabors are widespread and doubtless based on European models introduced in the early colonial period. Guaman Poma also includes an image of Pizarro and Almagro standing on either side of a pipe and tabor player in Spain, before setting sail for the Andes, suggesting strong Spanish associations with this instrument (1980 [c. 1615]:f.44).

[45] *Chay tiusninchis, chay imastas yawluritas tusun chaypi t'ullunmanta. Urqhuspa ruwasqanku a. Chay tukankupaq 'wish ish ish...' tusunkupaq chakinkumanjina tusurikunku chaylla.*

[46] *Chillchitha: Dançar* ('to dance'). Bertonio 1984 [1612], II:82.

Figure 7.6   **'Condor flute'** (*kuntur pinkillu*) **player during the feast of San Lazaro**

part of Bolivia? In Macha territory, as in most other parts of Northern Potosí, drums are rarely played outside the period between August and October.[47] Not only do we find them accompanying *siku* panpipes, the condor flute, and groups of *ch'unchus* with *quena* flutes, but also several lone drummers joined the cacophonous *rinuwa* processions during the feast of Mama Copacabana. Could such obsession with drums at this time imply a focus on boundaries; between inside and outside, or the endogenous and exogenous?

(D) ATTENDING TO MUSIC: MUSICAL BOUNDARIES

As Simon Frith points out for background music produced by modern technology, 'the meaning of music *as sound* depends, in the first place, on the quality of concentration given to it (1998:100).[48] For many participants in Kalankira's feasts, music serves as – albeit essential and 'consoling' – 'background noise' against which other sounds, such as conversation, are foregrounded. In ways reminiscent of street parades and outdoor festivals elsewhere, the general attitude seems to be the more music the better. As multiple groups play simultaneously, more or less consciously competing with one another, cacophony frequently emerges as a preferred modus operandi, or even aesthetic – conveying a sense of dynamism, excitement and activity (Allen 1988:195, Turino 1993: 65–67, Bigenho 2000:966). Yet, in these same events the attention of certain individuals – especially those actively participating in musical performance or dance – may be captured and focused by the music, perhaps leading to a powerful sense of mutual coordination or collectivity.[49]

In many highland regions, large consorts of wind players join together to 'play as one', sounding a shared melody in unison, octaves or other parallel intervals, which becomes emblematic of the particular *ayllu*, moiety, hamlet or

---

[47] In Inca times drums were played at the start of growing season, though it is sometimes specified that this was to frighten away droughts and frosts that would endanger the young maize plants (Murra 1978:43). Dynamite is also exploded (*tin!*) in Kalankira to 'frighten' away hail during the growing season. It should also be stressed that in many, if not most, other regions of Bolivia, drums accompany wind ensemble performance in both the rainy and dry season.

[48] Frith goes on to remark: 'Music becomes music by being heard as such by the listener; it follows that to make music is not just to put sounds together in an organised way but also to ensure that these sounds *make their mark*' (1998:100).

[49] Godlovitch compares musical attention to that of activities such as reading a novel or digging a garden that permit temporal punctuation without loss of integrity (1998:39). Also see Cook (1990:13) on the use of background music in industrial and office environments to enhance productivity, which when music is viewed as 'art' may be seen to devalue it. Such value judgements on music's surroundings are interesting when compared with Andean contexts, such as performances in mucky animal corrals without other human bystanders present.

patrilocal group the ensemble represents. As Turino has argued in his study of Conima, Peru, such musical solidarity is iconic of broader social values and behaviour, where equal opportunity to participate is paramount and individuals are encouraged to subordinate themselves to the collective. This leads to aesthetic priorities in which participation is often given precedence over musical accuracy, individual voices blend rather than dominate, and pitch discrepancies or differences in style are subsumed in a preference for a dense texture and wide unison (Turino 1989).[50] This 'wide unison', resulting from 'discrepancies' in tuning (from a Western perspective), is often seen to contribute to the richness and 'flavour' of the overall sound.[51] Kalankira's large *julajula* panpipe ensemble (Chapter 6) also included tuning discrepancies of up to a semitone between individual instruments, although in smaller ensembles of four to six players greater concern for 'accurate' tuning was usually observed.[52]

Alongside expressing solidarity for its members and social group, Andean wind ensembles are an important means of marking social difference and boundaries, a point already highlighted in the previous chapter. Feasts in the high Andes sometimes resemble musical battlefields, where ensembles explicitly compete to dominate the soundscape, to capture symbolically powerful spaces (Stobart 1988:84–5, Bigenho 2002:178–9). Consorts are occasionally reduced to silence by their competitors – their melody and rhythm rendered inaudible and lost. More often, melodies are maintained and no official winners recognized, although I have sometimes heard both ensembles privately claim victory (see Bigenho 2000:966). Distinguishing factors, such as emblem melodies, special cadential motifs, customized consort sizes and tunings, or distinct dress, sometimes serve to mark the identity of an ensemble. But at other times no specific musical markers may be in evidence – on one occasion in northern Bolivia I encountered two brass bands standing side by side and playing precisely the same piece just out of

---

[50] He also observes that in musical composition, which sometimes takes place communally, collective expression takes precedence over individual creativity. Thus individual composers are rarely acknowledged publicly. However, I found that among Aymara speaking *musiñu* flute players of Lahuachaka, Oruro department, the names of individual composers were often known. In Kalankira, by contrast, it was very rare for composers to be named.

[51] My friend and colleague Arnaud Gerard – a physicist, ethnomusicologist and instrument maker who lives in Potosí – once made a set of rural-style *siku* panpipes, tuned very precisely using an electronic tuning meter. A group of *campesinos* decided against buying this set of instruments after trying them out; when asked why, they explained that, although very fine instruments, they lacked 'flavour' (*sabor*).

[52] For example, great lengths were taken to bring *pinkillu* flutes into tune (see Chapter 8) and *siku* panpipe players sometimes placed pebbles inside certain tubes to improve tuning. Attitudes to wind tuning in the *altiplano* regions of departments La Paz and Oruro, where string instruments tend to be rare, may be somewhat different from those in Northern Potosí where men are very accustomed to tuning strings.

synchrony, a musically virtuosic feat.[53] Although cacophonous to my ears, it would have been unthinkable for the two bands to have joined forces and played together as one. Preserving the integrity and identity of their respective social groups, expressed in the form of albeit identical melodies, was paramount.

Despite sound's emanatory quality which directs attention to a central source, the cacophony or clash resulting from competing wind ensembles can be seen to express musical boundaries, which in turn are iconic of other forms of social or territorial limits. Indeed, it has been argued that the more immediate such boundaries, the more likelihood for such displays (Barth 1969). But as well as the assertion of social difference, musical multiplicity clearly also expresses the excitement and activity critical to festive performance. From this perspective, cacophony might be seen to evoke a sense of unity and collectivity.[54] Thus, on the one hand, 'playing as one' reflects participation in a single shared emblematic melody, in which individuals subordinate themselves to the collective, and where the musics of other ensembles represent a potential threat to the group. On the other hand, the collective and simultaneous performance of a multiplicity of musics can also invoke a sense of unity and homogenization, as the plethora of parts, people(s) or spirits that go to make up an imagined community, a powerful being, or even the world.

Concluding cacophony: *ch'ajwa*

Chhakhuani: Gossip, shouting or many talking together with raised voices without understanding one another[55] (Gonzalez Holguín 1989 [1608]:91).

Ch'ajwa: (1) Din, noise, disturbance, racket/confusion (2) Uproar resulting from an uprising, revolt, revolution, insurrection. By extension, also applied to the revolution itself[56] (Herrero & Sánchez 1983:59).

---

[53] Michael Sallnow describes a similar incident in the Cusco region of Peru (1987:187).

[54] Discussing the Amazonian group the Kalapalo, Ellen Basso translates the term *ail*, used to refer to playing multiple musics simultaneously, as 'feeling harmony' ('agreement in feeling') and characterizes such cacophony as 'a South American version of the experience of "communitas"'(1985:254) – in the sense of a 'homogenous, undifferentiated *whole*' (Turner 1974:237). As Lawrence Sullivan suggests, rather than being experienced as random and accidental, the clamour of multiple musics may aim 'to create a state of soundness or fullness of being' (1988:222). He cites Robin Wright's research on the Amazonian Baniwa who play over twenty different named pairs of flutes simultaneously to 'recompose the body' of the Kuai, a monstrous primordial human, 'whose every body part and orifice emitted a different sound at the moment of his disintegration in the cosmic fire' (Sullivan 1988:223; Wright 1981:586; Hill 1993:68, 84).

[55] *Hauer mormollo o griteria o hablar muchos juntos con bozeria sin entenderse.*

[56] *(1) Bullicio, ruido, alboroto, bulla (2) Alboroto resultante de un alzamiento, sublevación, revolución, motín. Por extensión, se aplica también a la misma revolución.*

In the previous chapter, I differentiated between two forms of warfare in Northern Potosí: the ritual battles called *tinku* – a form of 'violent harmony' in which 'winning' is almost entirely absent – and territorial battles called *ch'ajwa* – which are unconnected with calendrical feasts and are usually staged on boundaries or disputed territory. Weapons are used in *ch'ajwa*, especially sticks and slings, and the discourse explicitly concerns winners and losers. In contrast to *tinku*'s link with the maintenance of balanced relations, *ch'ajwa* is typically both asymmetrical and transformative in intent; potentially leading to the creation of a new order and a shift in the balance of power. Don Adrian's story of the water war clearly belongs to the *ch'ajwa* category, where through the combined efforts of the saints, the devil is defeated, his accumulated resources redistributed, and a new order created. The Quechua word *ch'ajwa* also means a noise, din, disturbance or confusion of different sounds, such as mass of people all speaking at once without understanding one another. This acoustic impression, and perhaps sense of communication breakdown, is clearly shared by the cacophonous music of the *rinuwa* feasts. Indeed, Paulino described the din (*ch'ajwa*) during these feasts in terms of competing musics 'defeating' or 'overcoming' one another:

puraq atipanakusjina ruwanku, chayrayku chajwa ruwanku. Gananakujina tukanku	they do this as if both are overcoming the other, that's why they make a racket/battle (*ch'ajwa*). They play as though defeating one another

The reciprocal action suffix *–naku-* in the verb stems meaning 'overcome' and 'defeat' (Quechua *atipa-* and Spanish *gana-*) suggest that, subjectively at least, all the musicians are victors and allied with the saints. As Paulino explains, the various musical forces are at war with one another. But are they attempting to disrupt or repress their various 'messages' and to silence one another?[57] As the ensembles stood outside the church door and then joined together during the procession, I encountered no explicit hostility between them. Indeed, to silence one another would negate the very notion of *rinuwa*, which is musically defined in terms of multiplicity. The various musical forces are at war with one another, their competing musical messages rendered mutually unintelligible, but simultaneously are unified in a common purpose, to 'pass on the message' of *rinuwa*.

The confused din (*ch'ajwa*) of *rinuwa* music vividly evokes the battle (*ch'ajwa*) of don Adrian's story of the saints' uprising against the devil's domination.[58] When I asked Asencio why so many drums were played during

---

[57] I have witnessed *tarka* ensembles explicitly attempt to silence others during Carnival in Eucalyptus, department Oruro.

[58] Violence and cacophony also coincide in Isbell's account of a 'celebration of chaos' from the Ayacucho region of Peru, which she suggests marks the end the month of August, when the earth opens and the subterranean deities of the inner earth escape and cause havoc. She describes how

the feast of Mama Copacabana, he simply replied *iskalaramus*, from the Spanish verb *descalabrar*. This can be glossed variously as 'we cause chaos, disruption, defeat an enemy, or injure somebody's head', vividly evoking the story's account of Mama Copacabana and Tata Turaqhari destroying the devil's horns and nose. Zuidema notes that in Inca times 'beating the drum with sticks … was done in imitation of beating their enemies with sticks'. He identifies the drum's association with political borders, political centres and the sun, relating both planting and harvest to warfare (1985:199, 183).

The victory and shift in power suggested by the *rinuwa* feasts coincides precisely with the spring equinox (21 September), the point in the year when, in a striking parallel with don Adrian's story, the power of darkness (devil, inner earth) is overcome by light (god, sun). In another conversation, don Adrian referred to the end of *amu timpu* ('silent time'), the epoch of the primordial *chullpas* who were destroyed by solar conflagration, as *rinuwa timpu* or 'renewal time' (Chapter 2). Once again this highlights the connection between the *rinuwa* feasts and the solar aspect of god's victory over the devil, where the cacophony surrounding the bodily destruction of the devil leads his accumulated energies to be released and circulated.[59] Andean devils are first and foremost accumulative in their relations to others, their acquired energies and resources dedicated to personal ends. This is also a necessary characteristic of humans, where such tendencies for personal accumulation can perhaps only be overcome with the final apotheosis of the process of dying (Chapter 9). As we shall see in the next chapter, the souls of recently deceased adult men are critical to the growth of crops during the rains.

This transition from a 'silent' (*amu*) primordium, via sonic multiplicity, to solar domination has obvious resonances with the way the dawn chorus articulates the passage from night to day (Chapter 2). Birds not only use song to mark boundaries in space but also in time. As Urton observes, for the village of Misminay in Southern Peru, 'the greatest amount of noise in the village occurs at dawn and dusk; unnecessary noise, even that of animals, is not easily tolerated at any other time' (1981:17–18). The word *amu*, which seems to have its roots in Aymara, also means a 'flower bud' and is linked with the notion of memory.[60] This suggests a pregnant silence, one that may highlight potential over the more ambiguous silence of the word *ch'in* associated with dangerous and deserted places.[61] The association of *amu* with a flower bud is especially

---

four different bands, dedicated to different saints, played in cacophony, while mock battles – sometimes escalating into real violence – took place (1997:288).

[59] This parallels the Amazonian Baniwa's use of musical cacophony to invoke the multiple sounds emitted from the body of Kuai, as he was destroyed in the solar conflagration (Wright 1981:586).

[60] Bertonio (1984 [1612], II: 17) includes the following entries: *Amu: mudo* ('dumb, silent, mute'), *Amu:Boton de la flor* ('bud of a flower'), and *Amutaatha: Acordar* ('to remember').

[61] The *apachita* (mountain pass) above Kalankira was described as *ch'in* ('silent') and I was

revealing, implying the containment of a multiplicity of sensory ingredients (sound, water, perfume, and colour). In short, the release and opening of this flower with the rise of the sun – a form of reversal or *pachakuti* ('world turning') – leading to new fruits might be seen as a powerful metaphor for the sensory release and circulation which characterize the entire period of the rains, or *karnawal timpu* ('Carnival time') as it is often known, leading to the new fruits of the year.

What is interesting here is that this invocation of sonic-sensory-hydraulic circulation is performed using dry season instruments, which are usually associated with attracting frost and blowing away the clouds. These instruments include *siku* (and *julajula*) panpipes, which I have related to body-like vessels evoking inner growth and accumulation (Chapters 2 and 6). Despite their brief appearance in Kalankira's patronal feasts, it is not until November that *pinkillu* flutes begin to be played in earnest, explicitly to attract the rain and help crop growth. With their own internal voices, regular wetting, and 'many holes', they richly evoke notions of unbridled circulation in contrast to the containment of panpipes. So should we see the sonic saturation of *rinuwa* music as the sound of things to come – heralding and invoking the circulation of water needed to saturate the landscape during the rains?

The practice of acquiring a multiplicity of *siku* panpipe melodies from exogenous sources and mixing them in *rinuwa* music has some interesting similarities with rain making rituals from several other parts of the Bolivian Andes. In these rites, acquiring and mixing waters from different, and sometimes widely separated, locations is thought to provoke the circulation of water and rainfall (Berg 1989:111; Rösing 1996; Sikkink 1997). I have already noted the close connection between water and ethnogenesis, where language, dress and music – key identity markers – are related to the water of specific places. In a ceremony called *cambio* ('change'/'exchange') in Condo, reported by Lynn Sikkink, the sense of identity attached to waters from different locations is particularly remarkable.[62] When ritually mixed in the centre of the village, the waters were said to fight and resist one another. Again when the mixed water was returned to the various sources from which it had been collected, the waters in these places were said to 'get angry' when the new foreign water was added, and to 'boil' because of the 'challenge', leading to a change in the environment and rainfall (1997:180). For all this discourse of violence and clashes of identity, Sikkink ultimately interprets the *cambio* ceremony in terms of the reopening and reinvigoration of communal exchange

---

warned that it was dangerous to walk there alone at night as you could be attacked or even murdered by evil people and thieves from the towns. In Quechua and Aymara 'silence' (*ch'in*) is synonymous with lack of life, such as a deserted or abandoned village. See for example Gonzalez Holguín 1989 [1608]:111, de Lucca 1987:49, Bertonio 1984 [1612]:86.

[62] Significantly, Alberto Camaqui also used the word cambio to explain the meaning of rinuwa to me.

channels, leading to the redistribution of communal resources, and the integration of the human community (1997:184).

The mixing of different musics during the *rinuwa* feasts seems to have a similar integrative function, linked to the redistribution of resources. Might *rinuwa* music and the *cambio* ceremony also be thought of as invocations of the common source from which new life must flow, thereby a generative 'imagined community'? Inca history stressed how locally differentiated waters, related to local identity, language and music, ultimately flowed from a common source: the creator god Wiracocha (*wira qucha*, literally 'fat sea'). Similarly, people in Kalankira asserted that the aqueous and musical *sirinus* travel along subterranean waterways from *lamar* – an inner or celestial 'sea' (Spanish: *la mar* 'the sea'), to arrive just as the new fruits of the year are beginning to take shape (Chapter 9). So, should we think of *rinuwa* music, and the miracle of renewal, from don Adrian's story, in terms of invoking this common ancestry (and sea) and setting in motion the subterranean flow that will ultimately lead to new life at Carnival?

I have suggested that on one hand *rinuwa* music concerns communication breakdown, and on the other invokes unity of expression and understanding – suggestive of Basso's 'feeling harmony' (1985:255) and the dynamics underpinning Anderson's 'imagined community' (1991). God's need to unify disparate forces to defeat the devil highlights the sense that this is by no means simply a mission of narrow local interest. Defeating the forces of darkness to bring rain, renewal and the rotation of the seasons is a project that unites multiple levels of Bolivian society, perhaps partly explaining the diversity, multiplicity and exogenous nature of the *siku* melodies played at this time of year. The rotation of the seasons does not emerge as a natural given, but as a hard fought campaign or revolution of perhaps national proportions. This contrasts vividly with the next two chapters, dedicated to the rainy growing season, where the focus shifts to the local: the *ayllu*, its ancestors, and the productivity of its fields.

November–January

Invoking the Dead and Crying for Rain

Souls, flutes, llamas and compassion

In a striking calendrical coincidence, the Catholic feast of All Saints (*Todos Santos*), rooted in European customs for the dead, falls at almost precisely the same point in the year as the principal prehispanic Andean festival for the dead. In Europe this feast occurs in autumn, where death is metaphorically related to dying plants, falling leaves and shortening days (Hutton 1996:426). By contrast, in the Bolivian Andes (southern hemisphere) it falls in spring and death is often connected with the sprouting of seeds and tubers, the destruction, consumption and mixing of life forms in order to invoke the potential for new life, and the release and circulation of regenerative water and energies. As described in Chapter 7, after prolonged negotiations all the saints finally joined forces to defeat the devil, releasing the water he had hoarded and permitting it to circulate once more, enabling God to resume his work creating new children. Whether this elegant connection between the combined efforts of 'all the saints' and the feast of 'All Saints' was consciously intended by don Adrian in his telling of this story I am unsure. What is for certain, however, is that people in Kalankira closely identified the feast of All Saints (1 November) and its invocation of the dead with the start of the heavy rains and the growing season proper. As is evident from several other ethnographic accounts from the central and southern Andes, the souls of the dead are widely seen to play a critical role in causing plants to grow and bear fruit (Harris 1982a:58, Allen 1988:56, Gose 1994:114).

In these next two chapters, dedicated to the rainy growing season, I contend that for Kalankira, at least, music and dance are critical to understanding these processes. This is supported by Olivia Harris in her pioneering study 'The dead and devils among the Bolivian Laymi' when she declares that 'only through music did it become clear that the dead remain in the world of the living during the season of rains' (1982a:58). A realization brought home to her with force when she innocently played back a recording of *wayñu* music of the rains, played on *pinkillu* flutes, a few hours after the final rites of Carnival, which mark the ritual end of the rains. A horrified audience immediately stopped her; these 'weeping' flute sounds would bring back the souls of the dead and devils that had just been safely despatched to the land of the ancestors. What sounds inspired such strong reactions? Why is *wayñu* music, especially that played on *pinkillu* flutes, so closely connected with the dead and devils? These are central questions of the next two chapters. In this chapter I focus on the first part of the rains and explore the sounds and sentiments of *pinkillu* flutes, and their connection with invoking the dead, weeping in the cemetery, calling for rain, and the hunger and copulation cries of llamas. I reserve my discussion of crops, Carnival and devils – especially the *sirinus* ('sirens') who bring new *wayñu* melodies and announce the new fruits of the year – for Chapter 9.

The entire rainy season or *paray timpu* (All Saints to Carnival) is often referred to as 'Carnival time' and the same instruments and genres are played throughout this period. With the ritual start of the rainy growing season at All Saints (1 November) the dominant imagery and focus of the music and dance shifts from associations with containment and accumulation, masculinity, balanced exchanges and *independence* of the dry winter months (Chapter 6) to those with release and flow, enclosing feminized space (dance), emplacement ('planting'), nurturing and *dependence*. More specifically, in the aural sphere of musical instruments, which evoke the shaping of *animu*, we move from containment and accumulation (panpipes) to release and flow (flutes). By contrast, in the visual realm of dance, as the external aspect of bodies, we pass from images of male gendered flow and movement (*link'u link'u*) to ones of feminine containment (*qhata*). Thus, instead of asserting their manhood through travelling and invoking images from beyond the boundaries of the community, men must now remain in their *ayllus* to work the fields. This is a nostalgic return to the sphere of their childhood and ancestors, and to the bounded female-gendered reproductive spaces of fields, corrals and the homestead itself (*thapa* 'nest'). Much of this imagery holds true for the entire growing season, but I suggest that the period between All Saints and early January – the build up and peak of the rains around the summer solstice – is, in many respects, the emotional climax of the year. Over this period – the theme of this chapter – pent-up tensions, emotions and desires are expressed and a powerful sense of 'coming together', familiarity and dependence are experienced. In a flood of tears, rain and seminal fluids, people, animals and the very landscape are consumed – a catharsis of death and destruction critical to subsequent regeneration at Carnival. To explore these themes, I begin with a descriptive account of the events and activities surrounding the feast of All Saints.

(A) FEASTING THE SOULS

Kalankira was a flurry of activity, as people tried to complete as much planting as possible before the feast of All Saints began. Before 8am on 27 October, the morning after my arrival from England after a year's absence, we had eaten our morning meal and together with Paulino, Asencio, his son Reneko, and a yoke of oxen, had set off on the 90 minute walk to Jalsuri to plant wheat for the day. Before starting work, we chewed coca leaves as an offering to the field's guardians and to various saints and other powers whose aid we required for the crops to grow successfully. This was a nostalgic moment for me, as I recalled the countless times we had shared this ritual together. I always deeply appreciated this way of entering into dialogue with the landscape, spirit guardians, ancestors and one's companions before getting down to work. On this occasion, we invoked:

Wirjin ('virgin')	Fields (cultivated land)
Sapiri	Principal mountain spirit (linked to condor)
Luriya kawiza ('glory head')	Celestial power: mountain (made offerings in *asintu*[2])
Luriya niñu ('glory child')	Celestial power, linked with piercing the earth
Sayjatkunkai	Power of mountain spirits ('similar to *sapiri*')
Kalsarinqa ('it will care for')[1]	Protects fields from frosts, hail and brings rain
San Marku (St Mark)	Patron of oxen: right side of yoke
San Isidro (St Isidore)	Patron of oxen: left side of yoke
Tata Wila Kurus ('True Cross')	Patron of harvest (3 May). Consort: Mama Candelaria
Mama Candelaria ('Candlemas')	Patron of flowers/'baby' fruits (2 February)
Mama Santisima ('Holiest Mother')	Moon
Tata Santisimu ('Holiest Father')	Sun
Mañapaq ('for requests/loans')	Souls of the dead
Tomás Jara	Asensio and Paulino's deceased father
Nicolas Jara	Asencio and Paulino's deceased grandfather

I helped Asencio with the ploughing while Paulino dug by hand in another nearby field, which was too steep for the oxen. The oxen were rather uneven in size and the smaller of the two often fell behind its partner. Periodically Asencio cried *TARA... TARA...* goading them to pull evenly and straight (*chiqan*), or – as he explained – 'to make [the two] equal' (*iwalanapaq*). We worked solidly through the day, stopping for occasional coca breaks and a few *kispiñas* (wholemeal dumplings) for lunch. The wheat (*qumu trigo*) was simply broadcast onto the fields by hand when the ploughing was complete, and eventually we set off back to Kalankira just after 6pm. The subsequent days were taken up with further planting alongside preparations for the feast of All Saints, including the brewing of corn beer (*aqha*) and making bread – a rare delicacy.

At last *uchu paqarin* ('chili pepper dawn') arrived – the morning of All Saints (1 November) – and each family busily prepared huge quantities of

---

[1] From the Spanish *calzar* – applied to providing forms of support or protection in the form of for example, a shoe, retaining wall, dam or wedge.

[2] See Chapter 5.

starchy foods. To every dish was added a blood red sauce made by grinding dried (red) hot *chili* peppers, known as *uchu*, and mixing them with water. Children tripped from house to house exchanging steaming bowls of *uchu*-flavoured foods between the homesteads, which I was told entice the souls of the dead (*almas*) back to the world of the living, because the ancestors (*awila achanchis*) especially appreciate this hot spicy flavour.[3] Following these meals, each household invited a few neighbours to join them in libations of corn beer in honour of their ancestors. I was invited to several houses and requested to bring along the *pinkillu* flutes I had just purchased en route to Kalankira. Besides very brief appearances during the patronal festivals in September, the sound of *pinkillus* had been banished from the soundscape for some nine months. The *wayñu* melodies we now played dated from the previous Carnival (February/March).

Although each family feasted and drank libations for their own specific ancestors, far more elaborate rituals and wider communal participation was underway in the home of doña Alicia Beltrán, whose husband had died just under a year before. I joined the long series of libations in the patio of her homestead, during which a black sheep was slaughtered in preparation for a communal meal consumed later that afternoon. Doña Alicia remained inside her cooking hut seated on the ground beneath a three level altar (*escalera* 'ladder/steps'), covered with a black cloth on which were placed candles, small sprouting onions with green stems, and small breads in the shape of babies, flowers, snakes, doves and other birds, called *tanta wawas* ('bread babies'). The altar was also decorated with two black and violet (*muray*) wreaths, and draped with chain-like rings of polythene ribbons (*sintay*) of the same colours. The sprouting onions, which were called *wirta mayku* ('garden authority'), were an especially important feature, which I was later to see placed on every grave of a deceased adult – highlighting the soul's association with the growth of crops.

Doña Alicia stayed under the *escalera* almost constantly through the day and then for an all-night vigil (*velatorio*), making libations to her deceased husband. Various people brought offerings that were added to the *escalera*, these included sprouting potatoes and maize cobs. On the following morning many more people joined the vigil, muttering prayers (*oraciones*) as they arrived, whilst everybody removed their hats. Several people said the Lord's Prayer in Spanish, but some also recited a local Quechua prayer, which doña Alicia's teenage son Ciprian dictated to me:

---

[3] Among the Laymis, to say that someone has gone to cultivate chili pepper is a common metaphor for death (Harris 1982a:62). In Kalankira I was told that although the souls delight in eating *uchu* they do not cultivate chilis; their only crop in *alma llajta* ('land of the souls') being the tiny Andean grain quinoa.

Lewqi-lewqi puka chaki	*Lewqi-lewqi* bird with the red legs[4]
Tiusnichischus rikusunqa	Perhaps our-god will see you
Chakiykita p'akisunqa	He will break your legs
Jamp'atitus laqanakun	The toads will hit one other
Kataris sikunakun	The snakes will whip one other
Tiusninchis quspachinakun	When god makes them give to one another
Amin.	Amen.

The *lewqi-lewqi* in the prayer, which resembles a black and white seagull with red legs, could be seen around Kalankira quite often during the rainy season. When I asked Asencio why God would want to break this rather pretty bird's legs, he explained that the *lewqi lewqi* is *saxra* ('evil/secret'), because it makes lots of noise (*ch'axwa*) at night. As a creature of the night, and along with toads and snakes, it is classified as a particularly evil and secret (*saxra*) part of the devil's (*supay's*) inner mountain sphere (Nash 1979, Harris 1982a:28, Platt 1987a:145).[5] God's assault on the *lewqi-lewqi* bird in this prayer is evocative of the saints' destruction of the devil in don Adrian's story (Chapter 7), forcing him to release and circulate the water he had accumulated. The reciprocal violence between toads and snakes is also suggestive of the moral imperative to 'give to one another'; share out accumulated resources rather than reserve them for individual benefit.

The next day, on the afternoon of All Souls (2 November), we made our way to the cemetery, a walled enclosure beside the church tower, where black cloths were laid out over the graves of the three adults who had died over the past three years. With the exception of doña Alicia's husband who had been in his forties, all of these adults had reached a ripe old age. However, nine white shrouds were placed over children's graves, which I found devastating. Rites in the cemetery are only performed for a single year for young children, or *angelitos* ('little angels') as they are known.[6] This meant that all these deaths had occurred during the past year, and I had known many of these infants and toddlers well. With the awareness that most of these children probably died from minor ailments, by Western standards, the contradictions between Kalankira and my own world suddenly seemed utterly impossible to reconcile.

For several hours people recited prayers at each grave and were offered maize beer and *t'anta wawas* ('bread babies') by the family in return, and then *pinkillu* flute *wayñu* music started up just outside the cemetery. The playing

---

[4] In various parts of Bolivia the cry of the *lewqi-lewqi* is said to announce the rain. Small marks on this water bird's eggs or a chestnut hue to its feathers are interpreted as a prognosis of a poor year, but large dark marks on the eggs and a brilliant green sheen to its feathers signal an abundant harvest (Berg 1989:49–51).

[5] All *khurus* ('wild creatures') belong to the devil's mountain sphere, although only certain species tend to be identified as 'evil' (*saxra*).

[6] Olivia Harris reports that among the Laymis the souls of infants (*angelitos*) are said to travel to heaven and to look after god's irrigation system, and send rain to earth (1982a:63). I found similar associations in Kalankira.

was desultory and, to my ears, disappointing – especially compared to the dynamic performances in cemeteries that I have encountered in other parts of Northern Potosí. In Kalankira that year, there was little sense of occasion or excitement as most young people had gone to the festivities and *tinku* in Macha. The remaining menfolk discussed at length whether also to go to Macha and eventually at about 10pm five men, including Paulino and Asencio, set off for town dressed in *muntira* fighting helmets, Macha-style jackets and waistcoats, and carrying the *pinkillus* and *kitarra* I had recently purchased. They planned to stay at a community near Macha for the night and aware that my arrival at a stranger's house in the middle of the night could be awkward, I arranged to catch them up in the morning. After a 3.30am rise and a high-speed walk I met them on the path just outside Macha at about 6am. They were all busily putting on five shirts beneath their thick woollen jackets and waistcoats, as well as three pairs of thick woollen trousers, in preparation for the *chuqay rumi* ('stone throwing'). There was a bitter dispute currently raging with the people of nearby *Q'illu q'asa* and some very violent scenes were predicted.

We headed into Macha, playing *pinkillus* as we walked, but had not gone far before Ciprian Beltrán (the son of doña Alicia) stopped us and asked me to refrain from playing because my large *q'iwa* size instrument was 'flat' (*astwan rakhu*) and 'out of tune' (*mana iwalasqa*) with his own – which was rather sharp.[7] Our two flutes were simply incompatible. Clearly the group was concerned about appearances as they entered Macha, and *pinkillu* tuning was a significant factor. This highlights the point that, despite Raul and Marguerite d'Harcourt's claim to the contrary (1959:14), Andean musicians are in general very conscious of tuning – even though there exists a widespread aesthetic for a 'wide unison' and priority of participation over precision in many contexts, as noted in Chapter 7.[8]

For my own safety Paulino suggested that I kept away from the *chuqay rumi* ('stone throwing'), so I wandered around Macha, playing *pinkillus* and drinking with other friends and acquaintances. The town was full of groups of young people singing and dancing *wayñu*, often with a dance called *qhata* that

---

[7] I had purchased this set of instruments, which had been made in the artisan village of Qala qala, in Llallagua en route to Kalankira. Unfortunately this was the only set on sale in the Sunday market and both its sound and tuning were poor. Also, the set only included four instruments, whereas those made in the Macha valleys usually included five or six sizes. By coincidence another *q'iwa* instrument, owned by Ciprian, happened to be reasonably well in tune with the other instruments in this set, but considerably sharper than the (somewhat flat) *q'iwa* of the consort I was playing.

[8] The pioneering work of Arnaud Gérard (1996a, 1996b, 1997, 1998, 2000, *c.* 2002) and Gérard Borras (1992, 1995) on the construction and tuning of Andean aerophones is of especial importance here and begins to give us a flavour of the sophisticated ethno-acoustic knowledge that underlies these instruments' construction and performance.

involves holding alternate and interwoven arms in a circle around a *pinkillu* flute consort or *kitarra* player.

In the afternoon I headed back towards Kalankira along with several other acquaintances from neighbouring communities, who – like me – were extremely intoxicated. En route we stopped at a house in Janqu'u Loma where a man had recently died. Many people from Kalankira and other nearby communities were already there, dancing *qhata* to *wayñu* music performed by a group of four *pinkillu* flutes and many female voices (CD track 22, Example 8.1). Like the vast majority of *pinkillu* flute *wayñus*, this consisted of two repeated sections, ending with an extended termination note and a brief moment of silence before repetition (AABB). This transcription does little justice to the rich heterophony, octave shifts, rhythmic feel, dense timbre and expressive pitch slides (the words of the first line are inaudible).

Hay si - way, si - way   ce - le - sta   (pur - ci - lay) ro - sas   t'i - ki - ta_____

Example 8.1   *Wayñu* played on four *pinkillus* (1 *q'iwita*, 2 *taras*, 1 *q'iwa*) with singing and dancing at the house of a recently deceased man in Janq'u Loma. The large circle of *qhata* dancers encircling the *pinkillus* includes 20 women and 10 men. (CD track 22)

A little later a large group of ten *pinkillu* players performed together without dancers (CD track 23, Example 8.2). I was struck by the integration of players from various communities in a single massed ensemble; a vivid contrast to the usual cacophony resulting from such encounters when musical independence is maintained (Chapter 7).[9] Alongside the usual loose heterophonic coordination between the various flutes, in this recording the shortening of the last note of each section gives rise to an interesting uneven pulse, which contrasts with the regularity of the dancers footfalls in the previous example. This shortening of the final note of the A and B sections may result from a slight anticipation of the repeat, which would not occur when regular footfalls are maintained by dancers. The economy of musical material is remarkable and typical of the genre. A four-note gesture dominates the piece and the second section is a precise transposition of the first (a 4th above or 5th below).

Paulino and Asencio arrived a little later, having escaped serious injury in the *chuqay rumi*, and together we gradually made our way back to Kalankira

---

[9] I have also encountered massed *pinkillu* consorts during All Saints in Toracari, Charka province, Northern Potosí.

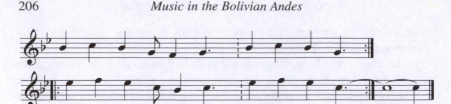

Example 8.2   Massed *pinkillu* flute *wayñu* at the house of a recently deceased man in Janq'u Loma. Transposed up about one semitone. (CD track 23)

dancing and playing *pinkillus* as we went. Ahead of us lay another three days of almost constant *wayñu* music to accompany the libations dedicated to animals and food crops (*turu ch'allas*).

Harnessing the souls: *wayñu* music

In Kalankira, as in other parts of Northern Potosí, death is accompanied by relatively little ceremony. Instead the main rites and celebrations are saved for the start of the growing season in November, when at All Saints 'death is tamed' and 'becomes cyclical' (Harris 1982a:56). Through music (*wayñu*) and dance (*qhata*) performance, perhaps more than any other medium, the power of recently deceased adults is harnessed to promote agricultural production, a point that is made especially explicit in the *alma kacharpaya* ('despatch of the soul') ceremony during Carnival (Chapter 9). The arrival of the *almas* ('souls of the dead') at All Saints was closely identified with the sound of *wayñu* music which the souls were said to constantly sing, play and dance in *alma llajta* ('land of the souls') – never performing dry season genres, such as *takis* (Chapter 5). The performance of *wayñu* by the living was evidently a means to invoke the perpetually green vegetation of the imagined landscape of *alma llajta*, decked in flowers and weeping willows – a sort of perpetual Carnival.[10] Thus, the powerful sensory contrast between the experience of the dry and rainy seasons, was underscored by a distinction between the worlds ('time-spaces') of the living and the ancestors.[11] It was specifically through the

---

[10] Paulino and Asunta vividly evoked images of *alma llajta* one evening as we sat chatting after supper. They described the flowers that grow there, including broom (*retama*), roses (*rosas*) and chamomile (*manzanilla*), and various kinds of trees, especially weeping willows, a potent metaphor for rain, greenery and death. By contrast with this vision of perpetual vegetation, Harris observes that among the Laymi the land of the souls was presented as seasonal and an inversion of the living – rainy for the living while dry for the souls, and vice versa (1982a:62).

[11] This incorporation of imagery and experience of the rainy growing season into descriptions of *alma llajta*, suggests the idea of the rainy and dry seasons as two distinct worlds or 'time spaces'. According to Paulino and Asunta, *alma llajta* is situated at the 'end of the world' (*mundu tukuypi*) and 'at the end of time' (*timpu tukuypi*). It is to the West – 'the direction of the setting sun' (*inti chinkayku ladu*), just out of human sight – but could potentially be seen with a telescope

medium of musical performance that this annual alternation of the seasons – or worlds – was invoked and articulated. It was through music and dance that people 'embodied' the sensorial, temporal and spatial dimensions of these distinct seasons of the year.

In a demonstration of how the *almas* sing, or literally 'weep' (*waqan*) *wayñu*, Paulino sang a verse invoking their sense of loss for the 'scorching' heat of the day. Doña Asunta also imitated the souls' music by singing *cholitay, cholitay, cholitay*... (girl, girl, girl...), highlighting the association of *wayñu* with love and desire as well as loss and grief. Several other people attributed the source of the *wayñu* music they played to the souls and typically referred to the act of playing it with the verb *waqay* 'to weep'.[12] In short, although Quechua and Aymara verbs meaning to 'weep' are applied to sounds emitted from any musical instrument, the *wayñu* music of the rains – especially when played by *pinkillu* flutes – carries especially close associations with the powerful sentiments and flow of tears associated with weeping – a theme developed later in this chapter.

Harris has suggested that despite the ritual expulsion of the souls of the dead, following the feast of All Saints, there is a sense that they 'do not depart', but remain as a 'collective presence' with the living through the rainy season (1982a:60). Perhaps this collective presence is best understood as a complex of sensory and emotional experiences associated with death and *alma llajta* which pervade the rainy season, alongside broader understandings about the relationship between the living and dead. This might help to account for why, despite the importance attributed to the role of the dead in musical discourse, a direct question such as 'Do the dead make the crops grow?' could, as Peter Gose found in Huaquirka, Peru, well receive a negative reply (1994:145).

Rather than stressing the generalized community of souls, the principal rituals for the dead at both All Saints and Carnival in Kalankira were focused on the individual souls of men who had recently died and who had yet to arrive or become fully socialized' into *alma llajta*. Harris implies this same point when she writes:'the transformation of individual death into collectivity is not completed until after the harvest' (1982a:60). *Alma llajta*, I was told, is surrounded by, and reached by crossing, a 'sea' (*mar*) or 'great river' (*jatun mayu*) (Harris 1982a:62, Izko 1986:144). For this journey, the soul sets off at

---

(*larga vista*). Surely I had seen it when I flew to Bolivia by airplane, they exclaimed. My feeble excuse for failing to do so was that I must have dropped off to sleep.

[12] For example, Pedro Chura observed that 'the *wayñus* they weep ['play'] come from the dead' (*wañusqamanta waqanku wayñusta*). Harris also observes that, among the Aymara speaking Laymi, '*wayñu* is said to weep (*q'asi*) while the *kirki* [*charango* song genre] of the dry season is happy (*kusisi*)'. She goes on to note that *pinkillu* 'flute music attracts rain; it is a dirge and thus will not cause offence to the dead whose co-operation is essential to bring the crops to fruition' (1982a:60).

All Saints with a llama and dog – the dog strangled and used 'like a mule' to ride across the 'great river'. Once there, in *alma llajta*, the souls wander around in new clothes (*musuq p'achasniyuq*) – indeed the dead are buried in new clothes – but over the years, as they become forgotten by the living, the souls' clothes, like the *wayñu* melodies from previous years, become old, worn and ragged (see Arnold 1992:31–2). For all its resonances with Greco-European accounts of souls crossing the river Styx to reach Hades, there is a sense that for people in Kalankira the 'sea' or 'river' that the soul must cross is the rainy growing season – a journey from All Saints to Carnival.[13] Arrival at Carnival is closely associated with 'new clothes', new *wayñu* melodies, and a vivid array of flowers – the imagery of Carnival and *alma llajta* merging as one. Only at this point, once the crops have grown to their peak and their first fruits have been tasted, are these individual male souls finally despatched to join the collectivity in *alma llajta*.

(B) THE *PINKILLU* FLUTE[14]

For many people in Kalankira, *wayñu* music is clearly closely connected with the souls of the dead and is sometimes even linked with the Quechua *wañu*, meaning 'die' (Chapter 5). The *wayñus* performed on *pinkillu* flutes at this time of year, which tend to be highly consistent in form and to be played by married and unmarried men alike, occupy a critical role in the community's ritual celebrations.

From the feast of All Saints onward, men played *pinkillu* flutes in earnest to 'call the rain' and 'make the crops grow'.[15] These heavy wooden duct flutes are not only played in consort during feasts but also sometimes singly by men as they walk to their fields. *Pinkillus* are found throughout Northern Potosí and its surrounds, they are played without drums, and it is likely that their construction is modelled on the recorders brought to the Andes by the Spanish during the early colonial period and played in churches (Stobart 1996b:42).[16] Locally these flutes are also often known as *lawuta* (from Sp. *flauta*, 'flute/recorder') and *tarka*, a reference to their hoarse and vibrant timbre, but

---

[13] It is also significant that a small *pinkillu* is often included in the soul's provisions for the journey, as I once witnessed during All Saints in Llallawita, *ayllu* Chayantaka.

[14] See also Stobart 1996a, 1996b and 1998a.

[15] The name *pinkillu* and its variants (for example, *pinkullu*, *pincollo*) is a generic term for 'flute'. Whilst in Bolivia this name is typically used in reference to duct flutes, it is also applied to tabor pipes (played during the dry season) and certain notched or transverse flutes (Stobart 2001). For discussion of other forms of *pinkillu* flutes from different regions see, for example, Stobart 1988 and Parejo-Coudert 2001.

[16] See Stevenson 1976 [1968]:279 and Turino 1991:263 concerning the use of recorders in churches, and Guaman Poma 1980 [c. 1615]:666 for an illustration of church recorder players..

Figure 8.1   A group of young *pinkillu* flute players in Wak'an Phukru (sizes, left to right: *q'iwa*, *q'iwita*, *tara*, *machu tara*, *tara*)

also a common name for the squared-off duct flutes played in many parts of the Central Andes, especially during Carnival.[17]

Most of the *pinkillus* played around Macha, I was told, were made near Huanuma, a popular destination for highland herders on their exchange visits to the valleys with llamas. Instruments are typically constructed from branches of the Andean Elder tree (*sawku*), which have a pithy core that may be easily scraped away to create a tube.[18] Red-hot irons (*multis*) are then forced along the tube's length to enlarge it, followed by water to inhibit further burning. Finally, six fingerholes (*qhaparina* 'shouting places') are drilled and burned, and a recorder-type duct mechanism carved with a knife.[19]

---

[17] For discussion of *tarkas* see INDICEP 1973:4, Baumann 1982a, Suárez 1984, Turino 1993:50–51, Stobart 1996a:79. On the border with Cochabamba department, *pinkillu* flutes are also sometimes called *charka* (Baumann 1982a:29) – a term also used for other duct flutes played in La Paz department, Bolivia (d'Harcourt & d'Harcourt 1959: 28).

[18] Latin name: *Sambucus Peruviana*. Other woods commonly used include: *turumi*, *balsa* (*Ochroma lagopus*), *chirimoya* (*Annona cherimola Mill*) and *tarku* (*Jacaranda mimosifolia*) – Calla 1995:55–56.

[19] See Figure 9.3 for a diagram of duct mechanism and comparison with notch flute construction.

The family of flutes

During feasts *pinkillus* are usually played together in a consort (*trupa*) of four to six sizes, certain of which may be doubled.[20] The various *pinkillu* sizes are linked to the growth cycle of animals; the terms *uña* ('offspring'), *malta* ('adolescent/medium') and *machu* ('old' or 'ancestor') used to refer to both llamas and *pinkillus*. The instruments of the *pinkillu* consort are also divided between paired *tara* and *q'iwa* sizes, the *q'iwas* pitched a fifth above the *taras*. Figure 8.2 shows a set of four instruments, although larger consorts of up to six sizes are also common, as in several other parts of Northern Potosí. These latter sets usually include a very large *machu* size, which includes a polythene tube (*manguera*) to enable the player to blow the instrument and reach the fingerholes (Figure 8.1).[21]

The terms *tara* and *q'iwa* refer to tone quality or timbre (Stobart 1996a:68–70). *Tara* is a hoarse vibrant sound, much appreciated, whereas *q'iwa* is clear, thin and relatively weak, and often considered aesthetically

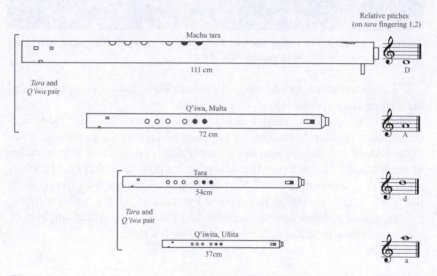

Figure 8.2   A *pinkillu* consort (*trupa*), showing relative sizes, pitches and names

---

[20] In some cases a complete consort was purchased by a single person, in others the various instruments of a set were purchased individually. As there is no pitch standard it is a matter of chance whether instruments from different consorts can be played together.

[21] A pair of smaller instruments are also sometimes added to these larger consorts: the *tarita* ('little *tara*') or *'juch'uy maltita* ('little *malta*'), pitched a fourth above the *q'iwita*, and the *juch'uycito* ('tiny one'), pitched one octave above the *q'iwita*. The tiny *juch'uycito* is sometimes made from plastic tube, rather than wood, and in practice is often discarded due to poor construction.

inferior. *Tara* tone quality is also found in other duct flutes of department Potosí, such as those made in Vitichi (Stobart 1988). Whilst playing in a *lawatu* duct flute consort in Yura I once swapped instruments with a fellow player. He strongly disapproved of my instrument's clear, thin sound (which I had rather liked at the time) and removed the block that he then trimmed with a sharp knife. He was very pleased with the resulting harsh and vibrant timbre; my initial reaction was that he had wrecked my instrument.

The *tara* and *q'iwa* instruments of the *pinkillu* consort, as played in Kalankira, are categorized according to the sound produced on the tuning/termination note which is heard at the end of every *wayñu* melody or for tuning before starting to play. (However, all sizes of *pinkillu* – except the large *machu tara* – are able to produce both *tara* and *q'iwa* sounds, dependent on fingering.) For the termination/tuning note, *q'iwa* (*q'iwita*) instruments use the fingering 23456, to create a thin, clear sound (*q'iwa*) one octave above their corresponding *tara* partner, which uses the fingering 12 to create a rich vibrant *tara* timbre (Figure 8.3).[22] CD track 25 demonstrates the sounds produced, using the respective *tara* or *q'iwa* fingering, on the termination/tuning note for the four main instruments of a consort: (1) *machu tara* (2) *q'iwa* (3) *tara* (4) *q'iwita*.

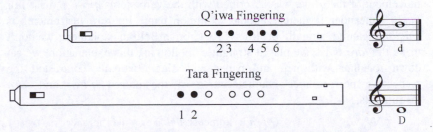

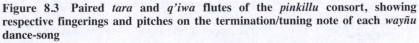

Figure 8.3 Paired *tara* and *q'iwa* flutes of the *pinkillu* consort, showing respective fingerings and pitches on the termination/tuning note of each *wayñu* dance-song

The *pinkillu* flutes of Northern Potosí are notable for their use of hocket or interlocking technique between the paired *tara* and *q'iwa* sizes, which in certain respects is comparable to that used in panpipe performance. This use of interlocking is most evident between the lower instruments of the consort, especially because the *machu tara* can only play three pitches. Strict interlocking between paired *machu tara* and *q'iwa* instruments is heard on CD track 26 (Example 8.3) recorded in Toracari (Charka province, Northern Potosí), where the two instruments only play together on the final termination notes. (However, on certain pitches the 'double' quality of

---

[22] In some cases it is necessary to shade or cover one of the lower finger holes in order to achieve this vibrant *tara* sound.

Example 8.3 Interlocking between two largest size *pinkillus*. *Machu tara* (downward stems), *q'iwa* (upward stems). (CD track 26)

tara timbre sometimes gives the false impression that two instruments are playing.)

The straight and the twisted [23]

Strict interlocking between *tara* and *q'iwa* instruments was less common in Kalankira, where instead people stress the contrast between the continuous melismatic performance style of the *q'iwa* (especially the small *q'iwita* flute) and the powerful sustained notes of the *tara*. The restless 'twisting' melodic movement of the *q'iwa* was described with the verb stems *q'iwi-* ('twist') or *link'u* ('meander') whereas another common name for *tara* instruments is *chiqan*, meaning 'straight' or 'true'.[24] As Ciprian Beltrán explained, 'we don't make the *tara* twist, we play it straight'.[25] Following this explanation, we sat down together with pen and paper and diagramatically contrasted the respective performance characteristics of the paired *q'iwa* and *tara* instruments:

ᴧᴧᴧᴧᴧ   *Q'iwa* instruments: *link'u* or *q'iwi* ('meander'or 'twist')
                    (melodic movement, restless fingers, continuity)

_____ _____   *Tara* or *chiqan* instruments: *chiqan* ('straight/true')
                    (sustained, little alternation, separation)

In practice only the smaller flutes of the consort, which cannot produce *tara* timbre, tend to play almost continuously and in a fluid melismatic style. This style of playing is especially associated with the *q'iwita*, which is referred to as the *ira* ('leader') of the consort, as it leads and states the melody – even when a higher pitched *tarita* size is present. People also described the *q'iwita* as the 'heart' (*sunqu*) of the consort, or its 'principal motor', in the words of

---

[23] See Stobart 1998a for further discussion of this theme in the context of kinship.

[24] *Chiqan* is the most common name for the *tara* category of instruments in the Macha valley areas that I visited.

[25] *Tarata mana link'uchinchis, chiqallanta tukanchis.*

Alberto Camaqui from *ayllu* Laymi.[26] Most *tara* and (large) *q'iwa* instruments, except the *machu tara*, are able to play all the notes of the pentatonic scale used in *wayñu* melodies, but players usually choose to leave out certain pitches. This enables them to create a fuller and richer sound and to stress the *tara* notes of their particular instrument, which need time and large amounts of breath to speak well. The contrast between the continuous melodic style of the *q'iwita*, which 'leads' the ensemble, and long sustained pitches of the *machu tara* is clearly audible on CD track 29 (Example 8.4). From this context it is clear that *q'iwa* should principally be associated with thin, plaintive, melismatic and higher pitched sounds, whilst *tara* is linked with vibrant, slower moving, sustained and lower pitched ones, where the name applied to the instrument itself is of secondary importance. Nonetheless, whereas the small *q'iwita* or *uñita* ('offspring') instrument 'leads' and provides melodic continuity, as the 'heart' of the consort, the larger *tara* instruments respond and dominate the final cadence – consisting of a characteristic drop of a minor third and a vibrant and sustained termination note (Example 8.4).

In certain other parts of highland Bolivia, high-pitched *pinkillu* duct flutes, made of cane, with a clear timbre – evocative of *q'iwa* – are played early in the growing season to attract rain. At Carnival, the climax of the growing season, heavy wooden duct flutes called *tarkas*, which produce a rich vibrant *tara*-type sound, replace them.[27] According to Hans Buechler, in Compi, near lake Titicaca, *tarkas* were considered to attract dry spells and their performance in the early part of the rains was prohibited, as their sound would endanger the young growing crops (1980:385). This suggests that the *q'iwa*-type sound was seen to provoke rainfall, and *tara*-like timbre to halt it. However, in Kalankira, people did not differentiate between the roles of *q'iwa* and *tara* sounds in this way; instead, according to Acencio, it was the very act of bringing the *tara* and *q'iwa* into 'tune' or 'agreement' (*iwalan*) with one another that caused it to rain. An exploration of the broader meanings surrounding the categories *tara* and *q'iwa* suggests that the challenge of bringing them into 'tune' or 'agreement' in *pinkillu* performance may lead us well beyond purely acoustic considerations.

---

[26] In *ayllu* Laymi the *q'iwita* is referred to in Aymara as *chuyma* or 'heart' (Camaqui 2001:13).

[27] It is likely that the design of *tarka* (or *anata*) flutes, which are now extremely widely played in the central and southern Andes, was originally based on a prototype similar to the *pinkillu* of Northern Potosí. The bore of most modern *tarkas* is drilled from a solid piece of wood, but older forms from department Oruro are constructed in precisely the same way as *pinkillus* – by burning out the pithy core of *tarku* wood. Also, the name *tarka* is undoubtedly etymologically related to the word *tara* which perfectly describes the distinctive quality of these instruments' sound. However, *tarka* makers from the instrument making village of Walata Grande (department La Paz) described this vibrant sound quality as *chirr* and were unfamiliar with the term *tara*.

Example 8.4 *Pinkillu* flute *wayñu* showing the interaction of parts, which vary on each repetition. The inner *tara* and *q'iwa* part are difficult to identify and very approximate. (CD track 29)

Rethinking harmony: the concept of *tara*

The concepts of *tara* and *q'iwa* provide a particularly good example of how musical experience of 'harmony' or 'dissonance' is socially constructed. In Chapter 6 we encountered the idea of 'violent harmony' in *tinku* fighting and a sense of diachronic harmony between paired *julajula* panpipes, but here the relationship between social and musical harmony becomes even more critical. That the sonorities of Andean flutes often seem 'harsh' or 'dissonant' to outsiders is hardly surprising given that the sounds literally are 'dissonant' from the perspective of Western acoustics. For example, the vibrant beating quality of *tara* is the result of difference beats – associated in Western music with two pitches being 'out of tune' or at a dissonant interval with one another. *Pinkillu* flutes are usually blown strongly and constructed in such a way as to create a rich multiphonic texture, often – according to Arnaud Gérard –

privileging the second and third harmonics and giving the effect of a chord at the octave and fifth (1997:67).[28] Indeed, this sense of a chord was highlighted when players described *tara* as 'two sounds' or as something which sounds with 'two mouths' (Stobart 1996a:58) – typically pitched approximately one octave apart, but not precisely so as to create a beating effect.

This aesthetic for a vibrant timbre appears to be widespread and very ancient in South America, and has been achieved through exploiting a range of musical technologies.[29] For example, José Pérez de Arce has identified an aesthetic for a 'dissonant' (from a Western perspective) vibrant timbre or 'torn sound' (*sonido rajado*) in the living performance tradition of the Chilean *pifilca*, and notes that this same form of sound production is evident from a number of pre-Hispanic instruments (1998).[30] Gerardo Reichel-Dolmatoff has also identified the opposing associations of whistling and buzzing sounds among the Amazonian Desana: sustained whistling (evocative of *q'iwa* timbre), he observes, has connotations of sexual invitation and the incitement of prohibited behaviour, and works in dialogue with buzzing sounds. According to one of his informants the 'buzzing is the result of accumulation' – as retained energy ready to explode or overflow (1971:115–16). As we shall see, this has close resonances with the *tara/q'iwa* contrast: the clear, thin and 'fluty' sound of *q'iwa* is associated with the build up and retention of energy, and the vibrant *tara* sound linked with its release; the two principles working in dialogue.

In Kalankira, the *tara* sound was intimately linked with concepts of pairing, social harmony, balance and equilibrium, as well as with high energy, abundance and exchange (Stobart 1996a:71–7). Perhaps this association is best conveyed by the example of the *tarka yuru*, a double drinking vessel used at weddings. The two halves are connected by a tube which enables fluid to pass freely and be equalized between the two vessels (ibid. 75). Similar implications of balance and equilibrium were also evident when Asencio shouted *TARA TARA* to the mismatched yoke of oxen while ploughing. Even if experienced as 'dissonance' by outsiders, it was evident that for people in Kalankira and many other parts of the Andes, the vibrant sound quality of *tara* powerfully conveys notions of social harmony and the expression or release of

---

[28] I am indebted to my friend and colleague Arnaud Gerard who, following up on my earlier research on *tara* and *q'iwa* (Stobart 1996a), has made an excellent study of *tara* from an acoustic perspective. He argues that *tara* refers specifically to the vibrant aspect of the timbre, resulting from difference beats, rather than to the rich and dense, multiphonic aspect of the sound, as implied in Stobart 1996a:70–71 (Gérard 1997:57–8).

[29] Prehispanic multiple chamber *ocharinas* (globular duct flutes) are sometimes constructed to produce two pitches that beat against one another (Olsen 2002:101).

[30] The 'secret' of vibrant sound production of the *pifilca*, which is played in the manner of a panpipe, lies in the way that the cylindrical tube is divided into two sections of approximately even length, the upper almost twice the diameter of the lower. This form of complex tube is found in several prehispanic instruments (Pérez de Arce 1998: 17–18, 25).

accumulated energies. While there are close similarities with the 'violent harmony' of *tinku*, in this case the dialectical tension is expressed in the timbre of a single instrument. Also, whereas the *julajula* panpipes of 'harvest time' take the form of vessels that contain and accumulate energies, *pinkillu* flutes are open ended and said to be 'full of holes' – evoking the free flow and circulation of animating energies or substances from within; an image with obvious resonances for the rainy season.

Deconstructing dissonance: the concept of *q'iwa*

The *q'iwa* sound consists of a single clear pitch, which would be very unlikely to be associated with dissonance, from a Western acoustical or musical perspective. Yet in Kalankira this timbre tended to be less appreciated aesthetically, and the word *q'iwa* was linked with notions of social dissonance or disagreement, imbalance, disequilibrium and certain forms of mediation. As already noted above, I often heard people who were considered 'mean' or 'stingy' described derogatively as *q'iwa*, suggesting that this sound quality was interpreted as 'failure to give', whereas the energized *tara* sound 'gives' freely and abundantly. Also in Chapter 6, I observed that people who do not wish to fight ('give') in *tinku* are dubbed *q'iwa*; disparaged not only as 'cowards' but as 'lazy, slack or feeble' (Sp. *flojo*).

The implication of individual accumulation was also suggested by the use of the term *q'iwa* in Kalankira to refer to castrated llamas because, as Paulino explained, through castration *q'iwa* llamas grow much fatter than their *machu* ('stud') counterparts, which use up energy in sexual activity or 'giving', as he put it. The accumulation of fat by *q'iwa* llamas is reminiscent of the hoarding of water by the devil in don Adrian's story (Chapter 7), and the widespread assertion that all devils are *q'iwa*. In this context it is also significant that devils are often claimed to inhabit rocks, which are considered sources of immense accumulated energy (*animu*) and sonic (musical) or reproductive potential, yet paradoxically are also among the most fixed, inert and ungiving objects in the landscape.

Whereas the word *tara* is etymologically linked to an old Aymara word for tuning the strings of a guitar (Stobart 1996a:74), I often heard *q'iwa* applied to an instrument that was 'out of tune' with others or with itself, such as a string instrument that could not be tuned properly.[31] This same sense of

---

[31] The *recto* consort of *musiñu* flutes, played in parts of departments Oruro and La Paz, includes a single instrument (*q'iwa* or *sobre requinto*) tuned to play a tone above a group of instruments (*requintos*) which are pitched an octave above the deepest (*saliwa*) instrument in the consort. All instruments in the consort play the same melody in parallel. Whilst the *q'iwa* instrument sounds at a 'dissonant' second above the *requintos*, it is also pitched a fifth above the *irasu* size

dissonance was also conveyed by the use of *q'iwa* to refer to awkward shaped fields or *adobes* (mud bricks); in short, things that did not fit and made life a trial.[32] Urban Bolivians commonly use the word *q'iwa* to mean 'homosexual' (Sp. *maricon*), but in Kalankira and other parts of rural Northern Potosí, it was said to be 'half-male, half-female', without necessarily carrying homosexual connotations. I witnessed several rituals in which men and women exchanged clothes (Chapter 9) where the participants were described as *q'iwa*, as were the *monos* during the *rinuwa* feasts when they spoke in falsetto voices (Chapter 7). This word carries a wide range of highly ambivalent or negative connotations, richly evoking notions of social and cultural dissonance. At the same time *q'iwa* seems linked with ideas of 'agency' and potentiality, and the mediation, destabilization or reconfiguration of relations between, for example, the living and the ancestors, or male and female. I suggest that the power and unsettling nature of the *q'iwa* sound may partly be understood if approached as an expression of dependency and distress. Indeed, another common use of the word *q'iwa* is to refer to a child who constantly whinges or wails.

(C) LOVE AND COMPASSION: THE CRIES OF DEPENDENCY

The hungry period of the year, between the usual onset of the rains (October–November) and their peak around the summer solstice (December–January), was referred to in Kalankira as *lapaka* or *khuyay timpu*. The term *lapaka* was related to hunger and scarcity, especially of pasture for the animals which, following heavy grazing and desiccation during the winter months, becomes increasingly sparse, not to be replenished until after the solstice. In Kalankira people often related the word *khuyay* to 'thin animals', but more generally this word is glossed as 'love' or 'compassion'. Whilst the other common Quechua word for 'love' – *munay* – appears linked with notions of desire, *khuyay* concerns the 'love' of, for example, a parent for his or her child, or to compassion for a distressed infant or animal. In his 1608 Quechua–Spanish dictionary Gonzalez Holguín glosses *ccuyay* [*khuyay*] as 'the love that gives good to somebody' and relates it to the idea of 'doing good and giving grace to something' (1989 [1608]:73).[33] *Khuyay* concerns the demonstration of compassion but the critical point is that this 'good' is an

---

instruments (themselves a fifth above the *saliwa*), thereby enriching the natural harmonics and overall density of sound.

[32] The word's explosive ejective (*q'i*), that shortens the vowel sound and concentrates the energy discharge into a reduced interval of time, also conveys notions of smallness, narrowness and thinness, which fit in well with *q'iwa's* association with meanness (Mannheim 1991:193–5).

[33] *Ccuyay. El amor que da alguin bien* and *Ccuyaycuni. Hazer bien y dar de gracia algo, y amar haziendo algun bien* (González Holguín 1989 [1608]:73).

expression of sentiment. Unlike such concepts of *ayni*, *minka* (labour prestation) or *tinku* (encounter), which have so dominated Andean ethnography, *khuyay* is not in essence reciprocal in a mechanistic sense but focuses on the empathetic feelings of the giver/helper.[34] In some senses it refers to an unequal relationship in which one party gives for the benefit of a needy, dependent or distressed other. Reciprocity may occur at a later stage – for example when an infant matures and begins to contribute to the economic welfare of a family.

I argue that a key medium through which such sentiments are aroused is sound and more specifically though distress or separation cries and weeping, or their invocation in music (see also Chapter 2). These affecting sounds highlight a sense of dependency and a powerful moral imperative to respond. Using distress cries to provoke compassionate responses from gods or ancestors appears to be widespread and ancient in the Andes, especially as a means to attract rain at the start of the growing season. Guaman Poma (c.1615) documents the prehispanic practice of tying up black llamas in public squares without food or drink during October. On the animal's body, in the drawing that accompanies his text, is written: *Carnero negro ayuda a llorar y pedir agua a dios con la hambre que tiene* – 'The black [llama] helps to weep and plead for water from god with its hunger' (Figure 8.4).

Guaman Poma's drawing (Figure 8.4) also depicts a sorrowful and tearful procession, which includes children, the infirm and elderly, who walk from peak to peak shouting and crying out 'with all their heart' to the god *Runa Camag* for rain (1980 [c. 1615]:254–5). One night during a period of severe drought in Kalankira, I watched a similar procession of small children make its way to a nearby peak to plead to God for rain.[35] While their voices echoed eerily overhead *awa tatay*, *awa tatay* ('water father, water father'), down in the hamlet I joined the men to play *pinkillus* late into the night. I was told that only young children were sent to plead for rain, as god would not listen to adults as they are *juchasapas*, or have lost their innocence.[36] Nonetheless, adult women powerfully aroused compassion and expressed dependence in laments to the dead, which I will suggest share close musical parallels with the *wayñu* music of *pinkillu* flutes.

---

[34] However, emotional pressure – especially expressed through a distinctive wheedling speech – is often exerted, when individuals are requested to participate in *ayni* or *minka* or when asking for favours. This vocal quality is also often used when addressing perceived social superiors. On occasion I found this affecting voice quality, which emulates weeping, extremely annoying. In retrospect my dislike of this sound can probably be attributed to the social asymmetry it invokes.

[35] I have been told about this practice in several other parts of Northern Potosí. Also see, for example, Berg 1989:112–13 and Rösing 1996:247–64.

[36] The Quechua *jucha* is often glossed as 'sin', but it also conveys the idea of participation in forms of business arrangement or contract.

Figure 8.4 A procession of weeping mourners and a llama tethered without food to help cry for rain in the month of October (Guaman Poma 1936 [c.1615]:254)

Deserted to wander weeping: laments in the cemetery

The second major series of rites in the cemetery were held almost a month after All Saints on the feast of St Andrew (30 November) and once again the black shrouds over the graves of adults were covered with sprouting green onions. On this occasion each grave was also decorated with three wreaths, made from green willow fronds and pink roses, and many women knelt beside the graves of deceased family members and performed distressingly sad laments.[37] While each woman wept – intensely absorbed in personal grief – people all around drank and talked with good humour, as though oblivious to her anguish. I recorded a few of these weeping songs in full view of the performer, troubled by deeply contradictory feelings; on the one hand I did not wish to invade their grief, on the other I felt it important to document these immensely powerful, poignant and poetic expressions. A short segment of text from one lament (Example 8.5) highlights both the richness of the poetry and the way in which the singer presents herself as a dependent (CD track 24):

1   *Mamitay nuqama kasqayniqa, ala wawitay*
     herman nuqama kayman kasqa
     mana hermanituyuq kayman kasqa,
     ay nuqama kaniqa

                              Mother, woe is me! Ah! my child.
                              Brother, here I endure
                              I am condemned to live without my little brother
                              Ah! such is my woe

2   *Jay ... wawitay nispa*
     chayarqamuq kanchu,
     ni maymanta, ni uraymanta,
     ni [wi]chaymanta chayarqamuq kanchu

                              Ah ... There is nobody who comes
                              [to me] saying 'my child',
                              not from anywhere, not from below,
                              nor from above. There is nobody who comes!

3   *Jay ... mamitaykita ama rikuq nuqa kusqayki*
     kanan rikuq nuqama kusqayki, mamay

                              Ah ... my mother, I cannot see you
                              Show yourself to me, mother

---

[37] Although I did not witness any, I was told that laments are also sometimes performed at All Saints.

4   *Jay ... mamitay mana qunqay atinata*
      puñuykuwaq kasqa, iki mamakita

> Ah ... mother I cannot forget
> I realize that your destiny was to go to sleep;
> is that not so mother?

5   *Jay ... mamitay nuqama kasqaniqa, mana mamitay*
      imallata mamitay mikhuykurqanki?
      misk'i puñuy jap'inayki[paq]

> Ah ... mother, woe is me!
> Mother, what was it that you ate?
> sweet sleep for you to grasp

6   *Jay ... mamitay, ni maymanta*
      chayarqamuq kanchu, wawitay nispa

> Ah... mother, there is nobody coming
> from anywhere saying 'my child'

7   *Jay ... mayllaman saqirpakuwanki?*
      tukuy lumapi wayq'upi
      waqas purinaypaq,
      ni maypi qunqay atinalla

> Ah ... where have you deserted me?
> to wander weeping
> on every hill and gully
> nowhere can I forget[38]

Perhaps these disturbing (female) outpourings of grief can be understood to be harnessed to productive ends, much as inherently disruptive (male) violence is shaped to socially constructive ends in *tinku* (Chapter 6). Both these powerful and potentially destabilizing expressions are subject to prescribed times, places and forms.[39] Like the plaintive cries of an infant for its mother, children's voices pleading for rain, or the pitiful wailing of a hungry tethered llama, the singer powerfully conveys her distress and sense of dependency in order to invoke pity and compassion. For all their verbal poignancy, it is perhaps ultimately the quality of sound that is the lament's most powerful and disturbing aspect. Any listener, no matter their language,

---

[38] I am grateful to Pedro Plaza and Rosaleen Howard for their help in interpreting and translating these poignant verses, and in particular for Rosaleen Howard's suggested use of the archaic English 'woe is me' to express heightened emotion implied by the use of the emphasizing suffixes *-ma* and *-qa* (*nuqama kasqaniqa*).

[39] Radcliffe-Brown's point (1964) that 'the sentiment does not create the act, but wailing at a prescribed moment and in the prescribed manner creates within the wailer the proper sentiment' seems relevant here (Huntington & Metcalf 1979:26).

Ma-mi-tay — nu-qa-ma kas-qa-ni-qa— a-la wa- wi - tay

(sob) her - ma - nu/nu - qa - ma kay - man ka - sqa ma - na her - ma

ni - tu - yuq— kay - man kas(sqa) Ay nu - qa ka - ni - qa

Example 8.5 Lament. Outline transcription, showing approximate rhythm and pitch, which stresses the characteristics of (a) an initial microtonal slide and (b) a drop of a minor third at phrase ends. Each bar represents approximately 1 second. Transposed up about one semitone. (CD track 24)

can identify the intense emotion that the sound conveys and can hardly fail to feel empathy or compassion (CD track 24). The Kalankiras associated this 'stirring' of the emotions with the *sunqu* ('heart'), which is locally identified with the core of the body, especially the liver (*q'iwicha*), rather than the organ the 'heart'. The word for *q'iwicha* ('liver') can literally be translated as 'make [something] twist/stir', where the verb stem *q'iwi* ('twist, stir, bend something straight') is widely used to refer to internal body pain as well as stirring the emotions. In this context it is significant that people also use *q'iwi* to refer both to the melismatic and restless playing style of the *q'iwa* (*q'iwita*) flute and to the act of acquiring or creating new *wayñu* melodies (Chapter 9), highlighting their connection with deeply felt emotions. I often heard people say *musuq wayñus q'iwinchis* – 'we collect/twist/stir new *wayñus*'.

   Like other laments I heard, this example shares several structural features with *pinkillu* flute *wayñus*, leading to a sense that both musically inform one another, as genres that 'weep' and explicitly express – and communicate with – the souls. The emotional high-pitched opening of the lament, with its undefined melismatic descent (Example 8.5), is evocative of the plaintive, thin and continuous 'twisting' line of the *q'iwita* flute, which leads and is the 'heart' of the *wayñu*. In turn, the more sustained and clearly articulated pitches which close each stanza of the lament, feature a drop of a minor third: a cadential formula characteristic of *wayñu* music (Example 8.4). While the first part (A section) of the *pinkillu* flute *wayñu*, including the cadence, is led by the *q'iwa* instruments, the second part (B section) and particularly the final cadence and sustained termination note is dominated by the vibrant *tara* instruments. There is a sense that both the *wayñu* and lament involve a kind of emotional journey or catharsis in which the twisting or undefined *q'iwa*, characterized as 'unbalanced/dissonant/out of tune' (*mana iwalasqa*), must be brought into agreement with *tara*, as 'well balanced/hamonious/in tune' (*sumaq iwalasqa*) – thereby provoking rainfall. Where the thin clear *q'iwa* sound appears to invoke feelings of sorrow, sympathy and desire, the vibrant *tara* timbre suggests the violent release and circulation of pent up energies and emotions, both an act of giving and an erotic climax.

(D) FLUTES AND LLAMAS: SEX AND SORROW

Llamas, like *pinkillu* flutes, are associated with two categories of sound: plaintive, thin, and high-pitched 'hungry' sounds, evocative of *q'iwa* timbre, and 'happy', full-throated, gurgling, vibrant and energetic mating cries, suggestive of *tara*. Asencio made a direct and surprising connection between llama and *pinkillu* sounds when I asked him why *pinkillus* are played outside the cemetery during the feast of All Saints:

> ... for mating, that's why they play... to copulate like llamas, that's why they play at the cemetery. So that men and women have sex, copulate like llamas. They sound-out *aarrr aarr eee* at All Saints during the libations until [everyone gets] drunk.[40]

A close connection between llama sexuality and the *pinkillu* flute was also highlighted in a ceremony I attended at the house of a recently deceased man during All Saints in *ayllu* Chayantaka (Map 2). In this fecundation ritual, the mating habits of the various domestic animals were hilariously imitated in turn. A different object was held in place of a phallus for each species and significantly for the llama it was a *pinkillu* flute. More generally, the phallic associations of *pinkillu* flutes were sometimes made blatantly obvious and I often heard imitations of llama mating sounds used humorously to refer to human sex.[41] Thus the passions associated with the early part of the rains not only concern sorrow and invoke the dead, but are also linked to sexual desire: the pent up fluids released are not only lachrymose but also seminal. Similarly, *wayñu* music and *qhata* dancing are particularly closely linked with sexuality. Paulino told me how an evening of *wayñu* singing and dancing from house to house during All Saints – in which we had both participated – had later transformed into a sexual frenzy on the hillsides. With a combination of disapproval, prurience and amusement, he described the girls as *arichas* ('easy morals') who just 'copulated like chickens'. In several other parts of Northern Potosí, I have heard how *qhata* dancing to *wayñu* music at All Saints

---

[40] *Arqikunanpaq, chayrayku tukanku chayta... Llamajina chajrukunanpaq chayrayku tukanku chaytaqa simintiriyupi. Qhariwarmis qukunankurayku a, llamajina chajrunankurayku. Chay sunashan aarrr aarr ee Turus santuspi chay ch'allaspi... machasqamanta*

[41] *Pinkillus* were said to be made from *jatuchus k'aspis* 'big branches' and the word *k'aspiwan* ('as a branch') is used to refer to a penile erection.

frequently leads to sexual encounters among young people. Thus, ideas of union in the early part of the rains must also, in part, be understood as sexual. However, the most influential sexual encounters of the year – which also undoubtedly shape ideas about human sexuality – are those between the male and female llama herds around the time of the summer solstice, the peak of rains.

Mixing the llamas

In Kalankira each family's llamas are organized into two herds according to gender and age category. The 'roaming' herd, consisting of adult stud (*machu*) and castrated (*q'iwa*) males, is left to roam on the high peaks, overseen from time to time by the men, and periodically rounded up to act as beasts of burden – especially for trips to the valleys during the dry winter months. Meanwhile, the 'reproductive' herd, consisting of females (*china*), immature males (*maltas*), and newborns (*uñitas* or *uñas*), are the responsibility of the women, who pasture them daily and return them to the corrals beside their homesteads each evening. The male and female animals are only brought together for the special mating ceremonies called *llama chajru* ('llama mixing') or *arqhichina* ('make mate') held around Christmas or New Year.[42] As the gestation period is approximately one year, I was told, it is desirable that the llamas give birth during the rains when there is adequate pasture.[43] The mating was performed in special double corrals on the highest mountain in Kalankira territory near a series of tall standing stones, called *San Francisco Qala Walaychu* (St Francis Rolling Stone lit. 'rock lout') that were noted for their immense sexual powers (see Chapter 5).

I attended one such llama 'mixing' ceremony on Christmas day in which some fifty pairs of animals were mated simultaneously (Figure 8.5).[44] It rained heavily for much of the day; the corral awash with flowing sound and regenerative fluids. The constant throaty sound of the sexually excited male llamas was remarkable and its vibrant quality highly evocative of the *tara* sound of *pinkillu* flutes. However, as can be heard from the recording I made

---

[42] The onomatopoeic verb *arqhiy* 'to mate' was explicitly linked with hoarse mating noises made by male llamas. In his Quechua–Spanish dictionary, Lara glosses *arqhëy* as 'death rattle' and 'breathe longingly with desire' (1978:51), which suggests that this vibrant release of substance (semen) might be seen as destructive to the male body. Elsewhere, of course, sexual climax is often connected with death – *la petit mort* (Falk 1994:61).

[43] In a study of the reproductive endocrinology of llamas and alpacas, Bravo gives the llama and alpaca gestation period as between 342 and 350 days (Bravo 1994:272).

[44] This ceremony was actually performed jointly by most of the familes of Wak'an Phukru. The families of Pata Kalankira tended to perform this ceremony individually and I attended Paulino and Asencio's own ceremony at New Year.

Figure 8.5 Llama mating ceremony on the rocky mountain peak of San Francisco Qala Walaychu above Kalankira on Christmas day

in the mixing corral of some seventy llamas mating simultaneously (CD track 30), a number of higher-pitched cries are also audible, which Paulino remarked 'balance like *pinkillus*, some are high-pitched (*nañu* 'narrow') and some are throaty and deep (*rakhu* 'broad')'. In some parts of Northern Potosí llama mating is accompanied by *pinkillu* music, however people in Kalankira told me that the already excessively excited male llamas needed no further encouragement. I also discovered that my host family's male llamas were far from reticent about enjoying their one opportunity of the year. While Paulino and Asencio went to round up some more males, during the family's own llama mating ceremony, I was asked to keep a dozen or so stud llamas from entering the females' corral. This was an extremely unpopular, difficult and dangerous task, which involved spending some thirty minutes frantically trying to push the stud males back into their corral and acting as the target of their foul smelling spittle. They were desperate to mix. The focus during this period on the creative 'mixing' of llamas might also explain why certain people identified the muddy timbre of *charka* tuning on the *kitarra* with the period between All Saints to late January, describing it as *chajru telmasqa* ('mixed-up tuning').

Hungry sounds: regenerative powers

Nobody objected in the least when I recorded the 'happy' vibrant and gurgling sounds of mating llamas, however I encountered a very different response when I set about making a recording of the 'hungry' cries my hosts' female and young llamas made every morning before being herded up to the mountain pastures for the day. When I innocently entered the corral and switched on my tape recorder, Evangelia rushed out of the cooking hut, unblocked the opening of the corral and started chasing out the animals, saying 'that's enough *compadre*' (*basta compadre*) (CD track 31). Asunta also emerged from the cooking hut looking annoyed and I quickly switched off my tape recorder in confusion. As Evangelia headed up the hillside behind the herd, I asked Paulino why the women had been so angry. He explained that if I took the llamas 'hungry' (*q'iwa*-like) sounds away to my country in my tape recorder this would stop them reproducing (Stobart 1996b:471).[45] Out of respect for this view, CD track 31 is based on a few seconds of llama sounds artifically duplicated (and considerably amplified) to give the impression of a much longer recording.

Guaman Poma's description and illustration (c. 1615) of the *warisqa arawi* ceremony (Figure 8.6), in which the Inka king learned a song from a 'red'

---

[45] He described this potential appropriation of their reproductive powers as *nasiunalismu* ('nationalism').

Figure 8.6 The Inka learns his song from the cries of the 'red' llama (Guaman Poma 1936 [c. 1615]:318)

llama, suggests that a link between the plaintive sounds of hungry llamas, reproductive powers, the flow of water and music is neither unique to Kalankira nor new in the Andes (Stobart 1996b:480). This ceremony, performed in April, when 'the food crops ripen', and when 'the people of this kingdom eat, drink and are filled at the expense of the Inka', involved the Inka king imitating the *y, y, y* distress cries of a tethered llama. The song was then taken up by the queens (*qoyas*) and princesses (*ñustas*), and gradually disseminated through the empire sung by both women and men and played on *pingollo* flutes (Guaman Poma 1980: 242).[46]

> In this festival they sang the song of the llamas, the red llamas and the song of the rivers – the sound they make. This natural sound, the Inka's own song, is like the llama sings and says '*yn*' many times with measure (loc. cit.).

According to other colonial sources consulted by Tom Zuidema, the aim of the *warisqa arawi* was 'to make the maize cobs have good grains' (1986b:58). This highlights both the sacred quality of the high-pitched *y, y, y* distress cries of llamas, and their powerful regenerative associations not only for llamas themselves, but also for the production of crops (Figure 8.6).

The distinction between the 'happy' (*kusi*) mating noises and 'hungry' plaintive sounds of llamas seems to be of great importance for appreciating the significance of the *tara* and *q'iwa* sounds of *pinkillu* flutes and their interaction in performance. Notably, it is the plaintive *q'iwa*-like sounds, rather than the vibrant *tara*-like mating noises, that are associated with regenerative power. This suggests that the *q'iwa* sounds signify the accumulation of reproductive potential – even among castrated *q'iwa* llamas. Although odd from a Western biological perspective, castrated *q'iwa* llamas were sometimes said to be more fertile than their stud *machu* counterparts.[47] Might this imply that the association of *tara* with the release, exchange and circulation of reproductive resources is analogous to the story of the bell stones in which the sound of god's black cockerel was released and dissipated, whereas that of the devil's red rooster remains contained and stored up for the future (Chapter 2). From this perspective *tara* might be understood not only as active release but also as spent force, in contrast to the craving and accumulative potential of *q'iwa*.

---

[46] It is unclear whether Guaman Poma's reference to the *pingollo* refers to duct or notched flutes; variants of this term (such as *pinkillu, pingollo, pinkayllu*) are used generically to refer to many different types of 'flute'. See Stobart 1996b:473–7, 2001.

[47] Isbell, among others, has also pointed out the common association of androgyny with fertility in the Andes (1997:256–7), reminding us that *q'iwa* is sometimes characterized as half-male, half-female.

(E) GRASPED IN THE PLAITED NEST: CORRALS, FIELDS AND THE *QHATA* DANCE

During the early part of the rains, after planting is completed, considerable time is dedicated to building up the walls around the fields to protect the tender young crops from domestic animals. Even the main footpath to Macha was blocked with several walls, made from rounded rocks precariously piled on top of one another. This sense of enclosure permeates the entire rainy season; travel is difficult and sometimes men remain in doors for long periods, unable to work waterlogged fields. One such day, I found Paulino in the cooking hut peeling potatoes. He looked up with a mixture of humour and resignation and remarked: 'I'm like a woman.' With this season he found himself imprisoned within feminine space and forced to adopt women's tasks.

This sense of enclosure in feminized space is also evoked by the principal dance of the rains in which a male *pinkillu* troupe or *kitarra* player are enclosed by dancers who hold alternate hands in a plaited ring. Although sometimes simply called *wayñu*, this dance was more specifically known as *qhata* or *simp'a* ('plaited') *wayñu*.[48] As *qhata* requires a large number of participants, its performance was generally restricted to larger feasts such as All Saints and, in particular, Carnival when groups could include as many as thirty dancers (Figure 9.7). This form of communal dancing is immense fun, and often boisterous as the different sides of the circle pull and push with great hilarity, dragging the enclosed instrumentalists this way and that across the hillsides. As in other parts of Northern Potosí, among the young, *qhata* also carries overt sexual connotations and is sometimes performed all night long – during which young couples slip away into the darkness for love-making. Whilst the flutes of the enclosed male instrumentalists are explicitly phallic, the young women whose singing dominates the circle of dancers suggests sexual union or uterine embrace. However, the more obvious imagery, as invoked in the *asintu* songs (Chapter 5), is that of enclosed fields (*wirjin* 'virgin'), the home (*thapa* 'nest') and the (female) llama corral.[49]

In discussing this dance, Alberto Camaqui from *ayllu* Laymi explained that the Aymara word *qhata* refers to braiding between 10 and 20 threads of wool (*q'aytus*) to form a strong cord such as the type used as an extension to women's hair braiding (*tullma*) or for tying woven belts (*chumpis*). Evoking similar imagery of feminized space, the nearby Qaqachakas refer to potatoes planted in the Virgin earth as gripped inside her waistband (Arnold 1988:439). Another name for the *qhata* dance in Kalankira is *simp'a wayñu*, where *simp'a*

---

[48] An identical dance termed *wayñu* is discussed by Arnold 1992. Circle dances are performed during the rains in many parts of the Southern Andes. The best documented is the *qhachwa* (*cachua*) with references dating back to colonial times. See for example Cobo 1990: 245, Carter & Mamani 1982:195, Berg 1990:98.

[49] See also Dransart 1997:90.

means the 'plaiting' or 'braiding' of women's hair. One sunny day when Evangelia was combing her long hair outside on the patio she commented, 'devils do not have plaits'. The associations of loose hair with the evil, secret (*saxra*) and ambiguous but regenerative powers of the inner world (*ukhupacha*) were further highlighted when she explained the word for combing hair is *saxrakuqtin* (lit. 'whilst evil') and the comb used to do this, which is made from the roots of the *qayara* cactus, is called a *saxraña* (lit. 'now evil'). It would seem that the plaiting of women's hair, which judging from the drawings of Guaman Poma ([c.1615] 1980) was not widespread before the European invasion, is synonymous with domestication and the control of both creative and destructive forces.[50] Whilst shaggy and disordered hair was associated with the wild grasses that grow naturally on the mountainsides, neat and ordered plaits evoke the enclosed plots of cultivated crops.[51]

The plaited arms in *qhata* dancing are described as 'strong' and 'not easily broken' and the male instrumentalists who dance wildly in the centre of the ring are likened to animals trapped in a corral, reminding us of 'circling in my nest' during the *asintu* wedding verses (Chapter 5). Indeed, Lucca glosses the Aymara *qhatalliña* as 'to chain, shackle, fetter or tie up' (1983:366). This idea of enclosure not only relates to the walls around fields and corrals but also to the reproductive female herd, a focus of interest during the rains, and evokes dependence, reproduction, nurturing and domestication.

The *qhata* dance is also connected with the offerings placed on mountain peaks to protect fields from hail. In the following extract, Alberto Camaqui links the protection of the fields in the *granizo jark'a* ('hail taming') ceremony to the *qhata* dance. To my immense surprise at the time, he went on to equate the *pinkillu* flute players with a plant.

> Let's say for protection… circled, no? It's the same with *pinkillu* players. With *pinkillus* when there is to be *qhata* where do they play? Well, they are grasped in the centre of the *qhata*. So they are in the centre, placed there. They whistle away there. But if the *pinkillus* were not grasped, for sure they would go off and play elsewhere. Well, the *qhata* dance keeps advancing this way and that … pulled every way. [HS: It's amusing, it makes you laugh.] Yes. So that's why it's like that. Like a plant, isn't it? [HS: The *pinkillu* players are like a plant?!] Yes![52]

---

[50] Olivia Harris, personal communication, suggests that the Spanish insistence on cutting men's pigtails during the early colonial era may have led women to adopt the cultural duty of wearing plaits (see Platt, Bouysse-Cassagne & Harris, 2006: document 21/f.5v).

[51] Another association of shaggy hair with devils was the llama fleece wigs, termed *taka uma*, worn by the *monos* (equated with *satanas colorados*) for the *rinuwa* feasts of September (Chapter 7).

[52] *O sea, jark'anapaq… sirkusqa kashan, mana. Pinkilleros kikillantaq; pinkilluyuq si qhatanaqtinqa maytapis [mayniqpis?] tukapullawan ichari i? Entonces uj qhata jap'ikusqa chawpipi, entonces chawpipi paykunaqa na… ari… asintan i? Khuyukun paykunan[kus?];*

His comment suggests an equation between the music and movements of the enclosed *pinkillu* players and the growth of plants enclosed in the soil. In his Aymara dictionary of 1612, Bertonio translates the word *Cahuatha* as both 'to dance in a circle of people holding hands' and 'to pile earth up to potato plants so that they grow' (1984 [1612], II:32). It is almost as though the ring of the *qhata* dance represents not only the enclosing earth and female liquidity, but also the sun, which rises to the peak of its annual cycle in late December. Both the burning sun and soil consume the matured (male) body they enclose or 'grasp', in the same way as I was told that women's blood 'grasps' (*jap'in*) male semen in human conception.

Conclusion: sentiment, flow and containment

The start of the growing season – between All Saints (1 November) and the peak of the rains at the summer solstice (Christmas–New Year) – is a time of especially intense emotions. We have seen how, in a surge of tears, rain and seminal fluids, death is invoked, forms break down and sediments or regenerative substances mix – in a search for new life in death. Among my vivid memories of Kalankira at this time are the transformation of the hill on which my hosts' homestead is built into a slippery sea of mud, and the roaring noise from behind my hut; the dry gully had become a raging torrent. The landscape was consumed by liquidity. Alongside the music of the rains – where sound literally flows out of the 'many holed' *pinkillu* flutes – dance choreography is associated with reproduction, nurturing and domestication within bounded female space – fields, 'nests' and corrals. Men are feminized in this enclosing reproductive space during the rains; forced to remain in the *ayllu* and unable to express their independence and manhood through travel.

With the alternation between the dry and rainy seasons, we discover a fascinating reversal between aural (musical) and visual (choreographic) expressions. During the dry season, fluid sound-like substances are contained and accumulated within (male) bodies as they grow, develop, circulate and express independence, whereas in the rains these fluid sound-like substances are released and circulate, with regenerative processes taking place in enclosing (female) space.

This seasonal distinction, and its articulation and invocation through dance, finds vivid parallels with the organization of each family's llamas into two herds according to gender and age category. On the one hand the male herd, which roams freely on the peaks and makes periodic exchange journeys to the valleys during the dry winter months, closely parallels ideas surrounding the

---

mientras mana pinkillu jap'ikuwan[chu] seguro pinkilluyuq wak trichumanta tukukusanman. Entonces qhataqa sigue avanzashan uj ladoman, mana? [HS: Planta jina kay pinkilleros?] Ari!

men's *link'u link'u* dance of harvest season. On the other, the close association of the reproductive female herd with the corral, to which it is returned each evening, and the rainy season when it becomes a special focus of interest, closely parallels the *qhata* dance. Not only do llama herding practices and ideas about human gender and sexuality mutually inform one another, but llama husbandry also appears to be an important model for understanding choreographic representations.

This chapter raises some fundamental questions about musical values and sentiment. In particular, the concepts of *tara* and *q'iwa* force us to question how broader notions of 'harmony' and 'dissonance' are expressed and perceived musically across culture. *Pinkillu* music is not immediately easy listening for outside ears, but I hope to have provided some tools to enhance appreciation. For local participants and listeners, this music is saturated in sentiment. This does not mean that I encountered people moved to tears through meditative listening as found in some cultures – where such modes of reception are in themselves forms of cultural performance. But, I was left in no doubt of *wayñu's* intimate association with weeping, nostalgia, passions and the deepest sentiments. The mechanisms for the invocation of such musical emotion may be understood in terms of tension creation (*q'iwa*) and release (*tara*) – in this case invoked through timbral relations (Meyer 1956:28). Yet, rather than identifying a specific theory of musical emotion, my focus is on locally relevant orientations to meaning and emotion that encounters with *wayñu* 'afford' individuals in Kalankira. In the next chapter we move forward to Carnival season proper and see that this, already wide ranging, exploration of potential 'affordances' to meaning in *wayñu* music has still left many critical stones unturned.

Chapter 9

January–February/March
Disembodied Voices and Dancing Potatoes

Carnival devils, sirens, musical creation and new potatoes

Music is prophecy. Its styles and economic organization are ahead of the rest of society because it explores, much faster than material reality can, the entire range of possibilities in a given code. It makes audible the new world that will gradually become visible, that will impose itself and regulate the order of things; it is not only the image of things, but the transcending of the everyday, the herald of the future (Jacques Attali 1985:11).

… if Indians saw potatoes that had a different form from the rest … or other crops with a different shape from the others, they had the custom of adoring them and making many ceremonies to venerate them, drinking and dancing and viewing these as signs of good fortune (Martín de Murúa 1946 [1590]:278).[1]

This fourth and final chapter of Part III, documenting the musical year, focuses on the Carnival season – an extraordinary period of sometimes about a month between the feast of St Sebastian (20 January) and *Tentación*, the final night of the moveable feast Carnival. Following the hunger, grief and passions discussed in the last chapter that characterize the early rains, the generation of new fruits miraculously begins with the feast of St Sebastian, often known as *yarqa kacharpaya* ('despatch of hunger'). This emergence of food crops is first revealed musically in the form of new *wayñu* melodies, transmitted to the musicians of Kalankira by St Sebastian's flock of sirens (*sirinus*) – a form of musical devil – which emerge from inside the earth and roam the hillsides at night during Carnival, only finally despatched back into the earth on the night of *Tentación*. These *sirinus* (or *sirinas*, implying female gender, as they are sometimes known)[2] are critically important to local ideas about musical creation, knowledge and seduction, and were often claimed to be both fatally dangerous and the source of 'all music'.

As in the often-riotous Carnival and Mardi Gras festivities elsewhere, Kalankira's celebrations include ideas of reversal, humour and parody, but above all the focus is agricultural. Carnival celebrates flowers and new fruits,

---

[1] English translation from Silverblatt 1987:24–5.

[2] The terms *sirinu* and *sirina* were used interchangeably in Kalankira, implying a Spanish male/female gender distinction. However, people insisted that *sirinus* include both males and females – just like the human community (see Stobart 2006).

particularly the potato, which are only harvested and consumed following the ritual despatch of the rainy season instruments (*pinkillus*, *kitarra*, *pututus*), the new *wayñu* melodies, and the feast's patron known as *tata pulurisa* ('Father Flowers'), *tata karnawal* ('Father Carnival') or *tata pujllay* ('Father Play'). It was the performances of Carnival season, more than almost any other time of the year, which enabled me to make sense of the relationship between music and agricultural production; and in particular the intimate links between the human life cycle and that of the potato.[3]

In the first part of this chapter I discuss local ideas about potatoes and how these relate to sound and music. Then I turn to the Feast of San Sebastian in late January, exploring the role of Kalankira's Carnival devils, especially the *sirinus* and their connection with musical creativity. Finally, I turn to the feast of Carnival itself, describing four ceremonies that are of critical musical importance.

(A) POTATO PEOPLE, SOUL MUSIC AND EMBODIED VOICES

As abundantly clear from Arnold and Yapita's 1996 Bolivian anthology of the Potato, *Madre Melliza y sus crias* ('Twin mother and her offspring'), an analogy between humans and potatoes as living sentient beings is widespread in the high Andes.[4] Domingo Jiménez, an Aymara speaking *yatiri* (shaman) from Northern Potosí, describes the potato in terms of a human 'baby' and 'person', and goes on to discuss the three elements of potato metaphysics, which must all be present for the plant to grow. Like humans, potatoes possess *animu* (or *espiritu*), *axayu* that is linked with the growth tips and the opening of flowers or 'eyes', and *janayu* that Jiménez relates to branching growth (Jimenéz, Yapita & Arnold 1996:145).[5] Similarly in Kalankira, I was often told that the potato – like all other food crops – possesses *animu*, and human-like sentiments. Thus, tubers that are abandoned or not cared for appropriately were said to 'cry' (*waqan*) 'just like human babies' (Chapter 2). This assocation was again highlighted when I once observed the first new potato of

---

[3] For further discussion of music and potatoes in Kalankira see Stobart 1994 or 1996c (Sp.). Key literature on the culture of potatoes includes Salaman 1985 [1949], Murra 1979, Arnold 1988, Harrison 1989 and Arnold & Yapita 1996.

[4] Allen 1982:182 also notes that in Sonqo, Peru, potatoes are considered 'living, sentient beings', and Isbell 1997 relates the human life cycle to the growth cycle and processing of the potato.

[5] Arnold observes that among the Aymara speaking Qaqachaka humans are said to have three metaphysical aspects: a name (*suti*), a spirit (*animu*) and a soul (*janayu*). The precise connection to these three of a further aspect, *ch'iwu* ('shadow'), which Arnold relates to potato growth and reproduction, is unclear (1988:435). The Quechua speaking Kalankiras were not forthcoming about metaphysical aspects, besides *animu* – which itself has multiple aspects depending on the type of body in question.

the year passed around an assembled family, tenderly kissed by each person in turn, and called *wawa* ('baby').[6] Similarly, when harvested potatoes were sorted, tubers resembling human form (*llallawas*) were carefully selected and put on one side, for use in libations (Figure 9.1). In addition to such analogies in form and metaphysics, I explore the interaction between human and potato life cycles in this chapter, focusing on how such relations or metaphoric processes are articulated through music.[7] Indeed, far from being a mundane spud, this enchanted tuber or *chaskañawi* ('one with the bushy eyebrows') – the name of endearment it is given in libations and a word used to refer to a 'lover' in song poetry – emerges as particularly appropriate and helpful for making sense of the musical year.

As the phases of the moon are intimately connected with the growth of crops, great care is taken to avoid harvesting potatoes during a full moon (*jurt'a*).[8] Any tubers dug at this time, I was told, would be deeply pitted with

Figure 9.1 Potato tubers ressembling human form, referred to as *llallawas*, carefully put aside while sorting and storing the harvest.

---

[6] See also Arnold 1988:445.

[7] See Isbell 1985 and Urton 1985 for ways in which comparable 'metaphoric processes' are played out between humans and animals.

[8] See Arnold 1988:423–37 for a discussion of connections between potato cultivation, human reproduction and the phases of the moon.

no 'eyes' (*ñawi*), and would be 'deaf' (*luqt'u*) and unable to grow; once again stressing the potato's human-like faculties and emotions. The importance of 'eyes', as the points from which sprouts emerge, is clear, but the significance of hearing to potato cultivation is less obvious. *Wayñu* music is explicitly played to make potatoes grow, so presumably a 'deaf' tuber would be unable to sprout and grow. However, faulty musical instruments that fail to sound correctly are also described as *luqt'u* ('deaf'), which implies a two way communicative or inter-animating process, where *luqt'u* potatoes neither express themselves nor respond through sound, while healthy sentient potatoes do both. I want to stress here that the lives of material things and their regeneration fundamentally concern the communication of *animu*, expressed most powerfully through sound – in such forms as music, weeping or speech.

As evident from previous chapters, the material body – whether, for example, human, a potato tuber or a bell stone – is characterized as a form of vessel, wrapping or a conduit that contains *animu*, and through its creative power communicates with other bodies (Allen 1982:193). The vessels or skins that enclose this *animu* appear to be commonly thought of as a form of ancestral wrapping into which *animu* or *espiritu* enters bringing the 'body' to life, perhaps partly explaining why potatoes are always peeled in the rural Andes and the consumption of their skins avoided, as if some form of taboo (Arnold 1988:406). In the case of humans, Arnold observes that at birth a person's *animu* enters the body through the fontanel (*p"uju*), on the top of the head, and at death leaves, with immense force and like a rush of wind, through this same point (1988:371). She also notes that with the arrival and departure of *animu* is also believed to come and go the power of speech, and presumably the ability to produce and respond to sound more generally – as suggested by the entry of *supay* into the bell stones (Chapter 2).

The idea of *wayñu* as a form of 'soul music' – as the genre that the souls of the dead constantly dance and sing in the 'land of the souls' (*alma llajta*) – was introduced in the last chapter. Importantly, this music is said to continue to sound in the hidden sphere of the souls during the dry winter months, although inaudible to the living. To hear *wayñu* in November, the start of the rains, signals death – as the emergence of soul substance from a 'body' or sprouts from a tuber. By contrast, the new *wayñus* brought by the *sirinus* for Carnival do not invoke death (unless an unwary listener is lured away by their beautiful seductive music), but announce new life. *Wayñus* might helpfully be thought of as the 'soul music' which animates living 'bodies' from within, whether human or potatoes, enabling them to communicate with others and thereby develop, mature and grow. Like the *axayu* of the potato, described by Domingo Jiménez, this inner music leads living bodies on their path through life, and then beyond the bounds of the body to flowering and rebirth. When the 'harnessed' male souls of the rains, which are invoked in November (Chapter 8), are viewed from this perspective, the peak of their afterlife at

Carnival appears as a glorious arrival and flowering as they become one with the spirit world.

In this chapter we see how powerful spirit beings – the custodians of powerful new melodies – associated with voice, identity and musical creation, are impersonated by dancers in the final despatches of Carnival. These devil dancers (*sirinus*) ritually act out entering the earth – as if filling a newly created vessel or material body with animating energy or spirit and bringing it to life. This takes place at the very moment the *wirjin* fields are said to be giving birth to baby potatoes; an identical process to a human becoming suffused with *animu* at birth. The new *wayñu* melodies from the *sirinus*, which dominate the soundscape through the feast of Carnival, appear to represent some form of disembodied or, more precisely, pre-embodied soul substance.

The Feast of St Sebastian

There are *sirinus* inside the earth... they will arrive here to [perform] *wayñu* for St Sebastian... then for *Tentación* [the end of Carnival] they will go off inside the earth (Asencio Jara).[9]

On 20 January 1991 many people from Kalankira walked to Titiri for the feast of St Sebastian, a journey of about an hour.[10] Titiri is now a rural peasant community, but in the early colonial period it was an important silver mining centre.[11] This accounts for the magnificent paintings, bells and statues in its large colonial church, which is situated far from habitation, and where the feast of St Sebastian is centred.[12] Following the parade of the patron's statue, I helped the sacristan and a few other people carry the bells back into the church. As we rested and chewed coca leaves in honour of the saint inside the church, I was surprised to be told that St Sebastian is the patron saint of the *sirinus;* musical demons that are consistently classed as 'devils' (*yawlus*). When I voiced incredulity at the idea of a patron saint of devils, everybody was quick to point out that this was quite normal and that St Sebastian even

---

9 *Sirinus jallp'a ukhupi tiyan ... chayamunqa kayman wayñuman San Sebastianpaq...chanta Tentacionpaq ripun jallp'a ukhupi.*

10 I was staying in Titiri at this time, before going to live in Kalankira. Many people from Kalankira later explained that this was the first occasion they had seen me.

11 According to Mendoza & Patzi 1997, the colonial town of Macha was originally situated in Titiri (in the present day community of Tirina, where a few walls from the old town are still visible) before being moved to its current warmer and lower altitude location (1997:101).

12 It is unclear how long the feast of St Sebastian has been celebrated in Titiri. An entry dated October 1914 from the parish records held by the Church in Macha only mentions the following feasts: Santisimo (Corpus Christi), Sta Teresa, Guadalupe y San Roque. However, it is possible that only those feasts at which a visiting priest performed mass are listed.

had a *pinkillu* flute.[13] To prove the point, Hilarion Gallego led me over to the statue and, in Spanish, insisted: 'He's got a *pinkillu*. See? The saint has a *pinkillu;* it's along his back. He's really the saint of the *sirinus*'.[14] Sure enough, the saint was tied to a large *machu* (bass) *pinkillu* flute, which stood vertically behind him.[15] This took the place of the tree to which, according to European legend and iconographic tradition, St Sebastian was tied and shot with arrows (Figure 9.2).[16]

The imagery of the Andean St Sebastian tied to a flute highlights how (wooden) *pinkillu* flutes and trees are both seen to communicate between 'this world' (*kay pacha*) and the powerful regenerative forces of the 'inner earth' (*ukhu pacha*), the realm of *supay* and other devils.[17] Don Hilarion's linking of a *pinkillu* flute with St Sebastian's status as patron of the *sirinus* highlights the flute's close connection with the *sirinus*. On several other occasions, when I asked 'what do *sirinus* sound like?' without hesitation, the reply always came 'like *pinkillus*'.[18] The fact that the *pinkillu* has its 'own voice' clearly underscores this connection. It is a duct flute with an internal whistle mechanism for which no embouchure is required, unlike the breathy panpipes or *quena* notched flute of the dry winter months.[19] The player simply blows the

---

[13] According to Antonia Caballero, who was born in Titiri and married in Kalankira, San Sebastian miraculously appeared, with 'a *pinkillu* flute on his back' (*pinkillu q'ipirisqa karqa*) in a thorn tree, situated in a river gully with *sirinus*, below the site of the church. He was carried into the church from this place, called *Kumpurtu*, which used to have a devil's church (*supay iglesia*) before it was carried away by the water. It also had a bridge, the foundations of which remain, where god defeated *supay* causing him to become *ll'uq'i* ('left') and, following the cockcrow, to disappear KUN!

[14] *El tiene pinkillu. Nove? El santo tiene pinkillu; en la espalda esta. El santo de sirinus siempre.*

[15] Concerned that this might cause offence I did not photograph this fascinating statue at the time. Tragically it was destroyed, together with the rest of this beautiful church's contents, in a fire some six months later.

[16] According to several Bolivian priests, Sebastian was a Roman soldier who declared his Christian faith. He is typically depicted tied to a tree and pierced with arrows. Some accounts of his life tell of how he cured the dumb-mute Zoe (wife of Nicostratus) (Delaney 1982: 512).

[17] In his description of a feast at St Marcos de Miraflores in the Macha valleys, Tristan Platt observes the regenerative associations of a fruit bearing *sawku* tree (*Sambucus Peruviana*) that formerly stood in the churchyard – (a species favoured for *pinkillu* flute construction). Despite being cut down by a priest 'in a fit of evangelical zeal', the tree continued to receive libations through a stone-covered hole, as if highlighting its role in connecting humans with powers of *ukhupacha* (1987b:146).

[18] This connection was brought home to me one evening when Paulino, Asencio and I were playing a fine set of *pinkillus* that I had just purchased. Pedro Beltrán arrived from the neighbouring homestead attracted by the music. Their sound was so beautiful, he exclaimed, that he thought it must have been the *sirinus* playing.

[19] A notable exception to a generalized association of duct flutes with the rainy season is the three-holed pipe and tabor, such as the *kuntur pinkillu* or 'condor flute', which is usually played at feasts during the dry winter months (Chapter 7).

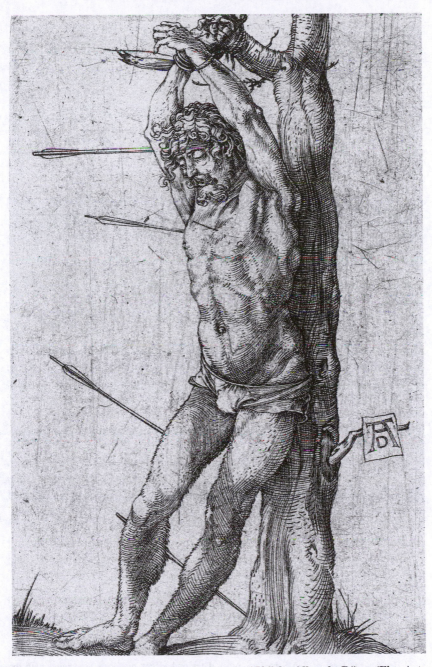

Figure 9.2   St Sebastian bound to the tree (c. 1501) by Albrecht Dürer (Fine Arts Museums of San Francisco, Achenbach Foundation for Graphic Arts 1963.30.19)

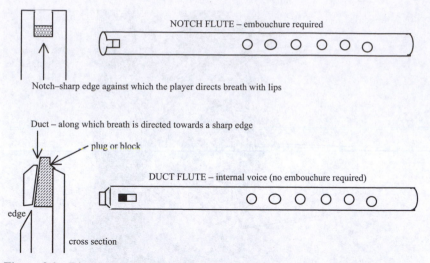

Figure 9.3   Diagram comparing the sound production of the dry season *quena*
(notch flute) with the rainy season *pinkillu* **(duct flute)**

pinkillu and sound magically appears – no further cultural knowledge or skill
is necessary (Figure 9.3).[20]

Significantly St Sebastian was sometimes referred to locally as *paracero*
('one who makes something appear').[21] In Titiri, I was told that if I waited in
the church for a few more minutes, the new *wayñu* music of the year, brought
by the *sirinus*, would start to rise up through the floor and the *pinkillu* players,
who had just entered the church, would play it. Hilarion explained that 'it
comes out of this church; that 'father' [Sebastian] places this *wayñu* [music].
Through him *wayñu* emerges.'[22]

Indeed, the band of highly intoxicated *pinkillu* players sounded their flutes
and danced wildly – presumably playing one of the *sirinus* brand new *wayñus*
– before suddenly lurching out of the church. Over the subsequent weeks I
discovered that the new *wayñu* melodies would continue to be collected until
a few days before 'Games Saturday' (*pujllay sawaru*), the start of Carnival.[23]
These melodies, which appear thanks to St Sebastian and the seductive but
fatally dangerous *sirinus* (or female *sirina* in the following example), also

---

[20] It is also notable in this context that the plastic green whistles played by dancers on the final
night of Carnival (two nights after the *pinkillus* had been despatched) were referred to as *sirinu*
(CD track 37).

[21] From the Spanish *aparecer* 'to appear'.

[22] *Kay iglesiamanta lluqsin; jaqay tata kay wayñu churan. Chaywantamanta lluqsin wayñu.*

[23] Besides the feast of San Sebastian, other dates and places my hosts associated with the
collection of *wayñus* for Carnival were the feast of Candelaria, 2 February in Pocoata, and the
feast of Comadres (Sp. 'Godmothers'), the Thursday before Carnival in Ocuri.

herald the emergence of the new miniature fruits (tubers, seeds) of the year, as Asencio so vividly explains:[24]

> [The *sirina*] emerges in just the same way as a plant from [the feast of] St Sebastian. Like a plant she stays down inside [the earth]. Then at this moment, as the fruits are emerging, she comes out in just the same way from [the feast of] St Sebastian. And from that moment she walks around, that's her time, you see. But that time is really dangerous. When we're drunk and not easily in control we might sleep anywhere and even end up with the *sirina*. During Carnival she [might] lead us away. In particular *Tentación* [the final night of Carnival] is really dangerous. And where might she lead us, drunk like that? Maybe to our deaths; tumbling down [dead]?[25]

Carnival devils and sirens

The Carnival season is widely associated with 'devils' (*diablos*) in the Bolivian Andes, as evident from the internationally famous devil dance (*diablada*) of the large mining town of Oruro.[26] The precursors of this urban dance phenomenon, linked to mining, lie in rural agricultural practices, where mineral was traditionally thought to 'grow' in the same way as potatoes. In several parts of Northern Potosí and its surrounds, devils are claimed to emerge from inside the earth and wander the hillsides during the nights of Carnival. Harris observes that among the Laymis these devils are 'in some form, the spirits of the dead', which during Carnival season:

> are personified as a source of danger – they make people ill, lead them astray and to their deaths if they remain alone instead of joining the collective celebration. But they are also celebrated as the abundance of natural increase, and [in the form of devil dancers] are festooned with the wild and domesticated plant life they have helped to grow (1982a:58).

Two forms of Carnival devil were identified in Kalankira: the *sirinus* and *satanos colorados* ('colourful satans').[27] In an interesting sensory division of

---

[24] It may be no coincidence that elsewhere in the Bolivian highlands offerings are made to potato plants during the festival of *Alacitas* on 24 January, just as miniature potatoes are beginning to form on the adult plants' roots. *Alacitas* is dedicated to the dwarf deity of abundance *Ekako* (*Iqiqu*) and is marked today by the sale of miniature objects in the national capital La Paz (Copana, Apaza & Hilaya 1996:287–8, Fernández 1998:154–5).

[25] *[Sirina]...Kikillantaq plantajina lluqsimun a. San Sebastianmanta, planta jinallataq entonces paypis entonces ukhullapi kakushan paypis kunan entonces kunan kay frutas lluqsishan, kikin lluqsimullantaq San Sebastianmanta ari. y hasta recien purin, y hasta timpu paypatapis a, pero chay timpo peligrosopuni. Machasqapis mana chiqa jasilta [facil?] maypipis puñullasunmanchu sirinawanchis ima. Karnawalespipis pusawasun, Tentacionpi a la menus ancha peligroso chayqa. Maymanpis pusallawasun ya machasqa tal vez wañusunraqpis a. chuqakukuspa i?*

[26] See Nash 1979, Vargas 1998, and Romero et al 2003.

[27] The Spanish *colorado* may be used to refer to the colour red. However, Paulino assured me that satanos colorados were multicoloured.

labour, the *sirinus* were connected with musical enchantment and creation (the aural), while the *satanos colorados* were associated with colours (the visual), such as growing plants and the various hues of llama fleece. Several people related *satanos colorados* to the jester-like *mono* dancers who perform during the *rinuwa* feasts in October (Chapter 7) and to growing plants, observing that, unlike *sirinus*, they have 'horns' and 'tails'.[28] Whereas the presence of the *satanos colorados* coincides with the growth of crops – from planting (or sprouting) to the peak of flowering, the emergence of the *sirinus* with their new *wayñu* melodies is related to the arrival of the year's new fruits (tubers). According to doña Asunta, *satanos colorados* are 'like plants' and *sirinus* are 'like fruits', suggesting the idea of distinct generations.

While the *sirinus* of Kalankira have much in common with other Carnival devils of Northern Potosí, they also share many similarities with specifically musical demons, often termed *sirena* (*sirina*), the Spanish word for 'siren/mermaid'. Many of the attributes of the terms *sirena* and *sirinu* appear identical and in turn have many resonances with Greco–European siren traditions.[29] For example, both tend to be considered a source of musical beauty, seduction, creation, knowledge, inspiration and danger, and are widely associated with nature (landscape), flowing water and altered consciousness, such as dreaming (Stobart 2006). According to Thomas Turino, in Southern Peru, near Lake Titicaca, the siren (*sirena*) is closely connected with mermaid imagery, string instruments and courtship (1983).[30] Elsewhere, forms and associated instruments vary considerably; for example, Kalankira's *sirinus* were said to resemble men, women and children in Carnival dress and, as we have seen, are closely connected with *pinkillu* flutes.[31] A gripping description of them by doña Asunta, which is full of verbal artistry and comments from the rest of the family, can be found in Appendix 2 (CD track 47). She tells how one day during Carnival she was pasturing llamas and had to shelter from the rain in a cave. As she sat 'daydreaming', lots of *sirinus* swarmed out of a gully

---

[28] This suggests certain parallels with the demonic *jira maykus* - spinning warrior spirits - of nearby *ayllu* Qaqachaka, who also have aqueous 'siren' (*sirina*) counterparts. Like the horned *satanos colorados*, the *jira maykus* arrive in the *ayllu* around early October, are despatched on the night of *Tentación*, and are obsessed with sharp horn-like points that lead them along their spiralling paths. Arnold and Yapita also relate the *jira maykus* to the 'breath' of the mountain spirits which are required to blow *pinkillu* flutes (1998b:71).

[29] The etymology of the word *sirinu* is unclear (Stobart 2006). It might be interpreted as a less gender specific version of siren (*sirinus* are by no means always female), derived from the Spanish *sereno* ('night-watchman, serene, clear sky') or connected with the Aymara *siri*, from the verb *saña*, which is glossed by Lucca as 'he who speaks' (1987:150). Arnold and Yapita have also identified this connection with the verb *saña*, noting that the termination *–irïna* expresses the idea of motivating a continuous action (1998b:51).

[30] Also see Gisbert 1980.

[31] This is exceptional as in most other contexts devils were said to be q'iwa (half-male, half-female). A likely explanation for this is that on the Monday night of Carnival men, women and children dance as sirinus.

together with Father Carnival and his flag, sounding their *pinkillu* flutes, *pututu* trumpets and singing '*sirina siwaysitu* violet violet ribbon'. She goes on to describe them as 'like people' but *challku* ('indeterminate colour'), perhaps implying rainbow-like chromaticism or the translucence of flowing water, with which they are often connected.[32]

Much of the ethnography of Andean sirens focuses on their aqueous associations and on how their powers are usurped by men for two main reasons, firstly to enchant or tune musical instruments especially for use in courtship, and secondly to acquire new powerful melodies. In several other parts of Bolivia I was told that men visit places associated with sirens late at night to leave their instruments together with offerings. When the instrument is collected, it is typically said to be perfectly in tune, to sound more beautiful than before, and to have the power to attract girls, rendering the male player irresistible (see Turino 1983:97). I was often told that such visits must be accomplished with great care in order to avoid potential illness, insanity or even death. Although such practices were well known, few people in Kalankira testified to having visited *sirinus* to 'tune' or 'enchant' instruments. For them, the *sirinus'* association with musical enchantment and danger was predominantly related to the Carnival season, a time that tales of fatal encounters and close escapes abound; and when I was regularly warned not to wander outside alone at night. For example, one night during Carnival Asencio once ventured outside alone whilst drunk and found himself in the company of a group of *sirinu*, playing flutes, singing and dancing. They were very friendly, he explained, just like normal people (*runa*) wearing Carnival dress and offered him corn beer before suddenly vanishing. Next morning he awoke to find himself outside on a mountainside, frozen to the bone, far from home and completely lost in Tinquipaya territory. Also, one night during Carnival 1991 I heard shouts emanating from beside the river below the nearby hamlet of Wak'an Phukru. I later heard that Feliciano Chura had been lured away by a child-like cry resembling the voice of his infant daughter. He would surely have been a victim of the *sirinus*, I was told, had he not been spotted and dragged home by a group of friends.

Sirens and musical creation

The *sirinus'* importance to musical creativity was frequently stressed, and on several occasions it was stated that they are the source of all music, including that heard on commercial recordings.[33] Whilst individuals occasionally

---

[32] See Solomon 1997 concerning connections between *sirinas* and flowing water.

[33] Certain of Turino's informants in Southern Peru have also characterized the sirena ('siren') as the source of all music (1983:96–97). The association of *sirinus* with recordings has grown over

claimed to have 'invented' (*inventado*) certain *siku* or *julajula* panpipe melodies, the idea of personal creativity seemed to be downplayed in the case of *pinkillu* flute *wayñus*.[34] Most *wayñu* melodies were claimed to be copied from other groups, but men also spoke of these highly formulaic tunes magically appearing in dreams or falling under their fingers while playing – pre-formed and communicated from the *sirinu* (see Harris 2000 [1980]:190). A new melody once came to me in this way whilst playing *pinkillu* flutes during a ceremony and in a state of considerable intoxication. The melody, which fitted the standard *wayñu* formula, was taken up by the rest of the ensemble and attributed to the *sirinus*.

A few individuals described making special journeys to waterfalls or rocks to collect tunes, often involving solitary contemplation of the natural environment reminiscent of the vision quests of certain North American groups. Don Adrian – the oldest man in the district – vividly evoked how new melodies gradually take form, 'as if in a dream', whilst listening to the sound of a waterfall (*p'akcha*). He vocalised the deep, rumbling drone of the water, with its mass of harmonics, as *booooo boooo*. Based on research in Chile, Claudio Mercado has described a similar shift in consciousness, when listening to water, where the *sirinu's* melodies emerge as 'phantom sounds' and 'metasounds' in the mind of the listener (1996:49). Don Adrian also observed that at first these phantom melodies are 'indistinct' (*charpu*). Only gradually do they take recognizable form, in a process of melodic perception referred to with the verb stem *q'iwi-*, meaning 'twist', which suggests a parallel process to that in which yarn is spun from a mass of raw wool (Stobart 1998a and 2006).[35] Such discourse about musical creativity needs to be balanced against individual expression – where individuals may identify themselves as the creators of particular compositions. Nonetheless, it highlights the connection of these melodies with the *sirinus* and their

recent years due to the annual release of commercial cassettes of *wayñu* music intended for musicians to learn and play during Carnival. The first recordings of this type were made by Gregorio Mamani, in 2000, with the group Zurazura which is named after a place associated with *sirinus*. Gregorio, who is one of the most prolific recording artists of the Northern Potosí region, was brought up in nearby Tomaykuri (his sister lives in Kalankira).

[34] I encountered no examples of collective composition in Kalankira, like that described by Turino for Conima, Southern Peru (1993:77).

[35] Elsewhere in Northern Potosí the verb stem k'uyu- also meaning 'twist' is used in reference to the perception of new melodies at a waterfall (Sánchez 1988:16). For the case of *ayllu* Qaqachaka, Arnold and Yapita have characterized the *jira maykus* (spinning warrior spirits) as the spinners of life and death (1998b:51 and 500, Arnold 1992:26). In many respects, the *sirinus* of Kalankira appear to fulfil a similar function; where the process of creating and giving form to new *wayñu* music parallels that of giving form and identity to the new generation of offspring (foodcrops). However, it would seem that whilst the *sirinus* might be metaphorically connected with spinning – as the creation of a thread from a mass of fleece, by contrast the *satanos colorados* (which have many resonances with the *jira maykus*) suggest a later phase; namely weaving, as the landscape is clothed in vegetation through the rains.

perceived power to bring transformations in other spheres.[36] This also helps to explain why people insisted that new *wayñus* must be acquired each year; those from previous years dubbed *q'ayma* ('tasteless' or 'insipid') and considered, as Paulino put it, 'unable to do anything'.

Song cycles and horny potatoes

In Kalankira, potato plants usually come into flower around late January and from this time on, new offspring tubers start to take form on the plants' root tips. The life cycles of *wayñu* melodies coincide precisely with those of cultivated crops, especially the potato. These melodies are heard almost constantly through the feast of Carnival until the Friday night when the *pinkillu* flutes and *kitarras* of the rains are hushed and packed away for some seven months.[37] I was told that when they reappear in the following November, the *wayñu* melodies from the previous Carnival are played once more, rather than new melodies.[38] As shown in Figure 9.4, these same tunes continue to be

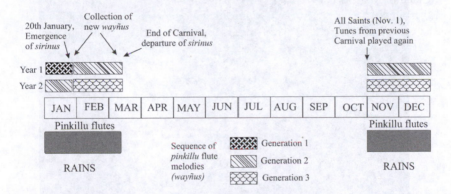

Figure 9.4   Seasonal renewal and performance of *pinkillu* flute *wayñus*

---

[36] Melodies attributed to individuals, like the 'make-up' tunes of the North American Flathead described by Merriam (1967:3–8), would presumably be thought to have less transformative power than those derived from ancestral powers of the landscape. However, despite such discourse, Bigenho highlights the role of individual creativity and the strategies used by a flute player-'composer' in Yura (Southern Potosí) to ensure that his *wayñu* was chosen as the ensemble's emblem piece (2000:966).

[37] In some other parts of northern Potosí new *wayñu* melodies only start to be collected from *Candelaria* (2 February), the Feast of Candlemas.

[38] The practice of playing *wayñus* from the previous Carnival at All Saints was widely confirmed in Kalankira, but it is possible that a few new *wayñus* are sometimes played. In the Sacaca region of Northern Potosí I was told that new *wayñu* melodies must be played for each feast during the rains.

performed until the following feast of St Sebastian (20 January) when the next new generation of melodies begin to be collected.

Figure 9.4 shows how *wayñu* tunes are linked with specific generations of potatoes. These melodies are sounded (a) during Carnival season, as the tubers take form, and (b) following All Saints, when sprouts burst out through the mature tubers and transform into growing plants. When I asked what would happen if I failed to respect the seasonal performance of *pinkillu* flutes, and played *wayñu* music during the dry winter months, I often received the same reply: 'You musn't play now, you would sprout horns like a devil.'[39] It took me some time to realize that this imagery related to the sprouts of potato tubers, which closely resemble horns (Figure 9.5). It is imperative that potatoes are not encouraged to sprout during the dry season, rather they must lie dormant in darkness and mature. Yet, during the rains *wayñu* music is explicitly said to 'make the crops grow'. This highlights the intimate connection between sprouting plants – as they burst from within tubers, seeds or the earth – and colourful devils (*satanos colorados*) emerging from *ukhu pacha*, the 'inner earth'.

Figure 9.5   A potato sprouting horns

The sprouting of a potato, where it sends out shoots, leaves and ultimately flowers, is not only the start of its life as a green plant but also signals the tuber's destruction and death. Its animating energy departs, much as *animu* is said to leave a human body at death, and passes into the tips of the plant.[40]

---

[39] *Amaña tukanachu asta uñasunqa yawlujina.*

[40] The parallel with human death and sprouting plants was also evident from the decoration of the graves in the cemetery at All Saints and St Andrew, for both of which sprouted onions littered the shrouds. One neighbour associated the purple decorations used on the graves at All Saints (1 November) with the purple sprouts of some *siwa* potatoes placed on a cloth altar (*mesa*) during

Also, like a buried human body, the tuber gradually decays and finally rots (*ismu*) in the soil; such parallels between human burial and the planting of crops are often noted in Andean ethnography (Bastien 1978:125, Harris 1982a:52, Arnold 1988:418).[41] The gradual redirection of energy of a sprouting tuber is encapsulated in the word *siway*, which was found in the refrain of almost every *wayñu* I heard sung in Kalankira. Thomas Solomon, working in *ayllu* Chayantaka, also identifies *siway* as 'the single word that most defines the *wayñu* genre through song texts', but characterizes it as 'nonsensical' (1997:122). Whilst some younger people in Kalankira were unable to gloss the word *siwa(y)*, most people immediately related it to 'sweetness', stirring sugar into hot drinks or, for example, old potatoes or apples on the verge of decay. Alberto Camaque (*ayllu* Laymi) was the first of several to specify that the verb stem *siwa-* refers to the phase when a potato tuber starts to send-out sprouts – a transformation provoked by the sounds of *wayñu* music. He explained that the tuber becomes 'watery', enters a state of 'transition' and, whilst still retaining its form, becomes 'sweet and tasty like water melon'.[42]

Sweetness, in this context, is a powerful metaphor for communication and redistribution of energies; items made from sugar are included in most ritual offerings as a means to ensure acceptance by spirit beings and subsequent reciprocity.[43] This language of sweetness, invoking notions of desire, redistribution and transformation, is especially critical to Carnival – the only feast in the year in which sweets (*confites*) are constantly shared around. Images of sweetness also appeared in the wept songs from the feast of St Andrew (Chapter 8), when the dead were said to grasp 'sweet sleep' (*miski puñuy*). As we have heard, the sounds of *wayñu* are included in this synaesthetic language; old, out of date, melodies from previous years described as *q'ayma* ('insipid, tasteless'). The power of transformation from one generation of embodied beings – such as potato tubers – to another (their

---

his family's Carnival libations. By contrast, the decorations placed on the graves at St Andrew (30 November), almost a month later when the potato plants had peeped out of the soil, were green and made from the fronds of willow and pink roses .

[41] I often noticed the rotted 'parent' tuber in the soil when I helped harvest potatoes. Billie-Jean Isbell also suggests that the rotting dead fertilize crops and contribute to future generations, whilst petrified forms – the mummified dead and *chuñu* (freeze-dried potatoes) – embody the regenerative process of renewal (1997:292).

[42] In his Aymara dictionary of 1612, Bertonio also links *sihuaratha* [*siwaratha*] with the uprooting of potatoes when they have started to sprout (1984 [1612], II:316). The 'sweetening' connected with *siwa* is similar to the process of malting barley grains, through spouting, for the preparation of corn beer.

[43] See Cereceda (1987:200–212), who relates sweetness to broader forms of beauty as aesthetic articulation or communication, such as colour chromaticism. See Fernández (1997:89, and so on) on the use of sweet ingredients in ritual offerings.

offspring) is intimately associated with sensory communication: taste, colour, aromas and sound (see also Isbell 1985:305). From this perspective, the potato plant may be seen to represent a phase of transition between embodied forms, but also one in which the life cycle reaches its ultimate expression, zenith or flowering, which is manifest in the feast of Carnival.

(B) GAMES AND FLOWERS: THE FEAST OF CARNIVAL

The moveable feast of Carnival or *pujllay* ('play'), in February or March, is often said to be the most 'joyful' festival of the year. It is the culmination of months of agricultural labour when fields and hillsides are carpeted with flowers and harvest begins. Even the omnipresent and dirge-like sounds of *pinkillu* flute *wayñus* now appear full of merriment: performed with immense vitality and exuberance and featured in almost every ceremony until their Friday night despatch.[44] The nine days of Carnival celebrations from *pukllay sawaru* ('Games Saturday') through to the Sunday of *Tentación* include a multiplicity of rites, ceremonies and music making but here I will focus on the four main community-level ceremonies – namely the three *kacharpaya* ('despatches') and the *salaki* ceremonies for the fields (*wirjin*) and offspring potatoes.

The Feast of Carnival

'Games Saturday'	('flowering' of male llamas)
Sunday	
Monday	*Alma Kacharpaya* ('despatch of soul')
Shrove Tuesday	
Ash Wednesday	
Thursday	
Friday	*Pinkillu Kacharpaya* ('despatch of *pinkillu* flutes')[45]
Saturday	*Salaki* or *Wirjin* ('virgin' = fields) ceremonies
'Temptation' Sunday	*Jatun Kacharpaya* ('great despatch')

On the morning of *pukllay sawaru* ('Games Saturday'), I helped Paulino hurl handfuls of wild flowers onto the roof of each hut of the homestead before the entire extended family set off for the llama corral on the high peak to perform the *t'ikachaku* ('flowering') ceremony for the male llama herd. In

---

[44] Unlike, for example *siku* panpipe music (Chapter 7), the same new *pinkillu wayñu* melody was often repeated over many hours or even days. Rather than becoming dull or boring, this repetition and familiarity enabled players to find each instrument's full voice and character, and to explore the melody's full range of gestures and expressive potential, as if developing its personality and defining its identity in the same way as a living being. This analogy seems especially appropriate if the melodies of *wayñu* are understood as a form of soul substance, which will be embodied in the emergent generation. See also Stobart 2002a:101.

[45] According to don Adrian, the *pinkillu kacharpaya* was formerly the final rite of Carnival, and probably performed on the Sunday night of *Tentación*, as it is in several other parts of Northern Potosí.

Quechua *t'ika* means 'flower' and for this ceremony, knotted red wools resembling and compared to flowers were sown into the llama's ears to make them 'multiply well' (*sumaq mirananpaq*), and flowers were sprinkled into the corn beer we drank in the libations.[46] Present at this *t'ikachaku* ceremony and the many others for the herds of female and young llamas, as well as almost every other Carnival ceremony, was a white flag (*wantira*). It was fixed in the wall at the entrance of the corral for the male llamas' ceremony, but in most other contexts it stood beside the bucket of corn beer in the centre of the corral around which the young *wayñu* musicians danced (Figure 9.6). Several people compared this flag to a potato flower and related it to the white flag carried by young unmarried women in the dry season *wayli* dance (Chapter 6). This flag, which seemed critical to the very ontology of Carnival, was always carried by women except in two notable contexts: the 'despatch of the soul' and the joint despatch of the *pinkillu* flutes and father St Flowers, when it was taken up by men.

Figure 9.6 *Wayñu* **musicians with** *pinkillu* **flutes dancing around a bucketan earthenware vessel of corn beer, beside which is placed a white flag, in a llama corral during Carnival**

---

[46] According to Denise Arnold *tikachaku* refers to coagulation or solidification, where the blood from the animal's ears is caused to flow and is then plugged with 'brightly coloured knotted threads of wool which represent coagulated blood' (1988:230). She observes that tika means adobe (Spanish 'mud brick') and refers to concepts of coagulation and solidification in both Aymara and Quechua (Arnold 1988: 230, and Arnold, Jiménez & Yapita 1992:53 fn.14). However, people in Kalankira insisted that this ceremony was connected with flowers and the idea of flowering and denied this association with blood and coagulation.

Despatching the soul (*alma kacharpaya*)

As in the feasts of All Saints and St Andrew (Chapter 8), the central focus of ritual activity during Carnival was the 'house of the dead' (*wañuq wasi*), where a married adult man had died during the previous year. In some years there may be several *wañuq wasi* in a community, but in other years none (Chapter 10). Late on Monday afternoon troupes of dancers and *pinkillu* flute players, referred to as *sirinus*, started arriving from neighbouring hamlets dressed in colourful newly woven traditional *ayllu* clothing. These troupes roamed the hillsides throughout the night, travelling from one *wañuq wasi* to the next, avoiding the footpaths travelled by living humans – in imitation of real *sirinus*. When I participated as a *sirinu* dancer and *pinkillu* player several years later we scrambled and danced well over twenty miles from one *wañuq wasi* to the next, arriving back in Kalankira just after midday on Tuesday. Even then, completely exhausted, I was told we should not rest because real *sirinus* never sleep.

The women carried several embroidered shawls (Sp. *rebozos*) on their backs, tied together with woven belts, and the men wore battle dress, including cow-hide fighting helmets (*muntiras*). This was the first occasion that these new clothes had been worn in public, suggesting that the new food crops, *wayñu* melodies and clothes were all new offspring of the *sirinus*. The beauty of the women's backcloths (*aksu*), painstakingly woven over the preceding months as the crops had grown, was particularly striking. Like the flowers that now decked the hillsides, these backcloths were a riot of colour, flapping enchantingly and exhibited in their full glory by the rings of *qhata* dancers (Figure 9.7).[47] This vision is nicely conjured up in the well-known libation formula: *sirinu Laymi aksu inkitu* ('Laymi *sirinu* restless backcloth'), which also alludes to the alleged practice of copying new Carnival *wayñu* melodies from people of *ayllu* Laymi, who were considered to have particularly powerful *sirinus* in their territory.[48]

---

[47] These new colourful textiles might be seen to evoke the idea of 'ancestral' wrappings created by the *satanos colorados* (the previous generation), that clothe the *sirinus* (the emergent generation) who, strictly speaking, invoke ideas of 'spinning' disparate sounds into *wayñus*, like fleece into yarn. In other words, the *sirinus* create new lines of (aural) communication across time and space and bring the animating energy of life (*wayñu*), whereas the *satanos colorados* bring the visible fabric of life, which will serve as the skins or wrapping of the new embodied generation. Arnold & Yapita (1998b:72) observe that among the Qaqachakas identical terms are used for the gradual wearing down of cloth and the time elapsed since a death. In the first year, souls are referred to as 'new' (*machaqa*), in the second 'used' (*murqu*), and in the third 'ragged' (*t"anta*). Accordingly, the new clothing of Carnival, like the flourishing vegetation, might be seen as the metaphorical product of the 'new' soul despatched in the *alma kacharpaya*.

[48] Harris observes that in practice the Laymis have lost their sirenas and copy melodies from the Chayantakas, Sikuyas and Jukumanis during the feast of Candelaria in Chayanta. She also notes that the Laymis consider one of the best *sirenas* for *wayñus* to be located in Pukwata

Figure 9.7 *Qhata* **dancing in a large ring with a view of the women's** *aksu* **backcloths. Rings of decorative** *rebozo* **shawls and weavings are carried on their backs together with bread rings (***pillus***).**

Through the course of the night some seven groups of '*sirinus*' from different hamlets visited Kalankira's *wañuq wasi*, the home of the recently widowed doña Alicia (Chapter 8). The *sirinus* arrived at an energetic trot, stamping the ground to the music of the year's new *wayñus* sung by women to the men's *pinkillu* flutes. These were often interspersed with *wayñu*, accompanied by the *kitarra*, such as the following that I recorded at about 3am, with its refrain of *siway* – discussed above – and Carnival imagery of multicoloured flowers (Example 9.1). The verses, which did not follow any set order (and are not all heard on the CD selection) vividly evoke the arrival of new life (CD track 34).

Ayranpuni kiyutanpuni	Surely now, surely it circles[49]
Chayqa viday chayanpuni	Here we are! my life always arrives
Siway misturas t'ikita	*Siway* confetti flower

(Pocoata) territory (1988:4). When I attended the feast of Candelaria in Pocoata I met several men from *ayllu* Pukwata who had recently collected *wayñus* from waterfalls, but encountered nobody from *ayllu* Laymi.

[49] Paulino interpreted *ayran* as 'now' (Sp. *ahora*) and *kiyutan* as a ring or circle, evoking the idea of *qhata* dance. *Ayrampu* and *kiyuta* are also both names of wild red berries used to symbolize blood in rituals. *Ayrampu* juice, from cactus berries, was poured over breads to symbolize 'heart' (*sunqu*) in the *waka ñakakun* ceremony during All Saints, when the red colour referred to as *Mama Copacabana* and linked with blood the concept of *sultira* ('unmarried woman'), symbolizing

Eso si pachan pachita	For sure, the same as before
Kaychu chay wachaq chulita	Can it be this girl who gives birth?
Siway misturas t'ikita	*Siway* confetti flower
Asintasun, asintasun	We shall place, we shall place
Chaki, maki asintasun	Foot, hand, we shall place [50]
Siway misturas t'ikita	*Siway* confetti flower
Pachallanpi pachallanpi	In the same place/time as before
Kinsa rusaq chawpillanpi	Three roses just in the centre[51]
Siway misturas t'ikita	*Siway* confetti flower
Esosi ñañay kasqanki	I realize that you are my sister
Nuqaymanta jamusqanki	Because of me you have come[52]
Siway misturas t'ikita	*Siway* confetti flower

Example 9.1   Ayranpuni: *wayñu* song with *kitarra*. (CD track 34)

female fertility. I have also witnessed *kiyuta* juice used to paint breads during All Saints in *ayllu* Chayantaka.

[50] In a song about potato cultivation from the Cuzco region of Peru, Harrison interprets a similar reference to hands and feet, as a 'reverie to other times when potatoes were sown by hand and using the footplow' (1989:192).

[51] Paulino related this to the centre of *qhata* dance. This imagery is also evocative of the three willow wreaths (*pillus*) placed on the graves and crosses in the cemetery at the feast of St Andrew (30 November).

[52] The use of the *sqa* suffix here suggests sudden realization (Pedro Plaza personal communication). This probably refers to greeting a new food product – 'as if they too were human' (Arnold, Jiménez and Yapita 1991:117).

Leading every band of *sirinu* dancers came one or two men carrying white flags, periodically making strange unpredictable movements and snorting like excited oxen. In several of the groups, these vibrant sounds were echoed, more loudly and lower in pitch, by *pututu* trumpets made from long wooden tubes (or rubber tubing) of some 3m in length with a bell made from several ox horns (CD track 33) (Example 9.2). On arrival, each group approached the altar (*misa*) of the dead man. Unlike any other ceremony in the year, this was set up to face west and on it was placed the fighting helmet and a bundle of clothes that had belonged to the deceased. Each dancer placed a large bread ring (*pillu*) on this helmet and then the group began to dance the most spectacular *qhata*, holding alternate hands in a circle enclosing the *pinkillu* flute players. After the *qhata* performance each dance group was served boiled meat (*kanka*) and maize (*mut'i*) in their hats and several bowls of *luqru* (potatoes and *chuñu* in broth). Prayers for the dead man and his ancestors followed the meal and then one or two men from the *sirinu* dance troupe put on the dead man's fighting helmet, and tied the bundle of clothes around his shoulders.[53] Immediately, as the men wearing the clothes of the dead man began to dance to the *sirinus'* music (CD track 33), the women seated near the altar, especially doña Alicia and her daughter Cenovia, began to weep and wail loudly. This was the climax of the *sirinus'* visit, when 'the soul is made to dance' (*almata tusuchin*) I was told (Figure 9.8).

In this dance, called *pukllay* ('game') or *karnawal* ('Carnival'), which is only performed on this Monday night of Carnival, the male dancer(s) wearing

Example 9.2 *Wayñu* with *pinkillu* flutes and voices. *Pututu* trumpets are also clearly audible on the recording. (See Example 9.3 below for translation of words.) Transposed up about one semitone. (CD track 33)

---

[53] The practice of dancing in honour of recently deceased men or women, and wearing their clothing, on the Monday of Carnival has been reported in other parts of Northern Potosí (Izko 1986:151). In Kalankira this observance was restricted to the memory of adult men.

Figure 9.8 The *pukllay* or *karnawal* dance in which the *sirinu* dancers make the soul dance to the left. Meanwhile the women, who are seated beside the altar to the dead man, wail.

the dead man's clothes were followed by the troupe of *sirinu* singers and flute players. In many respects, the *pujllay* dance encapsulates the central meaning and very ontology of 'Carnival'; the final despatch of the man's soul to *alma llajta* ('land of the souls'), sent on his way by the new emergent generation, represented by the *sirinus*. The dance of the male *pujllay* dancer was usually characterized by warlike shouts in descending glissandi of *su chacha* (Aym. 'I'm a man!') – as heard in *tinku* fighting (Chapter 6), strange burbling noises through vibrating lips *brrrrrr…* and sudden unpredictable movements. The white flag (*wantira*) was of central importance and was typically held midway along its handle and treated as though it had a life of its own rather than controlled by the dancer. It alternated between being: (a) held parallel to the ground, (b) positioned vertically, as though the dancer's partner, (c) moved gently in time with the music, or else (d) held almost completely still, before rushing off followed by the crazed steps of the dancer.[54] When the group returned to the altar, the man (or men) who had carried the dead man's clothes danced left (clockwise) around it before replacing the fighting helmet and bundle of clothes and being served from a pair *turu wasus* ('bull cups') of corn

---

[54] I participated in the dance myself alongside Victor Beltrán who demonstrated the movements in detail.

beer. I was told on several occasions that this is the only moment in the entire year that dancing or movement to the 'left' (*lluq'i*) is performed (outside the context of balancing movements to the right). Drinking from paired vessels may be seen as a reaffirmation of life, following the dance, as libations to the dead are drunk from a single vessel. In addition, this rite might also be seen to re-establish the distinction in orientation between the living (travel right) and souls of the dead (travel left) with the culmination of the rainy growing season.

Over the following four days, every household held *t'ikachaku* ('flowering') rites for their female and young llamas, hosted extended libation sequences for the various crops and animals, and, in some cases, organized special rites for newly built houses. Corn beer flowed constantly, coca leaves continually circulated, communal meals kept appearing, and *wayñu* music pervaded the soundscape.

Despatch of the *pinkillu* flutes (*pinkillu kacharpaya*)

On the Friday night of Carnival the *pinkillu* flutes were dramatically silenced and despatched along with 'father flowers' (*tata pulurisa*). Late on Friday afternoon, to the sound of constant *wayñu* music, we visited each homestead in turn and were invited to drink corn beer (*aqha*). During these visits a small cross decorated with flowering and fruiting potato, broad bean and barley plants was carried by a 9 or 10 year old boy referred to as the *uña alférez* ('offspring lieutenant').[55] Finally, at dusk, we visited the homestead of the *uña alférez* where, following a communal meal and *qhata* dancing, we climbed a nearby hill to the *pukara*, a stone construction with a niche, some distance from any habitation. An altar was set up on the *pukara*, a word meaning 'fortress', and libations poured in honour of *tata pulurisa*, the patron of Carnival and 'flowers', who takes the form of a warrior. Following another 40 minutes of *qhata* dancing a further meal was served. As it began to grow quite dark a stick of dynamite was exploded nearby, and with this signal a huge circle of *qhata* dancers was formed in which everybody participated. As we danced to the *pinkillu* flutes, the words sung by the women conveyed the vivid sensory exuberance of this final flowering of Carnival, the refrain amounting to a list of flower colours. The verses (first lines) are difficult to distinguish, except the line *Qanpaq nisqallaykis kachun* ('Let what you say be'), which was heard in many *wayñus* with *pinkillu* flutes, and powerfully evokes the idea of bringing new life into being[56] (Example 9.3, CD track 35).

---

[55] My description is based on the 1991 ceremony performed jointly by neighbouring Wak'an Phukru and Ura Kalankira hamlets which I attended by chance. I have since participated in this ceremony in Pata Kalankira, in which all the key activities were identical.

[56] This is reminiscent of the calls of Viracocha, the creator god, and his two servants who, in

Qanpaq nisqallaykis kachun, azucenitay　　Let what you say be, my lily [flower]
Pursilay siway[57] *celesta rosas t'ikay*　　　Orange, turquoise, blue, pink, my flower[58]

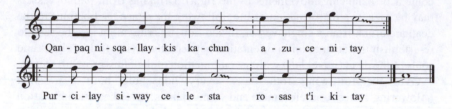

Qan - paq ni - sqa - llay - kis　ka - chun　　a - zu - ce - ni - tay

Pur - ci - lay　si - way　ce - le - sta　　ro - sas　t'i - ki - tay

Example 9.3 *Qanpaq nisqallaychis kachun* (**'Let what you say be'**). *Wayñu* with *pinkillu* **flutes and female voices.** *Qanpaq nisqallaychis kachun* (**'Let what you say be'**). **(CD track 35)**

In the centre of the circle of *qhata* dancers were six *pinkillu* players, an adult man with a white flag, who danced *pukllay*, side by side with his young son, the *uña alférez*. The circle of dancers slowly ascended the hillside above the *pukara*, the terrain becoming progressively steeper and more uneven. Suddenly, as it became almost impossible to continue dancing, the ring of dancers burst and the *pinkillu* players, *pukllay* dancer and *uña alférez* escaped into the darkness amid shouting and general confusion as they ran in all directions. Girls removed the rings of *rebozo* shawls, tied with belts around their backs, and placed them in ordinary carrying cloths (*llijllas*). Men tore off their *muntira* fighting helmets, which were festooned with colourful *serpentinas* (coiled confetti), and threw them to the ground – later comparing this with ripping off the horns of devils. Any remaining sweets (*confites*), a rare treat yet ubiquitous over the preceding days, were now cast away. The *pinkillu* flutes were packed away in cloths and *charangos* brought out and tuned up as a man shouted *luru, luru* ('parrot, parrot'), the bird depicted on the dry-season *charango* which is associated with the mythic coming of food crops (Chapter 4). As *charangos* were strummed in *natural* tuning, young unmarried men and women began to dance in couples (*parejas*) and sing *salaki*.

---

an account collected by Sarmiento de Gambóa in the colonial period, walked the length of the Andes calling life into existence. 'On hearing their calls, every place obeyed, and some people came out of lakes, others out of springs, valleys, caves, trees, caverns, rocks and mountains, and swelled the earth and multiplied' (Classen 1991:240).

[57] *Siway* sometimes refers to blue/green colour as well as sweetness.

[58] The following verses were also identified by Paulino:

　Pimintasqa kanilasqa azucenitay　　Peppered, cinnamoned my lily [flower]

　Palquyitusqa mintasqa azucenitay　　Cheated, confused my lily [flower]

(The word *palquyitusqa* was related to the idea of fermentation and is a play on a local place name.)

Salaki: **dancing potatoes**

Following the despatch of the *pinkillu* flutes and *tata pulurisa*, older people and children soon made their way home to bed, while unmarried men and women stayed up to sing and dance *salaki*. This playful genre, in which couples (*parejas*) dance arm in arm in a line (*comparsa*), is undoubtedly derived from the *salaki* music and dances performed almost every day during the week of Carnival in the nearby towns of Macha and Pocoata.[59] In Kalankira *salaki* was sung almost constantly for just two days and marked the transition between the Friday night of Carnival, as the end of the rains, and the final despatch of the Carnival devils on the Sunday night of *Tentacíon*, as the start of the dry season. *Salaki* appears neither truly to belong to the rains nor to the dry season, but articulates these two major epochs of the year.[60] The group of young dancers was given little respite by the dance master, or *cabecilla* (or *mayura*), who wore a fighting helmet and – often with great hilarity – controlled the choreography using a whip and stinging nettle.[61] Besides occasional sorties out to the *pampa* ('plain') nearby and visits to *salaki* ceremonies at other houses, most of the dancing and ritual activity was focused on the patio of the *wañuq wasi* ('house of the dead').

Through most of Saturday and Sunday, so-called *salaki* or *wirjin* ('virgin') libations were poured in honour of the new crop of potatoes and the 'fields' (*wirjin*) that give birth to them. With an immense sense of ceremony we were each handed small amounts of *uchu*, consisting of new 'baby' potatoes boiled and mixed with red chilli pepper sauce. Don Adrian, who sat next to me for some time, exclaimed:

I also drink here; we drink for *salaki*. '*Wir wiir*', I bellow, saying 'there's *sala*

---

[59] Couple dancing in lines, making right hand circles at crossroads, is also often performed during weddings in the towns of Pocoata and Macha.

[60] A transitional form is also played at this time accompanied by the *charango* in other parts of Northern Potosí. For example, according to Alberto Camaqui, in *ayllu* Laymi, *qhaana* style is played for about half an hour between the despatch of the *pinkillu* flutes and the start of the dry-season *kirki* song genre, during which young men and women dance together in couples. This genre is derived from *ayllu* Qhaana who are referred to as *puru centro* ('right in the centre') as their territory straddles the *chawpirana*, a 'middle' region of ecological transition between highlands and valleys – Map 3 (Harris 1985:320). Thus, in this transitional period between the end of the rains and start of the dry season the Laymis appear to invoke this pivotal transitional space. Might such invocation of 'centre' (*chawpi*) and focus on dancing in pairs serve as a means to reestablish binary balancing and exchange between, for example, the valleys and highlands? Balanced exchanges become a primary preoccupation of the dry winter months, as also suggested in the *julajula* music of this period that was described as *puru iwalasqa* ('perfectly balanced/in tune/agreed'). This transitional pairing is also reminiscent of the tying of young male (*malta*) llamas in (male) couples in the ceremonial rite of passage from the female to the male herd (Chapter 6) – highlighting the gendered aspect of seasonal change.

[61] The dead man's nephew on his wife's side (WBS) performed the role of *cabecilla*.

salaki'.[62] All the young people come together and dance here. We dig up the potatoes and eat *uchu* well.

Now we drink for the virgin. Wow! such fine 'starry eyed ones' [potatoes] the mother is giving birth to you; you're being made to grow beautifully. Wow! now this is fortune! Let's drink corn beer and make libations. And, carrying these potatoes on our backs, let's make them dance![63]

As we drank, don Adrian went on to explain that the *wirjin*, as large and small, and 'elder and younger' plots of land (pedazos) is asked to 'grasp' the offerings of uchu potatoes and corn beer made to her.[64] 'Everything that was planted in her is now grown', he exclaimed. Then, addressing the *wirjin* herself, and evoking the way a human mother carries her child, he exclaimed: 'carry all the products of the earth on your back in a carrying cloth' (*llallawata tukuyniqpi q'ipishanki*).

The following *salaki* verses were sung for me by doña Asunta, accompanied by Paulino on the *charango*, as especially representative of the style (Example 9.4, CD track 36).

Jovencita masi salaki bailarikus[unchis]	Young people together, let's dance
Rishani, rishani salaki larqa pati[tanta]	I'm off to above the irrigation canal
Chaypi tarishani salaki mejor paloma[sta]	There I'll be finding a better lover[65]
Esosi charanku salaki kusta quri[wanki]	That's it charango! you please me
Maypi aqha tiyan salaki rantirqapus[asqayki]	Where's the corn beer? I'll buy you some
Chala patitaywan[66] salaki chalarqapusq[ayki]	Change my old coins, I'll swap you
Cincomanta, cinco salaki yasta kapusq[ayki]	Five to five; you'll have from me x 2
Rishani, rishani salaki larqa pati[tanta]	I'm off to above the irrigation canal
Chaypi tarishani salaki mejor paloma[sta]	There I'll be finding a better lover x 2
Esosi ahora si salaki gusta quri[wanki]	That's it, yes now! you please me
Maypi rikuq tiyan salaki rantirqapusq[ayki]	Where's there a seer?[67] I'll buy you one
Chala patitaywan salaki chalarqapusq[ayki]	Change my old coins, I'll swap you

---

[62] The cry *wir wiir* was specified at another time to be that of the *samiris*, the horned and bull-like forces of the mountain peaks (*lumpris*) which, according to the nearby Qaqachakas, can engender female animals through 'breath' (*samay*) alone (Arnold 1992:63). This suggests that the new baby potatoes were engendered by the powerful cries or breath of the stones on the mountain peaks, reminding us how the *wirjin* ('fields') were married to the *jurq'u* ('mountain') in the *asintu* ceremony in August (Chapter 5).

[63] *Nuqapis kaypi tumani salakipaq tumayku 'wer wee' ulikuni, 'ay sala salaki' nispa. Mastucha tantakuspa, kaypi tusuyku a. Papitasta allarkamuyku chay uchurpitasta sumaq mikhuyku a. Tumayku a wirjinpaq kunanqa. Way! sumaq ch'askañawi mamata paqarichishanki qan; sumaqta wiñachishanki. Way! kunan kayqa surti. Aqhata tumayku ch'allayku a. Chay papataq q'ipirikuspa tusuchiyku a.*

[64] 'Elder and younger' possibly relates to crop rotation which varies according to altitude, land quality and access to irrigation. The most usual cycle in the fields near Kalankira is three years cultivation (years: 1 potatoes, 2 barley, 3 barley) followed by four years fallow (*samashan*).

[65] *Paloma*, literally 'dove'. A metaphor for 'lover' with male connotations.

[66] *Patita* or *'pata qullqi'* name for old currency (money).

[67] 'Seer' in this context may refer to a healer who reads coca leaves (and is paid); grammatically it may also simply refer to any person who is able to see.

Maypi rikurqanki salaki pisq'u wañusq[ata]	Where did you look? Dead bird x 2
Nuqa rikurqani salaki pukllay saykusq[ata]	I looked, tired of playing x 2
Rishani, rishani salaki larqa pati[tanta]	I'm off to above the irrigation canal
Chaypi tarishani salaki mejor palom[asta]	There I'll be finding a better lover

Charango tuning: *salaki*

Example 9.4   *Salaki* song with *charango* accompaniment. (Asunta Beltrán: voice, Paulino Jara: *charango*). Transposed up about one semitone. (CD track 36)

Salaki verses, like those of the dry season, consist of paired six syllable couplets, separated by the word *salaki* or *pastita* ('shepherdess'), which I have not translated. These lines focus on 'young women' (*jovencita masi*), whose concerns dominate dry season songs (*takis*). The allusions to going 'above the irrigation canal', 'finding a better lover' and being 'tired of playing', suggest leaving the rains, childhood and Carnival (*pujllay* 'play') behind. Exchanging old, out of date and worthless coins or lovers for new ones, and the image of a dead bird, also convey the idea of creating distance from the past and former intimacies, and thus presumably from ancestral guardians and the rains.[68] Paulino related the image of the 'dead bird' to a girl's loss of interest in boys, who now appear 'unpleasant' and 'weak' – where 'bird' and 'playing' clearly evoke erotic connotations.[69] In the context of this shift in modes of relating to others, it is notable that in his 1612 Aymara dictionary, Bertonio not only glosses *wayñu* (*huayñu*) as a circle dance but also as: 'friend, companion, familiar, applies to men and women who treat one another with familiarity' (1984 [1612], II:157). Through the various despatches of Carnival, we discover the tactile and erotic familiarity of *qhata* (*wayñu*) dancing gradually replaced by independence in the dance genres of the harvest season.

---

[68] Frequent changes in Bolivian currency, including rapid devaluation or complete replacement, means that peasants often experience the loss of considerable savings. For example, one peasant man I spoke to in the valleys lost the value of two oxen he had sold by not exchanging the old currency with which he was paid before it became obsolete and worthless.

[69] Catherine Allen describes the placing of a dead bird inside stores of *chuñu* (freeze-dried potatoes) as a guard in Sonqo, Southern Peru (1982:182), and observes that birds act as 'intermediaries between the worlds of life and death' (1982:188).

The great despatch (*jatun kacharpaya*)

On the final Sunday evening of Carnival, called *Tentacíon*, the adolescent
salaki dance troupe was joined by several other dancers. This enlarged group,
accompanied by Paulino on the *charango*, visited each homestead of the
hamlet in turn, starting and finishing at the *wañuq wasi*.[70] Among the additions
to the group of dancers were five 'devil' figures, consisting of two men
dressed as an urban miner and his wife, two men dressed as a peasant couple
(man and wife) and a *satanusitu* ('little satan'), a boy of about 12 years, who
ran behind the row of couples. The two principal girl singers (Sabasta and
Margara Beltrán), one who danced beside the *charango* player and the other
beside Ciprian Beltrán, the dead man's son, wore the jackets of the men who
were dressed as women.

The dress of the 'devil' *pandilla* ('gang')

(1) Urban mining couple

Machu (miner)   *Q'iwa* (*cholita*)
miner's helmet, rubber boots   man in drag: *pollera* (a wide
yellow waterproof dungerees,   pleated urban-style skirt), shawl,
sirinu whistle   bowler hat, headscarf over face

(2) Peasant couple

Machu   *Q'iwa*
muntira, fighting helmet,   man in drag: *almilla* (woollen dress)
waistcoat, jacket, boots   *llijlla* (carrying cloth on back),
sirinu whistle   white felt hat, headscarf over face

(3) *Satanusitu* (little satan)
large colourful shirt, tied with belt but
not tucked in at waist, large hat with
colourful polythene decorations

The mining couple, in particular, constantly mimed hilarious sexual
horseplay; for example, the miner (*machu*) often searched desperately for his
q'iwa partner, called *doña Elena*. On finding her he would throw her to the
ground to ravish her, only to be stopped by the *cabecilla* with his whip.
Similarly, both men in drag (*q'iwas*) would frequently throw other men to the
ground and mime copulation with them. A strong sense of parody pervaded the
performance, in which I was also discreetly included.[71] Between these antics

---

[70] As official *charango* player Paulino, who was only recently married at the time, was required
to perform for three consecutive years. He had also recently completed his three years contract as
mono dancer (September). Similarly, participants in urban dance groups, such as Oruro Carnival or
San Miguel in Uncia, make a 'contract' with the Virgin (or other patron) to dance for three years.

[71] The *q'iwa* urban miner's wife (in drag) was referred to as (*doña*) *Elena*, the name of my then
girlfriend in England, as many people knew.

the group danced from house to house, singing *salaki* verses and the two *machu* men blowing green plastic whistles, called *sirinu* (CD track 37). The group gradually swelled as the visits continued and it began to grow dark. In the patio of one homestead we formed a large 'circle' (*muyu*), without holding hands, and one by one, each dancer took a turn to move right, circling right around each person in turn (Figure 9.9).

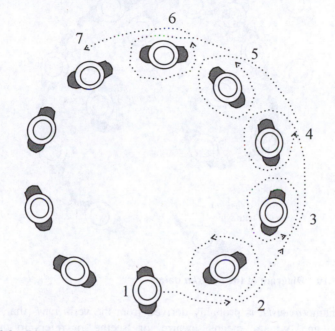

Figure 9.9   Diagram of *muyu* dance

Once we had visited every homestead and made final libations in the *wañuq wasi*, we danced out onto the *pampa* (flat ground) below the hamlet for another half hour of very vigorous *salaki* dancing, spurred on by the whip of the *cabecilla*. We then held hands in a circle, facing the centre, to perform the *aywisku* dance in which Cenovia Beltrán, the dead man's daughter, led the line of dancers back on itself in a zigzag path, moving in and out of the arches of held hands. Reminiscent of the shuttle moving in and out between the warp threads in weaving, this results in the dancers facing outwards, away from the centre of the circle. After dancing this way for a time, Cenovia led the line through the arches again until once again we faced inwards towards the centre. The whole sequence was then repeated. This dance, as I discovered, is extremely difficult to perform without losing grip of your partners' hands; and anyone who does so is likely to be whipped and berated by the *cabecilla* (Figure 9.10).

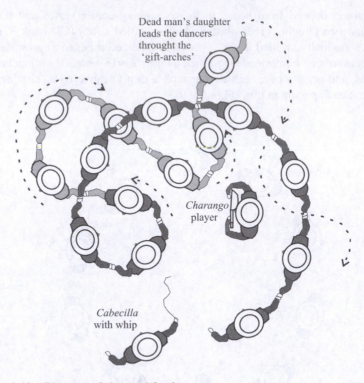

Dead man's daughter
leads the dancers
throught the
'gift-arches'

Charango
player

Cabecilla
with whip

Figure 9.10   Diagram of the *aywisku* dance

The name *aywisku* is probably derived from the verb *aywi-* that, both in Quechua and Aymara, means 'swarm' or 'seethe' or refers to the rapid multiplication of, for example, insects or rabbits in one place.[72] *Aywisku* was formerly danced at night during the potato harvest (April–June) in order, I was told, to 'make the potatoes grow' (*papa puqunanpaq*).[73] Doña Asunta, vividly evoked the imagery of giving birth, describing the dance as *siwil sik'iy* meaning 'to extract from a ring or hoop' and observing that three people were involved, 'two hold the arch and one passes through' (Figure 9.10):

> We used to dance beautifully, as if [making] holes. Grasping [hands] in doors of gift-arches[74] we passed through, extracted from the ring it is said… Thus we were dancers in *qhaliyu* [dry season *charango* music].[75]

---

[72] Lara 1978:56, Herrero & Sanchéz 1983:24, Lucca 1987:33.

[73] *Aywisku* was also formerly danced at harvest time by *cholo* agriculturalists in the nearby town of Macha.

[74] In the word *arku*, the Aymara *arku* meaning 'gift', for example at weddings, and Spanish *arco* 'bow, hoop or arch', which are both in common usage in Kalankira, creatively merge as one.

[75] *Tusuq kayku sumaqta chay jusq'us ajinas. Jap'inakuspa arkupunkus sut'uq kayku, siwil sik'is nisqa kaq nin… Chayqa tusuq kayku chay qhaliyupi.*

The 'gully' dance (*wayq'u*) or 'despatch' (*kacharpaya*)

Finally for the *kacharpaya* or 'farewell' itself, called *wayq'u* ('gully'), the dancers firmly held hands in a circle, enclosing the two *machu* and *q'iwa* couples (urban miners and peasants), and the *satanusitu*, *cabecilla* (dance master) and *charango* player. As Paulino strummed the final *salaki* on the *charango*, the *machu* and *q'iwa* dancers hurled themselves against the enclosing ring of hands and the members of the circle encouraged one another to hold hands with all their strength: 'don't let them escape!' After a few frenzied minutes the *machus* and *q'iwas* suddenly burst their way out of the ring and yelling at the tops of their voices leapt down into the nearby gully. Amidst wild shouting we removed our outer garments (for example jackets or waistcoats), shook them, turned them inside out and replaced them. A few seconds later the other dancers emerged from the gully, now dressed in their own appropriately gendered clothes.

'Did you hear the sound KUM! as they leapt into the gully,' people excitedly commented to one another – onomatopoeia often used by storytellers to refer to evoke the devil entering the earth or a rock (Chapter 2). Meanwhile Paulino tuned the *charango* from *natural* into *cruz* and, as he began to strum, was joined by the girls singing the *cruz* songs associated with harvest time and the feast of the Holy Cross (3 May). We formed a circle (*rueda*) around him and the *cabecilla*. However, this time we danced singly without holding hands and a girl directed the choreography; it was Cenovia Beltrán, daughter of the dead man, who was also identified as an *imilla wawa* ('baby girl') – the unmarried girls who control the male *wayli* dancers during *cruz* (Chapter 6). Invoking the choreography of *cruz*, Cenovia used her whip to send us in alternating directions around the circle, to stamp the ground violently in *zapateo*, and then to form a meandering single file (*link'u link'u*).[76] Through the darkness, the line of dancers snaked its way back across the *pampa* and into the hamlet, to sing *cruz* verses, dance in circles (without holding hands), and to drink corn beer in the patio of every homestead. Through music and dance performance, we had despatched the Carnival devils back into the earth and been transported to the harvest season.

Conclusion: Apotheosis and Embodiment

The three *kacharpaya* ('despatch') ceremonies of Carnival were in many respects quite distinct, but all clearly involved reversal and invoked the

---

[76] The file was led by Pedro Beltán who had acted as the lead *machu* dancer, dressed as a miner, in the *pandilla*. He took the lead role because he was to be the *alférez* for the patronal feast of Guadalupe in the following September.

separation between the living and the ambiguous ancestral and chthonic forces brought together during the rains. The focus of the first *kacharpaya* was clearly human – a celebration and farewell to the 'harnessed' male soul who had helped bring crops to fruition through the rains – while the second for 'father flowers' and the wooden *pinkillu* flutes was more agricultural in outlook. In many parts of Northern Potosí, this despatch of the *pinkillu* flutes into the mountain sphere is the final rite of Carnival, as it was in Kalankira before about the mid 1960s. Elsewhere, the silencing of the flutes is sometimes followed by a few hours of couple dancing in a distinct 'transitional' *charango* song genre, before performing the standard dry season genre to return to the sphere of habitation. The two days of *salaki* music of Kalankira and Sunday's *jatun kacharpaya*, might be understood as an extension of this 'transitional' phase of the *pinkillu kacharpaya*. It might even make sense to think of the Friday and Sunday *kacharpayas* as the opening and conclusion of a single ceremonial despatch.

Despite the human focus of the *alma kacharpaya*, which took place in the sphere of human habitation, its metaphorical connection with the life cycle of crops, especially the potato, is critical. From this perspective, the journey of the harnessed adult male soul through the course of the rains parallels the growth of plants to flowering. In this equation of human with plant life, Carnival emerges as the peak and flowering of the human lifecycle and afterlife – a glorious apotheosis reserved for male adults, who are presented as warriors.[77] The reversal in orientation, so vividly acted out by the *pujllay* dancers accompanied by the *sirinus*, leads these male souls to leave the growth pathway of the living (to the right) and embark on the pathway of the souls (to the left), as well as to join the ancestral community in *alma llajta* ('land of the souls') – singing and dancing perpetual *wayñu*.

Andrew Canessa has suggested that in Pocobaya, Bolivia, human life may be viewed 'as a process by which an unsocialised creature becomes fully human and ultimately reaches the apotheosis of humanity: becoming merged with the ancestral spirits'. He relates this to an individual's 'progressive integration into the life of the community', where through, for example, holding increasingly onerous community offices a person comes to 'approximate more and more the state of the mountain ancestors' (1998:239). This notion of an 'apotheosis' is especially apt for the *alma kacharpaya*, in which the *sirinus* accompany the male soul to the ancestral spirit world; it marks the glorious culmination of both the growing season and the man's participation in the living community – for whom his redistributed energies have brought new life. For many annual crops, such as the potato, growth culminates with flowering, which also signals the onset of decline – a vertical,

---

[77] However, ceremonies for deceased adult women are held during All Saints and Carnival in certain other parts of Northern Potosí.

as well as a horizontal, reversal in orientation. The plant's sap descends to feed and swell the new generation of tubers below the soil, and the colourful vegetation that clothed the earth during Carnival gradually begins to desiccate, shrivel and to be consumed as a new cycle of consumption commences, initiated by the mouse *charango* (Chapter 3).

Until despatched with 'Father Flowers' and the *wayñu* music of the rains on Friday night, the white flag was ubiquitous during Carnival. Women usually carried it, but in the hands of men in the *pujllay* dance it took on a life of its own, as if symbolic of male mortality – and perhaps a representation of soul substance, such as *axayu*.[78] Several people compared this flag to a potato flower and related it to the white flag carried by the unmarried girls (*imilla wawa*) in the men's snaking *wayli* harvest war dance (Chapter 6). In the *wayli*, the *imilla wawa* typically flank the lead male dancer, called *punta* ('tip' or 'peak'), and several people told me the *imilla wawa* and their flags symbolize the *punta's* arrival at the peak or flowering of the life cycle; the apotheosis and reversal suggested the *alma kacharpaya* – perhaps symbolizing the entire Carnival season. This choreography evokes fertility, where this male conjunction with the *imilla wawa* is symbolic of the fecundity of the earth (*wirjin* 'virgin') and of the food crops called *mamas* ('mothers').[79] According to Denise Arnold, the La Paz Aymara refer to the buds of sprouting potatoes as *imill wawa* ('girl child'), a name also used elsewhere to describe the most fertile tubers with most eyes (1988:419, 447). However, despite this female gendering of potato tubers and their buds there is a strong sense that the pointed tips, which force the way forward through life – like the *punta* ('tip', 'point') of the *wayli* dance – are intensely male and warlike. They are also evocative of the potato's *axayu*, as described by Domingo Jiménez, which is linked with the growth tips and the opening of flowers or 'eyes'.

Although *tinku* battles are not held during Carnival and fighting is supposedly forbidden (Harris 1982a:57), male warrior imagery was especially notable in the first two *kacharpayas*.[80] In these ceremonies the departing male

---

[78] Elsewhere in Bolivia white flags have been related to a pact with the spirit world and bringing peace and abundant harvests (Oblitas Poblete 1978 [1960]:214), or to inviting neighbours to attend *k'illpa* ceremonies during Carnival (INDICEP 1973:5). Most relevantly, in Sullka Titi Titiri (near Jesús de Machaca, Ingavi province, department La Paz) the *axayu* or 'soul' of a powerful rock on a nearby mountain peak, was ritually carried down to the community in *pañuelos* ('cloths, hankerchiefs') resembling flags on the first of January (personal communication Astvaldur Astvaldsson).

[79] See Torrico (1989) for an extensive discussion of the exchanges between different form of *mamas*, as food and exchange products, which are described as falling in love with one another (1989). Also see Arnold, Jiménez & Yapita (1991) who describe how most food crops are called *mamas* in the songs addressed to them and explain that mamas also often relates to *imillas* ('girls').

[80] Despite the theoretical prohibition on fighting during Carnival, a violent scuffle broke out immediately behind my hut between the respective *pinkillu* ensembles of Pata Kalankira and

soul, *tata pulurisa* ('Father Flowers'), the *uña alferéz*, and male *sirinu* dancers were all represented as warriors wearing *muntira* fighting helmets. During the Friday *kacharpaya* when these helmets are dramatically removed and thrown to the ground, metaphorically preventing the emergence of 'devilish horns', the simultaneous silencing of the *pinkillu* flutes ensures that no further sprouting of horns can take place until these Carnival *wayñu* melodies are sounded again, some seven months later. Both *wayñu* music and the imagery of *muntira* fighting helmets appear intimately associated with the energy that impels both human and plant growth towards flowering. I gained the impression that both the *uña alferéz* and the boy at the tail of the *wayli* dance (Chapter 6) represent the start of a new (male) growth cycle from youth to adulthood. Indeed, Paulino suggested that ideally this should be the same boy of around 10 years old. The boy's father, dancing *pujllay* with a white flag, might in turn be considered the head of the *wayli* dance and to embody 'Father St Flowers' (*tata san puluris*).

Imagery of birth, release and separation was omnipresent in many other aspects of the Carnival celebrations, such as the *wayñu* sung during the *alma kacharpaya* to *kitarra* accompaniment (Example 9.1, CD Track 34). In particular the idea of escape from enclosed feminized space, or uterine embrace (Chapter 8) was vividly evoked in the *pinkillu kacharpaya* by the bursting of the tightly interwoven ring of the *qhata* dance, followed immediately by the removal of the women's rings of shawls. This imagery of enclosing feminine space (especially corrals), associated with the growing season, was also richly evoked in the words of the *asintu* songs (Chapter 5). With the completion of the ceremony two days later in the *jatun kacharpaya*, the ring of dancers – now only holding single hands – was again burst asunder as the devils escaped into the gully. This was followed immediately by dry season *wayli* dancing in which each person danced 'separately' (*sapallan*) in a single snaking file, highlighting the vivid choreographic contrast between the rains and dry season. This shift in choreographic imagery (the visual) from enclosing feminized space to a meandering pathway of male growth and maturation was made explicit in subsequent conversations. It was accompanied by another almost equal and opposite process suggesting sonic containment (the aural), as the Carnival devils leapt into the gully at the climax of the *jatun kacharpaya*. This dramatic performance not only invoked the despatch of the ambiguous Carnival devils from the community, but was also a vivid re-enactment of god's mythic defeat of the devil when their two cockerels competed to be the first to crow as the sun rose for the first time (Chapter 2).

Wak'an Phukru hamlets. Although the disagreement did not concern me, I was forced to intervene as their use of these heavy wooden flutes as weapons threatened to lead to serious injury (as well as damaging my own set of *pinkillus*).

At the time of the *jatun kacharpaya* I presumed that the devils who entered into the earth were the *satanos colorados* but in subsequent conversations people insisted that these were the *sirinus*. Just as the devil's defeat and entry 'inside' brought resonance to the bell stones, the *sirinus* entry 'inside' at the climax of Carnival infused the new offspring (potato tubers) with life. This is reminiscent of the way that *animu*, which is connected with the power to communicate through sound, enters human infants through the fontanel (Arnold 1988:371). Finally this imagery parallels the shift in wind instruments from 'many-holed' *pinkillu* flutes, linked with the circulation of water and sound, to the vessel-like *julajula* panpipes of the dry season, connected with containment, accumulation and 'inner' growth (Chapter 6). The silencing of the *wayñu* melodies at the culmination of Carnival is not so much a cessation of this soul music, but its embodiment as the animating energy of living bodies, potatoes and humans alike. Like the *axayu* described by Domingo Jiménez, this inner soul music leads these bodies forward through life, eventually breaking through their wrapping in a burst of audible – but deathly – *wayñu* music on their ever-upward (and 'right' orientated) journey to Carnival. Here, having reached the summit of the growth pathway, they open their flowers (eyes) in a glorious apotheosis.

Part IV

Kacharpaya – 'Despatch'

Chapter 10

The Fragile Community

Epilogue

The last four chapters dedicated to the musical year have taken us in many directions, but certain concepts, themes and values have remained central, stressing the interdependence of musical, choreographic and other forms of production. These include notions of: containment and circulation; 'inner' and 'outer' growth; the concepts of *q'iwa* and *tara;* the roles of the 'devil' and 'god'; and the place of *animu* and *alma* in local ontologies of musical sound (see also Chapter 2). In a poetics of production, Kalankira's musical and choreographic expressions draw upon and articulate a range of models from people's experience. Music and dance invoke and set into communicative mode connections between, for example, potato cultivation, llama reproduction, the human life cycle, and a range of imagined communities or identities, often alongside powerful sentiments. Indeed, music as sonic sentiment powerfully embodies local notions of fertility and (re)production, as vividly brought home when my recording of llama distress cries was interpreted as an attempt to capture these animals' power to reproduce in my tape recorder (Chapter 8).

Rather than bringing the disparate themes and arguments of this book together into a neatly unified conclusion, this final epilogue intentionally destabilizes some of the apparent certainties of earlier chapters. Although constructed with great care and commitment, these seeming certainties are, of course, no more than ethnographic illusions; they are partial, highly subjective and woven together from disparate and often idiosyncratic sources.[1] Accordingly, I have resisted any expectation or temptation to conclude grandly with what might be interpreted as *the* shared way of understanding music's relationship to production and the unfolding year of the Kalankiras – itself an ethnographic fiction (Chapter 1). This book is, after all, a subjective, personal account and a snapshot of a particular moment in history; it does not aspire to, nor can possibly, adequately represent the multiplicity of views, knowledge and practices of the people of Kalankira. In place of a conclusion, this chapter creates a wider frame and explores a few of the events and developments over the subsequent decade, some of which cast a rather different light on earlier parts of the book.

---

[1] This reference of 'ethnographic illusion' intentionally leads us to question the notion of reality.

The previous chapter ended on a high note; the exuberance of Carnival as the apotheosis of the musical year when one life cycle reaches its zenith and a new one is ushered in, heralded by the *sirinu's* new *wayñu* melodies. It was Carnival and the discourse surrounding it which, more than any other event, gave me a sense that Kalankira's annual sequence of music might helpfully be conceived as a life cycle or integrated performance; its various movements, defined by feasts, motivating progression from one stage of development to the next – expressing and mutually informing understandings of human and plant maturation and fertility. But how much does such a conception of the musical year depend upon Carnival and its performance?

Cancelled Carnival

In February 1996 I returned to Kalankira for Carnival after a gap of just over three years, during which no communication had been possible. In the meantime, this community had lived on in my imagination, notebooks and writings. The Kalankiras of my memories were a dynamic group, one that had become an important aspect of my own sense of self. On this three-month visit, my key objective was to work on the analysis of song texts with some of the unmarried singers, such as Victor Beltrán's daughters Sabasta, Gregoria and Margara. After initially treating me with great suspicion, these girls had gradually grown increasingly helpful and friendly. Full of hopes, but also with some trepidation, I arrived in the hamlet late at night and exhausted following a particularly arduous journey. Paulino and Asencio's families greeted me warmly and over the next few days I gradually caught up with the news. The most obvious physical change was that a new elementary school had been built half a mile below Pata Kalankira, meaning a walk of a few minutes rather than well over an hour for local children. Several deaths had occurred while I had been away, tragically including Paulino and Evangelia's two youngest children, Hilaria and Francisco, as well as several older people. No adult men had died over the previous twelve months and for this reason, I was told, 'Carnival would not happen' in the hamlet that year, highlighting Carnival's close connection with rites for recently deceased adult men (Chapters 8 and 9). Nonetheless, in years without an adult male death community and family ceremonies are still performed.

But Carnival did not really happen in 1996 for other reasons. Many of (Pata) Kalankira's families were not speaking to one another, and the community had all but disintegrated; the feast's desultory music and dance were far from 'collective'. If anything these few half-hearted performances only served to emphasize community conflict and dysfunction. Individual family rites were observed, but they too seemed insipid and lifeless. Gone was the gaiety and exuberance I so fondly remembered – the visions and sounds of young people rushing from one family's corral to the next, playing flutes, singing and dancing. The final despatches of the feast, which people always insisted must include the entire community, involved just a few individuals and no shortage of argument. Carnival was a damp squib; it had no *sunqu* or 'heart'/'sap' (Chapter 2). Without the manifestation of unity in music and dance, so often invoked in local discourse about Carnival, the idea of community could not be realized.

Behind these soured relations lay immense tragedy, which directly involved my host family. Its roots lay in the seductive powers associated with music; which on the one hand may 'produce' sociality by bringing couples or communities together into stable reciprocal relationships, and on the other may threaten or destroy it by destabilizing such relations (Turino 1983:95, Martínez 1998:18). Like many young married men, Paulino continued to play the *charango* and accompany girls of the community in courtship songs. Hardly surprisingly, this was unpopular with his wife Evangelia who, as a married woman, was essentially 'prohibited' from singing such songs (Chapter 5). Precise details are unclear, but apparently a heated confrontation with a group of singers led to a fight with one of Victor Beltrán's daughters in which Evangelia's baby boy fell from her back and subsequently died. Instead of seeking redress through community authorities, Paulino took the matter to a civil court in the mining town of Colquechaka – selling six llamas to pay the legal costs. According to some people's version of the story, this led Victor's wife to spend two months in jail in Colquechaka, in place of her daughter. Whatever the truth, these terrible events destroyed any sense of cooperation or collective feeling in the hamlet. The 'imagined community' of my memory had been violently shattered, in turn compromising my own loyalties and friendships. Speaking with other families had to be handled with immense sensitivity and my research aim of working with Victor's daughters was unthinkable. Much of my energy was taken up in peacemaking, literally breaking up fights and arguing against the need for guns, rather than what might traditionally be conceived as ethnomusicological research.[2]

Ancestors and renewal

Paulino directly attributed his family's misfortunes and the collapse of the community to the breakdown of relations with his deceased father, who had died in Paulino's infancy. His father was angry (*piñakun*) with them, he explained, because they had failed to provide adequate offerings and respect.

---

[2] See Cooley (2003), Hellier-Tinoco (2003) and other essays in *British Journal of Ethnomusicology* (2003) 12/1 on 'Fieldwork impact' for perspectives on ethnomusicologists' roles and relationships in the communities studied.

This brought home just how tangibly Paulino (and presumably other people in Kalankira) believe the ancestors influence the fortunes of the living – and how this contrasted with my own perceptions.[3] In order to redress the situation, Paulino travelled to the town of Sucre to have mass said in his father's honour. Back in Kalankira, we then performed a complex series of rituals in which his father and other ancestors were richly feasted and remembered. Finally, in the middle of the night the feasted ancestors were exorcised from the sphere of the living and returned to *alma llajta* ('the land of the souls') – a task considered far too dangerous for Paulino or Asencio. Together with another man from nearby Titiri, I was called upon to burn the offerings on the western edge of the hamlet, and to smash the earthenware jugs used to serve corn beer to the souls. Once these powerful spirits had been safely despatched, we returned to the assembled family to drink libations from paired vessels until dawn.

On my next visit to Kalankira, just over one year later in 1997, I discovered that the worst of the community's crisis was past. Even if relations remained cool between certain families, a degree of communication and cooperation had resumed, which grew over subsequent years. At this time, many families began to move out of the central and increasingly deserted hamlet of Pata Kalankira, to build new and widely dispersed homesteads which, it was claimed, provided better access to water and mountain pastures. But I acquired a sense that the distance between homesteads reflected more than the purely economic concerns, indeed in nearby Wak'an Phukru – with its strong sense of community – this fashion for building second homes nearer pastures resulted in more concentrated, rather than dispersed, dwellings. From 1996 to 2002, Paulino and Evangelia's fortunes seemed to improve considerably and three more boys were born, who constantly enlivened their homestead with their antics. By 2002, their big bother Mario – my responsible and assured 11 year old godson – was rapidly turning into a competent *charango* player and Paulino was describing Victor Beltrán's family as *amigos* ('friends'). The deep and long-standing tensions between them were, at least temporarily, submerged in favour of a mutually beneficial climate of reciprocity.

Alongside the rites to appease his ancestors, Paulino attributed this resumption of community relations, and his own reintegration, to his participation as the *alférez* (sponsor) of the feast of the Holy Cross – which

---

[3] As beliefs and perceptions about relations with the ancestors are so diverse, even in the same places (for example, the UK), comparisons should perhaps only be made on the basis of personal experience. A few days before travelling to Bolivia in 1996 I gave a concert in Ingleton in Yorkshire, close to Ingleborough Hill, a favourite haunt of my own grandfather on which his ashes were scattered. As we approached the town, Ingleborough's peak stood out in the evening sun invoking powerful and benign memories of my grandfather, and the sense that some part of him had found a fitting home. When Paulino told me about his father's anger, it struck me that I did not share the conviction that my grandfather or any other ancestor could actively impact on my destiny and fortunes.

necessarily involved setting up webs of reciprocity and lines of communication, as this feast's music and dance so vividly manifest (Chapter 6). I was struck by how the basic structure of collective rituals, music and dance I had encountered a decade earlier appeared essentially unchanged.

There is sometimes a tendency for outsiders to romanticize the idea of rural communities as stable or even timeless and as sharing a common purpose, but like all human relationships they are riven with conflicts and complex power relations, and are subject to constant fluctuations, cycles of change and differences in priorities. The trauma and tragedy of 1996 and the subsequent healing brought home both the fragility of community relations and the critical role of music and dance performance in their expression. Rather like *tinku*, as imagined – if violent – 'harmony' (Chapter 6), the reproduction of musical traditions in places such as Kalankira enables people to imagine, and even represent in sound and motion, the idea and possibility of community and cooperation, as if temporarily forgetting their conflicts. Music and dance are a powerful force in the (re)production of a sense of community, although – as we have seen – they may also destroy what they create, or serve as the arena in which violent conflicts are played out. Kalankira's music is powerful, ambiguous, and potentially both productive and destructive.

Musical mobilization

One unfortunate consequence of the unfashionability of extended ethnographic fieldwork in rural communities (Chapter 1), is the tendency to view such communities as either 'isolated' or subject to 'outside influences', and thereby to fail to recognize their creativity, agency and view of the outside. For example, at first sight the urban and national repertoires played by *siku* panpipes during the *rinuwa* feasts in September, might be interpreted as an example of outside influence, and in certain respects they are. But, by drawing on don Adrian's story of the Water War, a much more interesting, emic picture emerges, which also acknowledges the agency and creativity of peasant musicians. Through this music, exogamous social groups and the nation are invoked for productive ends. Achieving the circulation of water as rain and the turning of the seasons is a shared project, which – like a military campaign or revolution (*ch'axwa*) – can only be achieved through bringing together and mobilizing a large disparate body of people: an 'imagined community'. Instead of viewing *siku* panpipes as an example of top-down *modernity*, we are presented with a dynamic vision of bottom-up *musical mobilization*.

It is also notable here that although panpipes are widely recognized as a global emblem for indigenous Andean people, having deep prehispanic roots in the region, for the Kalankiras they tend to be associated with outsiders –

external urban identities.[4] In a similarly counter-intuitive way, the instruments they connect most closely with local production (*pinkillu* flutes) and ethnic identity (guitars) turn out to be modelled on European music technology introduced to the Andes in the sixteenth century (Chapters 4 and 8).

These examples suggest that so-called 'indigenous' values, knowledge and ways of approaching the world are far from inward-looking; rather they are dynamic and precisely articulate between inside and outside. For example, in the feast of the Holy Cross (May) the peasant participants wear purchased factory-produced clothes and adopt aspects of *mestizo* identity. This dynamic vision of production – connected with the exchange journeys beyond the *ayllu's* boundaries during May and June – juxtaposes the 'reproduction' of the *ayllu* at Carnival, when traditional *ayllu* dress is worn. However, for the Tinku-Macha project (Chapter 6), with its focus on heritage and aim to transform the feast of the Holy Cross into a congenial tourist attraction, innovations such as the wearing of factory-produced clothes are seen as a contamination of the tradition, rather than as a dynamic expression of indigenous notions of production (see Boyes 1993:12). On similar lines, I have argued that the fads, fashions, modernity and market forces that fuelled guitar makers' innovations through much of the twentieth century, have contributed to the reinforcement and indigenization of seasonal performance practices, and the strengthening of *ayllu* identity. The connection between guitars, seasonality and agricultural practices is not some relic from a bygone age, but a dynamic, ongoing process in which indigenous values and identity are deeply interwoven with market forces and a demand for shifting fashions (Chapter 4).

An ear to the future

Will Kalankira's music continue to interact with and acquire meaning and power from the productive processes discussed in this book? Will children learn their lessons well at school, and – like much of the rest of the world – come to view the idea that music promotes plant growth or causes rain as primitive superstition? Kalankira's musical life depends on a lively population of fashion-conscious young people, who keep music dynamic and are motivated – through amorous interests and self-expression – into providing *kunswilu* or 'consolation' (Chapter 5). If too many young people migrate and fail to return to help with productive tasks and participate in feasts – leaving the responsibility for performance to older people – music will doubtless begin to lose its *sunqu* ('heart', 'sap'), as it has in many other parts of the Andes (see

---

[4] For information on prehispanic panpipes see d'Harcourt & d'Harcourt 1925, Stevenson 1976 [1968]:245–55, Bellenger 1982:40–43, Olsen 2002.

Turino 1993). Will young people continue to see performance as worth the effort? During Carnival in 1996, a cassette of commercial Cumbia music was played on a recently purchased radio-cassette player during a ritual for the llama herd in Wak'an Phukru. The young men were enthusiastic about this recent acquisition – 'it saves us having to play "consolation" on the *pinkillus*'. Even so, at the climax of the ceremony a group of *pinkillu* players arrived and the cassette was switched off.

On a recent trip to Kalankira I asked Paulino 'what is the best present I could bring you?' Without reflection he replied, 'two large speakers to put on the roof of the house so I can play loud music all over the hamlet'. The idea filled me with horror, betraying my own musical sensibilities and intense dislike of the blaring speakers found in many Bolivian towns. Was Paulino's intention to appropriate modern technology to achieve productive ends? – Just think how much *kunswilu* could be produced with two big speakers! Might this be part of a process of resignification similar to Renaissance recorders' transformation to *pinkillu* flutes? Whatever the answer, I have little enthusiasm for indulging this project, and it is well beyond Paulino's economic resources. However, it does bring home the issue of economics. Most families in Kalankira own radio-cassette players (which were frequently displayed when I took family photographs), but these are very rarely heard because batteries are expensive and not a priority. Doubtless they would regularly play such machines, delight in electricity and hot running water, consume MTV and the other trappings of modern affluent society if these were open to them.

Kalankira's musical traditions and way of life are in part preserved by the same economic and social disadvantages that defines them as peasants in relation to, for example, urban *mestizos*. But is their belief and pride in their own identity as Kalankiras and Machas powerful enough for them to keep taking on the world, as they do in the violent harmony of *tinku* battles? Will they continue to return home from these encounters bruised, but strengthened in the knowledge of their own agency, courage and future?

Sorting the harvest

We come to a kind of *kacharpaya* ('despatch') and turning point (*pachakuti*); an end and a new beginning. With the 'production' of this book comes a kind of apotheosis: the Carnival-like culmination of one phase, which carries in its wake the new fruit of the next. Brimming with energy (*animu*) and sounds, the fruit of this labour now sets off alone on its twisting pathway to unimaginable destinations. Will it be abandoned and forgotten to weep, like discarded broad bean husks, or will people care for it? Will they open their ears to its voice, with love and compassion, and find joy, wonder, enchantment and consolation in its messages? Might it grow and enter into dialogue with others in balanced and reciprocal exchanges, to promote mutual understanding and a more equitable global community?

It is a time to take stock, to look over and sort this harvest. Perhaps a few of these fruits might be set aside and prized, and even celebrated with song, dance and libations – like the strange shaped tubers called *llallawas* that embody the power of future production. Others I hope will nourish, and provide food for thought, and a taste for ethnomusicology and Andean ethnography for future students and scholars. Using these seeds, not all of which will grow, let new generations dig deeper and achieve yet greater abundance from their labours. Finally, I hope that an appetite for the fruits of this harvest will also be shared and enjoyed by anybody with a desire to understand more about music, the Andes, or just hungry for knowledge.

Appendix 1

The Battle for Water – a Quechua story (Adrian Chura)

See Chapter 7. The first part of the story is included on CD Track 46.

[HS: *Maymanta tukuy kay instrumentos … kay julajulas. Maymanta? ima timpumanta? kay waukus.*]

[HS: Where do all the different instruments come from? For example, the *jula-jula* panpipes. From where? From what time [epoch] do they come – those *wauku* [*julajula*] panpipes?]

1

Ahh … kay julajulas [HS: wayli] Ahh … chayqa, kay diosninchis … fiestata munankichischu kay jina tusukuyta nispa, tapullasqata ninma; bueno, kunan nataraq kwintarikusqayki a. Bueno kay jinaraq chaymantamá chay waukusta kwintasqayki.

1

Oh? Those *julajulas*? [HS: the *wayli* dance] Oh that, our-god's feast, you want to know about that, with all that dancing, is that the question? Well, now then I'll tell you the story. Well, this is the way it is with those *wauku* [*julajula*] panpipes. I'll tell you the story.

2

Chaymantaqa diosninchisqa ajina sapallanchá jina qhawarqa chaymantaqa: Karaju! wawasniytaqa tukuy lomapi turayta munashan karaju kay yawlus Karaju kunan imanasunmantaq, bueno karaju imaynata ruwayman.

2

Then god just like that, all by himself, watched:

    [God] 'Dammit! those devils are wanting to pester my children on every mountain. What will become of us? Well, damn it! how can I do it?

3

Bueno, nichu kunanqa waway … naman qhawaq sapa lomaman lluqsiwaqchu waway wawasta wartaq. Karaju wawasta kay karaju yawlu sujitay munashallanpuni, saruyta munashallanpuni nisqa.

3

Well, my son … why don't you go out onto the mountains and look after my children. This damn devil keeps wanting to control the children, he always wants to dominate [trample] them.

4

Bueno, intunsis milagrus kasaqkun [kashaqtin] nuqayku na … qhawaq risaqku, yastá.

4

Well then, as the miracles are being performed we will go and watch them, that's it.

5

Chaymanta kay Killakas quchata pusamusqa nin lamarmanta. Chay quchatari kay Potosi cerroman risqa nin ya hasta … Y chaypiri … nasqa nin.

5

And then Killakas, it's said, led the lake from the sea [*lamar*]. And this lake went to the mountain of Potosí, right there. And right to that place […] they say.

6

Karaju walliman riqta wawasniyta, chantá qan imapaq jark'ashanki kay quchatari? Ah mulinuta karaju … napi, Wardalupi [Guadalupe] sumaqta llank'achimuq rishani mulinuta, chaypaq yakutaqa pusashani.

6

[God to Devil]
'Dammit, my children go to the valleys, so then why are you holding back this lake? Gosh, the watermill at Guadalupe I'm going to make the watermill work and that's why I'm leading the water there.'

7

Qulluqa kustunmanta tintikusqa nin. Karaju ima puntascha uranta kustunmanta pampiyakusqa nin. Kayjina urqusqa mayu pura tinkuspa khuskita yaku lamanapaq ajina ruwakusqa nin.

7

It is said that the hill spread-out of its own accord. The peaks flattened themselves down. In this way the mountains brought their respective rivers intimately together to make water capable of carrying sediments.

8

Ari, chaymantaqa diosninchisqa, bueno. Karaju mirta! wawasniy mayta purinqari, a ver kunan kay yaku jark'aykuqtiykiri karaju mulinu importan mana wawasniyki importanchu. Wawasniykiqa uj ch'aqchata ruwaykusqa chayta latashankachari nisqa.[1] Ma[na] rinqachu karaju mirtas! Ukhutacha qan chay murupaq ruwashanki karaju. Bueno karaju tinkusun.

8

Well, then god [said]
'Damn and shit! where will my children be able to go now that you've held up the water? What matters is the mill, not your children. When your children have wallowed in filth[2] they will crawl along there anyway. [The watermill] won't go damn and shit! All that stuff [building, hardening] you are doing deep inside is [just making work] for the millstone damn it! We shall come face to face, damn you!'

9

Tinkuyusqanku nin.

9

It is said they met with determination.

10

Bueno chantari karaju qanpipuni kanki, qan jinata karaju kay wawasniywan enimigota hap'inakuspa qan. Karaju yakusta jark'anaykipaq majinachu kanqa Yastá karaju waqtakusun ya esta.

10

[God] 'Who do you think you are? – making enemies with my children and holding up the water like that. It will not be like that! All right, let's fight! All right that's it!'

---

[1] End of CD recorded excerpt.
[2] 'done that messy thing'.

11

Tata santu Killakas, tata primiruta
ukhurisqa chaytaqa maqasqa yawluqa
apamusqa nin sapitallan nin.

11

Father Saint Killakas appeared first and
was beaten up by the devil who carried
him just by himself.

12

Bueno, chaymantaqa sapitayta sujitawan
pero nispachá paruma willakullantaq
diosninchismanqa, ya hasta, bueno.

12

[Killakas] 'Well, he held me up all
by myself' complained that *paruma*
[saint] to god.

13

Karaju manajinachu kanqa. Bueno,
sujitan musunkipunichá.
Ari sujitamuwan.
Bueno karaju tawa phishka
kankichisriy tukuy lomaman tiyaq
rinkichu karaju. Karaju majinachu
kanqa karaju nispa.

13

[God] 'It must not be like this! He
grabbed you?'
[Killakas] 'Yes, he grabbed hold of
me'.
[God] 'There are four or five of
you, go and live in [take over] all the
mountains. It's not going to be like
this!

14

Fuera chaymantaqa nuqaq mastruyta
tata Manqhiri tatata ujta ruwasqa.

14

Well, then my master father Mankiri did
something.

15

Nuqaqa chay watulk'ulkupi
nuqaqa sayamusaq tatay. A chaypaq
nuqata juntaway nisqa.
'Bay rinki waway, chayman'.

15

[Mankiri] 'I will go and stand in
the narrow *watul* place
(*watulk'ulku*) father', he said. 'You
can recruit me for that'.
[God] 'Alright go there my child'.

16

Bueno nuqataq karaju Panakachi kasqa,
tata Panakachiqa kayman jamusqa nin;
kinsa hermanos.

16

Well then there's Panakachi; it's said
father Panakachi – three brothers came
here. Then Panakachi [said]:

17

Chaymantaqa achay Panakachiqa chay
yawlus chay susirawanchiqpuni [...]
runapis maqanakuspa
susiranakushanchis, achay janpiq nuqa
kasaq chayta nuqa thanichisaq jampispa,
karaju nisqa nin.

17

'Those devils always trap/infect
us.[3] Also when people fight we
hurt one another. Damn it! I will
be a healer and relieve the pain
through curing', he said.

18

Chaymanta mama jatun Qupaqawanaqa
[Copacabana] quchallapita kasqa nin.
Chay mama Qupaqawanaqa.

18

So then there was the great mama
Copacabana and she lived in the lake
it's said, that mama Copacabana.

---

[3] *Susuri* was translated as 'trap' or 'infect' with illness by Pedro Plaza. In Kalankira it was used
to refer to illness or loss of animals when, for example, correct offerings had not been made.

19

Bueno, karaju nuqaqa, quri wastunwan waqtasaq karaju, a ver karaju, kunan rikunqa nispaqa quri wastunta [baston] tatay juntapuway nuqapaq.

20

Bay juntapusqayki waway karaju. Mayta rejintinki karaju? Wawasmanta rejintinki karaju. Qan waqta kasp'iwan waktanakanki kay quri wastunwan nispa.

21

Bueno tatay nisqa. Ah ya esta.

22

Chaymantaqa tata Turiqhariqa nillasqataq nin:
Bueno nuqapaq tatay fundapuway qulqi muntirata sumaq … qulqi muntirata, ñukutawan ruwapuway sumaq qulqi ñukuta, karaju. […?] Ñukuta kayman karaju wayk'usqata ruwa … junt'apuway tatay.

23

Yastá karaju, chaywan qukunki, karaju nispa …

24

Ajinata diosninchis tantaykuraykusqa nin tata Mankiri nin, chaymanta kay tata Killakas nin, tata Panakachi nin, tata Eskaltasiyun nin, chaymanta tata Turaqhari nin; chaykuna tata Eskaltasiyun chaykuna juntaykuspaqa yawlumanchu chimpasqanku nin.

25

Bueno karaju nipunichu kunan yakutaqa nipunichu yakuta kunanqa karaju … nanki, kacharinki nipunichu?

19

'Well, I will hit [the devil] with a golden staff damn it! Let's see damn it! Now he'll see' she said, saying 'give me a golden staff father'.

20

[God] 'Alright, I shall bring it to you my child dammit! Who's going to guard dammit? You have to safeguard the children'. Saying, 'You will strike with the stick, hit with the golden staff'.

21

[Copacabana] 'Alright father, 'she said, 'that's it'.

22

And then in the same way father Turaqhari said:
'Forge me a silver helmet, a good quality silver helmet, and also make me knuckle-dusters, good quality silver knuckle-dusters. Forge knuckle-dusters for me, bring them to me father'.

23

[God] 'Alright, with those you will fight [give]'.

24

So it was that in this way god brought together father Mankiri, then father Killakas, father Panakachi, father Exaltación, and then father Turaqhari it is said. Along with father Exaltación they all got together and approached the devil.

25

[Saints] 'All right, you bastard, still no water? Are you still not going to liberate the water?'

26

A pusanallaypuni tiyan karaju trabaju tiyan astawan; karaju mana wawasniyki importanchu, karaju.

26

[Devil] 'I still need to drive it, damn you! There's more work to be done. Your children are not important'.

27

Mana kacharinkichu karaju, Yastá karaju intunsis waqtakusun karaju.

27

[Saints] 'So you are not going to let the water out? That's it then, we'll fight'.

28

Yawlupis jinallataq sayaykusqa nin a...Bueno chaymantaqa yawluwanqa tinkuykusqanku nin. Chaymanta chay tata Turiqhariqa qulqi ñukuyuq kaq ujta yawluta waktasqa kaypi nin llint'a sinqanpi 'k'iq um' pampaman chuqasqa nin. Chaymanta mama Qupaqawanataq wastunwan waktasqa.

28

The devil also stood up [and faced them] it is said. Well then they had an encounter with the devil it is said. Then father Turaqhari, the one with the silver knuckle-dusters, gave the devil a blow here on his twisted nose *k'iq umm!!* knocking him to the ground. Then mama Copacabana hit the devil with her staff.

29

Imanayta qan munanki? imanayta munanki porque es karaju kay yakuta kacharpanki karaju! Qunki wawaspaq qan kasharqanki nuqayku dueño kayku wawasmanta Ya a ver, ruway a ruway.

29

[Copacabana] 'What do you want to do? What do you want? Release this water, damn you! Give it for the children; we are the owners of the children. You'll see! Do it! do it!'

30

Yawlutaqa karaju waktasqa llimp'u chamusqa sinqa nin astas nin llimp'u nin. Chaymanta Yastá karaju. Intirumanta ch'ipanku kusqanku nin. Qan jinapuni kanki machu-machu karaju ya hasta wataychis kay karajuta, wataychis wataychis. Yastá watasqanku maqaykuspa. Yastá nataq chay Killakaswan tata Mankiriwantaq. Bay luqhisun kay karajutaqa sarunakasqanku 'pum poow'. Yastá yakuqa ukhuman chinkaykupusqa nin 'kum!'

30

The devil was completely smashed up, his nose and horns completely destroyed, it's said. That's the way it was dammit. They all grabbed him, [saying] 'You're like a lout damn you,' and all tied the bastard up. They beat him as they tied him. Those fathers Killakas and Mankiri [said] 'We'll puncture him, that bastard.' He was trampled down *'pum puuw'*. Right then the water disappeared into the depths – *KUM!*

31

Yastá wataykusqanku chaymanta kunanqa tata Killakasqa chay yawlutaq sarushan nin a. Fierro watasqata ajina sarushan nin a. Chaymanta Killakasqa napiqa kan a chay santuwayrusqa chaymanta[ma] diosninchisqa naqa kay wartaqkunaqa.

31

They tied him up, and from then to this day it is said that father Killakas treads down the devil. Like that, horribly tied-up he's trodden down. Because of this Killakas exists and those sanctuaries, and thus god and those guardians.

32

Bueno nuqaykutari kunanqa nuqaykuta imaynapitaq wawas kunswilawasaqku. Bueno kunanqa waway qantaqa watusunqa kayjina milakruman kunan qunqa. Nuqataq qanman qusqayki tukuy milakruta chaywanqa watusunqa sumaq rispiliwan watusunqa mana jinallachu, sumaq rispitasqa kanki.

33

Bueno tatay intunsis kulukawanki, intunsis chay lugarpi kanaypaq. Bueno nuqa tata Mankiriqa nuqa k'ulkupi sayamusaq karaju kurus chakatasqa kasaq nuqa karaju. Chaypi nuqa paytaqa sarusaq nisqa nin a.

34

Yastá t'akanaqakamusqanku nin chaynaqa Killakaspiqa partakuspa. Chaymanta tukuy lomapiqa tata mamaqa tiyan a sinuchus niya ni kanmanchu karqa nin qanpaq. Chaymanta santa wila kurus tatapis chaymantama diosninchisqa.

35

Bueno qanmanqa kulukashayki milagru kanaykipaq. Bueno, kunan tukuy wawasman jaywanki. Willakuqtinqa qanman willakusunqa como tatan mamanman.

36

Chaymantaqa nuqamanta qan willawanki, ajina nisqa bueno nisqa. Chaymanta waukus, chaymanta sikus, chaymanta musikas [banda], chaymanta chay kenitas chunchitus tukuy kunswiluwan willakuq rinchis. Chaymanta rinuwantin nisqa a. Chaymanta wauku julajulas a.

32

[God] 'Well, how are the children going to console us? Now my child, you will be taken and such miracles will be given. I will give you all these miracles and with that you will be looked after with great respect, taking special care, with great respect.'

33

[Mankiri] 'Well father, you will determine a place for me to reside. Well, I father Mankiri, will stand in a ravine and bridge it with the arms of my cross. There I will trample on him [the devil]'.

34

So they scattered about in the Killakas place, dividing themselves. Because of that in every hill there are mother and father from that time, if not there would not have been any [parents] for you. And then there is the father saint of the True Cross (*santa wila cruz*) and there is god.

35

[God?] 'Well I'm placing you [saint of the True Cross] to be a miracle. Well, now you will pass this on to all the children. When they give you this news, let us have it told as if to their mothers and fathers.

36

So I've told you all this, said like that. Well, there it is! That's why *waukus* [*jula jula* panpipes], why *sikus* [panpipes], why brass bands, and why those *ch'unchu's* quenas [notch flutes] go passing on this message with consolation. That's why there is 'renewal' it's said. That's why there are *wauku julajula* [panpipes].

Appendix 2: Encounters with *Sirinus*

A discussion in my hosts' cooking hut one evening after supper (19.5.1991).

AB   Asunta Beltrán   EA   Evangelina Anarata
PJ   Paulino Jara   HS   Henry Stobart

HS   Wak kwintus yachanki kay sirinusmanta?

HS   Do you know any other stories about the *sirinus?*

AB   Sirinusmanta?

AB   About the *sirinus?*

HS   Ari.

HS   Yes.

AB   Sirinusmantaqa yachani.

AB   Yes I know some. About the *sirinus*.

HS   Ima kwintu

HS   What story?

AB   Sirinumantaqa. Karnawal jamuq nin… pukllay wantirawan. Wayq'umanta lluqsimun, wantira carnivaljina uuuuhhh… ma[nara]situn rupa ujlitu. 'Sirina siwaysitu sintay muray muray' nispa nin wayñuq nin. sirinuqa.

AB   About the *sirinus* They come for Carnival it's said, with the *pukllay* flag. They emerge from a gully, like the Carnival flag. *Uuuuuu* …[4] a huge noisy troupe of them! (sung) 'Sirina siway, violet violet ribbon', that's what the *sirinu's wayñu* says.

Karnawal p'utumiriq [sabaj kay] nuqanchis imaynatachus purishanchis jina jamun nin. Chay sirinu siwaysitu nispa wayq'uspi wayñu … Wayq'uspi, qaqaspi, pututus.

Bursting Carnival comes [?] and walks around just as we do, it's said. [Singing] *wayñu* in the gullies 'siway sirinu'. In the gullies and rocks, *pututu* [trumpets resound].

Kay qala walaychu?

You know that *Qala walaychu?* [rock on mountain peak, where llamas mated].

HS   Ari.

HS   Yes.

AB   Chay uran wayq'upi tiyan. Nuqa jinata chuqushaq kuni. Pututu 'uj …' pinkillu 'uj …' wayñu lluqsimuq.

AB   Well, just below it there's a gully. I was sitting there, just as I am now [sitting]. The *pututu* [trumpet sounded] uj … the *pinkillu* uj … The *wayñu* emerged.

'Sirinu nuqa rikuni a. Ajina parapi chuqurkuspa. Ajina puñuyta chuturqurikasqani. Chaymanta

I saw the *sirinu* for sure. Just like that, as I was sitting there in the rain. As though I was day dreaming.[5] And then *wuuu* …

---

[4] Long vocal slide downward from high to low pitch.

[5] *chuturqurikasqani:* literally; 'as though removed, (like a garment,) in sleep'. *Chuturqokuy* refers to removing an article of clothing such as trousers or a skirt (Herrero & Sánchez 1983:50).

*wuuu … wuu … miiiiii …' Wayñu
junt'arkurimushasqa chay mirkata…*

wuu … wu … miiiiii …[6] The *wayñu*
came completely filling that hollow.

EA   *Libristuta?*

EA   Really?

*AB   Libristuta! Challtikujina rikuq
kani.
Challku kay kinray kay kinray
challkujina. Chay Lurin arqiñan chaypi
kuywapi parapi chukusaq kani, chaypi
jinapi puñuyta chutushasqani, puñuta
chutushaqtirqa.
'Wuu … wuu … aaaata.' pinkillus uj …
Chay mirkamantaq sunarqamun
kanpaq, carnivalqa.*

AB   Honest! As indefinite colour I
saw them. Undefined colour on that
slope, on that slope as though of
indefinite colour. There, by Lorenzo's
[llama] mating [corral] in a cave I sat,
while it was raining, as though carried
off in sleep, when day dreaming. *Wuu
… wuu … aaaata …*[7] the *pinkillus*
[sounded] *uj*… From that hollow it
sounded out, Carnival!

*Chaymanta chay sirinuyuq chay
mirkaqa. Chayta uyariq kani chayta
mana piru rupatapuni rikuqchu kani,
mana rupatapuni rikunichu. Imapaq
rupata rikuni nispa llullakusaq. Uj
juñarkamushaspajina chayta rikuq
kani. Chayta rikuq kani. Sirinuyuq chay.*

Well, that hollow has *sirinus*. I've
witnessed them, but I didn't see them in
a troupe, definitely not in a group. If I
were to say they were [together] in a
troupe I would be lying. Like a
stampede, running all over the place, I
saw them.[8] That's what I saw. That
place is inhabited by *sirinus*.

HS	*Ima sonashan?*		HS	What did it sound like?
PJ	*Sirinu*		PJ	*Sirinu*
AB	*Pinkillus, pututus a sirinus a.*		AB	*Pinkillus, pututus, sirinus,*
HA	*Pinkillujina? pututujina ?*		HS	Like the *pinkillu*? like the *pututu*?
AB	*Pinkillujina, sirinu a.*		AB	Yes, [the] *sirinu* is like the *pinkillu*
HS	*Kay sirinu – kay runajina?*		HS	That *sirinu* – is it like a person?
AB	*Runajinapuni a! runajinapuni sirinu a.*		AB	Absolutely, just like people, the *sirinu* are just like people
PJ	*Supay piru, yawlus*		PJ	But they're *supay*, devils
AB	*Yawlus chaypaq, chayqa.*		AB	Devils they are, that's what they are
HS	*Nuqaykujina o aswan jatun, aswan juch'uy?*		HS	Are they like us, or bigger or smaller?
PJ	*Qanjina*		PJ	Like you[9]
AB	*Kay … qankunajinas a.*		AB	Like all of you
HS	*Tukuy runa jina*		HS	Like everyone?
AB	*Tukuy runajina, .kay imillasjina*		AB	Like everyone … like girls.

Paulino explained this phrase as 'asleep when awake', suggesting day dreams.

  [6] The *wuuu* … sounds were of low and fixed pitch. The *miiiii* … sound started fairly high in pitch and glided downwards.

  [7] Two low pitches and closed vowel sounds (*woo*) contrasted by a violent and open vowel sound (*ahh*).

  [8] This was associated with a flock of animals running in different directions, it may also be related to the idea of the circular movement of winding skeins of wool (*juñi*).

  [9] In my question I mistakenly used the exclusive suffix *-yku*, meaning 'us, not you'. Accordingly my hosts were forced to answer in the second person although I really wanted to

AB *Mamay rikullasqataq kaq jaqay Titiripi wasinpi. Waychuqaqa nisqa chay qaqata, martispi ujlitu juyñurkamun nin, kurrispa nin, kurrispa nin, kurrispa nin hasta wasi uranta junkatakamun y hasta recien chinkapun nin. Libristuta chaypi rikuq kani. Chay Waychu qaqa.*

AB My mother also saw them once at the herding-house in Titiri. At *waychu* rock[10] she said. At that rock on [Carnival] Tuesday, one by one they came swarming out she said, running, running, running down to below the house where they collected together, and then suddenly disappeared. It's the truth I've also seen it myself [at] that *waychu* rock.

Chay Silistinu wasi uran wayq'u sumaq sirinuyuq nin. Chaymanta lluqsirqamun chay pampata 'ahh ...' imillas, lluqallas, rupa, pututus, pinkillus nin. Iskay wantirayuq kurrimushan nin, sut'ipi jamushan nin. Jinata rikuq kani nin mamay.[4]

The gully below Celestino's house has plenty of *sirinus* she said. From there they come out onto the flat ground 'ahh ...' girls, boys, [clothing/troupe],[11] *pututu* trumpets, *pinkillu* flutes she said. With two flags they came running, she said, in broad daylight they came she said. My mother said that's what she saw.

PJ *Mayumanta chayqa lluqsimusqa. Mayumanta, wayq'umanta, qaqa wayq'upunita, ukhu wayq'u. Jinatalla k'ullkitu pasan chay wayq'uqa. Pataman lluqsin kay wayq'uqa; chay wayq'umanta lluqimusqa.*

PJ [The *sirinu*] come out from the river. From the river, from gullies, especially those rocky gullies, those deep inner gullies. It passes through narrow passages into the gullies. It comes up and out into the gullies; from the gullies it emerges

AS *Unquchin sirinus a. lukuyachin. Uj wata Asencio luquiyachin sirinu: hasta chinkaspa Tinquipaya.*

AB The *sirinus* can make you ill or send you mad. One year Asencio was sent mad by the *sirinu*, when he disappeared all the way to Tinquipaya.

know if *sirinus* are like humans in general, as was confirmed later.

[10] This place, I was told during transcription, has 'two stones'. *Waychu* is the name of a common local bird whose call is equated with the wind (*wayra*).

[11] As Paulino confirmed during transcription, doña Asunta often uses the Spanish loan word *tropa,* common word for a group of musicians and dancers, pronouncing it *ropa* (*rupa*). She may be referring to 'clothing' (Spanish *ropa*) here, although it would have been more usual for here to use the Quechua *p'acha*.

Appendix 3

Variants of Cruz tuning on the charango (Chapter 4)

Variant tunings on the large laminated *panti charango*

(Alternative names for this form of *charango* include:
yana, bombo, samba, tabla and *ubandu*)

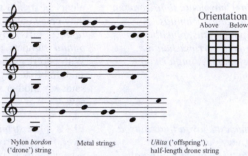

Orientation
Above   Below

Nylon *bordon*
('drone') string   Metal strings   *Uñita* ('offspring'),
half-length drone string

Variant tunings on the small Betanzos and Pocoata produced *k'ullu* ('wooden') *charango*

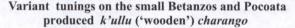

8va

8va

8va

Nylon

The names *cruz* ('cross'), *kinsa temble* ('three tuning'), *tres de mayo* ('third of May') and *Macha temble* ('Macha tuning') are widely applied to most of these tunings. The same basic left hand position is used, forming the basis for a wide range of variation.

Tunings played on the larger *panti charango* are sometimes termed *pascua* ('Easter'), especially when played in feasts at that time. Some players differentiate *pascua* from *cruz,* others insist these tunings are identical.

Two common names for the tunings played on the small *k'ullu charango* include: *churi qala* (Churicala) and *san lazaro* (San Lazaro), after the villages of the same names situated between Macha and Colquechaka. These names were used (in various contexts) to refer to all the above *k'ullu charango* tunings.

Character Glossary

Family relationships of some of the principal characters referred to in the text. Approximate ages in 1991.

(1) Families with main residence in Pata Kalankira *(Pata Cayanquira)*

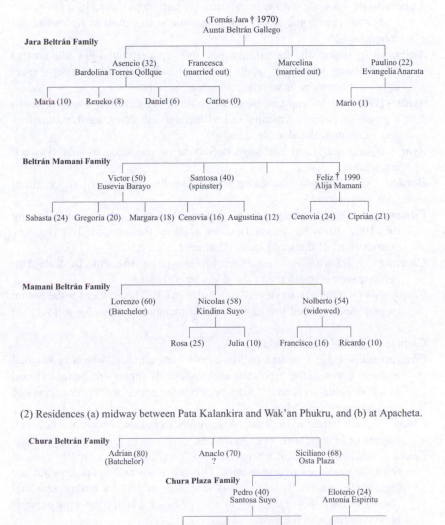

(Tomás Jara † 1970)
Aunta Beltrán Gallego

Jara Beltrán Family

Asencio (32)
Bardolina Torres Qollque

Francesca
(married out)

Marcelina
(married out)

Paulino (22)
Evangelia Anarata

Maria (10)   Reneko (8)   Daniel (6)   Carlos (0)

Mario (1)

Beltrán Mamani Family

Victor (50)
Eusevia Barayo

Santosa (40)
(spinster)

Feliz † 1990
Alija Mamani

Sabasta (24) Gregoria (20) Margara (18) Cenovia (16) Augustina (12)

Cenovia (24) Ciprián (21)

Mamani Beltrán Family

Lorenzo (60)
(Batchelor)

Nicolas (58)
Kindina Suyo

Nolberto (54)
(widowed)

Rosa (25)   Julia (10)

Francisco (16)   Ricardo (10)

(2) Residences (a) midway between Pata Kalankira and Wak'an Phukru, and (b) at Apacheta.

Chura Beltrán Family

Adrian (80)
(Batchelor)

Anaclo (70)
?

Siciliano (68)
Osta Plaza

Chura Plaza Family

Pedro (40)
Santosa Suyo

Eloterio (24)
Antonia Espiritu

Simona (17)   Alija (14)   Justo (12)

Emiliano (1)

Glossary

Alférez – a Spanish military term: 'ensign' or 'second lieutenant'. It is used in Kalankira to refer to various feast sponsors and translated here as 'sponsor'or 'senior sponsor'.

Anhemitonic – a scale without semitones (or half steps), used in reference to a (5 note) pentatonic scale. All pentatonic scales used in Kalankira are anhemitonic.

Animu – (Sp. *animó*) the animating aspect or energy (sound, light, movement) of all living beings or other phenomena/objects with autoresonance, internal movement or which are sources of light.

Ayllu – (Que.) an Andean unit of socio-political organization which refers to a group of people, typically linked through ethnicity, kinship, territory and a common 'head' or leadership.

Ayni – (Que.) reciprocal exchange of labour or products, usually between households.

Bordón – (Sp. 'drone') bass drone string, usually made of nylon, on guitar type instruments.

Campesino – (Sp.) 'country person' or peasant. A term introduced following the 1952 Bolivian Revolution to replace the supposed derogatory connotations of the word *indio* ('Indian').

Charango – (*charanku*) a small mandolin-type instrument. In Kalankira performance is restricted to the dry winter season.

Chaskañawi – (Que.) 'starry-eyed' or 'bushy-eyed'. The epithet for the potato (*papa*) used in ritual invocations and a metaphoric term for a 'lover' in song.

Chawpi – (Que.) 'centre, middle'.

Chawpirana – (Que.) central region of medium altitude, which is situated midway between the highlands and valleys. It appears to be understood as a conceptual axis articulating between the upper and lower regions of *ayllu* territory (see Map 3).

Chiqa – (Que.) 'straight' or 'true'. Also refers to balanced relations between objects or beings, such as even halves.

Cholo – inhabitant of local towns (*vecino* 'neighbours'), culturally distinct from the *campesinos* or peasants. The *charango* and Spanish guitar are commonly played by *cholos* but are not subject to strong seasonal considerations. For example, in the town of Macha the *charango* is played throughout the year.

Ch'ulla – alone, without its partner. For example, a single shoe.

Ch'ulu – woollen hat with ear-flaps worn and knitted by men.

Chuñu – (Sp. *chuño*) freeze-dried potatoes, an important staple food, soaked overnight before cooking. Made by leaving potatoes outside for several nights during the bitterly cold months of June or July and trampling to squeeze out moisture during the day.

Compadre – 'co-parent'. Relationship through which the godparent of a child is bound in reciprocal obligations with the child's family (*compadrazco* 'co-parent hood').

Huayño – Spanish spelling of Quechua/Aymara word *wayñu*. I use it (in contrast to the rainy season *wayñu*) to refer to the (more) urban associated *siku* panpipe genre and songs (*huayño*) of this name.

Jalq'a – name of an ethnic group with highly distinctive dress that lives on the South Eastern border of Macha territory.

Julajula – (*wauku*, *suqusu*) a form of bamboo panpipe especially associated with the feast of the Holy Cross in May.

Qhaliyu – a general term for dry season *charango* music, and the name of an near obselete dry season song genre accompanied on the *charango* which was replaced by the *cruz* and *san pedro* genres in the 1950s.

Kawiltu – (Sp. *Cabildo*) unit of socio-political organization and a ceremony performed in August and presided over by alcalde when (now symbolic) land tax (*tasa*) is collected.

Khuyay timpu – (Que.) 'time of love/compassion'. Hungry period of the year between August and December when there is a shortage of pasture. Also called *Lapaka*.

Kitarra – (Sp. *guitarra*) the Macha guitar of the rains. This Quechua spelling is used to avoid confusion with the Spanish guitar (*guitarra*) played in more urban contexts.

Khuru – any wild or undomesticated creature. Domesticated, that is 'nurtured' creatures are termed *uywa*.

Kuti – notion of reversal, change, or a turn. Expressed graphically by an angle or change in direction.

Kuwla – (*kupla*, *kulwa* Sp. *copla*, *cobla*) a piece performed (often whilst kneeling) on *julajula* or *siku* panpipes or the *qina* flute in 'adoration' or to request forgiveness from, for example, a saint, the church or the sun.

Lapaka – hungry period of the year between August and December when there is a shortage of pasture. Also called *khuyay timpu*.

Link'u – the concept of connection and rhythmic alternation or exchange. Represented visually by a curve or zigzag, snaking or meandering line (*link'u link'u*). Used to refer to the fluid (melismatic) shape of melodies that flow smoothly between pitches or to steady, balanced and regular strumming.

Machu – (Que.) 'old' or 'ancestor'. Used to refer to old men, male stud llamas and the largest size in a family of musical instruments.

Malta – (Que.) 'medium'. Used to refer to yearling (adolescent) animals, and to medium size within a family of musical instruments.

Mama Santisima – (Sp. 'Holiest Mother') name used for the moon in ritual invocations, such as coca chewing and libations.

Mayura – (probably derived from Spanish military title such as *mayordomo* 'steward'). In Kalankira the title is used for the music sponsor for the feast of the Holy Cross.

Melisma – fluid movement between pitches in a song or melody, as opposed to recitative or declamatory styles.

Mink'a – (Que.) labour reciprocated with products or food, such as part of the day's harvest.

Mono – (Sp. 'monkey') pantomime dancers who perform at the *rinuwa* feasts in September, dressed as fools or jesters (sometimes wearing monkey masks). They also speak in falsetto voices and wear llama fleece wigs.

Oca – (Que. *uqa*) a sweet Andean tuber.

Padrino – (Sp.) 'godfather' (see **compadre**)

Panti – dark saturated colour such as deep purple, burgundy, black, browns and reds, which are connected with fertile land.

Pentatonic – a scale that divides the octave into five intervals.

Pinkillu – (Que. Aym.) a generic term for 'flute'. Principally used today to refer to (recorder type) duct flutes, played during the rainy growing season.

Pututu – (Que. Aym) a natural trumpet made from several cow or bull horns attached to a long wooden tube (c. 3m) or rubber tube. Played during Carnival.

Quena – (Kena) a form of Andean notched flute played by *mono* dancers in *rinuwa* music in September.

Quinoa – (*qinuwa*) an Andean grain noted for its diminutive size. It is said to be the only crop cultivated by the souls of the dead.

Qunquta – a large deep bodied guitar, traditionally played during the rainy growing season, in the northerly *ayllus* of Northern Potosí.

Rinuwa – (probably derived from the Spanish *renovar* 'to renew'). A term used both to refer to cacophonous music, such as many drums or *siku* panpipe bands playing at once, and the period between mid September and October (*rinuwa timpu* 'renewal time').

Salaki – a vocal genre sung to the accompaniment of the *charango* on the final two days of Carnival.

Sapiri – the principal and unique mountain spirit of Kalankira *ayllu* that is evoked in shamanic rites and takes the form of a condor.

Siku – (*sikura*) a form of panpipe made from thin fragile cane played with drums and closely associated with patronal feasts of August to October.

Sinsiru – (Sp. *cencerro*) bells hung around the necks of leading male llamas when highland herders make trading journeys to the valleys during the dry winter months. The *sinsirus* are only worn on the return journey to the highlands so their sound charms the *animu* of the maize back to the highlands.

Sirinu – (*sirina* Sp. *sirena* 'siren') spirit beings or demons connected with musical creation and the flow of water, and a term used for certain Carnival dancers.

Suna – marching melody played on *wauqu* (*jula-jula*) panpipes. The name is possibly derived from the Spanish *sonar* 'to sound'.

Sunqu – (Que.) inner core or metaphorical 'heart' of a body, the sap or pithy centre of a branch, and the kernel of a seed. In animals *sunqu* usually refers to the liver, lungs or viscera, rather than the organ the heart, as the seat of the emotions.

Supay – (Que.) custodian of the inner space and hidden regenerative potential who is typically represented as a near equal and opponent to god. In Kalankira *supay* is usually synonymous with *yawlu* (Sp. *diablo* 'devil').

Suqusu – (Que. Aym.) 'bamboo'. A common term for *julajula* (*wauqu*) panpipes.

Taki – (Que.) song and the verb stem to 'sing' (*takiy*). More specifically *takis* are the songs of the dry season, as distinct from the *wayñu* songs of the rains.

Tambora – (Sp.) a military style side drum (often with a snare).

Tasa – 'land tax' paid each year in the *kawiltu* (Sp. *cabildo*) ceremony (now almost purely symbolic).

Tata Santisimu – ('holiest father') name used for the sun (Que. *inti*) in ritual invocations, such as coca chewing and libations.

Tinku – 'encounter', such as between lovers, meeting on a footpath or opponents in battle (*tinku*) and connected with the notion of equilibrium, harmony or concord.

Tiusninchis – 'god of us all' (Sp. *dios* 'god' and Quechua 2nd person plural inclusive possessive suffix *–nchis*). Solar god associated with the Catholic Church; equal and opponent of *supay*.

Tunay – (from Sp. *tunar* 'to lead a licentious life') a verb commonly encountered in courtship song texts, which refers to partying (dancing, singing and drinking).

Uña (*uñita*) – (Que.) 'offspring'. Used to refer to baby animals, the smallest size in a family (consort) of musical instruments, or the half-length drone string used on certain guitars (e.g. *panti* or *bombo charango*).

Wauku – (*julajula*, *suqusu*) bamboo panpipes, especially associated with the feast of the Holy Cross in May and *tinku* battles.

Wayli – snaking dance in a single file associated with the harvest season and performed by *julajula* (*wauku*) panpipe players.

Wayñu – the musical genre of the rainy season (closely connected with weeping and the soul), sung by women and played on *pinkillu* flutes or the *kitarra* by men.

Wirjin – (Sp *virgen* 'virgin') the female place spirits associated with cultivated fields, synonymous with *pachamama* (Que. 'earth mother'), a name more commonly heard among *cholos* in the nearby town of Macha.

Yanantin – concept of reciprocal and structured relations, such as 'helper and helped combined' – where parts suggest mirror images of one another (Platt 1986).

Zapateo – (Sp.) stamping dance.

Bibliography

Abercrombie, Thomas (1986). *The Politics of Sacrifice: An Aymara Cosmology in Action*. Ph.D. Thesis. University of Chicago: Illinois.

Abercrombie, Thomas (1998). *Pathways of Memory and Power: Ethnography and History Among an Andean People*. Madison: University of Wisconsin Press.

Albo, Xavier (2002). 'Bolivia: From Indian and Campesino Leaders to Councillors'. In *Multiculturalism in Latin America: Indigenous Rights, Diversity and Democracy*. Ed. R. Sieder. Houndhills, Basingstoke, Hampshire and New York: Palgrave Macmillan. (74–102).

Allen, Catherine (1982). 'Body and Soul in Quechua Thought'. *Journal of Latin American Lore* 8 (2):179–96.

Allen, Catherine (1988). *The Hold Life Has: coca and cultural identity in an Andean community*. Washington & London: Smithsonian Institution Press.

Anderson, Benedict (1991). *Imagined Communities*: *Reflections on the Origin and Spread of Nationalism*. London & New York: Verso.

Anderson, David (2000). *Identity and Ecology in Arctic Siberia*. Oxford: Oxford University Press.

Appadurai, Arjun (ed.) (1986). *The Social Life of Things: Commodities in cultural perspective*. Cambridge: Cambridge University Press.

Appadurai, Arjun (1986). 'Introduction: Commodities and the Politics of Value'. In *The Social Life of Things: Commodities in cultural perspective*. Ed. A. Appadurai. Cambridge: Cambridge University Press.

Arguedas, José Maria (1985 [1956]). 'Puquio: A Culture in Process of Change' [1956]. Included with novel *Yawar Fiesta* (same author). Translated by Frances Horning Barraclough. Austin: Texas University Press. (149–200).

Armstrong, Gweneth (1988). *Symbolic Arrangement and Communication in the Despacho*. Ph.D. thesis, University of St Andrews, Scotland.

Arnold, Denise (1987). 'Kinship as Cosmology: Potatoes as offspring among the Aymara of Highland Bolivia'. Working Paper No. 21. Centre for Latin American Linguistic Studies. University of St Andrews, Scotland.

Arnold, Denise (1988). *Matrilineal Practice in a Patrilineal Setting: rituals and metaphors of kinship in an Andean ayllu*. Ph.D. Thesis. University College, London.

Arnold, Denise (1992). 'At the heart of the woven dance floor: The wayñu in Qaqachaka'. *Iberoamericana* 16 Jahrang (1992). No 3/4 (47/48): 21–66.

Arnold, Denise, Domingo Jiménez A. & Juan de Dios Yapita (1991). 'Scattering the Seeds: shared thoughts on some songs to the food crops from an Andean ayllu'. *Amerindia* 16: 105–178.

Arnold, Denise, Domingo Jiménez A. & Juan de Dios Yapita (1992). *Hacia un orden andino de las cosas*. La Paz, Bolivia: Hisbol & ILCA.

Arnold, Denise & Juan de Dios Yapita (eds) (1996). *Madre Melliza y sus crias (Ispall Mama Wawampi): Antología de la papa*. La Paz, Bolivia: Hisbol & ILCA.

Arnold, Denise & Juan de Dios Yapita (1998a). '*K'ank'isiña:* Trenzarse entre la letra y la musica de las canciones de boda de Qaqachaka, Bolivia'. In *Gente de carne y hueso: las tramas de parentesco en los Andes*. Ed. D. Arnold. La Paz: CIASE/ILCA.

Arnold, Denise & Juan de Dios Yapita (1998b). *Río de vellon: río de canto: cantar a los animales, una poética andina de la creación*. La Paz: ILCA/HISBOL.

Arnold, Denise, Juan de Dios Yapita & Cipriana Apaza (1996). 'Mama Trama y sus crías: Analogías de la producción de la papa en los textiles de Chuiñapi, Bolivia'. In *Madre Melliza y sus crias (Ispall Mama Wawampi): Antología de la papa*. Eds D. Arnold & J. de Dios Yapita. La Paz, Bolivia: Hisbol & ILCA.

Arriaga, Pablo Joseph de (1999). *La extirpacíon de la idolatría en el piru (1621)*. Preliminary study and notes by H. Urbano. Cuzco: Centro de Estudios Regionales Andionos 'Bartolomé de Las Casas'.

Arzáns de Orsua y Vela, Bartolomé (1965). *Historia de la Villa Imperial de Potosí*. (1735). 3 vols. Eds L. Hanke & G. Mendoza. Providence, R. I.: Brown University Press.

Attali, Jacques (1985). *Noise: The Political Economy of Music*. (Trans. Brian Massumi). Manchester: Manchester University Press.

Ayo Saucedo, Diego (1999). *Los desafíos de la participación popular*. La Paz: Cebem.

Bachelard, Gaston (1994 [1958]). *The Poetics of Space*. Boston: Beacon Press.

Baily, John (1985). 'Musical Structure and Human Movement'. In *Musical Structure and Cognition*. Eds P. Howell, I. Cross & R. West. London: Academic Press Ltd.

Baily, John (1991). 'Some cognitive aspects of motor planning in musical performance'. *Psychologia Belgica*. 31(2):147–62.

Baker, Geoffrey (2001). *Music and Musicians in Colonial Cuzco*. Ph.D. Dissertation. Royal Holloway, University of London.

Bakewell, Peter (1984). *Miners of the Red Mountain*. Alburquerque: University of New Mexico Press.

Baptista Gumucio, Mariano (1988). 'Patrimonio cultural de la humanidad'. In G. Ugalade & F. Arce (comp.) *Potosí: patrimonio cultural de la humanidad*. (La Paz & Potosí): Compañía Minera del Sur S.A.

Barth, Fredrik (1969). *Ethnic Groups and Boundaries: The Social Organization of Cultural Difference*. Oslo: Universiteitsforlaget.

Basso, Ellen (1985). *A Musical View of the Universe: Kalapalo Myth and Ritual Performance*. Philadelphia: University of Pennsylvania Press.

Bastien, Joseph (1978). *The Mountain of the Condor: Metaphor and Ritual in an Andean Ayllu*. St Paul: West Publishing Company.

Baumann, Max Peter (1979). *Música andina de Bolivia*. (LP record with notes). Centro Portales and Lauro Y Cia (Records). LPLI/S-062.

Baumann, Max Peter (1981). 'Dance, music and Song of the Chipayas (Bolivia)'. *Latin American Music Review* 2/2:171–222.

Baumann, Max Peter (1982a). *Bolivien: Musik im andenhochland/Bolivia: Music in the Andean highlands*. (2 LP records with notes) 14 Museum collection Berlin (West) Editor Artur Simon. MC14.

Baumann, Max Peter (1982b). 'Music of the Indios in Bolivia's Andean Highlands (Survey)'. *The World of Music* 25/2:80–98.

Baumann, Max Peter (1985). 'The Kantu Ensemble of the Kallaway at Charazani (Bolivia)'. *Yearbook for Traditional Music* 19:146–65.

Baumann, Max Peter (1996). 'Andean Music, Symbolic Dualism and Cosmology'. In *Cosmología y Música en los Andes*. Ed. M. Baumann. Frankfurt am Main & Madrid: Vervuert & Iberoamericana. (15–66).

Beaudry, Nicole (1997). 'The Challenge of Human Relations in Ethnographic Inquiry: Examples from Artic and Subartic Fieldwork'. In *Shadows in the Field: New Perspectives for Fieldwork in Ethnomusicology*. Eds G. Barz & T. Cooley. New York & Oxford: Oxford University Press. (63–83).

Becker, Judith (1988). 'Earth, Fire, *Śakti*, and the Javanese Gamelan'. *Ethnomusicology* 32/3:385–91.

Bellenger, Xavier (1982). 'An Introduction to the History of Musical Instruments in the Andean Countries: Ecuador, Peru and Bolivia'. *The World of Music* 24/2:38–51.

Bellenger, Xavier (1986 [1983]). *Ayarachi & Chiriguano: Peru*. CD recording with booklet. (Montreuil, France): GREM G7501 (Unesco Collection).

Bellenger, Xavier (1987). 'Musique des villes, musique des champs: Neofolkore et musique contemporaine dans les Andes'. (Bolivie: Fascination du Temps et Organisation de L'Apparence.). *Cahiers des Ameriques Latines* 6 (Nouvelle Série):119–30.

Berg, Hans van den (1989). *La tierra no da asi nomas: los ritos agrícolas en la religión de los aymara-cristianos*. La Paz: Hisbol – UCB/ISET.

Bertonio, P. Ludovico (1984 [1612]). *Vocabulario de la Lengua Aymara*, CERES, IFEA, MUSEF. Cochabamba: Bolivia.

Betanzos, Juan de (1968). *Suma y narración de los incas* [1551]. Madrid: Biblioteca de Autores Españoles, Vol. 209.

Bigenho, Michelle (2000). 'Sensing Locality in Yura: Rituals of Carnival and of the Bolivian State'. *American Ethnologist* 26:4 (957–80).

Bigenho, Michelle (2002). *Sounding Indigenous: Authenticity in Bolivian Music Performance*. New York & Houndhills, Basingstoke, Hampshire: Palgrave.

Blacking, John (1987). *'A common sense view of all music': Reflections on Percy Grainger's contribution to ethnomusicology and music education*. Cambridge: Cambridge University Press.

Blench, Roger (2001). 'Nigeria'. *The New Grove Dictionary of Music and Musicians (second edition)*. Ed. S. Sadie. London: Macmillan. Volume 17. (907–12).

Blum, Stephen, Philip Bohlman & Daniel Neuman (1993). *Ethnomusicology and Modern Music History*. Urbana & Chicago. University of Illinois Press.

Bohlman, Philip (1991). 'Representation and Cultural Critique in the History of Ethnomusicology'. In *Comparative Musicology and the Anthropology of Music*. Eds B. Nettl & P. Bohlman. Chicago: University of Chicago Press. (131–51).

Bohlman, Philip (1997). 'Fieldwork in the Ethnomusicological Past'. In *Shadows in the Field: New Perspectives for Fieldwork in Ethnomusicology*. Eds G. Barz & T. Cooley. New York & Oxford: Oxford University Press.

Borras, Gérard (1992). 'Analyse d'une medida servant a la fabricacion de syrinx Aymaras'. *Journal de la société des américanistes* 78/1:45–56.

Borras, Gérard (1995). *Les Aérophones Tradionnels Aymaras dans le Département de La Paz (Bolivie)*. Ph.D. Dissertation. Université de Toulouse-le-Mirail, Toulouse.

Bourdieu, Pierre (1977). *Outline of a Theory of Practice*. Cambridge: Cambridge University Press.

Bourque, Nicole (1995). 'Developing People and Plants: Life-Cycle and Agricultural Festivals in the Andes'. *Ethnology* 34/1:75–87.

Bouysse-Cassagne, Thérèse (1987). *La Identidad Aymara: Aproximación histórica (Siglo XV, Siglo XVI)*. La Paz, Bolivia: Hisbol-IFEA.

Bouysse-Cassagne, Thérese & Olivia Harris (1987). 'Pacha: En torno al pensamiento Aymara'. In *Tres reflexiones sobre el pensamiento andino* (with T. Platt, V. Cereceda). La Paz, Bolivia: Hisbol. (pp. 11–60).

Boyes, Georgina (1993). *The Imagined Village: Culture, Ideology and the English Folk Revival*. Manchester & New York: Manchester University Press.

Bradby, Barbara (1987). 'Symmetry around a centre: music of an Andean community'. *Popular Music* 6/2:197–218.

Bravo, P. Walter (1994). 'Reproductive Endocrinology of Llamas and Alpacas'. In *The Veterinary Clinics of North America* 10/2 (Update on Llama Medicine: Guest Editor: LaRue W. Johnson).

Buechler, Hans (1980). *The Masked Media*. The Hague: Mouton.

Burgoa Coria, Tito (2002). *Perfil de proyecto fundación 'Tinku-Macha'*. Unpublished document. La Paz.

Calla, Ricardo (1995). *Aproximaciones etnográficas a la cubierta vegetal en Potosí*. Potosí, Bolivia: 'Desarollo Forestal Comunal en el Altiplano Boliviano'.

Calvo, Luz Maria & Wálter Sánchez (1991). *Música autóctona del norte de Potosí* (LP record with notes). Centro Pedagógico y Cultural de Portales. Centro de Documentación de Música Boliviana (CENDOC-MB). Cochabamba, Bolivia. PLP-029.

Camaqui M., Alberto (2001). *Cultura con esperanza: sumaq – ñan*. (Unpublished document – 33 pages). Potosí – Bolivia.

Cánepa Koch, Gisela (1993). 'Los *ch'unchu* y las *palla* de Cajamarca en el ciclo de la representación de la *muerte del Inca'*. In *Música, danzas y mascaras en los Andes*. Ed. R. Romero. Lima: Pontificia Universidad Católica del Peru/Instituto Riva-Aguero. (139–78).

Cánepa Koch, Gisela (ed.) (2001). *Identidades Representadas: performance, experiencia y memoria en los andes*. Lima: Pontificia Universidad Católica del Perú, Fondo Editorial.

Canessa, Andrew (1998). 'Procreation, Personhood and Ethnic Difference in Highland Bolivia'. *Ethnos* 63/2:227–47.

Canessa, Andrew (2000). 'Fear and loathing on the *kharisiri* trail: alterity and identity in the Andes'. *Journal of the Royal Anthropological Institute* (N.S.) 6:705–20.

Carsten, Janet (ed.) (2000). *Cultures of Relatedness: New Approaches to Kinship*. Cambridge: Cambridge University Press.

Carter, William & Mauricio Mamani (1982). *Irpa Chico: Individuo y comunidad en la cultura aymara*. La Paz, Bolivia. Librería-Editorial Juventud.

Cavour, Ernesto (1988). *El Charango: su vida, costumbres y desventuras*. La Paz, CIMA.

Cavour, Ernesto (1994). *Instrumentos Musicales de Bolivia*. La Paz: Producciones CIMA.

Cereceda, Verónica (1987). 'Aproximaciones a una estetica andina: de la belleza al tinku'. In *Tres reflexiones sobre el pensamiento andino*. (with T. Bouysse-Cassagne, O. Harris & T. Platt). La Paz, Bolivia: Hisbol. (133–231).

Cereceda, Verónica (1990). 'A Partir de los colores de un pajaro...'. *Boletin del museo Chileno de arte precolombino* 4:57–104.

Christian, William (1981). *Local Religion in Sixteenth-Century Spain*. Princeton: Princeton University Press.

Classen, Constance (1991). 'Creation by Sound/Creation by Light: A Sensory Analysis of Two South American Cosmologies'. In *The Varieties of Sensory Experience*. Ed. David Howes. Toronto: University of Toronto

Press. (239–55).

Classen, Constance (1993). *Inca Cosmology and the Human Body*. Salt Lake City: University of Utah Press.

Clayton, Martin (2001). 'Introduction: towards a theory of musical meaning (in India and elsewhere). *British Journal of Ethnomusicology* (special issue: *Music and Meaning)* 10/1:1–17.

Clifford, James (1986). 'Introduction: Partial Truths'. In *Writing Culture*. Eds J. Clifford & G. Marcus. Berkeley, Los Angeles & London: University of California Press. (1–26).

Coba, Carlos (1992). *Instrumentos Musicales Populares Registrados en el Ecuador*. Quito: Ediciones del Banco Central del Ecuador.

Cobo, Bernabe (1990). *Inca Religion and Customs*. Translated and edited by Roland Hamilton. Austin: University of Texas Press.

Cole, Jeffrey (1985). *The Potosí Mita, 1573–1700: Compulsory Indian Labor in the Andes*. Stanford: Stanford University Press.

Cook, Nicholas (1990). *Music Imagination and Culture*. Oxford: Oxford University Press.

Cooley, Timothy (2003). 'Theorizing fieldwork impact: Malinowski, peasant-love and friendship'. *British Journal of Ethnomusicology* 12/i:1–17.

Copana G., Norberto & Cipriana Apaza M. with Emiliana Hilaya M. (1996). 'Ofrendas a la papa en la región del lago'. In *Madre Melliza y sus crias (Ispall mama wawampi): Antología de la papa*. Eds D. Arnold & J. Yapita. La Paz, Bolivia: Hisbol & ILCA. (223–310).

Dawe, Kevin (2001). 'People, Objects, Meaning: Recent Work on the Study and Collection of Musical Instruments'. *The Galpin Society Journal* 54:219–31.

Dawe, Kevin (2003). 'The Cultural Study of Musical Instruments.''. In *The Cultural Study of Music: a critical introduction*. New York & London: Routledge. (274–83).

Dawe, Kevin & Moira (2001). 'Handmade in Spain: The Culture of Guitar Making'. In *Guitar Cultures*. Oxford & New York: Berg. (63–87).

Delaney, John (1982). *Dictionary of the Saints*. Kingswood, Tadworth, Surrey: Kaye and Ward Ltd. Windmill Press.

Diamond, Beverley, M.S. Cronk & F. von Rosen (1994). *Visions of Sound: Musical Instruments of First Nations Communities in Northeastern America*. Chicago and London: Chicago University Press.

Diaz Gainza, José (1988). *Historia Musical de Bolivia*. La Paz: Editorial Puerta del Sol.

Dransart, Penny (1997). 'Cultural Transpositions: Writing about Rites in a Llama Corral'. In *Creating Context in Andean Cultures*. Ed. R. Howard-Malverde. Oxford: Oxford University Press. (85–98).

Dougherty, Carole & Lelie Kurke (eds) (1998). *Cultural Poetics in Archaic Greece: Cult, Performance, Politics*. New York: Oxford Univerity Press.

Douglas, Mary (1970). *Natural Symbols: Explorations in Cosmology*. New York: Pantheon.

Douglas, Mary (1994 [1966]). *Purity and Danger: an analysis of the concepts of pollution and taboo*. London & New York: Routledge.

Dunkerley, James (2003). 'The Origins of the Bolivian Revolution in the Twentieth Century: Some Reflections. In *Proclaiming Revolution: Bolivia in Comparative Perspective*. Eds M. Grindle & P. Domingo. (Institute of Latin American Studies, University of London & David Rockefeller Center for Latin American Studies, Harvard University). Cambridge, Mass. & London: Harvard University Press. (135–63).

Escobari de Querejazu, Laura (1985). *Produccion y comercio en el espacio sur andino en el siglo XVII: Cuzco – Potosí 1650 – 1700*. La Paz, Bolivia: Embajada de España en Bolivia. (Talleres Gráficos de Industias Offset Color).

Escobari de Querajazu, Laura (1996). 'Producción y comercio colonial en Charcas. S. XVII–XVIII', *DATA: Revista del Instituto de Estudios Andinos y Amazónicas* No. 6, 1996. (55–69).

Falk, Pasi (1994). *The Consuming Body*. London: Sage Publications.

Feld, Steven (1990 [1982]). *Sound and Sentiment: Birds, Weeping, Poetics and Song in Kaluli Expression*. Philadelphia: University of Pennsylvania Press.

Feld, Steven (1991). 'Sound as a Symbolic System: The Kaluli Drum'. In *The Varieties of Sensory Experience*. Ed. D. Howes. Toronto: University of Toronto Press. (79–99).

Feld, Steven (1994). 'Aesthetics as iconicity of style (uptown title); or, (downtown title) "lift-up-over sounding": getting into the Kaluli groove'. In *Music Grooves*. By C. Keil & S. Feld. Chicago & London: University of Chicago Press. (109–50).

Feld, Steven (1996). 'Waterfalls of Sound: An Acoustemology of Place Resounding in Bosavi, Papua New Guinea'. In *Senses of Place*. Eds S. Feld & K. Basso, Santa Fe, New Mexico: School of American Research Press. (91–136).

Feld, Steven (2000). 'Sound Worlds'. In *Sound*. Eds P. Kruth & H. Stobart. Cambridge: Cambridge University Press.

Femenías, Blenda (2003). *Gender and the Boundaries of Dress in Contemporary Peru*. Austin: University of Texas Press.

Fernández Juáraz, Gerardo (1997). *Entre la repugnancia y la seducción: Ofrendas complejas en los Andes del Sur*. Archivos de historia Andina 24, Cusco (Peru): CBC (Centro de Estudios Regionales Andinos 'Bartolomé de las Casas').

Fernández Juárez, Gerardo (1998). 'Iqiqu y Achanchu: Enanos, demonios y metales en el altiplano aymara'. *Journal de la Société des Américanistes* 84 (1):147–66.

Flety, Bruno and Rosalía Martínez (1992). *Bolivia: Calendar Music in the Central Valleys*. CD Recording. Paris: CNRS/Muséee de l'Homme.

Flores Ochoa, Jorge (1986). 'The classification and naming of South American camelids'. In *Anthropological History of Andean Polities*. Eds J. Murra, N. Wachtel & J. Revel. Cambridge: Cambridge University Press.

Foster, Susan (1997). 'Dancing Bodies'. In *Meaning in Motion: New Cultural Studies of Dance*. Ed. J. Desmond. Durham: Duke University Press. (235–57).

Friedson, Steven (1996). *Dancing Prophets: Musical Experience in Tumbuka Healing*. Chicago & London: University of Chicago Press.

Frith, Simon (1998). *Performing Rites: Evaluating Popular Music*. Oxford: Oxford University Press.

Fuks, Victor (1990). 'Waiãpi Musical Instruments: Classification, Symbols and Meanings'. *Selected Reports in Ethnomusicology* 8:143–74.

Garcilaso de la Vega, El Inca (1989 [1966]). *Royal Commentaries of the Incas and General History of Peru*. Translated by H. Livermore. Austin: University of Texas Press.

Gell, Alfred (1992). *The Anthropology of Time: Cultural Constructions of Temporal Maps and Images*. Oxford and Washington D.C.: Berg.

Gérard, Arnaud (1996a). *Mediciones Acúsicas de Sikus Andions de Uso Actual en Bolivia (Un aporte para el compartamiento de las escalas musicales autóctonas)*. Informe de investigacíon, Universidad autónoma Tomás Frías, Potosí, Bolivia. (unpublished).

Gérard, Arnaud (1996b). *Primera aproximación a la acúsica de la tarka*. Informe de investigacíon, Universidad autónoma Tomás Frías, Potosí, Bolivia. (unpublished).

Gérard, Arnaud (1997). 'Multifonias en Aerofonos Andinos de Bolivia'. *Revista Boliviana de Física*. 3 (año 3):40–59.

Gérard, Arnaud (1998). 'Acústica de los Ayarichis: una original sucesión de alturas de sonido'. *Revista Boliviana de Fisica* 4:136–51.

Gérard, Arnaud (2000). 'Acústica del Suri-siku: una genial acomodación de alturas de sonido que permite une muti-pentafonia'. *Revista Boliviana de Fisica* 6:68–78.

Gérard, Arnaud (c. 2002). *Acústica de las siringas andinas: de uso actual en Bolivia*. Informe de investigacíon, Universidad autónoma Tomás Frías, Potosí, Bolivia. (unpublished).

Gifford, Douglas (1986). 'Time Metaphors in Aymara and Quechua'. Working Paper No. 16. Centre for Latin American Linguistics, University of St Andrews, Scotland.

Girault, Louis (1987). *Bolivia: Panpipes*. CD Recording with booklet. Documentation and Recordings by Louis Girault. AUDIVIS AD 090 (Unesco Collection).

Gisbert, Teresa (1980). *Iconografia y Mitos en el Arte*. La Paz: Gisbert y Cia.

Godlovitch, Stan (1998). *Musical Performance: A Philosophical Study*. London & New York: Routledge.

Gonzalez Holguín, Diego (1989 [1608]). *Vocabulario de la lengua general de todo el Peru llamada Lengua Qquichua o del Inca (1608)*. Lima, Peru: Universidad Mayor de San Marcos.

Gori, Grahan (2003). 'Villagers battle, and sometimes die as tourists watch'. *Augusta Chronicle* July 3, 2003. http://www.augustachronicle.com/stories/060903/biz_124-6698.shtml.

Gose, Peter (1986). 'Sacrifice and the commodity form in the Andes'. *Man* 21:296–310.

Gose, Peter (1994). *Deathly Waters and Hungry Mountains: Agrarian Ritual and Class Formation in an Andean Town*. Toronto, Buffalo & London: University of Toronto Press.

Grebe Vicuña, María Ester (1980). *Generative Models, Symbolic Structures and Acculturation in the Panpipe Music of the Aymara of Tarapacá, Chile*. Ph.D. Thesis. The Queen's University, Belfast.

Grondin, Marcelo (1990). *Metodo de Quechua: Runa Simi (tercera edición)*. La Paz/Cochabamba: Los Amigos del Libro.

Guaman Poma de Ayala (1936 [c. 1615]). *Nueva Corónica y Buen Gobierno (codex péruvien illustré)*. Ed. P. Rivet. Paris: Istitut d'Ethnologie.

Guaman Poma de Ayala, Felipe (1980 [c. 1615]). *El Primer Nueva Corónica y Buen Gobierno*. Eds J. Murra & R. Adorno. Mexico: Siglo Veintiuno.

Gutiérrez, Ramiro (1991). 'Instrumentos Musicales Tradicionales en la Comunidad Artesenal Walata Grande, Bolivia. *Latin American Music Review* 12/2:124–59.

d'Harcourt, Raul & Marguerite d'Harcourt (1925). *La musique des incas et ses survivances*. Paris: Librairie Orientaliste Paul Geuthner.

d'Harcourt, Raul & Marguerite d'Harcourt (1959). *La musique des Aymara sur les hauts plateaux Boliviens d'apres les enregistrements sonore de Louis Girault*. Paris: Société des Américanistes, Musee de l'Homme.

Harris, Olivia (1978). 'Complimentarity and Conflict: An Andean View of Women and Men'. In *Sex and Age as Principles of Social Differentiation*. Ed. J. La Fontaine. London: Academic Press. (22–40).

Harris, Olivia (1980). 'The power of signs: gender, culture and the wild in the Bolivian Andes'. In *Nature, Culture and Gender*. Eds C. McCormack and M. Strathern. Cambridge: Cambridge University Press. (70–94).

Harris, Olivia (1982a). 'The Dead and Devils among the Bolivian Laymi'. In *Death and the regeneration of life*. Eds M. Bloch and J. Parry. Cambridge: Cambridge University Press. (45–73).

Harris, Olivia (1982b). 'Labour and Produce in an Ethnic Economy'. In *Ecology and Exchange in the Andes*. Ed. D. Lehmann. Cambridge: Cambridge University Press. (70–96).

Harris, Olivia (1985). 'Ecological Duality and the Role of the Center: Northern Potosí'. In *Andean Ecology and Civilization*. Ed. S. Masuda. Tokyo: University of Tokyo Press. (311–35).

Harris, Olivia (1986). 'From asymmetry to triangle: symbolic transformations in northern Potosí'. In *Anthropological History of Andean Polities*. Eds J. Murra, N. Wachtel & J. Revel. Cambridge: Cambridge University Press. (260–79).

Harris, Olivia (1987). 'De la fin du monde: notes depuis le nord-Potosí'. *Cahiers des Ameriques Latines, No 6 Bolivie: Fascination du temps et organisation de l'apparence,* Paris: IHEAL (Institut des hautes études de l'Amerique Latine). (93–118).

Harris, Olivia (1988). 'Etnomúsica en el Norte de Potosí'. *Jayma* (La Paz, Bolivia). Año VI, Marzo-Abril:26–7:3–4.

Harris, Olivia (1989). 'The earth and the state: the sources and meanings of money in Northern Potosí, Bolivia'. In *Money and the Morality of Exchange*. Eds J. Parry & M. Bloch. Cambridge: Cambridge Univeristy Press. (232–68).

Harris, Olivia (1994). 'Condor and Bull: The Ambiguities of Masculinity in Northern Potosí'. In *Sexuality, Violence and Cultural Difference*. Eds P. Gow and P. Harvey. London: Routledge. (40–65).

Harris, Olivia (1995a). 'Ethnic Identity and Market Relations: Indians and Mestizos in the Andes'. In *Ethnicity, Markets, and Migration in the Andes* Eds B. Larson & O. Harris. Durham & London: Duke University Press.

Harris, Olivia (1995b). 'Knowing the past: Plural identities and the antimonies of loss in Highland Bolivia'. In *Counterworks*. Ed. R. Fardon. London & New York: Routledge. (105–23).

Harris, Olivia (2000). *To Make the Earth Bear Fruit: Ethnographic Essays on Fertility, Work and Gender in Highland Bolivia*. London: Institute of Latin American Studies.

Harrison, Regina (1989). *Signs, Songs, and Memory in the Andes: Translating Quechua Language and Culture*. Austin: University of Texas Press.

Harvey, Penny (1998). 'Los "hechos naturales" de parentesco y género en un contexto andino'. In *Gente de carne y hueso: las tramas de parentesco en los andes*. Ed. D. Arnold. La Paz: ILCA/CIASE. (69–82).

Hellier-Tinoco, Ruth (2003). 'Experiencing people: relationships, responsibility and reciprocity'. *British Journal of Ethnomusicology* 12/i: 19–34.

Hemming, John (1983). *The Conquest of the Incas*. London: Penguin.

Herrero, Joaquín & Federico Sánchez de Lozada (1983). *Diccionario Quechua – Español* (2 vols) (estructura semantica del Quechua Cochabambino contemporaneo). Sucre, Bolivia: Edita C.E.F.CO. (Talleres Gráficos 'Quri Llama').

Herzfeld, Michael (1985). *The Poetics of Manhood: Contest and Identity in a Cretan Mountain Village*. Princeton: Princeton University Press.

Herzfeld, Michael (1997). *Cultural Intimacy: Social Poetics in the Nation State*. New York & London: Routledge.

Hill, Jonathan (1988). 'Introduction: Myth and History'. In *Rethinking History and Myth: Indigenous South American Perspectives on the Past*. Ed. J. Hill. Urbana and Chicago: University of Illinois Press. (1–17).

Hill, Jonathan (1993). *Keepers of the Sacred Chants: The Poetics of Ritual Power in an Amazonian Society*. Tucson & London: University of Arizona Press.

Hobart, Mark (ed.) (1993). *An Anthropological Critique of Development: The Growth of Ignorance*. London: Routledge.

Hobsbawm, Eric (1983). 'Introduction: Inventing Traditions'. In *The Invention of Tradition*. Eds E. Hobsbawm & T. Ranger. Cambridge: Cambridge University Press.

Hodder, Ian (1987). 'The contextual analysis of symbolic meanings'. In *The archaology of contextual meanings*. Ed. I. Hodder. Cambridge: Cambridge University Press.

Howard, Rosaleen (2002). '*Yachay*: The *Tragedia del fin de Atahuallpa* as Evidence of the Colonisation of Knowledge in the Andes'. In *Knowledge and Learning in the Andes: Ethnographic Perspectives*. Eds H. Stobart & R. Howard. Liverpool: University of Liverpool Press. (17–39).

Howard, Rosaleen, Françoise Barbira-Freedman & Henry Stobart (2002). 'Introduction'. In *Knowledge and Learning in the Andes: Ethnographic Perspectives*. Eds H. Stobart & R. Howard. Liverpool: University of Liverpool Press. (1–13).

Howard-Malverde, Rosaleen (1990a). '*Upa* – La conceptualisation de la parole et du silence dans la construction de l'identité quechua'. *Journal de la société des Américanistes* 76:105–20.

Howard-Malverde, Rosaleen (1990b). 'The Speaking of History: "*Willapaakushayki*" or Quechua Ways of Telling the Past'. Research Paper 21, Institute of Latin American Studies, University of London.

Howard-Malverde, Rosaleen (1995). '*Pachamama* is a Spanish word: Linguistic tension between Aymara, Quechua and Spanish in Northern Potosí (Bolivia)'. *Anthropological Linguistics* 37/2:141–68.

Howard-Malverde, Rosaleen (1997). 'Introduction: Between Text and Context in the Evocation of Culture'. In *Creating Context in Andean Cultures*. Ed. R. Howard-Malverde. New York & Oxford: Oxford University Press. (3–18).

Howard-Malverde, Rosaleen & Andrew Canessa (1995). 'The school in the Quechua and Aymara communities of highland Bolivia'. *International Journal of Educational Development* 15/3:231–43.

Huntington, Richard & Peter Metcalf (1979). *Celebrations of Death: The Anthropology of Mortuary Ritual*. Cambridge: Cambridge University Press.

Hutton, Ronald (1996). *The Stations of the Sun: A History of the Ritual Year in Britain*. Oxford & New York: Oxford University Press.

INDICEP (1973). 'El Carnaval en las Comunidades Aymaras del Departamento de Oruro'. (Instituto de investigacion Cultural para Educacíon Popular). Publicaciones Especializadas en Educacion Popular. Año IV, Vol. No. 7, Octubre 1973. Doc. No. 10, Serie A. Oruro, Bolivia. (1–9).

Ingold, Tim (ed.) (1996). *Key Debates in Anthropology*. London & New York: Routledge.

Ingold, Tim (2000). *The Perception of the Environment: Essays in livelihood, dwelling and skill*. London and New York: Routledge.

Isbell, Billie Jean (1978). *To Defend Ourselves: Ecology and Ritual in An Andean Village*. Austin: University of Texas Press.

Isbell, Billie Jean (1985). 'The Metaphoric Process: "From Culture to Nature and Back Again"'. In *Animal Myths and Metaphors in South America*. Ed. G. Urton. Salt Lake City: University of Utah Press. (285–313).

Isbell, Billie Jean (1997). 'De inmaduro a duro: lo simbólico femenino y los esquemas andinos de género'. In *Más allá del silencio: las fronteras de género en los Andes*. Ed. D. Arnold. La Paz, Bolivia: ILCA (Instituto de Lengua y Cultura Aymara, La Paz) & CIASE (Centre for Indigenous American Studies and Exchange, University of St Andrews, Scotland). (253–322).

Isbell, Billie Jean & Fredy Amilcar Roncalla F. (1985). 'The Ontogenesis of Metaphor: Riddle Games among Quechua Speakers Seen as Cognitive Discovery Procedures'. *Journal of Latin American Lore* 3/1:19–49.

Izko, Javier (1986). 'Condores y mast'akus: Vida y muerte en los valles nortepotosinos'. In *Tiempo de Vida y Muerte*. By J. Izko, R. Molina & R. Pereira. La Paz: CONAPO (Consejo Nacional de población) and CIID (Centro Internacional de Investigaciónes para el Desarollo, Canada).

Jacobson, Roman (1960). 'Linguistics and Poetics'. In *Style in Language*. Ed. T. Sebeok. Cambridge, Mass.: MIT Press. (350–77).

James, Jamie (1995 [1993]). *Music of the Spheres: Music Science and the Natural Order of the Universe*. London: Abacus.

JAYMA; Centro Cultural Jayma (1989). 'Calendario Andino'. *RAYMI* 7. (La Paz, Bolivia).

Joralemon, Donald & Douglas Sharon (1993). *Sorcery and Shamanism: Curanderos and Clients in Northern Peru*. Salt Lake City: University of Utah Press.

Keesing, Roger (1981). *Cultural Anthropology: A contemporary Perspective* (second edition). New York: CBS Publishing Asia LTD.

Keesing, Roger (1989). 'Exotic Readings of Cultural Texts'. *Current Anthropology* 30/4:459–79.

Keil, Charles & Steven Feld (1994). *Music Grooves*. Chicago & London: University of Chicago Press.

Klein, Herbert (1992). *The Evolution of a Multi-Ethnic Society*. New York & Oxford: Oxford University Press.

Kohl, Benjamin (1999). *Economic and Political Restructuring in Bolivia: Tools for a Neoliberal Agenda?* Ph.D. Dissertation. Cornell University.

Kopytoff, Igor (1986). 'The cultural biography of things: commoditization as process'. In *The social life of things: Commodities in cultural perspective*. Ed. A. Appadurai. Cambridge: Cambridge University Press. (64–91).

Krener, Era & Niels Fock (1977–8). 'Good Luck and the Táita Carnaval of Cañar'. *Folk: Sansk Etnografisk Tidsskrift* 19–20. (152–70).

Krims, Adam (2000). *Rap music and the poetics of identity*. Cambridge: Cambridge University Press.

Laime, Omar (2002). *Les guitarillas del norte de Potosí: 'carnaval y tinku'* Tesis en opción al título de licenciado en artes musicales. Universidad autónoma Tomás Frías, Potosí, Bolivia.

Langevin, André (1987). *La Production Sociale de la Musique de Kantu dans un village Quechua de la Province de Bautista Saavedra, Bolivie: Premiers Jalons D'une Ethnographie*. Memoire présente pour l'obtention du grade de maître des arts (M.A.). Ecole des Gradues, Universite Laval.

Langevin, André (1992). 'Las Zampoñas del conjunto de Kantu y el debate sobre la función de la Segunda hilera de tubos: datos etnográficos y análisis semiótico'. *Revista Andina* 10/2:405–40.

Lara, Jesús (1978). *Diccionario: Qhëshwa – Castellano. Castellano – Qhëshwa*. La Paz – Cochabamba: Editorial 'Los Amigos del Libro'. (Second edition).

Larson, Brooke (1995). 'Andean Communities, Political Cultures, and Markets: The Changing Contours of a Field'. In *Ethnicity, Markets, and Migration in the Andes*. Eds B. Larson & O. Harris. Durham & London: Duke University Press. (1–53).

Larson, Brooke & Olivia Harris (eds), with Enrique Tandeter (1995). *Ethnicity, Markets, and Migration in the Andes: At the Crossroads of History and Anthropology*. Durham & London: Duke University Press.

Laurie, Nina, Robert Andolina & Sarah Radcliffe (2002). 'The excluded "indigenous"? The implications of multi-ethnic policies for water reform in Bolivia'. In *Multiculturalism in Latin America: Indigenous Rights, Diversity and Democracy*. Ed. R. Sieder. Houndhills, Basingstoke, Hampshire and New York: Palgrave Macmillan. (252–76).

Leichtman, Ellen (1987). *The Bolivian Huayño: A Study in Musical Understanding*. Ph.D. Thesis. Brown University.

Leichtman, Ellen (1989). 'Musical Interaction: A Bolivian Mestizo Perspective'. *Latin American Music Review* 10/1:29–52.

Levine, Terry (ed.) (1992). *Inka Storage Systems*. Norman & London: University of Oklahoma Press.

Lienhard, Martín (1992). *La voz y su huella: escritura y conflicto etnico-social en America Latina 1492–1988*. Lima, Perú: Editorial Horizonte.

Ling, Jan (1997). *A History of European Folk Music*. Rochester, N.Y.: University of Rochester Press.

Lippman, Edward (1964). *Musical Thought in Ancient Greece*. New York & London: Colombia University Press.

Little, William, H.W. Fowler & Jessie Coulson (1973). *The Shorter Oxford English Dictionary on Historical Principles*. (Revised & Ed. C. Onions). Oxford: Clarendon Press.

Lloyd, Geoffrey (1990). *Demystifying Mentalities*. Cambridge: Cambridge University Press.

Lucca, Manuel D. De (1983). *Diccionario: Aymara–Castellano, Castellan–Aymara*. La Paz, Bolivia. CALA (Comisión de Alfabetización y Literatura en Aymara).

Lucca, Manuel D. De (1987). *Diccionario Practico: Aymara-Castellano*. La Paz, Bolivia: Amigos del Libro.

Lucca, Manuel D. De & Jaime Zalles (1992). *Flora Medicinal Boliviana: Diccionario Enciclopédico*. La Paz & Cochabamba: Editorial Los Amigos del Libro.

Lyèvre, Philippe (1990). 'Les guitarrillas du nord du departement de Potosí (Bolivie): morphologie, utilisation et symbolique'. *Bulletin de l'institut Français d'Études Andines* 19/1:183–213.

Mamani, Mauricio (1987). 'Los Instrumentos Musicales en los Andes Bolivianos'. (Reunion Anual de Etnologia: MUSEF. La Paz). (49–79).

Mamani, Mauricio (1988). 'Agricultura a los 4.000 metros'. In *Raíces de América: El Mundo Aymara*. Comp. X. Albó. Madrid: Alianza Editorial. (75–129).

Mannheim, Bruce (1986). 'Poetry song and popular grammar, poetry and metalanguage'. *Word* 37:45–75.

Mannheim, Bruce (1987). 'A Semiotic of Andean Dreams'. In *Dreaming: Anthropological and Psychological Interpretations*. Ed. B. Tedlock. Cambridge: Cambridge University Press. (132–53).

Mannheim, Bruce (1991). *The Language of the Inka since the European Invasion*. Austin: University of Texas Press.

Mannheim, Bruce and Krista ven Vleet (1998). 'The Dialogics of Southern Quechua Narrative'. *American Anthropologist* 100/2:326–46.

Manuel, Peter (1988). 'Evolution and Structure in Flamenco Harmony'. *Current Musicology* 42:46–57.

Manuel, Peter (1993). *Cassette Culture: Popular Music and Technology in North India*. Chicago & London: University of Chicago Press.

Martínez, Rosalía (1990). 'Musique et Démons: Carnaval chez les Tarabuco

(Bolivie)'. *Journal de la societé des Americanistes* LXXVI:155–76.

Martínez, Rosalía (1994). *Musique du désordre, musique de l'ordre: le calendrier musical chez les Jalq'a (Bolivie)*. Ph.D. Thesis. Université de Paris X.

Martínez, Rosalía (1996). 'El Sajjra en la músic de los jalq'a'. In *Cosmología y Música en los Andes*. Ed. M. Baumann. Frankfurt am Main & Madrid: Vervuert & Iberoamericana. (311–22).

Martínez, Rosalía (1998). 'Quand chanter c'est être femme: Voix et féminité chez deux groupes quechua de la Bolivie'. In *Musique d'Amerique Latine – actes du colloque des 19 et 20 octubre 1996 a cordes (Tarne)*. La Talavera, France: C.O.R.D.A.E.

Mendoza, Fernando & Felix Patzi (1997). *Atlas de los ayllus del norte de Potosi, territorio de los antiguos charka*. Potosí, Bolivia: Comisión Europea – delegación en Bolivia/Programma de autodesarollo campesino (PAC-C).

Mercado, Claudio (1996). 'Detrás del sonido, el mundo'. *Takiwasi* (Tarapoto, Peru) 4, (año 2): 46–61.

Mercado, Melchor María (1991). *Album de paisajes, tipos humanos y costumbres de Bolivia (1841–1869)*. Archivo y Biblioteca Nacional de Bolivia – Sucre. La Paz, Bolivia: Servicio Grafico Quipus.

Merriam, Alan (1967). *Ethnomusicology of the Flathead Indians*. New York: Wenner –Gren Foundation for Anthropological Research Incorporated.

Meyer, Leonard (1956). *Emotion and Meaning in Music*. Chicago & London: University of Chicago Press.

Miller, Terry & Sean Williams (1998). 'The impact of modernisation on traditional musics'. In Miller & Williams (eds) *Southeast Asia: The Garland Encyclopedia of World Music, Volume 4*. New York & London: Garland.

Miracle, Andrew & Juan de Dios Yapita Moya (1981). 'Time and Space in Aymara'. In *The Aymara Language in its Social and Cultural Context*. Ed. M. Hardman. Gainesville: University Presses of Florida.

Mitchell, William & David Guillet (eds) (1994). *Irrigation at High Altitudes: The Social Organization of Water Control Systems in the Andes*. Washington DC: American Anthropological Association.

Molina, Cristóbal de 'el Cusqueño' (1943). *Fabúlas y ritos de los incas* [1573]. Lima: Miranda.

Murra, John (1978 [1955]). *La organización económica del estado inca*. Translated by D. Wagner. Coyoacán, Mexico: Siglo Veintiuno-Instituto de Estudios Peruanos.

Murra, John (1979 [1955]). *The Economic Organization of the Inka State*. Greenwich, Conneticut: JAI Press Inc.

Murúa, Martín de (1946). *Historia del origen y geneología real de los Incas* [1590]. Ed. C. Bayle. Madrid: Consejo Superior de Investigaciones

Científicas, Instituto Santo Toribio de Mogrovejo.

Nash, June (1979). *We eat the mines and the mines eat us: dependency and exploitation in Bolivian tin mines*. New York: Columbia University Press.

Nercessian, Andy (2001). *The Duduk and National Identity in Armenia*. Lanham, Maryland: Scarecrow Press, Inc.

Nettl, Bruno (1985). *The Western Impact on World Music: Change, Adaptation, and Survival*. New York: Schirmer, London: Collier Macmillan Publishers.

Neuman, Daniel (1990 [1980]). *The Life of Music in North India: The Organization of an Artistic Tradition*. Chicago & London: University of Chicago Press.

Oblitas Poblete, Enrique (1978 [1960]). *Cultura Callawaya*. La Paz: Ediciones Populares Camarlinghi.

Olsen, Dale (2002). *Music of El Dorado: The ethnomusicology of ancient South American cultures*. Gainsville, Florida: University of Florida Press.

den Otter, Elisabeth (1985). *Music and Dance of Indians and Mestizos in an Andean Valley of Peru*. Delft, Netherlands: Eburon.

Page, Christopher (2000). 'Ancestral Voices'. In *Sound*. Eds P. Kruth & H. Stobart. Cambridge: Cambridge University Press.

Palisca, Claude (1993). 'Forward by the Series Editor'. In *Musical Poetics* by Joachim Burmeister. Translated by B. Rivera. New Haven & London: Yale University Press.

Paredes-Candia, Antonio (1980). *Folklore de Potosí*. La Paz: Ediciones Isla.

Paredes-Candia, Antonio (1988). *Cuentos populares bolivianos*. La Paz, Bolivia: Libreria Editorial 'Popular'.

Paredes-Candia, Antonio (1991 [1966]). *La danza folkórica en Bolivia: de la tradición oral*. La Paz: Libreria-Editorial 'Popular'.

Parejo, Raphaël (1991). 'Syrinx of Bolivia' (Trans. Jeffrey Grice). From *Bolivia: Panpipes* (1987). CD Recording with booklet. Documentation and Recordings by Louis Girault. AUDIVIS AD 090 (Unesco Collection).

Parejo-Coudert, Raphaël (2001). 'La Flûte *pinkuyllu* des provincias altas de Cuzco (Pérou): organologie et symbolique érotique d'un aérophone andin'. *Journal de la Société des Américanistes* 87:211–64.

Pelliot, Paul (1929). 'Neuf notes sur questions d'Asie centrale'. *T'oung Pao* 26.

Pérez de Arce, José (1998). '*Sonido Rajado*: the Sacred Sound of Chilean *Pifilca* Flutes'. *The Galpin Society Journal* 51:17–50.

Platt, Tristan (1982). 'The role of the Andean *ayllu* in the reproduction of the petty commodity regime in Northern Potosí (Bolivia)'. In *Ecology and Exchange in the Andes*. Ed. D. Lehmann. Cambridge: Cambridge University Press. (27–69).

Platt, Tristan (1986). 'Mirrors and Maize: the concept of *yanantin* among the Macha of Bolivia'. In *Anthropological History of Andean Polities*. Eds: J.

Murra, N. Wachtel & J. Revel. Cambridge: Cambridge University Press. (228–59).

Platt, Tristan (1987a). 'Entre *ch'axwa* y *muxsa*: para una historia del pensamiento politico aymara'. In *Tres reflexiones sobre el pensamiento andino* (with T. Bouysse-Cassagne, O. Harris & V. Cereceda). La Paz, Bolivia: Hisbol. (61–132).

Platt, Tristan (1987b). 'The Andean Soldiers of Christ: Confraternity organization, the mass of the sun and regenerative warfare in rural Northern Potosí (18th–20th centuries)'. *Journal de la societé des Américanistes* LXXIII:139–92.

Platt, Tristan (2002). 'El feto agresivo: Parto, formación de la persona y mito-historia and los Andes'. *Estudios Atacameños* 22:127–55.

Platt, Tristan, Thérèse Bouysse-Cassagne & Olivia Harris (eds) (2006). *Qaraqara-Charka: Mallku, Inka y Rey en la 'Provinicai de Charka' (siglos XV–XVII)*. La Paz: Ediciones Plural.

Plaza, Pedro (2002). 'Why Nazario is Leaving School: Community Perspectives on Formal Schooling in Rural Bolivia'. In *Knowledge and Learning in the Andes: Ethnographic Perspectives*. Eds. H. Stobart & R. Howard. Liverpool: University of Liverpool Press. (141–65).

Poole, Deborah (1991). 'Rituals of Movement: Rites of Transformation, Pilgrimage and Dance in the Highlands of Cuzco, Peru'. In *Pilgrimage in Latin America*. Ed. R. Crumrine & A. Morinis. New York: Greenwood Press. (307–38).

Price, Richard & Sally (1980). *Afro-American Arts of the Suriname Rainforest*. Los Angeles: Museum of Cultural History/University of California Press.

Radcliffe-Brown, Andrew D. (1964). *The Andaman Islanders*. New York: New York Free Press.

Rasnake, Roger (1989). *Autoridad y poder en los Andes: Los Kuraqkuna de Yura*. La Paz: HISBOL.

Reichel-Dolmatoff, Gerardo (1971). *Amazonian Cosmos; the sexual and religious symbolism of the Tukano Indians*. Chicago: University of Chicago Press.

Rivera Cusicanqui, Silvia (1990). 'Liberal Democracy and *ayllu* Democracy in Bolivia: The Case of Northern Potosí'. *The Journal of Development Studies* 26/4:97–121.

Rivera Cusicanqui, Silvia & equipo THOA (1992). *Ayllus y proyectos de desarollo en el norte de Potosí*. La Paz, Bolivia: Ediciones Aruwiyiri.

Romero, Raúl (ed.) (1993). *Música, danzas y máscaras en los Andes*. Lima: Pontificia Universidad Católica del Peru/Instituto Riva-Aguero.

Romero, Raúl (2001). *Debating the Past: Music, Memory, and Identity in the Andes*. New York: Oxford University Press.

Romero, Raúl (2002). 'Popular music and the global city: huayno, chicha and tecno-cumbia in Lima'. In *From Tejano to Tango*. Ed. W. Clarke. New

York & London: Routledge. (217–39).

Romero, Carlos, Marco Romero & Javier Romero (2003). *The Oruro Carnival: images and narratives*. La Paz: Muela del Diablo.

Rösing, Ina (1996). *Rituales para llamar la lluvia: Rituales colectivos de la región Kallaway en los Andes bolivianos*. La Paz: Los Amigos del Libro.

Rowell, Lewis (1983). *Thinking about Music: An Introduction to the Philosophy of Music*. Amherst: University of Massachusetts Press.

Saignes, Thierry (1995). 'Indian migration and social change in seventeenth-century Charkas'. In *Ethnicity, Markets, and Migration in the Andes*. Eds B. Larson & O. Harris. Durham & London: Duke University Press. (167–95).

Salaman, Redcliffe (1985 [1949]). *The history and social influence of the potato*. Cambridge: Cambridge University Press.

Sallnow, Michael (1987). *Pilgrims of the Andes: Regional Cults in Cusco*. Washington D.C. & London: Smithsonian Institution Press.

Samson, Jim (1999). 'Analysis in Context'. In *Rethinking Music*. Eds N. Cook & M. Evarist. Oxford & New York. Oxford University Press.

Sánchez, Wálter (1988). 'El proceso de creacion musical: Musica autoctona del norte de Potosí'. Boletin No 7. Centro Pedagogico y Cultural de Portales/Centro de documentacion de musica Boliviana (Cochabamba, Bolivia). (1–18).

Sánchez, Wálter (1989a). 'Circuitos Musicales'. Boletin No 11. Centro Pedagogico y Cultural de Portales/Centro de documentacion de musica Boliviana. (Cochabamba, Bolivia). (1–10).

Sánchez, Wálter (1989b). 'El calendario musical e instrumental: Musica autoctona del norte de Potosí'. Boletin No 12. Centro Pedagogico y Cultural de Portales/Centro de documentacion de musica Boliviana. (Cochabamba, Bolivia). (1–37).

Sánchez, Wálter (1996). 'Algunos consideraciones hipotéticas sobre música y sistema de pensamiento. La flauta de pan en los Andes bolivianos'. In *Cosmología y Música en los Andes*. Ed. M. Baumann. Frankfurt am Main & Madrid: Vervuert & Iberoamericana. (83–106).

Sánchez, Wálter (2001). *Luz Mila Patiño Festival: 30 years of cross-cultural encounters through music*. Geneva, Switzerland: Simon I. Patiño Foundation.

Schechter, John (1992). *The Indispensable Harp: Historical Development, Modern Roles, Configurations, and Performance Practices in Ecuador and Latin America*. Kent & London: Kent State University Press.

Schneider, Marius (1949). 'Los cantos de lluvia en España: estudio etnológico comparativo sobre la ideología de los ritos de pluviomagia'. *Annuario Musical* (Barcelona) 4:3–57.

Schramm, Raimund (1992). 'Ist'apxam! – Escuchen! Tradiciones musical y oral aymaras'. In *La Cosmovision Aymara*. Eds H. van den Berg &

N. Schiffers. La Paz: Hisbol & UCB.

Schueller, Herbert (1988). *The Idea of Music: An introduction to musical aesthetics in antiquity and the Middle Ages*. Kalamazoo, Michigan: Western Michigan University Press.

Seeger, Anthony (1987). *Why Suyá Sing: A Musical Anthropology of an Amazonian People*. Cambridge: Cambridge University Press.

Seeger, Anthony (1993). 'When Music Makes History'. In *Ethnomusiology and Modern Music History*. Eds S. Blum, P. Bohlman & D. Neuman. Illinois: Illini Books.

Sharon, Douglas (1978). *Wizard of the Four Winds: A Shaman's Story*. New York: The Free Press (Collier Macmillan Publishers).

Sherbondy, Jeanette (1992). 'Water Ideology in Inca Ethnogenesis'. In *Andean cosmologies through time: Persistence and emergence*. Eds R. Dover, K. Seibold & J. McDowell. Bloomington & Indianapolis: Indiana University Press. (46–66).

Sikkink, Lynn (1997). 'Water and exchange: the ritual of *yaku cambio* as communal and competitive encounter'. *American Ethnologist* 24/1:170–89.

Sillar, William (1994). *Pottery's Role in the Reproduction of Andean Society*. Ph.D. dissertation. University of Cambridge.

Sillar, Bill (1996). 'The Dead and the Dying: Techniques for Transforming People and things in the Andes'. *Journal of Material Culture*. 1/3:259–89.

Silverblatt, Irene (1987). *Moon, Sun and Witches: Gender Ideologies and Class in Inca and Colonial Peru*. Princeton, New Jersey: Princeton University Press.

Slobin, Mark (1993). *Subcultural Sounds: Micromusics of the West*. Hanover & London: Wesleyan University Press.

Solomon, Thomas (1994a). 'Coplas de Todos Santos in Cochabamba: Language, Music, and Perfomance in Bolivian Quechua Song Duelling'. *Journal of American Folklore* 107/425:378–414.

Solomon, Thomas (1994b). 'Creando etnicidad por medio de la música en el norte de Potosí'. *Reunion annual de etnología 1993. Serie Anales de la Reunión de Etnología. Tomo II*. La Paz, Bolivia: MUSEF (Museo de Etnografía y Folklore).

Solomon, Thomas (1997). *Mountains of Song: Musical Construction of Ecology, Place, and Identity in the Bolivian Andes*. Ph.D. Thesis. University of Texas at Austin.

Solomon, Thomas (2000). 'Duelling Landscapes: Singing Places and Identities in Highland Bolivia'. *Ethnomusicology* 44/2:257–80.

Soto, Ileana (1996). 'La interculturalidad en la educación básica ecuatoriana'. In *Educación e interculturalidad en los Andes y la Amazonía*. Ed. J. Godenzzi. Cusco: CERA BC:139–48.

Spek, Miranda van der (1994). *The Devil's Horn: a documentary about brass* bands in the Andes. (Video documentary). Amsterdam.

Stern, Steve (ed.) (1987). *Resistance, Rebellion, and Consciousness in the Andean Peasant World: 18th to 20th Centuries*. Madison: University of Wisconsin Press.

Stevenson, Robert (1976 [1968]). *Music in Aztec and Inca Territory*. Berkeley, Los Angeles & London: University of California Press.

Stobart, Henry (1987). 'Primeros Datos sobre la musica campesina del norte de Potosí. Reunion anual de Etnologia'. MUSEF (Museo Nacional de Etnografia y Folklore). La Paz, Bolivia. (81–96).

Stobart, Henry (1988). *The Pinkillos of Vitichi* (unpublished document, to accompany instrument collection, 137 pages). Horniman Museum, London.

Stobart, Henry (1994). 'Flourishing horns and enchanted tubers: music and potatoes in highland Bolivia'. *British Journal of Ethnomusicology* 3:35–48.

Stobart, Henry (1996a). '*Tara* and *Q'iwa*: Worlds of sound and meaning'. In *Cosmología y Música en los Andes*. Ed. M. Baumann. Frankfurt am Main & Madrid: Vervuert & Iberoamericana. (67–82).

Stobart, Henry (1996b). 'The llama's flute: musical misunderstandings in the Andes'. *Early Music XXIV/3*, August 1996:470–82.

Stobart, Henry (1996c). 'Los wayñus que salen de las huertas: Música y papas en una comunidad campesina del Norte de Potosí'. In *Madre Melliza y sus crias (Ispall Mama Wawampi): Antología de la papa*. La Paz, Bolivia: Hisbol & ILCA. (413–30).

Stobart, Henry (1998a). 'Lo recto y lo torcido: La música andina y la espiral de la descendencia'. In *Gente de carne y hueso: las tramas de parentesco en los andes*. Ed. D. Arnold. La Paz: ILCA/CIASE. (581–604).

Stobart, Henry (1998b). 'Bolivia'. In *The Garland Encyclopedia of World Music: Volume 2, South America, Mexico, Central America, and the Caribbean*. Eds D. Olsen & D. Sheehy. New York & London: Garland Publishing. (282–99).

Stobart, Henry (2000). 'Bodies of sound and landscapes of music: a view from the Bolivian Andes'. In *Musical Healing in Cultural Contexts*. Ed. P. Gouk. Aldershot: Ashgate. (26–45).

Stobart, Henry (2001). 'Pinkullu'. *The New Grove Dictionary of Music and Musicians (second edition)*. Ed. S. Sadie. London: Macmillan. Volume 19. (757).

Stobart, Henry (2002a). 'Sensational Sacrifices: Feasting the Senses in the Bolivian Andes'. In *Music, Sensation and Sensuality*. Ed. L. Austern. New York & London: Routledge. (97–120).

Stobart, Henry (2002b). 'Interlocking Realms: Knowing Music and Musical Knowing in the Bolivian Andes'. In *Knowledge and Learning in the Andes: Ethnographic Perspectives*. Eds H. Stobart & R. Howard.

Liverpool: University of Liverpool Press. (79–106).

Stobart, Henry (2006). 'Devils, Daydreams and Desire: Siren Traditions and Musical Creation in the Central-Southern Andes'. In *Sirens and Music*. Eds I. Naroditskaya & L. Austern. Bloomington & Indianapolis: Indiana University Press.

Stobart, Henry (forthcoming). 'Wind and Water: Musical instruments, Fertility and Gender in the Bolivian Andes'. In *The Sounds of Power*. Ed. V. Doubleday.

Stobart, Henry & Ian Cross (2000). 'The Andean Anacrusis? rhythmic structure and perception in the Easter songs of northern Potosí, Bolivia'. *British Journal of Ethnomusicology* 9/2:63–92.

Stokes, Martin (1994). 'Introduction'. In *Ethnicity, Identity and Music*. Ed. M. Stokes. Oxford: Berg. (1–27).

Strathern, Marilyn (1981). 'Self-interest and the social good: some implications of Hagen gender imagery'. In *Sexual Meanings: The Cultural Construction of Gender and Sexuality*. Eds S. Ortner & H. Whitehead. Cambridge: Cambridge University Press.

Strathern, Marilyn (1991). *Partial Connections*. Savage, Maryland: Rowan & Littlefield Publishers, INC.

Suárez Eyzaguirre, Nicolás (1984). *La música autoctona para tarkas y su caracter repetitivo*. Tésis de grado para optar al título de licenciatura en música. Universidad Católica Boliviana, (La Paz).

Sullivan, Lawrence (1988). *Icanchu's Drum: An Orientation to Meanings in South American Religions*. New York & London: Collier Macmillan.

Thorrez Lopez, Marcelo (1977). *El Huayño en Bolivia*. La Paz: Instituto Boliviano de Cultura.

Titon, Jeff Todd (1997). 'Knowing Fieldwork'. In *Shadows in the Field: New Perspectives for Fieldwork in Ethnomusicology*. Eds G. Barz & T. Cooley. New York & Oxford: Oxford University Press. (87–100).

Titon, Jeff Todd (2004). 'Homesick for Heaven: Distance and Nostalgia in Ethnomusicological Fieldwork'. Keynote address. Annual conference: British Forum for Ethnomusicology, University of Aberdeen 15.4.2004.

Torrico, Cassandra (1988). 'Toads and doves: the symbolism of storage sack's design amongst Macha herders. Northern Potosí, Bolivia' (unpublished; earlier draft of Torrico 1989).

Torrico, Cassandra (1989). 'Living Weavings: the symbolism of Bolivian herders sacks'. (unpublished).

Turino, Thomas (1983). 'The Charango and the Sirena: music, magic and the power of love'. *Latin American Music Review* 4 (Spring/Summer): 81–119.

Turino, Thomas (1984). 'The Urban-Mestizo Charango Tradition in Southern Peru: A Statement of Shifting Identity'. *Ethnomusicology* 28/2:253–69.

Turino, Thomas (1989). 'The Coherence of Social Style and Musical Creation

Among the Aymara in Southern Peru'. *Ethnomusicology* 33/1:1–30.

Turino, Thomas (1990). 'Structure, Context and Strategy in Musical Ethnography'. *Ethnomusicology* 34/3:399–412.

Turino, Thomas (1991). 'The State and Andean Musical Production in Peru'. In *Nation States and Indians in Latin America*. Eds G. Urban & J. Sherzer. Austin: University of Texas Press.

Turino, Thomas (1993). *Moving Away from Silence: Music of the Peruvian Altiplano and the Experience of Urban Migration*. Chicago: Chicago University Press.

Turino, Thomas (1996). 'From Essentialism to the Essential: Pragmatics and Meaning in Puneño *sikuri* Performance in Lima'. In *Cosmología y Música en los Andes*. Ed. M. Baumann. Frankfurt am Main & Madrid: Vervuert & Iberoamericana. (469–82).

Turner, Victor (1974). *Dramas, Fields and Metaphors: Symbolic Action in Human Society*. Ithaca & London: Cornell University Press.

Tyler, Stephen (1986). 'Post-Modern Ethnography: From Document of the Occult to Occult Document'. In *Writing Culture*. Eds J. Clifford, G. Marcus. Berkeley, Los Angeles & London, University of California Press. (122–40).

Urioste, Miguel (1987). *Segunda reforma agraria: campesinos, tierra y educació?n popular*. La Paz, Bolivia: Centro de Estudios para el Desarrollo Laboral y Agrario.

Urton, Gary (1981). *At the Crossroads of the Earth and the Sky: An Andean Cosmology*. Austin: University of Texas Press.

Urton, Gary (1985). 'Animal Metaphors and the Life Cycle in an Andean Community'. In *Animal Myths and Metaphors in South America*. Ed. G. Urton. Salt Lake City: University of Utah Press. (251–84).

Urton, Gary (1986). 'Calendrical cycles and their projections in Paqariqtambo, Peru'. *Journal of Latin American Lore* 12/1. (45–64).

Valencia Chacón, Américo (1981). 'Los Chiriguanos de Huancane'. Separata del 'Boletin de Lima' Nos. 12–13–14 (May, June, Sept 1981). Lima, Peru. Editorial Los Pinos.

Valladolid Rivera, Julio (1998). 'Andean Peasant Agriculture: Nurturing a Diversity of Life in the *Chacra*'. In *The Spirit of Regeneration: Andean Culture Confronting Western Nations of Development*. Ed. F. Apffel-Marglin with PRATEC. London & New York: Zed Books Ltd. (51–88).

Van Cott, Donna Lee (2002). 'Constitutional Reform in the Andes: Redefining Indigenous-State Relations. In *Multiculturalism in Latin America: Indigenous Rights, Diversity and Democracy*. Ed. R. Sieder. Houndhills, Basingstoke, Hampshire & New York: Palgrave Macmillan. (45–73).

Van Kessel, Juan (1981). *Danzas y estructuras sociales de los andes*. Cusco: Centro Bartolomé de Las Casas.

Van Vleet, Krista (2002). 'The intimacies of power: rethinking violence and affinity in the Bolivian Andes'. *American Etnologist* 29/3:567–601.

Vargas Luza, Jorge (1998). *La Diablada de Oruro: sus máscaras y caretas*. La Paz: Plural editores.

Veiga de Oliviera, Ernesto (1995). *Festividades Cíclicas em Portugal*. Lisbon: Publicações dom Quixote.

Vellard, Jean & Mildred Merino (1954). 'Bailes folklóricos del altiplano'. *Traveaux de l'Institut Français d'Études Andines*. (Paris & Lima):4:59–132.

Wara Céspedes, Gilka (1993). 'Huayño, Saya and Chuntunqui: Bolivian identity in the music of "Los Kjarkas"'. *Latin American Music Review* 14:52–101.

Wright, Robin (1981). *History and Religion of the Baniwa Peoples of the Upper Rio Negro Valley*. (2 vols.) PhD dissertation. Stanford University.

Yampara Huarachi, Simón (1992). '"Economia" Comunitaria Andina'. In *La Cosmovision Aymara*. Eds H. van den Berg & N. Schiffers. La Paz: Hisbol/UCB.

Zegarra, Erlinda & Eduardo Puma (c. 1997). *Danza de los Wauqös (en la fiesta de la virgen de Guadalupe) – primer ensayo* (undated, unpublished)). Instituto Boliviano de Etnomusicología (Universiteit 'Gent' Belgica; Universidad Autoónoma Tomás Frías, Potosí, Bolivia).

Zorn, Elayne (2004). *Weaving a Future: Tourism, Cloth and Culture on an Andean Island*. University of Iowa Press.

Zuidema, R. Tom (1977). 'The Inca Calendar'. In *Native American Astronomy*. Ed. A. Aveni. Austin: University of Texas Press. (219–59).

Zuidema, R. Tom (1985). 'The Lion in the City: Royal Symbols of Transition in Cuzco'. In G. Urton (ed.), *Animal Myths and Metaphors in South America*. Salt Lake City: University of Utah Press. (183–250).

Zuidema, R. Thomas (1986a). 'Inka dynasty and irrigation: another look at Andean concepts of history'. In *Anthropological History of Andean Polities*. Eds J. Murra, N. Wachtel & J. Revel. Cambridge: Cambridge University Press. (177–200).

Zuidema, R. Thomas (1986b). 'The place of the *chamay wariqsa* in the rituals of Cuzco'. *Amerindia* 11:58–63.

Zuidema, R. Tom (1992). 'Inca Cosmos in Andean Context: From the Perspective of the Capac Raymi Camay Quilla Feast Celebrating the December Solstice in Cuzco'. In *Andean Cosmologies through Time: persistence and emergence*. Eds R. Dover, K. Seibold & J. McDowell. Bloomington & Indianapolis: Indiana University Press.

Zuidema, R. Tom (1997). 'The Incaic Feast of the Queen and the Spanish Feast of Cabañuelas'. *Journal of Latin American Lore*, 20:1. (143–60).

Zulawski, Ann (1995). *They Eat from their Labour: Work and Social Change in Colonial Bolivia*. Pittsburgh: University of Pittsburgh Press.

Index